MW00786803

A Staircase to Standards Success
for English Language Arts

The Shape of Story
Yesterday and Today

Pam Allyn

Executive Director of LitLife and LitWorld

PEARSON

Boston · Columbus · Indianapolis · New York · San Francisco · Upper Saddle River
Amsterdam · Cape Town · Dubai · London · Madrid · Milan · Munich · Paris · Montreal · Toronto
Delhi · Mexico City · São Paulo · Sydney · Hong Kong · Seoul · Singapore · Taipei · Tokyo

Vice President, Editor in Chief: Jeff Johnston
Executive Editor: Meredith Fossel
Editorial Assistant: Maria Feliberty
Senior Marketing Manager: Chris Barry
Production Editor: Cynthia DeRocco
Program Manager: Karen Mason
Text Design: Electronic Publishing Services, Inc., NYC
Project Coordination and Editorial Services: Jouve
Art Rendering and Electronic Page Makeup: Jouve
Cover Designer: Diane Lorenzo
Grade Band Opening and Lesson Set Illustrations: Steve Morrison

Text Credits: The Common Core State Standards for the English Language Arts are © Copyright 2012. National Governors Association Center for Best Practices and Council of Chief State School Officers. All rights reserved. Page xxi, "Five Principles for Teaching Content to English Language Learners," by Jim Cummins. Retrieved from www.PearsonELL.com. Reprinted with permission.

Photo Credits: All photos not credited are courtesy of the author.

Library of Congress Preassigned Control Number
2014949747

10 9 8 7 6 5 4 3 2 1

ISBN 10: 0-13-290748-8
ISBN 13: 978-0-13-290748-4

About the Author

Pam Allyn is an authority in the field of literacy education and a world-renowned expert in home and school literacy connections. As a motivational speaker, expert consultant, author, teacher, and humanitarian advocating for children, she is transforming the way we think about literacy as a tool for communication and knowledge building.

Pam currently serves as the executive director of LitLife, a national literacy development organization providing research-based professional development for K–12 educators. She founded and leads LitWorld, a groundbreaking global literacy initiative that reaches children across the United States and in more than 60 other countries. Her methods for helping all students achieve success as readers and writers have brought her acclaim both in the United States and internationally. Pam is also recognized for founding the highly acclaimed initiative Books for Boys for the nation's most struggling readers.

Pam is the author of many books for educators and parents, including the award-winning *What to Read When: The Books and Stories to Read with Your Child—And All the Best Times to Read Them* (Penguin Avery), *Pam Allyn's Best Books for Boys* (Scholastic), and *Your Child's Writing Life: How to Inspire Confidence, Creativity, and Skill at Every Age* (Penguin Avery). Her work has been featured on "Good Morning America," the "Today Show," and "Oprah Radio," as well as in the *Huffington Post*, in the *New York Times*, and across the blogosphere.

About the Core Ready Series

Core Ready is a dynamic series of books providing educators with critical tools for navigating the Common Core State Standards. The foundational text, *Be Core Ready: Powerful, Effective Steps to Implementing and Achieving the Common Core State Standards*, provides practical strategies for how to implement core ideas to make all students college- and career-ready scholars. The Core Ready Lesson Sets, including three grade bands with four books per grade band, provide an easy-to-use way to access and organize all of the content within the standards. Readers see how to take complex concepts related to the standards and turn them into practical, specific, everyday instruction.

Acknowledgments

I thank the many members of the team at Pearson for believing in the Core Ready vision. I also thank the Jouve team for their careful eye and diligent work toward the editing and design of these books.

Thanks to my colleagues at LitLife, most especially to the middle school dream team on this project: Carolyn Greenberg, Rebekah Coleman, Debbie Lera, and Jen Scoggin. They are teachers, leaders, and big thinkers who never forget it is about children first. I am blessed to work with them. Many, many thanks to Rebecca Bascio, Christa Begley, Erin Harding, Megan Karges, Ingrid O'Brien, David Wilcox, and Jim Allyn for glorious input at every step.

I would like to thank our reviewers who provided valuable feedback: Christine H. Davis, Hillcrest Elementary (Logan, Utah); Wendy Fiore, Chester Elementary School in Connecticut; Keli Garas-York, Buffalo State College in New York; Karen Gibson, Springfield Public Schools in Illinois; Timothy M. Haag, Greater Albany Public Schools, New York; Katie Klaus Salika Lawrence, William Paterson University of New Jersey; Edward Karl Schultz, Midwestern State University (Wichita Falls, TX); Elizabeth Smith, Saint Joseph's College in New York; and Rhonda M. Sutton, East Stroudsburg University in Pennsylvania. Finally, I thank Steve Morrison for his extraordinary illustrations, which were, like everything else about everyone who has participated in the creation of this series, so perfect all together.

Contents

Grade 6 Packing a Punch: The Art and Craft of Short Stories 2

Reading Lessons 10

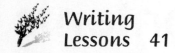

Writing Lessons 41

Grade 7   Examining Past Perspectives: Historical Fact and Fiction 70

Reading Lessons 79

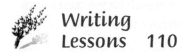

Writing Lessons 110

Grade 8 *Revealing Character: The Hero's Journey* 136

Reading Lessons 143

Writing Lessons 174

Appendixes

Additional Resources in PDToolKit

Grade 6

PARCC Frameworks

Core Support for Diverse Learners

Language Companion Lesson

Speaking and Listening Checklist

Grade 7

PARCC Frameworks

Core Support for Diverse Learners

Language Companion Lesson

Speaking and Listening Checklist

Grade 8

PARCC Frameworks

Core Support for Diverse Learners

Language Companion Lesson

Speaking and Listening Checklist

Welcome

Welcome to the *Core Ready Lesson Sets for Grades 6 to 8:*
A Staircase to Standards Success for English Language
Arts—The Shape of Story: Yesterday and Today. Here you
will find rich and detailed lesson plans, and the specifics and
daily activities in them, that you can use to make your Core Ready
instruction come to life.

The Four Doors to the Common Core State Standards

We have synthesized the expanse of the Common Core State Standards document into four essential doors to the English Language Arts. These Four Doors organize the CCSS into curriculum, identifying the most critical capacities our students need for the 21st century—skills, understandings, and strategies for reading, writing, speaking, and listening across subject areas. "The Four Doors to the Core" group the CCSS into lesson sets that match the outcomes every college- and career-ready student must have. The magic of the Four Doors is that they bring together reading, writing, speaking, and listening skills together into **integrated lesson sets**. Rather than face an overwhelming array of individual standards, teachers, students, parents, and administrators together can use the Four Doors to create the kind of curriculum that simplifies the schedule and changes lives. Here are the Four Doors to the Core:

▶ The Road to Knowledge: Information and Research

This Door to the Core—The Road to Knowledge—encompasses research and information and the skills and strategies students need to **build strong content knowledge and compose informational text** as suggested by the Common Core State Standards.

▶ The Power to Persuade: Opinion and Argument

This Door to the Core—The Power to Persuade—encompasses instruction that explores the purposes, techniques, and strategies to **become effective readers and writers of various types of opinion text** as delineated in the Common Core State Standards.

▶ The Shape of Story: Yesterday and Today

This Door to the Core—The Shape of Story—encompasses exploration of a variety of genres with the corresponding craft, structures, and strategies one needs to be a **successful consumer and producer of literary text** as required by the Common Core State Standards.

▶ The Journey to Meaning: Comprehension and Critique

This Door to the Core—The Journey to Meaning—encompasses the strategies and skills our students need to **comprehend, critique, and compose literary text** as outlined in the Common Core State Standards.

Get Ready to Explore The Shape of Story: Yesterday and Today

We seek to develop students who approach reading with the experience that will allow them to know what to expect in a variety of genres and apply appropriate strategies to each with purpose and flexibility. In this lesson set, students will read closely to explore various types of writing and learn the terminology and structures that will enable them to read and speak with others about each one effectively. They will notice and discuss the choices that authors make and examine how various authors treat similar themes and topics across genres and generations.

Students will use literature from many genres as models for their own writing. They will explore the writing techniques and purposes of various literary text types and compose their own original pieces. They will analyze texts and create written responses as evidence of their discoveries and ideas. They will share their writing and thinking with others orally and/or using appropriate tools and technologies. The student who recognizes, appreciates, and writes in a variety of genres is truly entering a lifelong journey of deep literacy. The understanding of genres of many types and origins gives the student an anchor and a field guide for understanding how to "read the world."

Walk Through a Lesson Set

This section is meant to take the reader through the major features of the lesson set.

Why This Lesson Set?

This section establishes the rationale for the lesson set and provides helpful background information about the lesson set focus.

Common Core State Standards Alignment

All of the Common Core State Standards addressed in the lesson set are listed here, including the individual grade-level standards.

Essential Skill Lenses
(PARCC Framework)

This table provides specific examples of how, in this lesson set, Core Ready students will build the essential skills required by the Partnership for Assessment of Readiness for College and Careers (PARCC), a multistate coalition that is currently developing Core Standards–aligned assessments that are slated to replace many statewide assessments across the United States. This alignment helps to ensure that Core Ready students will be prepared when states begin to use these assessments (Available in the PDToolKit).

Core Questions

Core Questions are thought-provoking, open-ended questions students will explore across the lesson set.

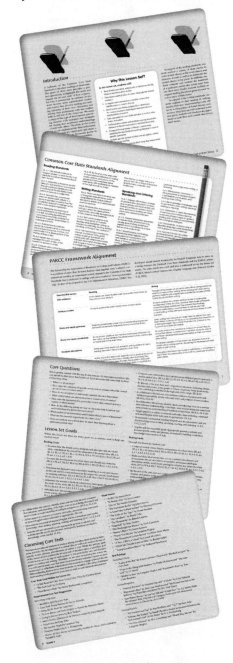

We expect students' responses to the Core Questions to evolve as their experience and understanding become richer with each lesson. For best results, post these questions somewhere in your classroom and use them to focus your instruction.

Lesson Set Goals

Here you will find a list of goals for student learning summarized in clear language in three to five observable behaviors for each reading and writing lesson set, listed with corresponding Common Core State Standards that the goals address.

Choosing Core Texts

For best practice to occur and for all our students to achieve success, all teaching of reading and writing should be grounded in the study of quality literature. Here you will find lists of books, poems, articles, and other texts for you and your students to use for modeling and close reading to achieve the instructional goals of the lesson set. We also explain the types of texts that will focus and enrich your students' reading and writing during this lesson set. Any text that is used specifically as an exemplar in a lesson appears here in the first list. We also recommend additional texts with similar features and qualities to supplement your work in this lesson set.

Teacher's Notes

This section relays a personal message from us to you, the teacher, meant to give the big picture of what the lesson set is all about, the impact we hope it will have on students, and tips or reminders to facilitate your teaching.

Building Academic Language

This section provides a list of key terms and phrases chosen to help your students read, write, listen, and speak during the course of the lesson set. Introduce these terms to your students in context and gradually; scaffold their use by making them visible to everyone, with bulletin boards and manipulatives; and encourage students to use the new words as they communicate during your study together. See the glossary at the end of each grade's lesson set for more information about important lesson vocabulary.

Recognition

The successful conclusion of each grade's lesson set is a time for recognition. Find specific suggestions for how to plan meaningful recognition opportunities for your students here.

Assessment

Reading and writing rubrics aligned to unit goals and the Common Core State Standards are provided in the Appendixes of each lesson set.

Also, see the Reading Lessons and Writing Lessons sections to find Milestone Performance Assessments—practical, reproducible checklists to monitor student progress on key skills.

Also see the Reading Lessons and Writing Lessons sections to find Milestone Performance Assessments for

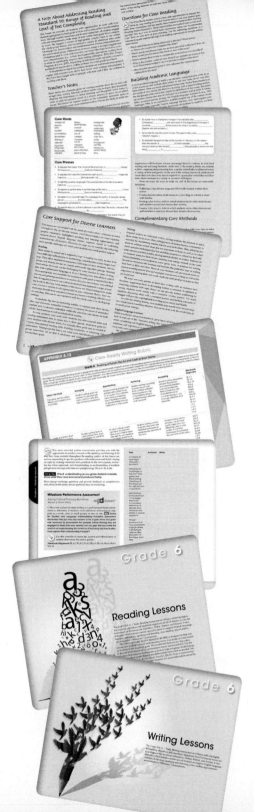

monitoring progress and for standards-aligned reading and writing rubrics.

Core Support for Diverse Learners

Here we provide guidance for how to pace and plan instruction and provide materials that will help all students in your class be successful during the lessons (Available in the PDToolKit).

Complementary Core Methods

This segment offers specific ideas for how to use key instructional structures (read-aloud, shared reading, shared writing, etc.) to reach the goals of the lessons.

Core Connections at Home

This section suggests ways to keep caregivers at home informed and involved.

The Reading and Writing Lessons

Each set of reading and writing lessons is separated into two sections with the following contents for either reading or writing:

- The Core I.D.E.A. / Daily Instruction at a Glance table
- Reading and writing rubrics aligned to unit goals and Common Core State Standards
- Detailed lesson plans (10 for reading, 10 for writing, and 1 Language Companion Lesson)

What to Look for in the Core I.D.E.A. / Daily Instruction at a Glance Table

Specifies the I.D.E.A. framework stage for each lesson

Lists any extra teacher support found in the lesson:
- Milestone Assessment
- Speaking and listening opportunities
- Suggestions for English language learner (ELL) support
- Technology suggestions
- Close reading opportunity

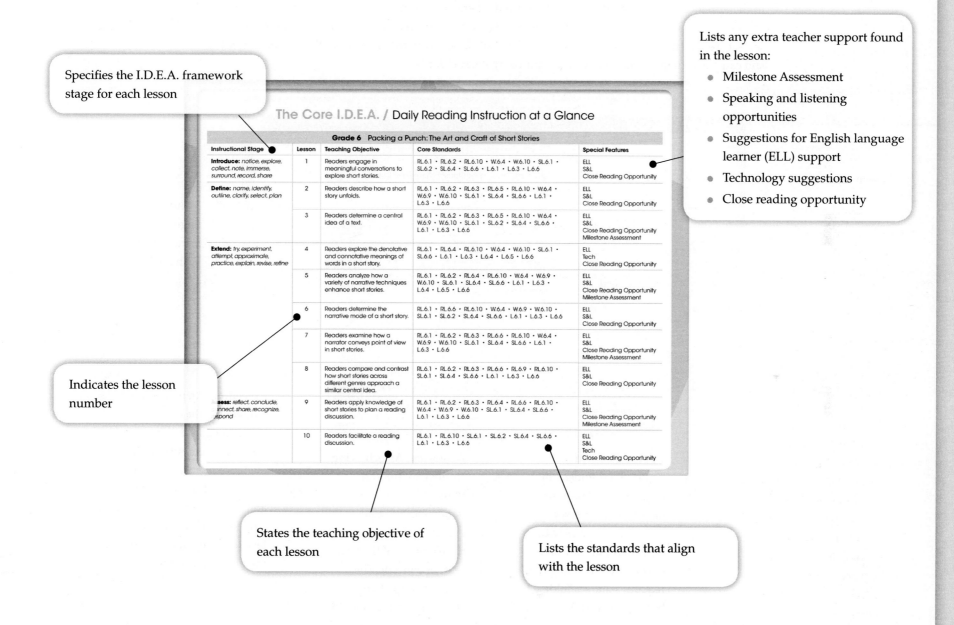

The Core I.D.E.A. / Daily Reading Instruction at a Glance

Grade 6 Packing a Punch: The Art and Craft of Short Stories

Instructional Stage	Lesson	Teaching Objective	Core Standards	Special Features
Introduce: notice, explore, collect, note, immerse, surround, record, share	1	Readers engage in meaningful conversations to explore short stories.	RL.6.1 · RL.6.2 · RL.6.10 · W.6.4 · W.6.10 · SL.6.1 · SL.6.2 · SL.6.4 · SL.6.6 · L.6.1 · L.6.3 · L.6.6	ELL S&L Close Reading Opportunity
Define: name, identify, outline, clarify, select, plan	2	Readers describe how a short story unfolds.	RL.6.1 · RL.6.2 · RL.6.3 · RL.6.5 · RL.6.10 · W.6.4 · W.6.9 · W.6.10 · SL.6.1 · SL.6.4 · SL.6.6 · L.6.1 · L.6.3 · L.6.6	ELL S&L Close Reading Opportunity
	3	Readers determine a central idea of a text.	RL.6.1 · RL.6.2 · RL.6.3 · RL.6.5 · RL.6.10 · W.6.4 · W.6.9 · W.6.10 · SL.6.1 · SL.6.2 · SL.6.4 · SL.6.6 · L.6.1 · L.6.3 · L.6.6	ELL S&L Close Reading Opportunity Milestone Assessment
Extend: try, experiment, attempt, approximate, practice, explain, revise, refine	4	Readers explore the denotative and connotative meanings of words in a short story.	RL.6.1 · RL.6.4 · RL.6.10 · W.6.4 · W.6.10 · SL.6.1 · SL.6.6 · L.6.1 · L.6.3 · L.6.4 · L.6.5 · L.6.6	ELL Tech Close Reading Opportunity
	5	Readers analyze how a variety of narrative techniques enhance short stories.	RL.6.1 · RL.6.2 · RL.6.4 · RL.6.10 · W.6.4 · W.6.9 · W.6.10 · SL.6.1 · SL.6.4 · SL.6.6 · L.6.1 · L.6.3 · L.6.4 · L.6.5 · L.6.6	ELL S&L Close Reading Opportunity Milestone Assessment
	6	Readers determine the narrative mode of a short story.	RL.6.1 · RL.6.6 · RL.6.10 · W.6.4 · W.6.9 · W.6.10 · SL.6.1 · SL.6.2 · SL.6.4 · SL.6.6 · L.6.1 · L.6.3 · L.6.6	ELL S&L Close Reading Opportunity
	7	Readers examine how a narrator conveys point of view in short stories.	RL.6.1 · RL.6.2 · RL.6.3 · RL.6.6 · RL.6.10 · W.6.4 · W.6.9 · W.6.10 · SL.6.1 · SL.6.4 · SL.6.6 · L.6.1 · L.6.3 · L.6.6	ELL S&L Close Reading Opportunity Milestone Assessment
	8	Readers compare and contrast how short stories across different genres approach a similar central idea.	RL.6.1 · RL.6.2 · RL.6.3 · RL.6.6 · RL.6.9 · RL.6.10 · SL.6.1 · SL.6.4 · SL.6.6 · L.6.1 · L.6.3 · L.6.6	ELL S&L Close Reading Opportunity
Assess: reflect, conclude, connect, share, recognize, respond	9	Readers apply knowledge of short stories to plan a reading discussion.	RL.6.1 · RL.6.2 · RL.6.3 · RL.6.4 · RL.6.6 · RL.6.10 · W.6.4 · W.6.9 · W.6.10 · SL.6.1 · SL.6.4 · SL.6.6 · L.6.1 · L.6.3 · L.6.6	ELL S&L Close Reading Opportunity Milestone Assessment
	10	Readers facilitate a reading discussion.	RL.6.1 · RL.6.10 · SL.6.1 · SL.6.2 · SL.6.4 · SL.6.6 · L.6.1 · L.6.3 · L.6.6	ELL S&L Tech Close Reading Opportunity

Indicates the lesson number

States the teaching objective of each lesson

Lists the standards that align with the lesson

What to Look for in the Reading and Writing Rubrics

In the appendixes, we provide a discipline-specific performance rubric, including performance descriptors for four levels of proficiency. A score of 3 ("Achieving") indicates that, by the end of the lesson set, a student has demonstrated solid evidence of success with the elements of the task or concept and can perform independently when required by the standards.

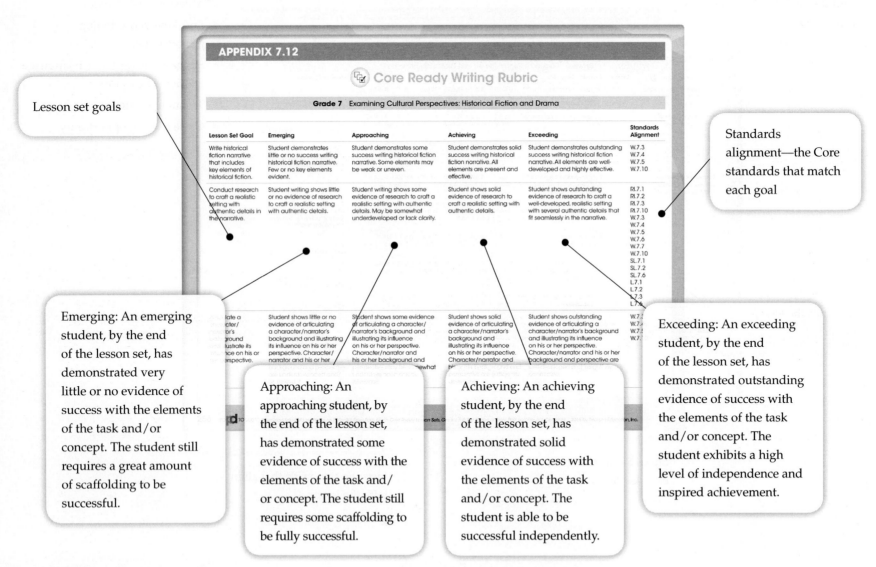

Lesson set goals

Standards alignment—the Core standards that match each goal

Emerging: An emerging student, by the end of the lesson set, has demonstrated very little or no evidence of success with the elements of the task and/or concept. The student still requires a great amount of scaffolding to be successful.

Approaching: An approaching student, by the end of the lesson set, has demonstrated some evidence of success with the elements of the task and/or concept. The student still requires some scaffolding to be fully successful.

Achieving: An achieving student, by the end of the lesson set, has demonstrated solid evidence of success with the elements of the task and/or concept. The student is able to be successful independently.

Exceeding: An exceeding student, by the end of the lesson set, has demonstrated outstanding evidence of success with the elements of the task and/or concept. The student exhibits a high level of independence and inspired achievement.

What to Look for in the Detailed Lesson Plans

Teaching Objective: A succinct statement that captures the primary focus of the lesson.

Standards Alignment: A list of the standards that the students will practice and apply during the lesson.

Materials: List of the texts, resources, equipment, and so on that you should gather in preparation for the lesson.

Indented text indicates scripted suggestions for what you might say to students.

Procedure: The instructional sequence divided into six segments: Warm Up, Teach, Try, Clarify, Practice, and Wrap Up. After a brief definition of the segment, we provide detailed guidance to inform your instruction.

Regular font indicates specific directions or explanations for you.

Charts and tables are provided as examples throughout the lessons.

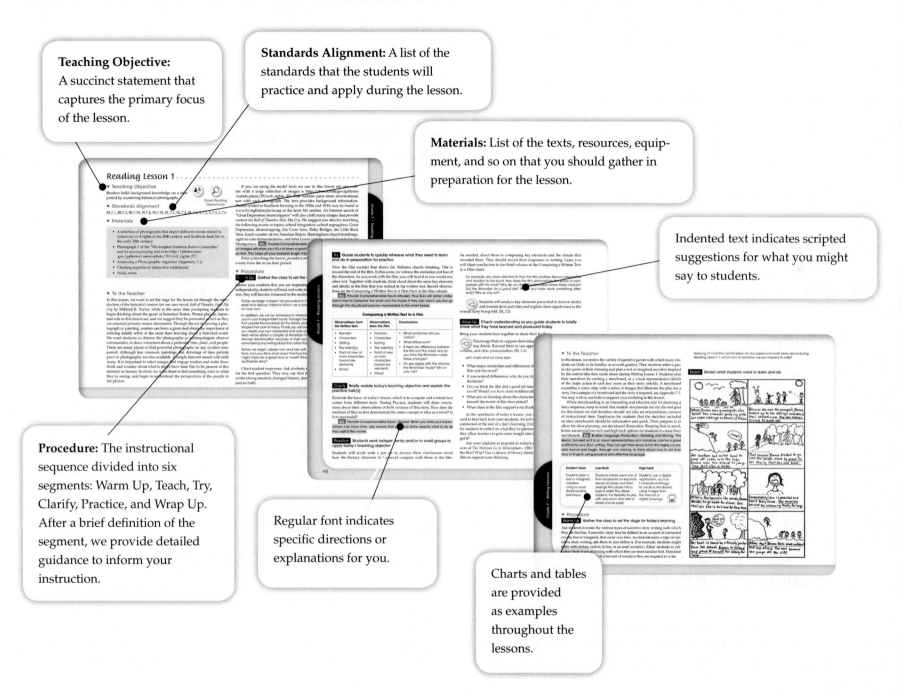

Special Features Marked with an Icon

Look for these icons to help you find the following important elements within each lesson set.

	Suggestions for English language learners
	Speaking and listening opportunity
	Suggestions for technology integration
	Assessment opportunity
	Close reading opportunity

ELL Support

Across the lesson set, we highlight specific strategies embedded in the lesson to shelter instruction for ELL students. Based on Jim Cummins's *Five Principles for Teaching Content to English Language Learners* (www.pearsonschool.com), these strategies will help ELL students participate successfully in the whole-group lesson and will support the development of their language skills. Wherever you see this icon, you can expect to find which of the Five Principles is being employed alongside helpful advice and information to support your English language learners in any lesson you teach. (See Figure 1 for a complete list with descriptions of the Five Principles for Teaching Content to English Language Learners).

Speaking and Listening Opportunities

Speaking and listening skills are essential for career- and college-ready students, yet these two capacities are frequently underrepresented in classrooms. We have embedded frequent opportunities for students to grow in these areas. Look for the speaking and listening icon to see where. Also, see the Core Ready PDToolkit for a grade level-specific standards-aligned checklist to help you assess student performance in these areas.

Technology Options

The Common Core State Standards require that students use technology strategically and capably, and for today's student, this is essential work across the disciplines. Each lesson set provides several suggestions, marked with the Technology icon, for how to build student technology skills and enhance the lessons with various technological tools. Beside each English language arts goal we list for students, we present both high- and low-tech options for your classroom. Although we strongly advocate using a high-tech approach, we recognize that circumstances of funding, training, or even those annoying times when equipment just refuses to function may make it difficult to rely completely on technology. Therefore, we also suggest a low-tech method to achieve the goal—tools that are easily available and inexpensive or free.

Milestone Assessments

Every lesson set includes several suggested Milestone Performance Assessments to assess students' progress toward the lesson set goals. Each of these performance-based assessments aligns directly with one or more Common Core State Standards for reading or writing. With each Milestone Assessment, we include a checklist of indicators for you to observe, with specific guidelines for where to gather the evidence. See each grade's appendix for "copy and clip" masters of these checklists.

Close Reading Opportunities

Every lesson set includes several lessons that require focused, text-based reading where teachers model, and then students practice reading closely to determine what the text says explicitly, making logical inferences from it and citing specific textual evidence when writing or speaking to support conclusions drawn from the text. This icon marks a close reading opportunity.

Figure 1 Five Principles for Teaching Content to English Language Learners

1. Identify and Communicate Content and Language Objectives

When presenting content objectives

- Simplify language (active voice, use same terms consistently)
- Paraphrase
- Repeat
- Avoid idioms and slang
- Be aware of homophones and multiple-meaning words
- Clarify (with simplified language, gestures, visuals)
- Check for understanding

When working with language objectives, focus on

- Key content vocabulary
- Academic vocabulary found across the curriculum
- Language form and function essential for the lesson

2. Frontload the Lesson

Provide opportunities to frontload or preteach lesson elements.

- Activate prior knowledge by connecting to students' academic, cultural, or personal experiences
- Build background by explaining new vocabulary or unfamiliar facts and concepts
- Preview text by reviewing visuals, headings, and/or highlighted text
- Set a purpose for reading by clarifying comprehension questions at the end of the lesson
- Make connections by helping students see relationships between the lesson and other aspects of their lives

3. Provide Comprehensible Input

Make oral and written content accessible by providing support.

- Visuals: photos, illustrations, cartoons, multimedia
- Graphics: graphs, charts, tables
- Organizers: graphic organizers, outlines
- Summaries: text, audio, native language
- Audio: recordings, read-alouds
- Audiovisual aids: videos, dramatizations, props, gestures
- Models: demonstrations and modeling
- Experiences: hands-on learning opportunities, field trips

4. Enable Language Production

Structure opportunities for oral practice with language and content.

Listening and speaking

- Make listening input understandable with a variety of support
- Model language
- Allow wait time for students to plan what they say

Reading and writing

- Tailor the task to each student's proficiency level
- Provide support and scaffolding
- Expect different products from students with different levels of proficiency

Increasing interaction

- Provide collaborative tasks so students can work together
- Encourage the development of relationships with peers
- Lower anxiety levels to enable learning, as indicated by brain research

5. Assess for Content and Language Understanding

Monitor progress and provide reteaching and intervention when necessary.

Diagnostic Assessment

- Determine appropriate placement
- Identify strengths and challenges

Formative Assessment

- Check comprehension in ongoing manner
- Use appropriate instruction and pacing

Summative Assessments

- Provide alternative types of assessment when possible, such as projects and portfolios
- Provide practice before administering formal tests

Accommodations

- Provide extra time
- Use bilingual dictionaries
- Offer oral presentation of written material

Source: Jim Cummins, "Five Principles for Teaching Content to English Language Learners." Retrieved from www.pearsoneLL.com. Reprinted with permission.

Language Companion Lesson

Available on the PDToolkit is a Language Companion Lesson that is a resource and model for explicit teaching of language standards within the context of each lesson set topic.

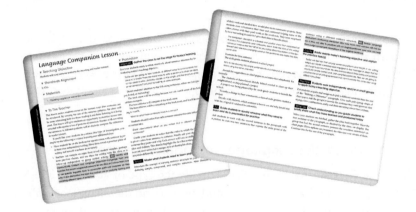

Glossary

A glossary of key terms is provided with each grade's lesson set.

Appendixes

We have provided a variety of resources in the appendixes, including masters for graphic organizers and charts, sample texts for close reading, a Speaking and Listening Performance Checklist, bibliographical information for the research and texts we mention within the lesson sets, Clip-Apart Milestone Performance Assessments that can be copied, and other resources specific to the lesson sets. The Appendixes pages, along with other teaching tools, will be available as downloadable PDFs in the PDToolkit. For information, visit the PDToolkit for Pam Allyn's *Be Core Ready* Series at **http://pdtoolkit .pearson.com.**

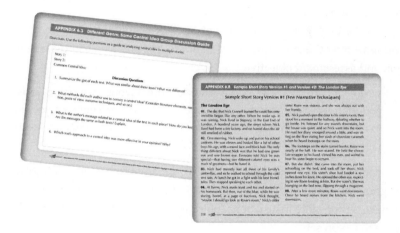

FAQs About the Core Ready Lesson Sets

Q How does Core Ready ensure alignment with the Common Core State Standards?

A We have carefully examined, analyzed, and synthesized the standards to create for all students rich, engaging learning experiences—many of which touch on multiple standards—with the goal that within a single grade level Core Ready students will experience the full breadth of the Core Standards in reading, writing, speaking, and listening. Every grade-level standard in these three areas is listed in one or more of the lessons for that grade level, and most appear in multiple lessons.

As the Common Core document on "Focus and coherence in instruction and assessment" states, not every standard appears as a stand-alone instruction and assessment objective:

> While the Standards delineate specific expectations in reading, writing, speaking, listening, and language, each standard need not be a separate focus for instruction and assessment. Often, several standards can be addressed by a single rich task. (CCSS, p. 5)

We consider every standard we list in the Common Core State Standards Alignment section to be an integral part of what students must do in order to achieve one or more instructional objective of the multifaceted tasks that make up each lesson set.

Q How do you address Language Standards?

A When applicable, Language Standards are listed with a lesson, however, the full range of Language Standards is outside the scope of these lesson sets. Regarding the teaching and application of language standards, we endorse the position statement of the National Council of Teachers of English:

> [T]he use of isolated grammar and usage exercises not supported by theory and research is a deterrent to the improvement of students' speaking and writing and . . . in order to improve both of these, class time at all levels must be devoted to opportunities for meaningful listening, speaking, reading, and writing. (NCTE Position Statement on the Teaching of Grammar, 1998–2009)

The primary goal of grammar study is to improve writing and speaking skills. Students best acquire such skills not from the isolated drill and practice of grammar rules, but from engagement in authentic language experiences requiring active participation in reading, writing, listening, and speaking.

> The inclusion of Language standards in their own strand should not be taken as an indication that skills related to conventions, effective language use, and vocabulary are unimportant to reading, writing, speaking, and listening; indeed, they are inseparable from such contexts. (CCSS, 2012, p. 25)

Q What are the Language Companion Lessons?

A The Core Ready Lesson Sets provide the type of authentic integrated experiences that will help all students expand their language skills. Explicit instruction in selected language concepts benefits students as they try to navigate the complex rules and requirements of conventional English. To this end, we have provided Language Companion Lessons, one per grade, as resources and models for the explicit teaching of language standards within the context of each lesson set topic. The Language Companion Lessons may be found in the PDToolkit.

When choosing teaching objectives for the Language Companion Lessons, we considered a few factors. First, we made sure to include a lesson for each of the standards listed in the Language Progressive Skills, which are specially marked in the standards as being particularly likely to require extended attention over time. The inclusion of these growth-targeted standards will help Core Ready teachers start addressing these important topics.

Second, we made sure that the lesson set and Language Companion Lessons were compatible in focus so that students could immediately connect and apply the language learning to their reading and writing experiences. For example, a lesson on punctuating dialogue would not be a very good match for a lesson set on writing editorials; while dialogue might be included in editorials, it is not very common. A lesson on using domain-specific words would be a better language match for that lesson set. Teaching this lesson would enhance your students' language use during the lesson set. The Language Companion Lessons can also be used as models for teaching other language standards that couple well with the content of the lesson set.

Q How do you address the Common Core State Standard requirements for text complexity (Standard 10)?

A We have reflected the Core requirements by suggesting texts that meet the standards' call for appropriate text complexity for the lesson set grade level. In addition to our own suggestions for grade-level-appropriate text, we have used many exemplars from Appendix B of the Common Core State Standards across each lesson set book.

We support the Common Core State Standards' assertion that the ability to read complex text independently and proficiently is essential for high achievement in college and the workplace and important in numerous life tasks. To this end, we also agree with the Core Standards tenet that all students deserve opportunities to read and engage with high-quality literature. We stand firmly, however, by years of research that suggests that students who are learning to read need extended practice (Allington, 2009; Kuhn et al., 2006) with texts that they can read with accuracy and comprehension (Allington, 2012; Ehri, Dreyer, Flugman, & Gross, 2007) in order to improve their abilities. This means time spent reading appropriately leveled text, which may be above, within, or below grade level depending on an individual's needs and skills. This type of differentiation typically takes place in small-group and independent settings.

It should also be noted that at times students can and should most certainly engage with complex texts above their levels when reading independently if they have been taught skills to grapple with texts and if they are confident in working with them.

Q Do I have to use the core texts recommended in the lesson set? What if I can't get a text or I have a different one in mind?

A Although we always provide specific suggestions for texts that we feel will serve you and your students well for each lesson, there is always room to make thoughtful substitutions. Can't find the text cited in the lesson? Already have a great piece in your classroom collection? No problem. Use the description of what to look for in the introduction to guide you to substitute texts you already own or already love.

Q Are teachers required to use the text exemplars listed by the Common Core State Standards in Appendix B?

A The writers of the Core Standards intended the text exemplars as models of appropriate texts for each grade band, not a required list, as stated below:

> The choices should serve as useful guideposts in helping educators select texts of similar complexity, quality, and range for their own classrooms. They expressly do not represent a partial or complete reading list. (Common Core, 2011, p. 2)

We have included some of the Appendix B texts in the lesson sets alongside our own choices of texts that meet the parameters suggested by the exemplars.

Q You include a special feature for speaking and listening opportunities and strategies to support ELLs in only some lessons, yet there seem to be lots of speaking and listening and similar ELL strategies in practically every lesson. Why don't you mark every instance with a special feature?

A Special features are added where we felt teachers should purposefully focus their instruction and attention on a particular element. Core Ready Lessons are rich with practices that strengthen speaking, listening, and language skills, such as conversing with a classmate, but we do not include a special feature in every instance. We hope that, by highlighting effective practices in selected lessons, we will increase teachers' awareness of how to build speaking, listening, and language skills in any lesson they teach.

Q Must the lesson sets be taught in any particular order?

A Each set of 10 reading and writing lessons has been designed to be modular; that is, the sequence in which you teach the lesson sets may vary in response to local curricular needs, testing schedules, or other factors that influence a school calendar.

Q Should the individual lessons be taught in the order they appear in the book?

A Yes. The lessons within the Core Ready lesson sets are arranged in a purposeful sequence that reflects respected models of how students learn, such as the "gradual release of responsibility" model (Pearson and Gallagher, 1993) and "cognitive apprenticeship theory" (Collins, Brown, & Newman, 1989). Across the lessons, the teacher guides the students toward increasing levels of independence with the lesson set goals. The teaching objectives of each lesson generally build on the knowledge gained in the previous lesson, and many student products are developed in a series of steps across multiple lessons. Therefore, the lessons are designed to be taught as a set and are best delivered in the sequence we provide. At times, it is helpful to pre-teach some of the reading lessons before beginning the writing lessons. When this is advisable, it is noted in the lesson set.

There are four stages in a Core Ready lesson set: Introduce, Define, Extend, and Assess. We use the acronym I.D.E.A. to refer to this structure. Each stage is described below. For a much more detailed description of these stages, please see the foundational book of this series, *Be Core Ready: Powerful, Effective Steps to Implementing and Achieving the Common Core State Standards*.

▶ **Introduce**   The Introduce stage activates students' background knowledge and builds a big-picture understanding of the topic of study.

▶ **Define**   The Define stage provides students with essential knowledge, terms, and structures that will guide their learning about the topic across the unit.

▶ **Extend**   If you compare the types of lessons found in the Define stage of the unit to a road map to learning, the Extend stage might be likened to a series of guided day trips designed to help students become increasingly independent travelers. This is the phase in which students apply and refine the skills and strategies they need to achieve the goals of the unit.

▶ **Assess**   The Assess stage serves to wrap up each lesson set in a meaningful way intended to encourage students to recognize and commit to how they have grown as readers, writers, listeners, and speakers.

Q Is it important to teach both the reading and the writing lessons?

A The reading and writing lesson sets are strategically connected, and we have long advocated teaching reading and writing in an integrated manner. That is, what we study with our classes in reading is directly related to what we study in writing. For example, a reading lesson set on the successful reading of folktales is taught alongside writing lessons on how to write folktales. Or a set of reading lessons on determining theme in traditional text is accompanied by lessons on the theme-related written response to literature.

We have found that the confluence of reading and writing benefits both students and teachers. Each area, reading or writing, helps students be more successful in the other via the natural connections that students make between the two disciplines. A reading experience helps students gain knowledge that helps them develop and enhance the content and structure of connected writing tasks. As students read folktales, for example, they gain a sense of the literary elements, author's purpose, and craft techniques that they will need to consider and include as they write folktales. Likewise, a close study of how to write folktales raises student awareness of what to expect in this genre, leading them be more confident and perceptive readers.

Teachers intuitively understand that such connections help students, but often, curricular materials do not align reading and writing together. Core Ready's dynamically integrated reading and writing lesson sets make it easy for teachers to help students see important connections clearly and immediately. "In reading yesterday, we talked about how folktales usually include magic and fantasy. Today in writing, you begin to imagine how magic and fantasy can be an important part of your original tale."

Because of the close relationship between our reading and writing lesson sets, we strongly recommend that they be taught side by side. Is it possible to teach just the reading lessons or just the writing lessons? In most cases, with some adjustments, this could be done, but again, we recommend that reading and writing be presented simultaneously to maximize the benefits for students and teachers.

Q You provide a lot of specific guidelines for what teachers should say aloud and do during the lessons. Should I follow those specifications exactly?

A It depends. There are all kinds of cooks out there. Some like to follow the recipe to the letter. Some like to refer to a recipe and immediately improvise with the ingredients and procedure. Others like to follow a recipe exactly the first time and figure out places they want to modify next time to suit their tastes and needs. It is much the same with teachers and lesson plans. We expect that some teachers will adopt these plans as written and others will adapt them to suit their teaching style, needs, and resources. The quotes and directions are there to model how the teaching might go. The most nonnegotiable elements by far are the teaching objectives and standards alignment. If you keep your eye on those as your ultimate destinations, there are many roads that will get you there. These lessons are designed to guide you along the way.

Q Are the lessons meant to be taught in one class period?

A Each lesson provides guidelines for six instructional segments: Warm Up, Teach, Try, Clarify, Practice, and Wrap Up. As your students become actively engaged in the rich content of the lessons, you are often likely to find that one class period will not be enough time to complete all of these segments thoroughly. It is perfectly OK to split the segments over two or more periods.

We encourage you to use your professional judgment to decide how to allocate your time teaching these lessons. There are, however, a few rules of thumb that will make your teaching more successful:

1. *Make every effort to include all six segments of the lesson.* There is a purposeful flow and gradual release of responsibility embedded in every lesson to guide students to build independence. Skipping sections interrupts this flow and reduces the likelihood that students will achieve the objectives of the lesson.

2. *Don't let the whole-group segments at the beginning of the lesson (Warm Up, Teach, Try, Clarify) eat up all of your time.* As a group, many teachers have a tendency to go on too long with the whole class lesson. Come on— you know we are talking to you! Nearly all of us are guilty of this from time to time. Just one more example, ask a couple more questions to check understanding, address a few more wayward student comments—we've all been there! Try to keep the whole-group instruction sharply focused with a succinct demonstration (Teach) and rehearsal (Try) of the teaching objective. Your students' attention span is limited, and you need to get "off the stage" so that they can get to what is arguably the most important part of the lessons. Which brings us to . . .

3. *Allow ample time for independent practice.* Courtside instruction and pep talks from the coach are helpful to a budding basketball player, but nothing builds a player's skills like playing the game. Likewise, while young readers and writers certainly need your teaching and guidance, what they really need most is to *read* and *write*—eyes on the text or screen, pencils on paper or hands on keyboard, actively thinking and engaging in the reading and writing process *themselves*. This is where the students get to apply the teaching objective of the lesson on their own using their own texts or writing. This is where they work through the hard stuff of reading and writing, which builds capacity, confidence, and stamina. Students need focused practice, collaboration with other learners, making and revising mistakes, making choices, and revising their thinking and understanding of how language works. It is perfectly okay, even necessary, for you to coach from the sidelines, but if students are to become independent readers and writers, they must have extended time working independently and semi-independently in teacher-led groups. While your students are working independently, you may be holding teaching conferences with individual students, working with small groups to differentiate instruction, or making assessment notes to inform your planning.

A variety of options for allocating lesson plan time are in the table on the next page. All are based on a 50-minute class period. If you have more or less time, scale up or down the number of minutes accordingly, keeping proportions similar. If you choose the options with lengthier practice times, planning a mixture of small groups, centers, and independent practice of the teaching objective will maximize young students' levels of engagement.

Timing Guidelines for a Lesson

	Days (Minutes)	Lesson Segment (Minutes)
A lesson that includes all six segments in one 50-minute session	Day 1 (50)	Warm Up (3), Teach (10), Try (5), Clarify (2), Practice (25), Wrap Up (5)
A lesson that spans 2 days	Day 1 (50)	Warm Up (10), Teach (20), Try (15), Clarify (5)
	Day 2 (50)	Practice (45), Wrap Up (5)
A lesson that spans 3 days, with extended time for the independent practice	Day 1 (50)	Warm Up (10), Teach (20), Try (15), Clarify (5)
	Day 2 (50)	Practice (50)
	Day 3 (50)	Additional Practice (40), Wrap Up (10)
A lesson that spans 2 days, plus a reteach based on Milestone Performance Assessment data to allow students more time to achieve the teaching objective	Day 1 (50)	Warm Up (10), Teach (20), Try (15), Clarify (5)
	Day 2 (50)	Practice (45), Wrap Up (5)
	Day 3 (50)	Reteach Based on Milestone Data: Warm Up (3), Teach (10), Try (5), Clarify (2), Practice (25), Wrap Up (5)

PD TOOLKIT™

Accompanying *Core Ready for Grades* 6–8, there is an online resource site with media tools that, together with the text, provides you with the tools you need to implement the lesson sets.

The PDToolkit for Pam Allyn's *Core Ready* Series is available free for 12 months after you use the password that comes with the box set for each grade band. After that, you can purchase access for an additional 12 months. If you did not purchase the box set, you can purchase a 12-month subscription at **http://pdtoolkit.pearson.com**. Be sure to explore and download the resources available at the website. Currently the following resources are available:

- Pearson Children's and Young Adult Literature Database
- Videos
- PowerPoint Presentations
- Student Artifacts
- Photos and Visual Media
- Handouts, Forms, and Posters to supplement your Core-aligned lesson plans
- Lessons and Homework Assignments
- Close Reading Guides and Samples
- Children's Core Literature Recommendations

In the future, we will continue to add additional resources. To learn more, please visit **http://pdtoolkit.pearson.com**.

Common Core State Standards Alignment

Available in the PDToolkit is a matrix that details the Common Core State Standards alignment for each Core Ready lesson set in all of the Core Ready books. See sample shown below.

Common Core Language Arts Standards Alignment

Standard Number	Standard	The Road to Knowledge (RK)	The Power to Persuade (PP)	The Shape of Story (SS)	The Journey to Meaning (JM)
Reading: Literature					
RL.3.1	Ask and answer questions to demonstrate understanding of a text, referring explicitly to the text as the basis for the answers.	•			•
RL.3.2	Recount stories, including fables, folktales, and myths from diverse cultures; determine the central message, lesson, or moral and explain how it is conveyed through key details in the text.	•			
RL.3.3	Describe characters in a story (e.g., their traits, motivations, or feelings) and explain how their actions contribute to the sequence of events.				•
RL.3.4	Determine the meaning of words and phrases as they are used in a text, distinguishing literal from nonliteral language.			•	
RL.3.5	Refer to parts of stories, dramas, and poems when writing or speaking about a text, using terms such as *chapter*, *scene*, and *stanza*; describe how each successive part builds on earlier sections.	•	•		•
RL.3.6	Distinguish their own point of view from that of the narrator or those of the characters.				•
RL.3.7	Explain how specific aspects of a text's illustrations contribute to what is conveyed by the words in a story (e.g., create mood, emphasize aspects of a character or setting).				•
RL.3.8	(Not applicable to literature)				
RL.3.9	Compare and contrast the themes, settings, and plots of stories written by the same author about the same or similar characters (e.g., in books from a series).	•			
RL.3.10	By the end of the year, read and comprehend literature, including stories, dramas, and poetry, at the high end of the grades 2–3 text complexity band independently and proficiently.				•

PD TOOLKIT™ Common Core Language Arts Standards Alignment for Pam Allyn's *Core Ready Lesson Sets: A Staircase to Standards Success for English Language Arts*, Copyright © 2014 Pearson Education, Inc.   1

Grade 6

Packing a Punch: The Art and Craft of Short Stories

Introduction

A hallmark of the Common Core State Standards is the close readings of short texts. The genre of short story provides a perfect opportunity to highlight this work and unpack the art and craft of how a powerful story is constructed. In addition, as students become more sophisticated readers and writers, they develop reading and writing identities of their own, discussing and sharing their preferences with one another both in and out of the classroom. We want to support this type of development, providing students with examples and strategies for sharing their newfound understandings of texts with others. Therefore, in this lesson set, we ask students to take their understanding of the craft of a short story and create a series of questions or discussion points to lead a group of other interested readers.

Why This Lesson Set?

In this lesson set, students will:

- Read closely and think analytically to determine the big ideas in narrative short stories
- Determine a central idea of a text, citing specific textual evidence
- Compare and contrast how a similar central idea unfolds across a variety of texts
- Read closely and think analytically to determine the various narrative techniques and word choices employed by an author
- Infer the point of view of the narrator as well as other major characters
- Collaborate to create and facilitate a group discussion focused on the art and craft of a selected short story
- Compose formal pieces of literary commentary, applying the standards for reading literature to answer specific questions
- Include specific textual evidence to strengthen written responses to reading
- Craft a central idea-driven short story that incorporates several narrative techniques
- Revise and edit writing in accordance with an understanding of the genre and the conventions of standard English

In support of the reading standards, students analyze a variety of short stories in order to look closely at the word choices and elements of craft as well as to determine the central idea(s) of the piece. In addition, students compare and contrast the treatment of a particular central idea across more than one short story. Finally, students facilitate an original reading discussion group focused on a short story of their choice.

In support of the writing standards, students respond to their reading in writing, sharing their new understandings with others by writing pieces of formal literary commentary. Once they are well immersed in this new genre, students will also have the opportunity to craft their own central idea-driven short stories.

Common Core State Standards Alignment

Reading Standards

RL.6.1 Cite textual evidence to support analysis of what the text says explicitly as well as inferences drawn from the text.

RL.6.2 Determine a theme or central idea of a text and how it is conveyed through particular details; provide a summary of the text distinct from personal opinions or judgments.

RL.6.3 Describe how a particular story's or drama's plot unfolds in a series of episodes as well as how the characters respond or change as the plot moves toward a resolution.

RL.6.4 Determine the meaning of words and phrases as they are used in a text, including figurative and connotative meanings; analyze the impact of a specific word choice on meaning and tone.

RL.6.5 Analyze how a particular sentence, chapter, scene, or stanza fits into the overall structure of a text and contributes to the development of the theme, setting, or plot.

RL.6.6 Explain how an author develops the point of view of the narrator or speaker in a text.

RL.6.9 Compare and contrast texts in different forms or genres (e.g., stories and poems; historical novels and fantasy stories) in terms of their approaches to similar themes and topics.

RL.6.10 By the end of the year, read and comprehend literature, including stories, dramas, and poems, in the grades 6–8 text complexity band proficiently, with scaffolding as needed at the high end of the range.

Writing Standards

W.6.3 Write narratives to develop real or imagined experiences or events using effective technique, relevant descriptive details, and well-structured event sequences.

W.6.4 Produce clear and coherent writing in which the development, organization, and style are appropriate to task, purpose, and audience.

W.6.5 With some guidance and support from peers and adults, develop and strengthen writing as needed by planning, revising, editing, rewriting, or trying a new approach.

W.6.6 Use technology, including the Internet, to produce and publish writing as well as to interact and collaborate with others; demonstrate sufficient command of keyboarding skills to type a minimum of three pages in a single sitting.

W.6.9 Draw evidence from literary or informational texts to support analysis, reflection, and research.

W.6.10 Write routinely over extended time frames (time for research, reflection, and revision) and shorter time frames (a single sitting or a day or two) for a range of discipline-specific tasks, purposes, and audiences.

Speaking and Listening Standards

SL.6.1 Engage effectively in a range of collaborative discussions (one-on-one, in groups, and teacher-led) with diverse partners on grade 6 topics, texts, and issues, building on others' ideas and expressing their own clearly.

SL.6.2 Interpret information presented in diverse media and formats (e.g., visually, quantitatively, orally) and explain how it contributes to a topic, text, or issue under study.

SL.6.4 Present claims and findings, sequencing ideas logically and using pertinent descriptions, facts, and details to accentuate main ideas or themes; use appropriate eye contact, adequate volume, and clear pronunciation.

SL.6.6 Adapt speech to a variety of contexts and tasks, demonstrating command of formal English when indicated or appropriate.

Language Standards

L.6.1 Demonstrate command of the conventions of standard English grammar and usage when writing or speaking.

L.6.2 Demonstrate command of the conventions of standard English capitalization, punctuation, and spelling when writing.

L.6.3 Use knowledge of language and its conventions when writing, speaking, reading, or listening.

L.6.4 Determine or clarify the meaning of unknown and multiple-meaning words and phrases based on grade 6 reading and content, choosing flexibly from a range of strategies.

L.6.5 Demonstrate understanding of figurative language, word relationships, and nuances in word meanings.

L.6.6 Acquire and use accurately grade-appropriate general academic and domain-specific words and phrases; gather vocabulary knowledge when considering a word or phrase important to comprehension or expression.

Core Questions

Before getting started with the day-to-day lessons, it's important to consider the core questions that drive this lesson set. Each lesson should come back to these overarching ideas:

- What is a short story?
- How does the selection of specific words and/or phrases affect the overall mood or tone of a short story?
- How do we recognize or determine a central idea in a short story?
- What central ideas are common across a variety of short stories?
- How does the treatment of a particular central idea compare across a variety of short stories?
- How do the differing points of view of characters help to inform our understanding of a particular short story?
- What makes for an interesting conversation about a piece of literature?
- What are the essential ingredients of a short story?
- How can authors use a short story to share their thinking about a particular central idea?

Lesson Set Goals

Within this lesson set, there are many goals we as teachers want to help our students reach.

Reading Goals

- Examine how the details (story elements and plot episodes) of a short story contribute to the overall development of the central idea. (RL.6.1, RL.6.2, RL.6.3, RL.6.5, RL.6.10, W.6.4, W.6.9, W.6.10, SL.6.1, SL.6.2, SL.6.4, SL.6.6, L.6.1, L.6.3, L.6.6)
- Examine the development of a short story and identify key elements. (RL.6.1, RL.6.3, RL.6.5, RL.6.10, W.6.4, W.6.9, W.6.10, SL.6.1, L.6.1, L.6.3, L.6.6)
- Determine the figurative and connotative meaning of words and phrases as they are used in a text and analyze the impact of a specific word choice on meaning and tone. (RL.6.1, RL.6.4, RL.6.10, W.6.4, W.6.9, W.6.10, SL.6.1, SL.6.4, SL.6.6, L.6.1, L.6.3, L.6.4, L.6.5, L.6.6)
- Determine the narrative mode of a short story and explain the impact of the mode on the story. (RL.6.1, RL.6.6, RL.6.10, W.6.4, W.6.9, W.6.10, SL.6.1, SL.6.2, SL.6.4, SL.6.6, L.6.1, L.6.3, L.6.6)
- Articulate how the narrator or a main character's point of view develops across a story. (RL.6.1, RL.6.2, RL.6.3, RL.6.6, RL.6.10, W.6.4, W.6.9, W.6.10, SL.6.1, SL.6.2, SL.6.4, SL.6.6, L.6.1, L.6.3, L.6.6)
- Compare and contrast how short stories across different genres approach a similar central idea. (RL.6.1, RL.6.2, RL.6.3, RL.6.6, RL.6.9, RL.6.10, SL.6.1, SL.6.4, SL.6.6, L.6.1, L.6.3, L.6.6)
- By the end of the year, read and comprehend literature, including stories, dramas, and poems, in the grades 6–8 text complexity band proficiently, with scaffolding as needed at the high end of the range. (RL.6.10)
- In collaborative discussions, demonstrate evidence of preparation and exhibit responsibility for the rules and roles and purpose of conversation. (SL.6.1a, SL.6.1b)
- In collaborative discussions, identify, share, and develop ideas in a manner that enhances understanding of the topic, text, or issue being discussed and demonstrate an understanding of multiple perspectives. (SL.6.1c, SL.6.1d)
- Adapt speech to a variety of contexts and tasks, demonstrating command of formal English when indicated or appropriate. (SL.6.6)
- Demonstrate command of standard English and its conventions and use the knowledge when writing, speaking, reading, and listening. (L.6.1, L.6.2, L.6.3)
- Acquire and use accurately grade appropriate general academic and domain-specific words and phrases, strategically building vocabulary knowledge when needed. (L.6.6)

Writing Goals

Through this lesson set, students will:

- Compose formal written literary commentary of a short story. (RL.6.1, RL.6.3, RL.6.10, W.6.4, W.6.5, W.6.6, W.6.9, W.6.10, SL.6.1, SL.6.4, SL.6.6, L.6.1, L.6.2, L.6.3, L.6.6)
- Write and share short stories that convey a central idea (theme) and demonstrate the use of a variety of narrative techniques (dialogue, descriptive details, word choice, pacing) to enhance key elements of the story. (W.6.3, W.6.4, W.6.5, W.6.10, SL.6.1, SL.6.2, SL.6.4, SL.6.6, L.6.1, L.6.2, L.6.3, L.6.6)
- By the end of the year, read and comprehend literature, including stories, dramas, and poems, in the grades 6–8 text complexity band proficiently, with scaffolding as needed at the high end of the range. (RL.6.10)
- With some guidance and support from peers and adults, develop and strengthen writing as needed by planning, revising, editing, rewriting, or trying a new approach. (W.6.5)
- Use a variety of techniques, including the Internet, to publish and share writing with a larger audience. (W.6.6)
- In collaborative discussions, demonstrate evidence of preparation and exhibit responsibility for the rules and roles and purpose of conversation. (SL.6.1a, SL.6.1b)

- In collaborative discussions, identify, share and develop ideas in a manner that enhances understanding of the topic, text, or issue being discussed and demonstrate an understanding of multiple perspectives. (SL.6.1c, SL.6.1d)
- Adapt speech to a variety of contexts and tasks, demonstrating command of formal English when indicated or appropriate. (SL.6.6)
- Demonstrate command of standard English and its conventions and use the knowledge when writing, speaking, reading, and listening. (L.6.1, L.6.2, L.6.3)
- Acquire and use accurately grade appropriate general academic and domain-specific words and phrases, strategically building vocabulary knowledge when needed. (L.6.6)

Choosing Core Texts

This lesson set asks our students to analyze strong narrative short stories to determine and trace the development of a central idea as well as to analyze the use of specific words, phrases, and elements of author's craft. While the primary goal of this lesson set is to address the art and craft of the short story, a secondary goal of this lesson set is to expose sixth graders to this potentially new and dynamic genre of reading and writing. Therefore, in advance of teaching this lesson set, you will want to make sure that your classroom library includes a variety of short stories and/or collections of short stories for students to engage with and discuss. When collecting these texts for your students, be mindful of the range of independent reading levels present in your class as well as individual student interest.

Core Texts Used Within the Lesson Set

- "A Bad Road for Cats" from *Every Living Thing* by Cynthia Rylant
- "The Last Leaf" by O. Henry
- "Paul Revere's Ride" by Henry Wadsworth Longfellow

Supplemental Core Text Suggestions

Short Story Collections

- *Baseball in April* by Gary Soto
- *Guys Read: Funny Business* by Jon A. Scieszka
- *Living Up the Street* by Gary Soto
- *The Lone Ranger and Tonto Fistfight in Heaven* by Sherman Alexie
- *Losing Is Not an Option* by Rich Wallace
- *Mara's Stories: Glimmers in the Darkness* edited by Gary Schmidt
- *Petty Crimes* by Gary Soto
- *The Rainbow People* by Laurence Yep
- *Throwing Shadows* by E. L. Konigsburg
- *Visions: 19 Short Stories by Outstanding Authors for Young Adults* edited by Donald R. Gallo

Short Stories

- "Araby" by James Joyce
- "To Build a Fire" by Jack London
- "Eleven" by Sandra Cisneros
- "The Enormous Radio" by John Cheever
- "A Good Man Is Hard to Find" by Flannery O'Connor
- "The Lady, or the Tiger" by Frank Stockton
- "The Landlady" by Roald Dahl
- "The Moustache" by Robert Cormier
- "Nightfall" by Isaac Asimov
- "The Rockinghorse Winner" by D. H. Lawrence
- "Sonny's Blues" by James Baldwin
- "Thank You Ma'am" by Langston Hughes
- "The Treasures of Lemon Brown" by Walter Dean Myers
- "A Tree, a Rock, a Cloud" by Carson McCullers
- "When Mr. Pirzada Came to Dine" by Jhumpa Lahiri
- "Young Goodman Brown" by Nathaniel Hawthorne

Text Pairings

Poem/Short Story

- "Casey at the Bat" by Ernest Lawrence Thayer and "Baseball in April" by Gary Soto
- "Hope Is the Thing with Feathers" by Emily Dickinson and "The Last Leaf" by O. Henry
- "Mother to Son" by Langston Hughes and "Raymond's Run" by Toni Cade Bombara

Fiction/Nonfiction

- "Natural Enemies" by Laurence Yep and "A Globe" by Gary Schmidt
- "Raymond's Run" by Toni Cade Bombara and "We Found Our Son in the Subway" by Peter Mercurio (from *The New York Times*)
- "Just Before Recess" by Jim Van Pelt and "Chalk Face" by A.J. Jacobs (from *The Moment: Wild, Poignant, Life-Changing Stories from 125 Writers and Artists Famous & Obscure* by Larry Smith)

Fantasy/Realistic

- "All Summer in a Day" by Ray Bradbury and "1,2,3" by Gary Soto
- "Ozioma the Wicked" by Nnedi Okorofor (found in *Unnatural Creatures* by Neil Gaiman) and "At the Home" by E. L. Konigsburg
- "No Pets Allowed" by M.A. Cummings and "Thank You, Ma'am" by Langston Hughes

A Note About Addressing Reading Standard 10: Range of Reading and Level of Text Complexity

This lesson set provides all students with opportunities to work with texts deemed appropriate for their grade level as well as texts at their specific reading level. Through shared experiences and focused instruction, all students engage with and comprehend a wide range of texts within their grade-level complexity band. We suggest a variety of high-quality complex texts to use within the whole-group lessons and recommend a variety of additional titles under Choosing Core Texts to extend and enrich instruction. During independent practice and in small-group collaborations, however, research strongly suggests that all students need to work with texts they can read with a high level of accuracy and comprehension (i.e., at their developmentally appropriate reading level) in order to significantly improve their reading (Allington, 2012; Ehri, Dreyer, Flugman, & Gross, 2007). Depending on individual needs and skills, a student's reading level may be above, within, or below his or her grade-level band.

It should also be noted that at times students can and should most certainly engage with complex texts above their levels when reading independently if they have been taught skills to grapple with texts and if they are confident in working with them.

Teacher's Notes

Short stories are a fantastic genre for teaching students about the art and craft of tight story writing. Not only are short stories easy to digest, they beautifully illustrate the importance of careful planning and thoughtful word choice in order to pack the greatest punch in a shorter amount of space. As an added bonus, this lesson set exposes readers to this potentially unfamiliar genre of reading and may excite more reluctant readers who are less likely to tackle longer texts independently.

In advance of teaching this lesson, you will want to select several short stories that illustrate how an author uses techniques such as word choice, dialogue, and point of view to craft a piece with a strong central idea. There are a wide variety of grade-level appropriate short story collections available, many of which are included in the Choosing Core Texts section of this lesson set.

During the writing portion of this lesson set, we ask students to compose two distinct types of writing. We begin with the writing of formal literary commentary in which students must express their understanding of key literature standards in writing. This writing focuses on the use of specific textual evidence, particularly in the form of direct quotations, to strengthen student work. Later in the lesson set, students are asked to write a short story inspired by one of

the central ideas prominent in their own reading. Students work to incorporate many of the strong elements of craft they have observed as readers into their own writing.

Questions for Close Reading

The Core Ready lessons include many rich opportunities to engage students in close reading of text that require them to ask and answer questions, draw conclusions, and use specific text evidence to support their thinking (Reading Anchor Standard 1). These opportunities are marked with a close reading icon. You may wish to extend these experiences using our recommended Core Texts or with texts of your choosing. Use the following questions as a resource to guide students through close reading experiences in sharply written short stories.

- What central idea(s) are being addressed in this text? What textual evidence can you provide to support this claim?
- Which words and phrases stand out as most powerful in this text? How do these words/phrases impact the mood or tone of the story?
- Which sentence best reveals or captures the central ideas you identified?
- What is the narrator's point of view toward key episodes or events in this text? What textual evidence can you provide to support this claim?
- How does the narrator's point of view influence the central idea(s) addressed in this story?

Building Academic Language

A list of academic language to build your students' comprehension of the focus of this lesson set and facilitate their ability to talk and write about what they learn follows. There are words and phrases listed here. Rather than introduce all the words at once, slowly add them to a learning wall as your teaching unfolds. See the glossary at the end of this chapter for definitions of the words. Also listed are sentence frames that may be included on a sentence wall (Carrier & Tatum, 2006), a research-proven strategy for English language learners (Lewis, 1993; Nattinger, 1980), or as a handout to scaffold student use of the content words. Some students, especially English language learners, may need explicit practice in using the sentence frames. Encourage all students to regularly use these words and phrases in their conversations and writing.

Recognition

At the end of the lesson set, it is important to recognize the hard work your students have put into their learning and the way they have thought about themselves and others. This individualized recognition will enhance students'

Core Words

antagonist	literary	protagonist
central	commentary	resolution
idea	memoir	secondary
conflict	metaphor	characters
connotation	mood	setting
denotation	narrator	short story
dialogue	narrative	simile
episode	mode	third-person
figurative	narrative	narrator
language	technique	theme (i.e.,
first-person	personification	central idea)
narrator	point of view	tone

Core Phrases

- *To express the mood:* The mood of this short story is _____. I know this because _____[textual evidence]_____.

- *To express the tone:* The tone of this short story is _____. I know this because _____[textual evidence]_____.

- *To identify powerful language:* This word/phrase of the text is powerful because _____.

- *To express a central idea:* A central idea of this text is _____. I know this because _____[textual evidence]_____.

- *To expand on a central idea:* The message the author is trying to convey about _____[central idea]_____ is _____. This message is conveyed by _____[text evidence]_____.

- *To explain how an author addresses a central idea:* The author conveys the central idea of _____ by _____.

- *To identify a scene that connects to the central idea:* This scene is key to understanding the central idea because _____.

- *To articulate an experience that changed a character:* After _____ [experience]_____, _____[Character]_____ changes. [Explain how.]

- *To explain how a character changes:* _____[Character] _____ is no longer _____. Now, he/she is _____. This change is evident because _____[textual evidence] _____.

- *To explain how a character changes:* If I could describe _____ [Character]_____with one word at the beginning of the story, it would be _____. At the end of the story, it would be _____. [Explain with text evidence.]

- *To identify the narrative point of view:* This scene/story uses _____ narration. [Explain.]

- *To articulate the point of view of the narrator in the story:* In this scene/ story, the narrator is _____ [name narrator]_____. The narrator's point of view toward _____ [key episode or event from the story]_____ is _____.

experiences with the lesson set and encourage them to continue to work hard reading and analyzing literature. At the end of the reading lesson set, students will be comparing and contrasting how a similar central idea is addressed across a variety of texts and genres. At the end of the writing lesson set, students will create their own short story that is inspired by a particular central idea and illustrates their command of a variety of narrative techniques.

There are many fun ways to make the end of this lesson set memorable, including:

- Publishing a class literary magazine filled with student-written short stories.
- Posting student-written short stories to a class blog or website to share with families.
- Hosting a day of story clubs in which students invite other students and staff members to read and discuss their writing.
- Hosting a day of story clubs in which students invite other students and staff members to read and discuss their favorite short stories.

Complementary Core Methods

Read Aloud

Take this opportunity to share additional short stories with your class in order to provide a variety of models for students as they craft their own short stories. Use your knowledge of students' interests to select texts focused on central ideas that will inspire and excite your class. Be sure to highlight and include pieces of writing that include strong examples of narrative techniques such as use of dialogue, a strong narrator, clear pacing, and interesting and dynamic word choice. Consider multiple reads of these short stories to emphasize the importance of returning to key readings to discover new elements. In your first read, you are providing a foundation for the content of the piece as a whole, and your students may benefit from a read-aloud without repeated interruption. In your second read-aloud of the text, pausing to think aloud or asking for students' thoughts allows for deeper understanding of the text.

When appropriate, use your read-aloud as another chance for students to practice one or two of the following skills:

- Identify the central idea being addressed.
- Analyze how a central idea develops across the beginning, middle, and ending of a piece of text.
- Identify the narrator's point of view and how this informs the reader's understanding of the central idea.
- Identify and discuss examples of narrative techniques used by the author and how these techniques enhance the mood, tone, or treatment of the central idea.
- Compare and contrast the treatment of a similar central idea across a variety of familiar short stories.

Shared Reading

Shared reading provides a wonderful opportunity to look closely at excerpts from grade-level appropriate short stories, allowing students to zoom in and focus on an isolated portion of a text. Shared reading is a large- or small-group reading experience where everyone has a clear view or individual copy of the text to read closely and discuss with the group. In this lesson set, use shared reading of key moments within short stories to help students develop the ability to determine the central idea being expressed as well as the examples of narrative techniques such as dialogue, pacing, specific word choice, and strong imagery. Here are some prompts you may want to use in your conversations about these texts:

- Identify the central idea being addressed.
- Analyze how a central idea develops across the beginning, middle, and ending of a piece of text.

- Identify key scenes or moments related to the central idea.
- Identify examples of specific narrative techniques and discuss how they function within the reading.

Shared Writing

During shared writing, the teacher collaborates with students to create a piece of writing. While the teacher is in control of the pen and acts as the scribe, he or she also guides students through the process they will need to ultimately use independently. The content for the writing is facilitated by the teacher yet reflective of students' ideas. In this lesson set, shared writing can be viewed as an opportunity to provide additional practice or scaffolding with the following:

- Crafting a strong statement about the central idea of a particular short story.
- Summarizing a shared reading or read-aloud.
- Planning for writing.
- Practicing a particular narrative technique, such as dialogue or descriptive detail.
- Composing a written response that analyzes the aspects of craft used by the author of a particular short story.

Core Connections at Home

Have students share their favorite short stories from their reading with their families during a special recognition. Invite family members to share a short story or a selected stand-alone excerpt from a favorite narrative text of their own and discuss the central idea being addressed. Use this as an opportunity to build community around the power of narrative storytelling. Family stories, written or oral, also often convey strong central messages. Honor and encourage students and their families to share these as well!

Reading Lessons

The Core I.D.E.A. / Daily Reading Instruction at a Glance table highlights the teaching objectives and standards alignment for all 10 lessons across the four stages of the lesson set (Introduce, Define, Extend, and Assess). It also indicates which lessons contain special features to support English language learners, technology, speaking and listening, close reading opportunities, and formative ("Milestone") assessments.

The following CORE READY READING RUBRIC is designed to help you record each student's overall understanding across four levels of achievement as it relates to the lesson set goals. We recommend that you use this rubric at the end of the lesson set as a performance-based assessment tool. Use the Milestone Performance Assessments as tools to help you gauge student progress toward these goals. Reteach and differentiate instruction as needed. See the foundational book, *Be Core Ready: Powerful, Effective Steps to Implementing and Achieving the Common Core State Standards,* for more information about the Core Ready Reading and Writing Rubrics.

The Core I.D.E.A. / Daily Reading Instruction at a Glance

	Grade 6	Packing a Punch: The Art and Craft of Short Stories		

Instructional Stage	Lesson	Teaching Objective	Core Standards	Special Features
Introduce: *notice, explore, collect, note, immerse, surround, record, share*	1	Readers engage in meaningful conversations to explore short stories.	RL.6.1 • RL.6.2 • RL.6.10 • W.6.4 • W.6.10 • SL.6.1 • SL.6.2 • SL.6.4 • SL.6.6 • L.6.1 • L.6.3 • L.6.6	ELL S&L Close Reading Opportunity
Define: *name, identify, outline, clarify, select, plan*	2	Readers describe how a short story unfolds.	RL.6.1 • RL.6.2 • RL.6.3 • RL.6.5 • RL.6.10 • W.6.4 • W.6.9 • W.6.10 • SL.6.1 • SL.6.4 • SL.6.6 • L.6.1 • L.6.3 • L.6.6	ELL S&L Close Reading Opportunity
	3	Readers determine a central idea of a text.	RL.6.1 • RL.6.2 • RL.6.3 • RL.6.5 • RL.6.10 • W.6.4 • W.6.9 • W.6.10 • SL.6.1 • SL.6.2 • SL.6.4 • SL.6.6 • L.6.1 • L.6.3 • L.6.6	ELL S&L Close Reading Opportunity Milestone Assessment
Extend: *try, experiment, attempt, approximate, practice, explain, revise, refine*	4	Readers explore the denotative and connotative meanings of words in a short story.	RL.6.1 • RL.6.4 • RL.6.10 • W.6.4 • W.6.10 • SL.6.1 • SL.6.6 • L.6.1 • L.6.3 • L.6.4 • L.6.5 • L.6.6	ELL Tech Close Reading Opportunity
	5	Readers analyze how a variety of narrative techniques enhance short stories.	RL.6.1 • RL.6.2 • RL.6.4 • RL.6.10 • W.6.4 • W.6.9 • W.6.10 • SL.6.1 • SL.6.4 • SL.6.6 • L.6.1 • L.6.3 • L.6.4 • L.6.5 • L.6.6	ELL S&L Close Reading Opportunity Milestone Assessment
	6	Readers determine the narrative mode of a short story.	RL.6.1 • RL.6.6 • RL.6.10 • W.6.4 • W.6.9 • W.6.10 • SL.6.1 • SL.6.2 • SL.6.4 • SL.6.6 • L.6.1 • L.6.3 • L.6.6	ELL S&L Close Reading Opportunity
	7	Readers examine how a narrator conveys point of view in short stories.	RL.6.1 • RL.6.2 • RL.6.3 • RL.6.6 • RL.6.10 • W.6.4 • W.6.9 • W.6.10 • SL.6.1 • SL.6.4 • SL.6.6 • L.6.1 • L.6.3 • L.6.6	ELL S&L Close Reading Opportunity Milestone Assessment
	8	Readers compare and contrast how short stories across different genres approach a similar central idea.	RL.6.1 • RL.6.2 • RL.6.3 • RL.6.6 • RL.6.9 • RL.6.10 • SL.6.1 • SL.6.4 • SL.6.6 • L.6.1 • L.6.3 • L.6.6	ELL S&L Close Reading Opportunity
Assess: *reflect, conclude, connect, share, recognize, respond*	9	Readers apply knowledge of short stories to plan a reading discussion.	RL.6.1 • RL.6.2 • RL.6.3 • RL.6.4 • RL.6.6 • RL.6.10 • W.6.4 • W.6.9 • W.6.10 • SL.6.1 • SL.6.4 • SL.6.6 • L.6.1 • L.6.3 • L.6.6	ELL S&L Close Reading Opportunity Milestone Assessment
	10	Readers facilitate a reading discussion.	RL.6.1 • RL.6.10 • SL.6.1 • SL.6.2 • SL.6.4 • SL.6.6 • L.6.1 • L.6.3 • L.6.6	ELL S&L Tech Close Reading Opportunity

Reading Lesson 1

▼ Teaching Objective

Readers engage in meaningful conversations to explore short stories.

Close Reading Opportunity

▼ Standards Alignment

RL.6.1, RL.6.2, RL.6.10, W.6.4, W.6.10, SL.6.1, SL.6.2, SL.6.4, SL.6.6, L.6.1, L.6.3, L.6.6

▼ Materials

- Charting supplies or interactive whiteboard to create a list of behaviors and skills necessary for successful collaborative discussions
- "A Bad Road for Cats" in *Every Living Thing* by Cynthia Rylant
- A selection of short stories for independent reading (see Choosing Core Texts section for suggestions)

▼ To the Teacher

We launch our exploration of the short story by immersing students in the genre, asking them to develop a definition of the genre through their observations and collaborative small-group conversations. While creating an understanding of the genre of short story is a key focus of this lesson, the behaviors and skills necessary to a successful collaborative conversation are also highlighted. Students are not only asked to follow the rules of a collegial conversation, but are also prompted directly to practice key speaking and listening skills such as making eye contact, speaking at an appropriate volume, and presenting ideas clearly and logically. **ELL** Enable Language Production—Reading and Writing. Middle-school ELLs tend to fall into two groups: those who have arrived in the country relatively recently and know little English but have prior schooling in their home language and those who have spent years in the United States and speak English fluently but have not yet developed the literacy skills that would allow them to be officially "reclassified" according to state or district criteria. (Of course, not all of your students will fit neatly into one of these two categories!) Each group has very different needs, particularly regarding their independent levels: Could your newcomers read stories in their home language and discuss them in English? Could your orally proficient students listen to a recording of a story before they analyze it? Look for adaptations that keep texts and tasks both rigorous and accessible for all your ELLs.

In advance of teaching this lesson, organize your students into small conversation groups, considering personality, reading levels, and varying interest to create groups that will be as successful as possible. **ELL** Enable Language Production—Increasing Interaction. Consider putting ELLs in groups with bilingual students who share their home language as well as with monolingual English-speaking peers so that their collaboration can occur in both languages.

▼ Procedure

Warm Up Gather the class to set the stage for today's learning

Select a short story to read aloud to the class. You can choose any story that is particularly illustrative of the short story genre. More specifically, the story you select should represent or include the following characteristics: It should span a short period of time and have a strong central idea and a clear narrator as well as other elements of a short story (characters, a strong narrator or clear point of view, setting, plot, conflict, and central idea). For the purposes of this lesson set, we have chosen to use "A Bad Road for Cats" from *Every Living Thing* by Cynthia Rylant.

 Before reading the selected short story to your students, provide them with a specific listening task. (SL.6.2)

> In a moment, I am going to read you a short story. As you listen to this short story, pay close attention to the elements, words, phrases, or moments that stand out to you. Jot notes about whatever stands out to you as you listen so you can recall these aspects during our discussion. After I finish reading the story, we will discuss the various items you jotted down as we work together to create a definition of short stories as a genre.

ELL Frontload the Lesson—Set a Purpose for Reading. This gives your ELLs a focus for their listening and helps them avoid getting bogged down by extraneous details.

Read your selected story aloud to the class.

Teach Model what students need to learn and do

Ask students to share what stood out as they listened to the short story being read aloud. As students share significant observations and moments from the story, note these ideas in writing as you work with the class to develop a definition of *short stories*. You may choose to record student observations as bullet points or in full sentences, depending on your teaching style.

Some of your students may comment on the language used or the very specific word choice of the author. In that case, highlight the importance of word choice and precise descriptive language in this shorter genre.

Christian Schwier/Fotolia

- Short stories include only a few important characters.
- Short stories use vivid, descriptive language to paint a clear picture in a small amount of space.
- Short stories usually convey one or more central ideas (themes).

Tell students that they will be diving into reading short stories themselves today. In addition, prepare students to work in small discussion groups to share what they noticed or observed in their own reading work. Each small group should aim to uncover a new aspect of short stories to share with the class.

Emphasize the importance of small-group conversation. Take a moment to outline several expectations for conversations as well as to highlight behaviors that facilitate successful collaborative conversation. Record these behaviors and rules on a chart for student reference throughout this lesson set.

Here is a sampling of some of the key speaking and listening behaviors and skills to cover in your teaching. (SL.6.1a, SL.6.1b, SL.6.1c, SL.6.1d)

However, the language and craft of short stories will be addressed more specifically in Reading Lesson 4, so it is not necessary to belabor this point if it does not come up organically in conversation. If necessary, use the following questions to advance the discussion and guide students toward recognizing several key characteristics of short stories.

What do you notice about the length of the story?

How much time passed in the short story we read?

What did you notice about the number of characters and settings included?

What powerful words or phrases stood out to you, if any?

Here is an example of what your class list might look like at this point in the lesson, although your specific work will reflect the words and observations of your own students specifically. As their understanding of the genre develops, we want students to notice the following about short stories:

What Do We Notice About Short Stories?

- Short stories can be read in one sitting. Typically only a few pages in total.
- Short story settings often span a short amount of time.
- Short stories often happen in one location (one setting).

Ground Rules for Collaborative Conversations

- Come to the conversation prepared: Do the reading! Jot notes about what you would like to share!
- Set a goal for the conversation: What will be the outcome of your conversation?
- Take on different roles: Do you need a notetaker? A timekeeper?
- Stick to the text: Ground what you are saying in the reading itself.
- Be an active listener: Keep your eyes on the speaker. Hear what he or she is saying. Don't just wait for your own turn to speak.
- Respond to others: Do you have a question about what someone just said? A comment? A way to link what he or she said to what you would like to share?
- Make sure you understand: Did you understand what the speaker said? Do you need another example? How can you ask for clarification when you need it?

Try Guide students to quickly rehearse what they need to learn and do in preparation for practice

Introduce the small conversational groups to the class. Provide each group with a few moments to get organized. Ask each group to gather and discuss the behaviors and skills you just listed during the Teach portion of this lesson.

> Are there any behaviors or rules that you would like to add to this list or discuss further?

Allow each group ample time to talk.

 As groups begin these initial conversations, take this time to circulate and reinforce some of the important speaking and listening behaviors outlined in this lesson. (SL.6.1a, SL.6.1b, SL.6.1c, SL.6.1d)

ELL Enable Language Production—Listening and Speaking. Keep in mind that even apparently basic listening conventions are culturally specific and may vary even among subcultures within the United States. For example, some children learn not to look at the speaker as a sign of respect; some cultures practice overlapping speech during conversation instead of strict turn-taking. Look for behaviors that may indicate your students have been socialized differently than you, and think about how to encourage them to be culturally flexible depending on the demands of the context.

Clarify Briefly restate today's teaching objective and explain the practice task(s)

Review the goal for each small group today.

> Today you will each dive into the exciting world of short stories! We will begin by reading independently. Remember to make note of things you notice in your reading that you would like to share in conversation with your small group. Once everyone has had time to read independently, we will move to working in our small groups to discuss the short stories we just read. As a group, your goal is to share at least one new observation about the genre of short stories with the class. I have also prepared a list of other discussion questions you can select from to keep your conversation going.

Provide students with the following list of discussion questions. Read through the questions with the class briefly, taking care that students understand the questions themselves before releasing them to work with their small groups.

Discussing the Short Stories: Guiding Questions

- Summarize the story.
- What are the basic elements included in this story (characters, setting, key events)?
- What interesting language did you notice while reading?
- What are you left thinking after finishing the story?
- Why do you think the author wrote this story?

Practice Students work independently and/or in small groups to apply today's teaching objective

Students read independently from the collection of short stories you have gathered (see the Choosing Core Texts section of this lesson set for more detail). Students should make notes as they read in order to make specific contributions to their small group's conversation. Once students have had ample time to read independently, direct students to meet in their small discussion groups to share their observations with one another. **ELL** Enable Language Production—Increasing Interaction. ELLs can use peer work to clarify their understanding of the lesson's goals. Additionally, language develops through use. The more your ELLs talk with their peers, the more their language and content knowledge will develop.

Wrap Up Check understanding as you guide students to briefly share what they have learned and produced today

Gather the class's attention. Ask members of each small group to share their observation(s) of short stories with the class. As necessary and appropriate, add these observations to your class definition of *short story*.

Reading Lesson 2 ·

▼ Teaching Objective

Readers describe how a short story unfolds.

▼ Standards Alignment

RL.6.1, RL.6.2, RL.6.3, RL.6.5, RL.6.10, W.6.4, W.6.9, W.6.10, SL.6.1, SL.6.4, SL.6.6, L.6.1, L.6.3, L.6.6

Close Reading Opportunity

▼ Materials

- Class list titled "What Do We Notice About Short Stories?" created during Reading Lesson 1
- Elements of a Short Story graphic organizer (Appendix 6.1)

- "A Bad Road for Cats" in *Every Living Thing* by Cynthia Rylant
- Charting supplies or interactive whiteboard
- A selection of short stories for independent reading (see Choosing Core Texts section for suggestions)

▼ To the Teacher

In this lesson, we introduce students to the common elements of the short story: character, narrator, setting, and major plot episodes (highlighting the conflict and resolution). While many of these elements may be familiar to your sixth graders, this lesson delves into how authors of short stories include and elaborate upon these key elements in a limited space, emphasizing the importance of word choice and thoughtful planning. Students practice the development of a brief summary that includes all key elements. In addition, as students begin to analyze short stories both with your guidance and on their own, continue to encourage them to return to the text itself, citing specific textual evidence and focusing their attention on the craft of the short story. This work provides a foundation for Reading Lesson 3, which focuses on determining the central idea(s) of a story.

This lesson involves a collaborative in-depth analysis of a short story as well as an opportunity for students to read and analyze a variety of short stories on their own. Therefore, this lesson may best be taught across more than one day of instruction to allow students ample time to read and closely study a number of short stories.

▼ Procedure

Warm Up Gather the class to set the stage for today's learning

Elements of a Short Story Graphic Organizer

Directions: Use the organizer to think about and record the key elements of a short story.

Character(s) (identify and describe protagonist, antagonist, and minor characters)	Narrator (identify narrative mode and narrator, if possible)	Setting (describe the time and place of the story)
Key Plot Episodes (include conflict and resolution)	Brief Summary of Story (include all elements)	Central Idea

Review the class list titled "What Do We Notice About Short Stories?" crafted in collaboration with your students during Reading Lesson 1. **ELL** Provide Comprehensible Input—Graphics. Class-created charts can help your ELLs recall key points and orient themselves to new learning as you proceed through this lesson set. Make sure you repeatedly return to familiar resources like these. Then tell the class that today you will go deeper by looking more closely at *how* the short story unfolds through the use of a series of common key elements.

Introduce the class to the literary elements of a short story using the list here to guide your discussion. Take time to define and discuss each element individually. **ELL** Identify and Communicate Content and Language Objectives—Key Content Vocabulary. While your ELLs may already be familiar with these concepts, they will absolutely need to be comfortable with the terms that label them in order to participate in this lesson. Explicitly discussing key terms ensures that all your students begin the lesson on the same page. Many of these terms, but not necessarily all of them, may be familiar to your students by this grade level.

- **Character(s)**: Short stories include a limited number of sharply drawn characters. Students should note the name of each character as well as several observations related to each character's major traits and personality.
  - **Protagonist:** The main character in a work of fiction whom the reader usually connects with the most.
  - **Antagonist:** Character(s) who opposes or comes into conflict with the main character.
  - **Secondary Characters:** Characters in addition to the main characters who may or may not be essential to the story.
- **Narrator**: Short stories have a narrator who recounts the events of a story. Students should determine narrative mode (first-person or third-person narration) as well as who is telling the story, if it is narrated by an identifiable character.
- **Setting:** The time and place in which the story is set. Typically, short stories take place in a single setting. Students should be able to name the setting, including some descriptive details.
- **Key Plot Episodes**: Short stories include a series of related events, or scenes, that lead toward some sort of conflict and resolution. Students should be able to identify these scenes, or episodes, which will include the conflict and resolution.
  - **Conflict:** Short stories usually include a conflict between two characters (protagonist and antagonist) or a single character and himself or herself. Students should be able to name the specific conflict as well as identify the specific lines or paragraphs that refer to the conflict.

- **Resolution**: Short stories usually include a resolution that wraps up or resolves the conflict presented earlier in the story. Students should be able to identify the resolution as well as identify specific lines or paragraphs from the text that represent the resolution itself.

- **Central Idea**: Short stories reflect a particular central idea. Students should use clues such as changes in character, emotional moments, and resolutions to conflicts to help identify the overall central idea of the short story.

Teach Model what students need to learn and do

Model how to fill out the Elements of a Short Story graphic organizer (Appendix 6.1) in order to identify each of the key elements of this short story. (You will leave "central idea" blank for now.) **ELL** Provide Comprehensible Input—Organizers. Graphic organizers can make lesson content more transparent for your ELLs and facilitate the discussions and writing that will come later on. Organizers visually show the relationships between the ideas you are teaching, making the verbal aspects of the lesson more understandable. Ask students to recall the short story you read during the Warm Up of Reading Lesson 1. Be sure to (1) identify the element in your notes and also (2) include details from the text to describe it. Begin by thinking aloud and naming the characters from this story. As you think aloud about the characters, take care to do more than simply name them; use specific textual evidence to highlight how the author reveals a variety of information about the character in a limited space. Highlight a key moment or moments from the story, asking students to identify the specific places where the author advances the character. Here is one way your modeling could unfold using the short story "A Bad Road for Cats" as an example. Start with Magda, the **main character,** or **protagonist**. Model recording important details the author reveals about Magda.

> We all agree that the main character in the story is Magda. She is the protagonist of the story. Let's take a minute and think about what we know about the woman—her personality, character traits, thoughts, and feelings. In just ten short pages, Cynthia Rylant manages to give us a very clear picture of Magda. Listen again as I read aloud a portion of this short story. Together we will highlight the places in which the author gives us information about the character.

Reread a portion of the selected short story. For the purposes of this lesson, we will continue to use "A Bad Road for Cats" and have selected to read the portion of the text where Cynthia Rylant clearly begins to describe the character Magda, providing the reader with some background information for this character as well as a scene in which Magda advocates for a stray animal found at a gas station. You may wish to display an enlarged copy for students to view as they follow along. As you read this portion of the text aloud, take care to stop and think aloud about the moments in which the author provides additional insight into the main character, highlighting the specific evidence from the text as you go. For example, in the selection from "A Bad Road for Cats," Cynthia Rylant provides us with the following information about Magda through the use of descriptive detail, vivid action, and strong dialogue:

- an idea of her heritage
- an image of how Magda carries herself
- details about Magda's personal life
- examples of Magda's concern for the welfare of animals

Emphasize the tightness of the short story—how authors take care to not waste any space or words within their storytelling.

> As we begin to identify the other various elements of this and other short stories, pay attention to the authors' use of space. No sentence or word is wasted. Instead, every line of the text is used to give the reader key information about one of these essential elements, particularly the characters and their actions.

Discuss the other important character: the boy. He may be considered the **antagonist** because he creates a conflict between Magda and himself by taking and selling the cat. Jot down some details about what the author reveals about the boy. Add the girl and the gas station attendant as **secondary characters**. Neither is really essential to the story, but both add interesting and believable detail as Magda asks others for help in finding the cat.

Introduce the identification of the **narrator**. (Narrator and point of view will be explored in more depth later in the lesson set, but for now expose students to the concept and encourage them to start trying to identify the narrator in their reading. If students do not yet master this, there will be more opportunity later.) Who seems to be telling the story? Magda? An unidentified observer? The absence of *I* in descriptions in the text quickly reveals that Magda is not telling the story. The story is recounted by an unidentified observer. This type of narration is called third-person narrative. Record this: Unidentified narrator—third person narration. Clues: *She*, not *I*, in descriptions of Magda. **ELL** Provide Comprehensible Input—Models. The clues authors provide about a character's personality are linguistic—that is, they appear in words. When you model analyzing these clues in the text, you make it easier for your ELLs to pick up on similar clues in their own texts.

Finally, define the terms **setting** and **plot episode** and discuss them. **Setting** refers to the time and place within a story. A narrative typically unfolds as a series of **plot episodes** (major scenes or incidents) that occur within the story. These episodes are carefully planned to relate logically to one another and to reveal clues about the characters. Episodes provide opportunities for the reader to experience the actions of characters in critical situations.

Try Guide students to quickly rehearse what they need to learn and do in preparation for practice

Next, ask students to collaborate with each other to identify and describe the **setting** and **key plot episodes** of the story in small groups or partnerships. After groups have had enough time to discuss setting and plot episodes, record their findings on the Elements of a Short Story Graphic Organizer as a whole class. When listing plot episodes, guide students as necessary to restrict them to only listing key scenes or episodes (not every detail of the story). Label and discuss the **conflict** and **resolution**. Note and emphasize the use of specific text details to describe the key episodes, as shown in the sample responses. Point out how Rylant establishes the conflict immediately to get the short story rolling quickly. This is a common approach in short stories.

Setting: The time is not identified specifically, but the mention of trucks and the highway lets us know that it's fairly modern. The location is a town that is most likely in the country because Magda has her own house and owns sheep.

Key Plot Episodes:

- Magda walks along the highway in search of her missing cat. She asks a gas attendant if he has seen Louis, but he says no. While walking, Magda recalls finding Louis injured as a kitten and how no one would help him. (conflict)

- Magda stops at a dairy barn, orders food, and sees a "4 Sal.CAT" sign in a window. The waitress directs her to a house.

- A strange boy is at the house and has Louis, who is weak, dirty, and skinny. Magda pays $20 for the cat, and the boy turns him over, crying.

- Magda brings Louis home, and he becomes healthy again. Magda's feelings change as she forgives the boy for taking Louis and makes a stuffed cat and brings it to the boy's house. (resolution)

Clarify Briefly restate today's teaching objective and explain the practice task(s)

Finally, use the elements discovered previously to compose a brief oral summary of the text by recounting the key episodes of the text. In addition to the key plot episodes, remind students to mention main characters by name, include the setting, and avoid including personal opinions about the story. Guide students to go *into* the text for evidence. **ELL** Provide Comprehensible Input—Models. When you directly demonstrate how to compose a summary, you make it clear for all your students, but especially ELLs, what you expect from them. This helps them to become more proficient at composing text.

For the next portion of the lesson, direct students to use the Elements of a Short Story Graphic Organizer (Appendix 6.1) to record evidence of these elements from a short story of their choosing. Emphasize how authors are able to weave each of these elements into a limited space through careful word choice and thoughtful planning.

Practice Students work independently and/or in small groups to apply today's teaching objective

Students read independently from the collection of short stories you have gathered for the class. Remind students that they must ultimately select a short story and identify its elements using the Elements of a Short Story Graphic Organizer (Appendix 6.1), filling in all of the sections *except* central idea, which will be addressed in Reading Lesson 3. In order to provide your students with ample time to read and study several short stories before selecting one to analyze, this lesson may be best taught across multiple days of instruction.

Wrap Up Check understanding as you guide students to briefly share what they have learned and produced today

Gather the class, asking students to have their Elements of a Short Story Graphic Organizer ready. Have a couple of students who wish to promote a story they enjoyed to others share some of the details of their stories, but remind them not to include the ending and spoil it for other readers!

Encourage students to include pertinent details and to use appropriate eye contact, adequate volume, and clear pronunciation. (SL.6.4)

Reading Lesson 3

▼ Teaching Objective

Readers determine a central idea of a text.

Close Reading
Opportunity

▼ Standards Alignment

RL.6.1, RL.6.2, RL.6.3, RL.6.5, RL.6.10, W.6.4, W.6.9, W.6.10, SL.6.1, SL.6.2, SL.6.4, SL.6.6, L.6.1, L.6.3, L.6.6

▼ Materials

- "A Bad Road for Cats" from *Every Living Thing* by Cynthia Rylant
- A selection of short stories for independent reading (see Choosing Core Texts section for suggestions)
- Elements of a Short Story Graphic Organizer (created with the class in Reading Lesson 2; Appendix 6.1)
- Common Central Ideas in Middle School Literature (Appendix 6.2)
- Charting supplies or interactive whiteboard to create Determining the Central Idea(s) of a Text chart
- Ground Rules for Collaborative Conversations (from Reading Lesson 1)

▼ To the Teacher

This lesson allows us to scaffold students' ability to closely analyze a short piece of text by using key details, story elements, and plot episodes to identify a central idea in a short story. Each small group must use information gathered from a shared short story, discuss how those details contribute to the overall development of a central idea, and infer what the author's deeper message about the central idea(s) may be.

In advance of teaching this lesson, you will need to determine how you wish to provide students with access to short stories for groups to read and analyze (either print or digital). Several short stories are suggested in the Choosing Core Texts section of this lesson set. However you may substitute them with any appropriate short stories that are aligned with the interests and reading levels of students in your class. Select a different short story for each group to study. When selecting short stories for each group, consider the specific independent reading levels of students within the group as well as student interest. In addition, each selected short story should clearly exemplify each element discussed in Reading Lesson 2 (character(s), narrator, setting, key plot episodes [including conflict and resolution], and central idea).

The terms *central idea* and *theme* are frequently used interchangeably. A central idea (or theme) of a piece of reading can often be expressed in one or two words, such as "friendship," "coming of age," or "family." However, a central idea (or theme) of a text may also be described in a longer, more specific sentence that describes the message or universal truth suggested by the events in the story. For example, "People should choose friends wisely" or "Growing up means making difficult choices." Throughout the remainder of this lesson set, we will rely mainly on the term *central idea*.

This lesson also emphasizes the importance of small collaborative conversations. Student groups will need to establish clear goals for completing an assignment and take on specific roles. In this lesson, students must read, complete a graphic organizer, and hold a focused conversation. Therefore, this lesson may be best taught across more than one day of instruction. Set a clear deadline for students so they may work to plan their time accordingly.

▼ Procedure

Warm Up Gather the class to set the stage for today's learning

Reread the text of "A Bad Road for Cats" from *Every Living Thing* by Cynthia Rylant.

Prior to reading the story aloud, remind your students to listen carefully as they will need to identify the various elements of a story. (SL.6.2) Also review the elements of this short story that were identified in Reading Lesson 2 and recorded on the graphic organizer. Explain that today's lesson will include using all of that information to identify the final and arguably most important piece: a central idea in the story. **ELL** Frontload the Lesson—Make Connections. It is important to explicitly draw students' attention to how today's lesson builds on their recent work. This will especially help your ELLs leverage what they already know to achieve this new work.

Teach Model what students need to learn and do

Introduce the concept of a **central idea**, asking students to volunteer their understanding of this term. Take a moment to fill in any gaps in their understanding. If necessary, clarify that *central idea* and *theme* are often used interchangeably. In Appendix 6.2, we provide a list of Common Central Ideas in Middle School Literature. Have students refer to this list as a foundation for their thinking. **ELL** Enable Language Production—Reading and Writing. A list of common themes will help your ELLs to home in on salient themes in their own stories. Additionally, note that central ideas are often phrased in terms of abstract nouns, like "friendship"—consider paraphrasing these for students with more familiar words like "having friends" so all students can see the connections between these concepts and their familiar experiences.

> Literary authors reveal their central ideas through carefully chosen details, elements, and episodes. A central idea rises above the concrete elements and details of the story and represents the larger idea or theme most prominent in the text. Sometimes a central idea may be expressed in a word or two such as "hope" or "love." One may also go further and expand a central idea into a sentence or two that conveys the author's implied commentary on the central idea: "Even in times of great strife, the human heart continues to hope." Many texts have more than one central idea. In today's lesson, we will learn some strategies to identify central ideas in short stories.

Think aloud about how a reader might go about determining a central idea of a text. The details included in the text, the story elements, and the plot episodes will all play a large role in this analysis. Although the work with your students thus far has included identifying and describing these items separately, successful readers realize that all of the details, story elements, and plot episodes in a well-written story are interrelated and should be viewed collectively during analysis. Any or all of these may serve as clues to reveal central ideas in the story.

Begin by soliciting ideas from students to get a sense of their command of the requirements of this work. Then review the list of clues in the Determining the Central Idea(s) of a Text list, giving brief explanations of each. Chart these items for students to use as a guide for today's lesson and future work with central ideas.

Determining the Central Idea(s) of a Text

Pay close attention to:

- the title.
- background knowledge of the author or time period.
- what main characters say, do, think, reflect on.
- what main characters learn or how they change.
- the setting.
- important events or episodes, especially conflict and resolution.
- strong emotions or mood.
- key lines or details (suggested through repetition, isolation, placement at end of a passage).
- powerful word choice, sensory imagery, figurative language.

Now, model for students how you might use some of these items to spark your thinking about a central idea in the story and the author's message about a central idea in "A Bad Road for Cats." Model using the Common Central Ideas in Middle School Literature list (Appendix 6.2) and the Determining the Central Idea(s) of a Text list as references. **ELL** Provide Comprehensible Input—Models. ELLs in particular need to see how you use the text to draw conclusions about the central idea of a story. When you think aloud, you are showing them how a proficient reader closely studies a text to understand its meaning.

When I think about this list of central ideas and the story we read, I think there is evidence that points to a few of these central ideas. For example, compassion. Based on what I remember from the story, I am pretty sure that compassion, or sympathy toward others, is a significant central idea. The items on the Determining the Central Idea(s) of a Text list remind me where I can find

evidence of a central idea. I should be able to find several pieces of evidence to support my thinking that compassion is a central idea. In this case, I think I can find evidence in what main characters think and do, how main characters change, and the resolution of the story. Remember what Magda thinks about the boy? While Magda is angry with the boy for harming her cat, she also notices his rotten teeth, tears when letting the cat go, and apparent need for money. She feels rage at first, but later she finds a way to let go of her anger and feel sympathy for him. She shows this by making the stuffed cat for him. This is compassionate behavior. These details (her actions, inner thoughts and reflections, how she changes, and how the story resolves) suggest that a central idea of the story is compassion. Magda is concerned and sympathetic toward the boy even though he has caused the cat to become ill.

Next, I want to expand my thinking about this central idea and consider the question, "What is the author saying about the central idea I have identified: compassion?" I think the author's message about compassion is that it is important to have compassion for others even when they may cause us harm.

Record the results of your thinking on the class's Elements of a Short Story Graphic Organizer under "Central Idea." Review your process. First, you thought about which ideas on the Common Central Ideas in Middle School Literature list seemed to relate to the story. Then you described several examples of evidence from the Determining the Central Idea(s) of a Text list that pointed to a central idea. Last, you expanded your thinking by inferring the author's message about the central idea you named. **ELL** Identify and Communicate Content and Language Objectives—Repeat. This repetition can help ELLs be totally clear about what is expected of them before they head off for their group work.

Try Guide students to quickly rehearse what they need to learn and do in preparation for practice

Place students in discussion groups. Have them use the clues on the Determining the Central Idea(s) of a Text list to analyze "A Bad Road for Cats" more deeply in search of another central idea in this story. The items on the list will help them frame evidence of a new central idea and the author's message about it. Encourage groups to look at the list of Common Central Ideas in Middle School Literature in Appendix 6.2 to scaffold the process.

Take this opportunity to highlight and reinforce the importance of drawing on explicit evidence from the text to support their thinking. (SL.6.1a)

Circulate and support students with their work. Remind students about the importance of text evidence and universality when working with central ideas.

In order to be considered a central idea, there should be multiple points of evidence to support it. Central ideas should be universal, relating to people in general, not just the characters in the story; for example, "It is important to have compassion for others" rather than "It was important for Magda to be nicer to the boy."

Have students share their findings. Possible student central ideas: loyalty, courage, friendship, love. Accept all logical answers for which students can provide several pieces of evidence from across the story, even if they are not on the list of common themes. Use the Determining the Central Idea(s) of a Text list to guide their thinking and provision of evidence. After students identify a central idea, be sure they expand their thinking into a statement by asking them, "What message do you think the author is sharing about a central idea?" Record students' thinking on the class's Elements of a Short Story Graphic Organizer under "Central Idea."

Clarify Briefly restate today's teaching objective and explain the practice task(s)

Distribute copies of the selected short story to each small group. Also, provide students with the Elements of a Short Story Graphic Organizer (Appendix 6.1) to help students organize their thinking before diving into their discussion.

Direct students to read the short story and then work collaboratively to identify and record evidence from the text in response to the questions on the graphic organizer. Students should complete a brief summary of the story as well. Finally, groups should use the gathered information to work collaboratively to identify a central idea in the story. Students may need more than one class period to complete this work.

> Once you have identified each of the elements from the short story with your group, use the information you gathered to identify a central message present in the story. Stay close to the text, using it as an example whenever possible, as you discuss how that particular element contributes to the development of a central idea. Each group should be prepared to share a summary of the story as well as a central idea and the author's message about that central idea.

Share your predetermined deadline for completing this work. Before releasing students to read and discuss the selected piece, take a moment to direct their attention to the Ground Rules for Collaborative Conversations chart (created during Reading Lesson 1), reminding them of these rules and behaviors. Also, emphasize the importance of assigning jobs and setting goals to complete their work. What is their goal for completing the reading? Who will record their thinking on the graphic organizer? What is their timeline for completing the graphic organizer? Who will take notes during the discussion? How will they work collaboratively to draft a short response that reflects their conversation?

Practice Students work independently and/or in small groups to apply today's teaching objective

Provide each small group with several minutes to set goals for completing this work and to assign task-based roles to each member as necessary. Circulate to assist in this process and to informally observe each small group's ability to do this work successfully. (SL.6.1b)

All students read the short story selected for their small group. Then each small group works collaboratively to identify and record each of the story elements using their Elements of a Short Story Graphic Organizer (Appendix 6.1). Next, small groups engage in a collaborative discussion in an attempt to identify a central idea and message in their shared stories, focusing on how the details, story elements, and plot episodes contribute to the overall development of the central idea. Finally, each group composes a short response to share with the class that reflects their conversation.

Wrap Up Check understanding as you guide students to briefly share what they have learned and produced today

Gather the class. Ask each small group to share the outcome of its time together. Specifically, one member of each group should share the following:

- a summary of the short story
- a central idea of the story and the author's message about it
- several points of evidence from the text that suggest the central idea described

As students share their findings, remind them to provide textual evidence to support their thinking and to use appropriate eye contact, adequate volume, and clear pronunciation. (SL.6.4) **ELL** Enable Language Production—Increasing Interaction. Peer sharing allows ELLs to hear many proficient language models and gives them a chance to hear the lesson focus interpreted from a variety of perspectives. Multiple sources of input are important for ELLs as they learn content while simultaneously developing English.

Milestone Performance Assessment

Identifying the Elements and Central Idea of a Short Story   PD **TOOLKIT**™

Collect and analyze the Elements of a Short Story Graphic Organizer as a performance-based assessment to determine if students need additional instruction or support as a whole class, in small groups, or one on one. **ELL** Assess for Content and Language

Understanding—Formative Assessment. Language and content are very bound up in the work of this lesson. Students need to comprehend the literal meaning of the text, interpret the significance of different parts of the text, and express that understanding clearly in writing. Look for examples of how your ELLs are mastering content even if they express that mastery in "imperfect" language.

 Use this checklist to assess student work on the Elements of a Short Story Graphic Organizer.

Standards Alignment: RL.6.1, RL.6.2, RL.6.3, RL.6.5, W.6.4, W.6.9, W.6.10

Task	Achieved	Notes
Identify and briefly describe character(s).		
Identify and briefly describe the narrator.		
Identify and briefly describe setting(s).		

Task	Achieved	Notes
Identify and briefly describe key plot episodes (including conflict and resolution).		
Provide a brief, accurate summary.		
Identify and briefly describe a central idea and the author's message about it.		
Cite several points of evidence that support thinking about the central idea.		

Reading Lesson 4

▼ Teaching Objective

Readers explore the denotative and connotative meanings of words in a short story.

Close Reading Opportunity

▼ Standards Alignment

RL.6.1, RL.6.4, RL.6.10, W.6.4, W.6.10, SL.6.1, SL.6.6, L.6.1, L.6.3, L.6.4, L.6.5, L.6.6

▼ Materials

- "A Bad Road for Cats" in *Every Living Thing* by Cynthia Rylant (or any short story with powerful word choice)
- Charting supplies or interactive whiteboard to create a list of questions titled "Evaluating Word Choice in Short Stories"

- Short stories students selected for independent reading in Writing Lesson 3
- Dictionary and thesaurus for students (hard copy or digital)

▼ To the Teacher

The purpose of this lesson is to increase student appreciation for the fact that great writers choose words with purpose and precision to convey meaning as clearly as possible. Students will focus first on the literal, or denotative, meaning of words and then consider the associations they make, or connotative meanings, and how these nuances affect the reader. Students will expand their vocabulary and become stronger at examining and evaluating word choice. **ELL** Identify and Communicate Content and

▼ Procedure

Warm Up Gather the class to set the stage for today's learning

Present the class with the following four sentences:

> I **strolled** down the street.
> I **strode** down the street.
> I **wandered** down the street.
> I **swaggered** down the street.

Ask students how the sentences are similar and how they are different. They should point out that all four sentences mean that the narrator "I" went down a street. Each sentence, however, creates a somewhat different image in one's mind. Focus on the verbs, which differ in each sentence. The literal meaning, known as the **denotation,** of the verb in each sentence is similar. However, the association and emotional connection we make, known as the **connotation,** to each word varies. Display and discuss the following chart.

Word	Denotation	Connotation
strolled	walked	walked in a leisurely way
strode		walked with speed and purpose
wandered		walked with confusion or lack of purpose
swaggered		walked with pride and arrogance

Teach Model what students need to learn and do

Explain the importance of denotation and connotation in literature.

> When writers compose short stories, they choose words with care and precision in order to convey meaning as clearly as possible to the reader. They are aware of both the denotation and the connotation of the words they use. *Stroll* and *swagger* may both mean *walk*, but the connotations are very different and affect the meaning of the sentence significantly. If a writer refers to a child in a story, the choice of *cherub, tyke, brat,* or *urchin* suggests very different things to the reader!

Explain that readers must have understanding of both denotations and connotations in a text. As a reader, one must first be aware of the denotation or dictionary meaning of the words in a story in order to attain basic comprehension of what the text literally says. Then one must consider the connotation of various words in order to more closely connect to the author's intended meaning. Remind students of the strategies available to them to determine the meaning of unfamiliar words. They should infer, then, if still unsure, to verify the meaning of unknown words. Strategies include:

1. Check context.
2. Look at word parts (Greek and Latin affixes and roots).
3. Consult reference materials.

Ask students to share which strategy they use most often and which one they find to be most effective. Responses will vary.

Now shift the focus to connotative meaning of words in a story. Short story authors choose words with purpose and precision to convey meaning as clearly as possible. They will choose the word with just the nuance they wish to convey. Showcase a few examples in the model short story.

> Let's consider the importance of precise word choice and connotation in "A Bad Road for Cats." In paragraph 3, Cynthia Rylant describes Magda *striding* up to the clerk at the gas station. Why did she choose *striding* instead of *strolling* or *wandering*?

Striding conveys Magda's anger and intense emotion over Louis. Guide students in a discussion that touches on how careful word choice can help to more clearly develop characters, setting, and events. Other possible words to examine in the first several paragraphs: *snapped, spit, pinched, marched, skinny, tracking.* Use the following process:

- Examine each word in the context.
- Discuss the basic meaning of the word. Use a reference tool if needed.
- Consider other words the author might have chosen.
- Discuss the connotation, or nuance, that particular word has for the reader. What does it tell you about the character, setting, or event to which it refers?

Goal	Low-Tech	High-Tech
Determine definitions and synonyms for unfamiliar words.	Use hardcopy reference materials such as dictionaries and thesauruses.	Use online tools such as: • Google Drive (see Tools/Research) • www.thesaurus.com • www.thefreedictionary.com • www.onelook.com (aggregates multiple sources) • www.en.wiktionary.com (multilingual)

Try Guide students to quickly rehearse what they need to learn and do in preparation for practice

Ask students to explore the denotation and connotation of a variety of words in partnerships. If using "A Bad Road for Cats," the section where Magda questions the waitress in the dairy barn and meets the boy who took Louis is rich with nuanced vocabulary. Some suggestions: *stringy, grinned, strange, pleading, leap, clutched, puckering.*

Have students record the results of their discussion of two words as follows.

Evaluating Word Choice in Short Stories

• What is the word?
• What is the basic definition of the word? (denotation)
• What other words might the author have chosen? (synonyms)
• What is the connotation of this word?
• Are there any words that might be equally effective, in your opinion?

Clarify Briefly restate today's teaching objective and explain the practice task(s)

Ask students to reflect on how considering connotation in addition to denotation is helpful in reading and writing short stories.

Explain that in Practice they will choose two more words from their independent reading to examine and evaluate for denotation and connotation.

Practice Students work independently and/or in small groups to apply today's teaching objective

Students read independently. They will choose two words to evaluate using the Evaluating Word Choice in Short Stories question list. They should record their findings in writing.

Wrap Up Check understanding as you guide students to briefly share what they have learned and produced today

Have a few volunteers share their word choice evaluations. Use this time to reinforce understanding of denotation and connotation as well as expand overall vocabulary. Be sure to call on at least one student who agreed with an author's choice and can explain why and one who has a different suggestion for an author and can justify it. **ELL** Enable Language Production—Increasing Interaction. ELLs will need to hear many examples, from both their teacher and their peers, of the denotations and connotations of words if they are to develop a broad and rich vocabulary.

Use the work on the Evaluating Word Choice in Short Stories question list as evidence for the Milestone Performance Assessment that follows Reading Lesson 5.

Reading Lesson 5

▼ **Teaching Objective**

Readers analyze how a variety of narrative techniques enhance short stories.

Close Reading Opportunity

▼ **Standards Alignment**

RL.6.1, RL.6.2, RL.6.4, RL.6.10, W.6.4, W.6.9, W.6.10, SL.6.1, SL.6.4, SL.6.6, L.6.1, L.6.3, L.6.4, L.6.5, L.6.6

▼ **Materials**

• "Paul Revere's Ride" by Henry Wadsworth Longfellow
• Charting supplies or interactive whiteboard to create a chart titled "How Short Stories Pack a Punch"
• Short stories students selected for independent reading in Writing Lesson 3

▼ To the Teacher

This lesson seeks to elevate student awareness of the tricks of the trade that short story authors employ to convey a powerful story to readers in a small amount of space—in other words, how short stories "pack a punch!" The class explores how writers use a variety of narrative techniques to enhance meaning, tone, and mood in a story. Students will comb a story in search of powerful phrases and passages, identify the narrative techniques used, and explain how the sample impacts the story for the reader.

▼ Procedure

Warm Up Gather the class to set the stage for today's learning

Read aloud a new story that has strong evidence of narrative techniques such as dialogue, figurative language, precise words and phrases, vivid sensory images, and/or descriptive details. For the purposes of this lesson set, we will use "Paul Revere's Ride" by Henry Wadworth Longfellow. "Paul Revere's Ride" is written in poetic form, but it also tells a compelling short story, a blend of historical fact and fiction that is rich with narrative techniques.

 Prior to reading the text aloud, remind your students to listen carefully, as they will need to identify the narrative techniques. (SL.6.2)

Teach Model what students need to learn and do

Tell the class that successful authors use a variety of narrative techniques, the tools of the storyteller, to make their writing more effective and powerful for the reader. Authors of short stories in particular must carefully select each word and phrase in their work due to the limited space of the genre.

Begin a chart titled "How Short Stories Pack a Punch." **ELL** Identify and Communicate Content and Language Objectives—Be Aware of Idioms. Note that the expression "pack a punch" is idiomatic and may be confusing for your ELLs. Be sure to explain its meaning. You will use this chart to record the various narrative techniques you would like students to become familiar with and explore. Name the general purpose behind an author's inclusion of narrative techniques.

> Authors use a variety of narrative techniques, such as character dialogue, to create a specific tone or mood and to create a vivid picture of what's happening in the story in the mind of the reader.

Introduce and define several narrative techniques commonly used by the authors of short stories. Introduce and define each one individually, taking the time to share examples or provide students with a concrete and clear idea of each device. **ELL** Provide Comprehensible Input—Models. Specific examples of each narrative technique will help your ELLs understand how they look in text. Strong examples are much more comprehensible than definitions alone. As your conversation unfolds, add each narrative technique to your chart. Include the following narrative techniques in your discussion. Each one is outlined in the completed table.

How Short Stories Pack a Punch

Narrative Technique	Description
Dialogue	When the author provides us with the exact spoken words of the character(s), usually in quotations. Dialogue can help provide important information about a character, a setting, or what is happening in the plot in an engaging way.
Descriptive details	When the author provides details about events, experiences, setting, character (appearance, actions, observations, inner thoughts).
Figurative language	When the usual (literal) meaning of a word or phrase is changed in order to compare, emphasize, or provide a clear image. Some common devices: • simile: when two unlike things are compared directly using *like* or *as* (Example: *She is as pretty as a rose.*) • metaphor: when one object is described as being the same as another seemingly dissimilar object (Example: *I am feeling a roller coaster of emotions.*) • personification: when inanimate objects are given human qualities (Example: *The sunlight danced across the floor.*)
Precise words and phrases	When authors carefully choose words, such as strong verbs and powerful phrases, to further drive home the desired meaning, mood, or tone of their work.
Vivid sensory images	When the author chooses words or phrases that appeal directly to one or more of the five senses: seeing, hearing, smelling, tasting, or touching.

By using narrative techniques effectively, a writer can strengthen the meaning, tone, and mood of a story. Define meaning, tone, and mood. The following box provides explanations as well as age-appropriate language to help students discuss each term.

Narrative Techniques Have an Effect on ...	Explanation	Helpful Language
Meaning	The text should convey meaning clearly to the reader. It should help the reader to visualize clearly what is happening in the story.	*This part makes me better understand . . .* *This part makes me be able to picture . . .*
Tone	Tone refers to the attitude or feelings the *author* or *narrator* seems to have toward the material or the reader.	*The writer/narrator seems to feel . . .* *The writer/narrator sounds as if . . .*
Mood	Mood refers to the effect of the author's words on the reader, how the piece makes the *reader* feel.	*This part of the story makes me feel . . .* *The mood of the story is . . .*

ELL Identify and Communicate Content and Language Objectives— Language Form and Function. Here you are showing your ELLs how authors use particular *forms* of language—dialogue, sensory images, figures of speech— to accomplish particular literary *functions*—affecting the meaning, tone, or mood of the text. When you make these connections explicit, you help your ELLs to analyze texts on their own for similar form–function relationships.

Use several short and powerful quotes from the story to illustrate each technique and discuss how it has an impact on meaning, tone, and/or mood. Begin with character dialogue. Ask a student to define *dialogue* for the class as well as to identify at least one line of dialogue from the short story provided. Take a moment to analyze the sample dialogue from the short story you have selected with the class. Think aloud about how dialogue can provide readers with important details that affect meaning, tone, and/or mood. See the chart for a suggestion of how this dialogue is important to "Paul Revere's Ride" by Henry Wadsworth Longfellow.

Longfellow is very adept at choosing words carefully, and his work is chock-full of words and phrases that pack a punch in terms of vivid meaning, tone, and mood. Work collaboratively with the class to read and reread your selected short story to identify powerful words, phrases, and sentences. For each text sample, name the narrative technique(s) and discuss the impact that the text has on the overall meaning, tone, and/or mood in the story. You will probably notice overlap when trying to identify narrative technique. (For example, descriptive details and vivid sensory images are closely related.) Choose whatever makes the most sense or list both, if both seem to fit well. Also, every story may not exemplify every narrative technique. In fact, it is important for students to understand that authors use these devices selectively and, therefore, not each short story will include examples of each. Create a chart with 3 columns: Example of Powerful Language, This Is an Example of . . . (narrative techniques) and How This Is Important to the Story (meaning, tone, mood).

Record your findings on the class chart. For your convenience, here are several examples of powerful use of language via the narrative techniques identified in "Paul Revere's Ride" by Henry Wadsworth Longfellow:

Example of Powerful Language	This Is an Example of . . . (narrative technique)	How This Is Important to the Story (meaning, tone, mood)
"'If the British march By land or sea from the town to-night, Hang a lantern aloft in the belfry arch Of the North Church tower as a signal light,— One if by land, and two if by sea; And I on the opposite shore will be, Ready to ride and spread the alarm Through every Middlesex village and farm, For the country folk to be up and to arm.'"	Dialogue	Explains Revere's plan with his friend to communicate the approach of British troops, which will prompt him to ride to warn the local citizens, the main focus of the story. Creates a suspenseful mood right from the beginning as the reader wonders whether the British will come and the people will need to fight.
"Then he said 'Good-night!' and with muffled oar Silently rowed to the Charleston shore . . ."	Vivid sensory imagery	This helps the reader imagine how quietly Revere rows, emphasizing the secretiveness of the mission.
"Beneath, in the churchyard, lay the dead, In their night encampment on the hill Wrapped in silence so deep and still . . ."	Figurative language: metaphor Vivid sensory imagery	The author compares the rows of graves below the bell tower to a military camp. Suggests the fine line between soldiers and death. Conveys clear image of silent rows of graves.

25

Example of Powerful Language	This Is an Example of ... (narrative technique)	How This Is Important to the Story (meaning, tone, mood)
"A line of black that bends and floats On the rising tide like a bridge of boats."	Descriptive details	Allows the reader to picture the British ships approaching in the darkness.
"Who that day would be lying dead, **Pierced** by a British musket ball."	Precise words and phrases	"Pierced" sounds quick and painful. (Compared to more common choices like "shot" or "hit.")
"...And yet, through the gloom and the light, The fate of a nation was riding that night; And the spark struck out by that steed, in his flight, Kindled the land into flame with its heat."	Vivid sensory imagery Figurative language: metaphor	The reader can picture the sparks from the racing horse's hooves. The spark from the horse that kindles the land into flame symbolizes the start of the revolution that this battle is fueling. In the line, "The fate of the nation was riding that night" Longfellow emphasizes how important he considers Revere's ride—if Revere had not warned the minutemen, the British may have defeated the American colonists.

Try Guide students to quickly rehearse what they need to learn and do in preparation for practice

Direct students to refer to their copies of the shared short story and to work with a partner to find and discuss powerful language in the text and how the use of particular narrative techniques contribute to the meaning, tone, or mood of the story. **ELL** Enable Language Production—Increasing Interaction. Discussing with peers can give ELLs a chance to hear proficient English speakers analyze the language of a text and gives them a low-pressure environment to practice articulating their own analyses. Note: It is not necessary that student partners be from the same small discussion groups. Rather, this partner conversation provides an opportunity to allow students to work with a broader range of peers from within the class.)

This is a good opportunity to reinforce the importance of posing and responding to specific questions with elaboration and detail by making comments that contribute to the short story under discussion. (SL.6.1c)

Take a closer look at our shared short story. Work with a partner to identify words or short sections of text that seem to "pack a punch." Identify the narrative technique that you think the author is using. Then explain how the narrative technique works to enhance the meaning, tone, or mood of the story.

Circulate as partners work together. Have a few volunteers chart their findings and discuss them.

Clarify Briefly restate today's teaching objective and explain the practice task(s)

Remind students of the purpose of narrative techniques in short stories.

Authors of short stories use various narrative techniques to pack a punch. They have limited space to set a tone and send the reader a clear message about the desired meaning of the short story. These narrative techniques not only help authors to do this but also make their writing much more interesting and exciting to read.

Direct students to closely read the short story they selected during Writing Lesson 3 with an eye out for samples of powerful language in the text, the narrative technique employed in the sample, and how the use of particular narrative techniques contributes to the meaning, tone, or mood of the story. Students should record their findings in the same format used in the Try segment of the lesson in order to prepare to discuss the story with their small group. Once their chart is complete, students can and should continue to read from the selection of short stories provided.

Practice Students work independently and/or in small groups to apply today's teaching objective

Students explore their selected short story (identified in Writing Lesson 3) to find and analyze powerful language samples. Once finished, students should read independently from the collection of short stories you have gathered for them. **ELL** Identify and Communicate Content and Language Objectives—Check for Understanding. Check in with your ELLs to make sure they know how to find narrative techniques in the text. Some students may struggle to identify the significance of particular uses of language or to sift out the interesting from the trivial when working in their second language. If they are struggling, consider having them work with a partner or encourage them to clarify the meanings of unknown words before trying to analyze them. Have students prepare for group discussion by recording the following for at least one story:

- a brief summary of the short story
- the exact words or lines from the text they highlighted as an example of a narrative technique
- the name of the narrative technique identified
- thoughts on how the use of this narrative technique contributes to overall meaning, tone, and/or mood of the story

Once students have had ample time to read, they should meet with their small groups to share their findings. Each member of the group should share what they discovered.

 Remind students to use appropriate eye contact, adequate volume, and clear pronunciation when sharing their findings. (SL.6.4)

Wrap Up Check understanding as you guide students to briefly share what they have learned and produced today

Gather the class. Ask several volunteers to share their discoveries with the class. As appropriate, add these student examples to a class chart to serve as additional concrete models of powerful use of language and narrative techniques.

Milestone Performance Assessment

Examining Powerful Language and Narrative Techniques

Collect and analyze student work as a performance-based assessment to determine if students need additional instruction or support as a whole class, in small groups, or one on one. **ELL** Assess for Content and Language Understanding—Formative Assessment. Examine your ELLs' work thoughtfully, looking for strengths and struggles in both language and content. Sometimes students have a strong grasp of the teaching objective but express their understanding in nonstandard language; alternatively, some ELLs might be struggling to understand the language of the text well enough to analyze it. In some cases, ELLs may not have fully understood the purpose of the lesson to begin with. Each type of challenge will require a different instructional response.

 Use the following checklist to assess student work analyzing the use of language and narrative techniques.

Standards Alignment: RL.6.1, RL.6.4, W.6.4, W.6.10, L.6.4, L.6.5, L.6.6

Task	Achieved	Notes
Choose two words from independent reading and examine and evaluate the words for denotation and connotation.		
Write a brief summary of the short story.		
Highlight the exact words or lines from the text as an example of a narrative technique.		
Name the narrative technique identified.		
Explain how the use of this narrative technique contributes to overall meaning, tone, and/or mood of the story.		

Reading Lesson 6 ·

▼ **Teaching Objective**

Readers determine the narrative mode of a short story.

Close Reading Opportunity

▼ **Standards Alignment**

RL.6.1, RL.6.6, RL.6.10, W.6.4, W.6.9, W.6.10, SL.6.1, SL.6.2, SL.6.4, SL.6.6, L.6.1, L.6.3, L.6.6

▼ Materials

- Photo or drawing of a person engaging in an activity
- "A Bad Road for Cats" by Cynthia Rylant
- A selection of short stories for modeling narrative mode and independent reading (see Choosing Core Texts section for suggestions)

▼ To the Teacher

When discussing point of view in literature, there are two common meanings for this term. The first type of point of view is often called the literary point of view and refers to how the author chooses to narrate the story. Is the voice telling the story a character who is a part of the action? Is the narrator addressing another character or the reader directly? Is the narrator an outside observer who is not part of the story? The answer to these questions will determine the literary point of view, or narrative mode, of the story. There are three possible narrative modes—first person, second person and third person. This is explored in more depth below. We will rely mainly on the term *narrative mode* to reduce confusion between this meaning for point of view and the other common meaning. This second meaning refers to how a particular character, who may or may not be the narrator, sees a situation—his or her attitude or way of looking at a particular set of circumstances. The second type of point of view—the point of view of specific characters—is the focus of Reading Lesson 7.

▼ Procedure

Warm Up Gather the class to set the stage for today's learning

Display a drawing or photo that depicts a person engaging in some type of activity. Example: A girl playing basketball, a scientist working in a lab, a lady catching a bus. Practically anything will do. Randomly assign each student a number: 1, 2, or 3. This is the prompt to which they should write.

1. Pretend you are the person in the picture. Write three to five lines about what happened to you in this scene. **Example:** I saw the bus starting to pull away from the curb. I sprinted down the road yelling, "Stop! Wait!" I almost lost a shoe, but I made it on the bus and took the last seat.

or

2. Pretend you are talking directly to the person in the picture. Write three to five lines telling him or her what happened in the scene.

Example: You woke up very late and rushed to the bus stop. You yelled for the bus to stop. The bus screeched to a stop and you boarded, relieved to find a seat and make it to work on time.

or

3. Give the character in the picture an imaginary name. Pretend you witnessed this scene as it happened to the character. Write three to five lines explaining what happened. **Example:** Mrs. Montgomery was late for work. She ran to the bus and hopped on. She sat down and took a deep breath. "Just made it!" said the driver.

Select a few students who have successfully completed the task to read their mini-stories aloud. Don't have them reveal which prompt they selected. Ask the rest of the students to listen carefully to determine which prompt the writer chose and explain how they knew. **Clues for #1:** Includes details as seen from the eyes of the person in the picture. Uses *I* to refer to himself or herself. The narrator participated in the scene and is telling the story as it happened to him or her. **Clues for #2:** Seems to be talking directly to the person in the picture. Uses *you* to refer to the subject of the picture. The writer appears to have watched the scene but did not participate in it. **Clues for #3:** Calls the character by name. Uses *he* or *she* to refer to the subject of the picture. The writer appears to have watched the scene but did not participate in it.

Explain to students that they are using clues to determine the "narrative mode" of the stories their classmates wrote. Each of the prompts requires writing in a different narrative mode. Another way to refer to "narrative mode" is "literary point of view." Narrative mode refers to the method the writer uses to tell, or narrate, the plot of a story. **ELL** Provide Comprehensible Input—Visuals. If you have students with beginning English skills in your class, consider "staging" the stories by having the reader either act out the story himself or herself, read it to another student who acts out the story, or read it to the class while another student acts on the side. This can turn the somewhat abstract, linguistic cues listed previously into something concrete and understandable so that all your students can grasp the idea of narrative mode.

Teach Model what students need to learn and do

Take a moment to ensure that all students are familiar with and can define the term *narrator*. A narrator is the person telling the story. Stories can be narrated in three modes: first person, second person, or third person, although second-person narration is quite rare. Provide the following explanations.

Narrative Modes

First person: Narrator reveals the plot through the character, usually the protagonist, who is part of the story and tells the story through his or her eyes. Uses pronouns *I* and *me* to refer to himself or herself.

Second person: Narrator reveals the plot by telling the story to another character, usually the protagonist, or directly addressing the reader. Refers to the addressee as *you*.

Third person: Narrator does not participate in the action and is not a character in the story. Tells the story as an outside observer. Uses the pronouns *he* or *she* or *it* (but never *I* or *we*) and proper names to refer to all characters in the story.

Limited: Narrator's knowledge is limited to the thoughts and feelings of only one character.

Omniscient: Narrator knows all of the thoughts and feelings of every character in the story.

Connect the writing prompts from the Warm Up with the explanations here. (The numbers line up with the mode: Example 1 is first person, Example 2 is second person, and Example 3 is third person.) Revisit the clues students used to determine the mode in the Warm Up.

Now, read an excerpt of a story aloud to the class and demonstrate how you would identify the narrative mode. Read enough of the story to identify the narrative mode. For the purposes of this lesson, we will model with the two stories used in the previous reading lessons as well as another story, "The Last Leaf," by O. Henry. You may, however, substitute this text with excerpts from any other short stories of your choice. Just be sure to select at least one example of first-person point of view and third-person point of view for students to identify. (Note: You may wish to distribute copies of the selected short stories to students so they can follow along as you read.)

> Let's look at "A Bad Road for Cats." How is the story narrated? Is it first person, second person, or third person? Remember that this is called the narrative mode, which may also be called the point of view of the story.

Read aloud a short segment, up to where Magda marches toward the door of the Shell station.

> I notice that in this section the author narrates what the woman is doing like an outside observer would. The woman does not seem to be telling the story in her voice. The text refers to her as *she* and *the woman*. Same with the gas station attendant. I see the pronoun *I* here where it says "I lost my cat," but this text is in quotations, which indicates she is speaking aloud, but it doesn't appear she is telling the story directly. I am pretty sure that this story is in third-person narrative mode.

If necessary, continue to read on to look for more evidence of third-person narrative mode, or point of view. **ELL** Provide Comprehensible Input— Models. When you demonstrate how to determine narrative mode, you help all your students see how to do this work on their own. Such demonstrations are particularly helpful for ELLs because authors signal narrative mode by using words in particular ways; students working in their second language may have a harder time picking up on these linguistic cues independently.

Try Guide students to quickly rehearse what they need to learn and do in preparation for practice

Next, ask students to identify the narrative mode of two more stories as you read excerpts from them aloud. Try to select at least one story in first person and one in third person.

Before reading to the class, charge the group with a specific listening task. Ask students to identify the narrative mode of the story. (SL.6.2)

> As I read this bit of the story, listen carefully for the narrative mode of the story.

When students think they have determined the mode, they should jot their response down and be ready to share the clues that helped them.

When stories are written in first person narrative mode, it is usually revealed by the frequent use of *I* in the opening lines. This shows that the main character is telling the story. When stories are written in third-person narrative mode, it is revealed by the lack of any character referring to himself or herself as *I* or *me*. All characters are referred to as *she* or *he* or directly by name.

Authors often choose their narrative mode for specific effect. First person allows an up-close-and-personal view of a key character in a story. Some people dislike it because it removes some suspense, giving away the fact that the main character survives the events of the story. Imagine if Harry Potter had been told from Harry's point of view. No one would have wondered if he would survive through the seventh book! Third person can be effective because it allows the reader inside the minds of many characters. Some people prefer third person because it allows the reader to be a distant and objective observer.

Clarify Briefly restate today's teaching objective and explain the practice task(s)

Review the three narrative modes. Remind students of the rarity of second-person narrative; it is difficult to even find authentic samples in literature, and students are unlikely to encounter it in their independent reading of short stories. First- and third-person narration, however, are both common, and students should be on the lookout for which narrative mode is employed in their independent reading stories. They should also consider why the author may have chosen first-person versus third-person narration.

Practice Students work independently and/or in small groups to apply today's teaching objective

Students read short stories independently. They should:

- Determine the narrative mode of the story they are reading and write it down.
- Jot down the clues they used to make the determination.
- Explain in writing how they think the particular narrative mode used affects the story.

ELL Identify and Communicate Content and Language Objectives—Check for Understanding. Check in with your ELLs to make sure they are able to use the pronouns found in their stories to determine narrative mode. If students seem confused, try to have a bilingual peer translate the English pronouns into the ELL's home language to reinforce the idea of certain words forming a natural class (e.g., *I*, *me*, and *my*, all associated with a first-person singular perspective, have analogues in most languages). If this is not possible, try using an online translator to find out the equivalents in your student's home language.

Wrap Up Check understanding as you guide students to briefly share what they have learned and produced today

Ask a few students to share their findings. Chart responses in four columns as shown.

Title and Author	Narrative Mode	Clues	Impact

Reading Lesson 7

▼ Teaching Objective

Readers examine how a narrator conveys point of view in short stories.

Close Reading Opportunity

▼ Standards Alignment

RL.6.1, RL.6.2, RL.6.3, RL.6.6, RL.6.10, W.6.4, W.6.9, W.6.10, SL.6.1, SL.6.4, SL.6.6, L.6.1, L.6.3, L.6.6

▼ Materials

- Determining the Central Idea(s) of a Text chart from Reading Lesson 3
- Common Central Ideas in Middle School Literature (Appendix 6.2)
- "The Last Leaf" by O. Henry or another high-interest text of your choosing
- Charting supplies or interactive whiteboard
- A selection of short stories for independent reading (see Choosing Core Texts section for suggestions)

▼ To the Teacher

In this lesson, we ask students to infer the point of view of a main character by looking closely at his or her dialogue, actions, and inner thoughts related to significant events within the text and considering how a character's point of view may suggest the central idea of the story. Prior to teaching this lesson, select a short story and read it aloud to the class in its entirety. Take care to select a text that clearly conveys the point of view of a main character. For the purposes of this lesson, we have selected to use "The Last Leaf" by O. Henry; however, you may choose to substitute this text with another of high interest for your class.

▼ Procedure

Warm Up Gather the class to set the stage for today's learning

If time has passed since you read "The Last Leaf," ask students to summarize the story using the basic elements: character, setting, and plot episodes (including conflict and resolution). Today's work will analyze how the details of the story reveal a character's point of view.

Teach Model what students need to learn and do

Introduce and define a new meaning for the term *point of view*. A character's point of view is how she or he views a particular situation—in other words, the attitude or feelings a character has toward key events or individuals in a story. Be clear that this is a different kind of point of view than in Reading Lesson 6. Reading Lesson 6 explored the narrative point of view of the *story*. This lesson explores the point of view of specific *characters*. The Common Core State Standards require that students need to understand and discuss both types of point of view by this grade level.

Reiterate the class's determination from Reading Lesson 6 that the story is written in the third-person narrative mode—the narrator is an unidentified outside observer who recounts the events of the story. This is in contrast to first-person narrative mode, in which the narrator is an actual character who recounts the story as he or she participates in it. In any narrative mode, the details of the story that the narrator describes will reveal various characters' points of view.

Now, model for students by thinking aloud how to determine the point of view of a main character (who, depending on the story, may or may not be the narrator) toward an important situation in the story by paying attention to what the character says, does, and thinks. As you look back at your selected short story, think aloud about the specific lines of the text that you are relying on to make your inference about a particular character's point of view. Use the following questions to structure the discussion.

Identify an important situation, such as the main conflict of the story, and a main character connected to the situation.

> I am going to focus on Johnsy, the woman who becomes ill with pneumonia, and her point of view toward this.

Examine what the main character says, does, and thinks about this situation. What does this information reveal about the character's point of view toward the situation?

> To recognize Johnsy's point of view toward her illness, I must pay attention to what she says, does, and thinks in connection to it. I read how she lies still looking out the window counting the leaves. "Johnsy lay, scarcely making a ripple under the bedclothes, with her face toward the window. . . . Johnsy's eyes were open wide. She was looking out the window and counting—counting backward." She seems to think that when the last leaf falls, she will die. "'When the last one falls I must go, too.'" She also refuses to drink and says that she is tired and ready to let go of life. "'. . . I'm tired of waiting. I'm tired of thinking. I want to turn loose my hold on everything, and go sailing down, down, just like one of those poor, tired leaves.'" This all tells me that her point of view toward her illness is one of exhaustion and despair. She clearly has given up hope and desire to live. Notice how I found and cited specific lines in the text that shaped my thinking about Johnsy's point of view.

Try Guide students to quickly rehearse what they need to learn and do in preparation for practice

Next, ask students to discuss the following question.

As students engage in their discussions, support them as they review the key ideas and demonstrate understanding of multiple perspectives through reflection and paraphrasing. (SL.6.1d)

As the story continues, does the character change his or her point of view toward the situation? (Again, examine what the character says, does, and thinks.)

In this case, the story depicts an important shift in the point of view of Johnsy, the main character. (Note: A change in point of view may not be evident in every story. A character's unyielding point of view may actually be significant in some stories.) As needed, guide students to notice that at first Johnsy clings to the idea that she will die when the last leaf falls. "'It will fall to-day, and I shall die at the same time.'" Johnsy even ignores Sue when Sue asks what she will do without her. When the last leaf fails to fall, however, Johnsy looks at it and then says, "'I've been a bad girl, Sudie . . . Something has made that last leaf stay there to show me how wicked I was. It is a sin to want to die. You may bring me a little broth now, and some milk with a little port in it, and—no; bring me a hand-mirror first, and then pack some pillows about me, and I will sit up and watch you cook.'" She now wants to eat and look at herself and sit up. She even regains her most important hope: "'Sudie, some day I hope to paint the Bay of Naples.'" Clearly her point of view has shifted from one of despair to a feeling of hope.

ELL Identify Content and Language Objectives—Check for Understanding. ELLs in particular may struggle with this language-heavy task, as they may not be familiar with the ways authors signal characters' attitudes and feelings or they may be focused on just figuring out what the text means. Listen carefully to the contributions they make, and check in with them to ensure they're following the lesson.

Now have students discuss the final question: Does the development of the character's point of view reveal a central idea of the text to you? How?

> Let's revisit the Determining the Central Idea(s) of a Text list from Reading Lesson 3. One of the clues listed is "what main characters learn or how they change." Our class has noticed a change in Johnsy's point of view toward her illness from one of despair to one of hope. This shift in point of view is not an accident and is an important clue to determining the author's overall intended message related to a central idea. What central idea or message about life does this change convey?

Responses will vary, but one possibility is that the author is saying that hope can help us find the strength to battle through hardships in our lives. Johnsy heard the doctor's prognosis and lost hope, but when the last leaf wouldn't fall, she regained hope and her will to live. Even though the last leaf was painted on the wall, she doesn't know that the leaf was painted, so she found the hope inside herself.

If students are struggling, encourage them to look at the list of Common Central Ideas in Middle School Literature to prompt their thinking. Ask questions such as: What might the author be trying to say about one of these central ideas in our lives? Why does the main character's point of view change? What does this say about the character? About human beings in general?

Clarify Briefly restate today's teaching objective and explain the practice task(s)

Again, share the purpose of looking at the point of view of a variety of characters in the story.

> As we examine the central idea of a short story, it is important that we understand it from all angles. Authors craft short stories very carefully and include details, such as characters with different points of view toward a topic, on purpose to make our reading experience more interesting and to drive home a specific message.

Review the process for examining point of view. Students will be applying this four-step process to their independent reading in Practice.

1. Identify an important situation, such as the main conflict of the story, and a main character connected to the situation.

2. Examine what the main character says, does, and thinks about this situation. What does this information reveal about the character's point of view toward the situation?

3. As the story continues, does the character change his or her point of view? (Again, examine what the character says, does, and thinks.)

4. Does the development of the character's point of view across the story reveal a central idea of the text to you? What is it? How do you know?

Practice Students work independently and/or in small groups to apply today's teaching objective

Students read independently from the collection of short stories you have collected. As students read, they use the four-step process listed in Clarify to focus on identifying an important character's point of view as it develops across the story. Students should jot notes on their findings and/or highlight the text as needed to track their thinking.

Students should compose a short paragraph that addresses all of the points in the four-step process, citing specific textual evidence as appropriate. **ELL** Enable Language Production—Reading and Writing. Check in with your ELLs to make sure they have the skills necessary to complete these analyses and composition tasks. Newcomers who are literate in their home language may be better off reading a text in that language and discussing it with a bilingual peer before attempting to compose in English. ELLs with high oral proficiency but who struggle with literacy may benefit from reading a text with you in a small group or may need extra scaffolding as they put their analyses down on paper. Look for adaptations that keep the rigor of the texts and task high for all your students while providing appropriate support so that they are successful with the work.

Monkey Business/Fotolia

Wrap Up Check understanding as you guide students to briefly share what they have learned and produced today

Gather the class. Ask volunteers to share their work with the class.

Milestone Performance Assessment

Determining Point of View and Central Idea

PD **pd** TOOLKIT™

Collect and analyze student writing as a performance-based assessment to determine if students need additional instruction or support as a whole class, in small groups, or one on one. **ELL** Assess for Content and Language Understanding—Formative Assessment. As you study your ELLs' work, try to look past nonstandard uses of English to assess how well these students understand the concepts of narrative mode, character point of view, and central idea. Additionally, think of ways you can support your ELLs to compose using standard English conventions for academic tasks..

 Use this checklist to assess student paragraphs based on the identification of narrative mode and use of the four-step process.

Standards Alignment: RL.6.1, RL.6.2, RL.6.3, RL.6.6, W.6.4, W.6.9, W.6.10

Task	Achieved	Notes
Identify the narrative mode of a story.		
Identify an important situation (possibly the conflict) in the text.		

Task	Achieved	Notes
Explain how a main character's point of view toward the situation develops across the text.		
Articulate how the development of the point of view connects to a central idea.		
Provide sufficient textual evidence to support thinking.		

Reading Lesson 8

▼ Teaching Objective

Readers compare and contrast how short stories across different genres approach a similar central idea.

Close Reading Opportunity

▼ Standards Alignment

RL.6.1, RL.6.2, RL.6.3, RL.6.6, RL.6.9, RL.6.10, SL.6.1, SL.6.4, SL.6.6, L.6.1, L.6.3, L.6.6

▼ Materials

- Different Genre, Same Central Idea Group Discussion Guide (Appendix 6.3)
- "The Last Leaf" by O. Henry and "Hope Is the Thing with Feathers" by Emily Dickinson or any other pairing of texts of different genres and common central ideas for modeling
- Pairings of texts of different genres and common central ideas for independent reading (see Choosing Core Texts section for suggestions)

▼ To the Teacher

Prior to teaching this lesson, gather pairings of texts of differing genres with a common central idea. See the Choosing Core Texts section for several suggestions. Another option is to ask students to gather in advance two texts of different genres but the same central idea. There should be enough copies of the texts to facilitate small-group work. It is OK for different groups to be working on the same texts if necessary. Small groups will read and discuss, comparing and contrasting how a similar central idea unfolds across two different genres. In order to provide small groups with plenty of time to read and articulate their conclusions regarding how a particular central idea was addressed across two texts, this lesson may be best taught across a few days. Select and set a clear goal or timeline for this work to share with your students during the Teach portion of the lesson.

▼ Procedure

Warm Up Gather the class to set the stage for today's learning

Show the class the text pairings you have selected prior to teaching this lesson. Focus on the pairing of "The Last Leaf" by O. Henry and "Hope Is the Thing with Feathers" by Emily Dickinson. Ask students to recall central ideas in "The Last Leaf." Be sure that "hope" is mentioned. Read the poem "Hope Is the Thing with Feathers" by Emily Dickinson aloud. Point out that both of these texts deal with a common central idea—hope—yet their treatment of this theme is quite different.

Teach · Model what students need to learn and do

Tell students that they will be working in new small groups to read and discuss these freshly organized texts.

> You will notice that I have included in our reading collection pairings of texts that address a similar central idea. Different authors address the same central idea in a variety of ways. You will work with a new group to compare and contrast how each of these authors deals with a similar central idea in their text using a set of specific discussion questions.

Introduce the class to the Different Genre, Same Central Idea Group Discussion Guide (Appendix 6.3), discussing and clarifying each question as necessary. The questions included in this list are copied here for your convenience.

Discussion Questions

1. Provide a brief summary of each text. What was similar about each of these texts? What was different?

2. What methods did each author use to convey a central idea? (Consider literature elements, narration, point of view, narrative techniques.)

3. What is the author's message related to a central idea of the text in each piece? How do you know? Are the messages the same in both texts? Explain.

4. Which text's approach to the central idea was more effective in your opinion? Why?

ELL Identify and Communicate Content and Language Objectives—Set a Purpose for Reading. Focus questions like these can help your ELLs zero in on the most important ideas as they read so they can avoid getting bogged down by trying to understand every word and sentence.

Use the discussion questions to compare "The Last Leaf" to "Hope Is a Thing with Feathers." Emphasize some items as the type of thing that groups could share after analysis:

- O. Henry writes about hope in the form of a realistic fiction short story. Dickinson uses rhyming poetry to convey the same central idea.

- O. Henry conveys a central idea of hope through Johnsy's shifting point of view as she reacts to events in the story. At first she has little

hope because of the doctor's pessimism, but when the last leaf doesn't fall, she regains her hope and decides to fight and live.

- Dickinson uses the narrative technique of metaphor to compare hope to a bird.

- Dickinson says that hope is within us all through the use of strong imagery: "the thing with feathers that perches in the soul." She feels that hope is always in us—"and never stops—at all."

- O. Henry also feels that hope comes from inside us. The final leaf inspires Johnsy to find hope in her soul that she will live.

- The opinions on which text was more effective will vary, but encourage students to use specific evidence from the text to support their reasoning.

Try · Guide students to quickly rehearse what they need to learn and do in preparation for practice

Remind students that they are to use the discussion questions as a way to compare and contrast how a similar central idea is addressed in two different texts. Their goal, as a small group, is to come up with some conclusions regarding the treatment of this central idea to share with the class. **ELL** Enable Language Production—Increasing Interaction. Group collaboration will help your ELLs comprehend the text, grasp the objective, and try out their analyses in a low-pressure environment.

Finally, outline the various roles that may be necessary to the successful functioning of each small group as well as the timeline groups have to complete this work together.

Allow students the opportunity to organize themselves into small groups, each with a selected central idea and related collection of short stories to study. Then provide students with time to discuss and delegate the following roles and responsibilities in their small groups:

- What are your goals for finishing reading?
- Who will read what?
- Who will keep track of the time?
- Who will record any relevant notes?
- Who will keep everyone on topic?

Circulate as these newly formed small groups begin to interact, taking this opportunity to reinforce the key speaking and listening skills that have been discussed throughout this lesson set. These skills include, but are not limited to, following rules for collegial discussions, taking on various roles, staying on topic, and coming to discussions prepared. (SL.6.1a, SL.6.1b, SL.6.1c)

Clarify Briefly restate today's teaching objective and explain the practice task(s)

Remind students of the focus for their small group work.

> You will work in small groups to explore and discuss how a similar central idea is addressed in texts of different genres. Remember to use the discussion questions to guide your thinking. Your goal is to compare and contrast these texts to come up with some conclusions about how this central idea has been addressed, not to just talk about each text individually.

Practice Students work independently and/or in small groups to apply today's teaching objective

Students read independently from the selection of texts available to their small group. Then students move to discussing their reading with their small group, focusing their conversation on comparing and contrasting how a similar central idea is addressed in the two texts. Students may record their group's thinking on their copies of the discussion questions.

Wrap Up Check understanding as you guide students to briefly share what they have learned and produced today

Gather the class. Ask students to share the results of their analysis with a focus on question 4 from the discussion guide. If students have differing opinions within a group, all the better! Encourage students to use text evidence to support their ideas as they answer the following questions:

- What texts did you compare?
- What was the common central idea?
- Which story did you think addressed the central idea more effectively and why? (Use text evidence related to questions 1 to 3 from the discussion guide to support your answer.)

ELL Enable Language Production—Increasing Interaction. Comparing and contrasting and forming and defending arguments are communicative functions that are considered most effective when they take particular forms. For example, contrasting involves taking two parallel but distinct aspects of the two texts and highlighting their differences; arguing involves asserting an opinion (inherently subjective) and backing it up with textual evidence (inherently objective, in that everyone has the same text). ELLs need to hear many examples of how their English-proficient peers accomplish these linguistic tasks, and they need many opportunities to practice them as well.

Reading Lesson 9 . . . .

▼ Teaching Objective

Readers apply knowledge of short stories to plan a reading discussion.

Close Reading Opportunity

▼ Standards Alignment

RL.6.1, RL.6.2, RL.6.3, RL.6.4, RL.6.6, RL.6.10, W.6.4, W.6.9, W.6.10, SL.6.1, SL.6.4, SL.6.6, L.6.1, L.6.3, L.6.6

▼ Materials

- Charting supplies or interactive whiteboard to jot quick notes during the class review in the Warm Up portion of the lesson
- Example(s) of discussion guides designed for facilitating a conversation about a particular text
- "The Last Leaf" by O. Henry or any other familiar short story for which you have created a sample discussion guide
- Sample Short Story Discussion Guide (Appendix 6.4)

▼ To the Teacher

Students continue to work in the same small groups as in Reading Lesson 8. However, for the work of this lesson, students will form partnerships within their group. Each partnership will select a short story from the collection they have read in independent reading. Then partners will collaborate to create a discussion guide designed to help other readers comprehend and engage in rigorous discussion of the text. Students should demonstrate their learning about the various elements and techniques that make up an artful short story as well as their knowledge of the particular story to be discussed through the questions they create for the discussion guide.

In advance of teaching this lesson, you will need to find at least one example of a discussion guide that is included within a text to facilitate a book club or other conversation. A good discussion guide asks thought-provoking questions about key details of a text. The questions tend to be text-specific but open-ended enough to inspire lively discussion. The sample you share does not need to be from a grade-level appropriate text; rather, any text from your own life or one that clearly demonstrates the question format typical of these discussion guides will work. We have included a sample in Appendix 6.4.

▼ Procedure

Warm Up Gather the class to set the stage for today's learning

---

Sample Short Story Discussion Guide: "The Last Leaf" by O. Henry

1. Why do you think O. Henry called the story "The Last Leaf?"

2. The author uses lots of figurative language, descriptive detail, and imagery in the story. What do you think are the strongest examples?

3. Why do you think O. Henry chooses to personify pneumonia? Was this an effective use of figurative language? Explain.

4. How would you describe the mood of the story after Johnsy becomes sick? What actions, dialogue, and language help convey the mood?

5. How would you describe the relation between Johnsy and Sue? How is their relationship important to the story?

6. Do you think Johnsy really believes that she will pass away with the last leaf? Why or why not? Cite evidence from the text to support your thinking.

7. This story was published in 1907 and takes place around that time. Does the time period have an impact on the story? If the story took place today, would anything be different or not? Explain.

8. How does Johnsy's point of view change across the story? How is this important to the central idea(s)?

9. O. Henry is famous for writing stories with a "twist," or surprise at the end. What was the twist in this story? Were you surprised? Explain?

10. The author describes Behrman as a failed artist. Why is this significant to the story? Do you agree?

11. One of the central ideas of the story is hope. How is hope an important theme? What do you think O. Henry message is about hope? What other central ideas may be found in this story?

12. What is your overall opinion of the story? What other comments do you have to share?

Review the various aspects of a short story that you have studied during this lesson set. **ELL** Frontload the Lesson—Activate Prior Knowledge. Highlighting what students have already learned about short stories will help your ELLs mentally organize themselves for the work they will undertake today. Use any classroom charts or other artifacts of your teaching to guide this conversation. Jot student responses in a quick list for reference later in this lesson. Some aspects of your teaching to take care to highlight or include in this conversation include:

- Short stories share common literary elements (character, narrator, setting, key plot episodes, often including conflict and resolution and central idea).

- There are usually many details in a story that convey a central idea and the author's message about it.

- A story may have more than one central idea.

- Words have both denotations and connotations, and because of this authors must choose words carefully.

- Authors use many narrative techniques (dialogue, figurative language, precise words and phrases, vivid sensory images, descriptive details) that have an impact on meaning, tone, and mood.

- Authors choose a narrative mode that may have an important impact on the story.

- Development of the point of view of the narrator or main character is usually connected to a central idea of a story.

Reiterate for students that awareness of each of these aspects of the short story is helpful for deep comprehension and enhances the overall reading experience.

> As readers of short stories, we need to pay attention to these important elements and details to fully connect with all a text has to offer. This is sometimes hard work, but it also can be a very engaging and enjoyable challenge, especially when we can explore a great story together with friends. This is why people form book clubs and publishers often provide discussion guides to challenge readers to think about and discuss compelling pieces of the story.

Teach Model what students need to learn and do

Explore the idea of using discussion guides to facilitate a conversation about a particular book or text.

> Often, books or other texts are accompanied by a discussion guide that can help facilitate a conversation. These discussion guides ask a variety of interesting questions that help future readers dig into and think about some of the most important aspects of the text. All of our learning thus far will inspire dynamic questions that will push the thinking of other readers.

Share the model discussion guide you selected to show the class **ELL** Provide Comprehensible Input—Visuals. ELLs will be more successful at creating a strong discussion guide if they can actually see one and study how it is put together. We have included a sample in Appendix 6.4.

Tell the class the goal of today's work.

> Today you will work in partnerships to create a discussion guide for one of the stories you have read in Practice. Later, we will use your work to host discussion groups focused on your selected short stories.

Model for the class how to generate thought-provoking open-ended questions based on a specific short story. For the purposes of this lesson, we will use the story "The Last Leaf." Emphasize the need to use your knowledge of the target story as well as the list of important aspects of the short story genre you discussed with the class during the Warm Up portion of this lesson. The questions should ask readers to think critically about key elements and details of the text and use specifics from the text to develop and support their thinking. Phrases like *Why do you think . . .* and *How does the . . .* will come in handy. **ELL** Identify and Communicate Content and Language Objectives—Language Form and Function. Phrases like these (forms) show your ELLs how to accomplish the task of posing thought-provoking, open-ended questions (function). Complex question stems can support language learners to go beyond basic questions that take more familiar forms.

Also, state the importance of keeping questions open-ended to provoke lively, prolonged discussion. Good question for discussion: Why do you think the author chose a city park for the setting? Poor question for discussion: What is the name of the park?

> You want to make sure that the questions you create challenge your discussion group to think about all of the aspects of a short story we have studied together over the past few weeks. Take a look at this discussion guide for "The Last Leaf." The first question asks readers to talk about the significance of the title, which would hopefully generate discussion about the plot and maybe even the central idea of the story. Notice how the second question presents how the story is narrated but then asks the readers to think about why the author chose that narrative mode. Good discussion guides focus on key elements and details and ask readers to share their thinking about why these things are important to the story.

Continue to read through and discuss the remaining questions included on this sample guide, drawing attention to the difference between each question, the elements and details addressed, and what each question asks the discussion group to think about. Take care to emphasize that many of these questions are intended to spark an interesting conversation to which many can contribute. Also, highlight that while a few of the questions are applicable to all short stories, there are several questions that are highly specific to this short story. The students' guides may include general questions that could apply to any story (e.g., Who was your favorite character and why?) but should also address specific details from the story (e.g., Why do you think the author chose the word *shrieked* in the last paragraph?)

Try Guide students to quickly rehearse what they need to learn and do in preparation for practice

Plan logistics and goals for the partner work in Practice. Allow small groups a moment to organize themselves into partnerships. Then direct each partnership to select a short story about which it will create a discussion guide. Finally, review the goals and timeline of this work for students so that they may set specific goals for themselves.

As you work together to set goals for your time and work, think about each of these tasks. Each of you must read or reread the selected short story. Together, you need time to craft at least eight questions that help future readers engage with key aspects of this short story. Several of your questions need to be specific to your story and not general questions that could be asked of any short story.

Check in on partnerships to be sure they are on track with their planning. Have a few groups share their decisions.

Clarify Briefly restate today's teaching objective and explain the practice task(s)

Remind students of the purpose of today's work.

> Creating these discussion guides with a partner not only will demonstrate your own understanding of the short story, but it also will help future readers consider each of the important elements of a short story and benefit from your expertise.

Reiterate the timeline for the completion of the work. Remind students of the expectations:

- Develop at least eight discussion questions for a selected short story.
- Content of questions should demonstrate knowledge of the short story genre and the teaching objectives of the lesson set.
- Content of several questions should demonstrate comprehension of the target short story by including references to specific elements and details.
- Questions should have potential to engage others in open-ended discussion of the target short story.

ELL Enable Language Production—Listening and Speaking. This lesson supports the development of your ELLs' oral language skills. Clear guidelines for the discussion guide can scaffold their ability to lead and participate in complex conversations.

Practice Students work independently and/or in small groups to apply today's teaching objective

Students read their selected short story independently, highlighting or marking the text as necessary to note key elements and details they may want to address in a discussion guide. Then partners shift to collaborate in order to generate original questions that reflect their own understanding of the story as well as their knowledge of the craft of short stories. When the questions are developed, the partners should test out answering their own questions orally to check that the questions make sense and can be answered.

This more extended partner conversation provides you with the opportunity to reinforce several of the speaking and listening skills that have been essential throughout the reading portion of this lesson set, such as responding to specific questions with elaboration and detail, staying on topic by making comments that contribute to the conversation, reviewing key ideas expressed, and demonstrating an understanding of multiple perspectives through reflection and paraphrasing. (SL.6.1c, SL.6.1d)

Wrap Up Check understanding as you guide students to briefly share what they have learned and produced today

Have groups exchange questions and provide feedback on completeness and clarity to the group whose questions they are reviewing.

Milestone Performance Assessment

Asking Critical-Thinking Questions About a Short Story

 PD **pd** TOOLKIT™

Collect and analyze student writing as a performance-based assessment to determine if students need additional instruction or support as a whole class, in small groups, or one on one. **ELL** Assess for Content and Language Understanding—Formative Assessment. Remember that ELLs may lack mastery of the English words and grammar necessary to demonstrate the complex critical thinking they are engaged in. Study their work carefully: Are any gaps that you notice the result of not understanding the content or of not being sure how to effectively express their understanding in English?

Use this checklist to assess the content and effectiveness of student short story discussion guides.

Standards Alignment: RL.6.1, RL.6.2, RL.6.3, RL.6.4, RL.6.6, W.6.4, W.6.9, W.6.10

Task	Achieved	Notes
Compose at least eight discussion questions.		
Demonstrate knowledge of the short story genre and the teaching objectives of the lesson set through content of questions.		
Demonstrate comprehension of the target short story by including references to specific story elements and details in several questions.		
Include questions that have potential to engage others in prolonged open-ended discussion of the target short story.		

Reading Lesson 10 ·

▼ **Teaching Objective**

Readers facilitate a reading discussion.

Close Reading Opportunity

▼ **Standards Alignment**

RL.6.1, RL.6.10, SL.6.1, SL.6.2, SL.6.4, SL.6.6, L.6.1, L.6.3, L.6.6

▼ Materials

- Short story discussion guides (created by student partnerships in Reading Lesson 9)

▼ To the Teacher

In this final lesson, the discussion guides partners created during Reading Lesson 9 are used by students to either participate in or facilitate reading discussions. These discussions may be either virtual or in person. In advance of teaching this lesson, select a method for these discussion groups. Several options, both high-tech and low-tech, are outlined in the table.

Goal	Low-Tech	High-Tech
Student discussion guides are used to facilitate a book club–style discussion.	Short story discussions are held in person. Consider: • asking students within your class to sign up to participate in one or more story discussions with their classmates. • organizing story discussions with your students and students from other classes at the same grade level. • having your students facilitate invitational story discussions for staff members and/or family members.	Short story discussions are held virtually: Consider: • posting a reading with discussion questions on a classroom blog for participants to engage with through the comments function. • hosting story discussions with classrooms in other schools via Skype, FaceTime, or Google Hangout.

▼ Procedure

Warm Up Gather the class to set the stage for today's learning

Share with the class your selected method for hosting short story discussions. See the technology box within this lesson for low-tech and high-tech suggestions.

Teach Model what students need to learn and do

Lay out the logistics for hosting the story discussions. Here are some logistics for you to consider for each of the options outlined in the preceding table.

Presentation Type	Considerations
Students within your class sign up to participate in one or more story discussions using the discussion guides created by classmates.	• How many discussion groups will occur at one time? • How many people will be in each group? • When will students read the target stories? • How many different story groups will students participate in?
Students participate in story discussions with students from other classes at the same grade level.	All of the questions in the section above, plus: • What classrooms will be involved? • Where will the discussions be hosted? • What are the dates for the discussions?
Students facilitate invitational story discussions for staff members and/or family members.	• How will you invite/advertise the story discussions to staff members and families? • How will you provide the stories for participants to read in advance? • How many people will be able to sign up for each discussion to ensure that all students have some participants? • What date will work for this event?
Students post a short story with discussion questions on a classroom blog for participants to engage with through the comments function.	• How will students invite others to read the story and engage with the questions posted on the classroom blog? • How/when will students moderate comments?
Students host short story discussions with classrooms in other schools via Skype, FaceTime, or Google Hangout.	• What classrooms will you connect with? (Consider finding other classes with www.epals.com.) • What technological means do you need to support this?

ELL Enable Language Production—Listening and Speaking. Consider that if you have many ELLs with the same home language who are only beginning to learn English, they may benefit from working in a group that holds its discussion in their shared language. These students may be able to engage in more complex thinking and conversation in their home language than in English. If you are connecting with other schools via the Web, could some of your ELLs work with students in their home country? Also, consider that if you are inviting ELLs' family members, it is important to find a way to include them in the celebration by using the languages they are most comfortable with as much as possible: How can you make the invitations, stories, and discussions accessible? Multilingual practices show students and their families that your school is a place for people from all different backgrounds.

Try Guide students to quickly rehearse what they need to learn and do in preparation for practice

Lead the class in a discussion of how they can and should prepare for this experience. Use the following questions to guide your conversation.

- What can you do to prepare for your literature discussion (either as a guide or a facilitator)?
- What tasks need to be completed?
- What speaking and listening skills will be important to each participant?

Clarify Briefly restate today's teaching objective and explain the practice task(s)

Based on the results of the planning in Teach and Try, reiterate the required tasks and timeline for students to prepare for and engage in their discussions.

Practice Students work independently and/or in small groups to apply today's teaching objective

Over one or more days, students collaborate with their partners to complete the necessary tasks prior to the short story discussions. These tasks may include, but are not limited to, reading new short stories, creating and issuing invitations, scheduling discussions, posting or delivering discussion questions, and distributing copies of the selected short story for others to read.

Then the discussions take place as planned.

As students engage in discussions remind them to incorporate the important tasks of speaking at an appropriate volume, using appropriate eye contact, speaking clearly and using formal English when appropriate, and using a logical sequence and relevant details that support their central idea. (SL.6.4, SL.6.6) Instruct the listeners to carefully listen to the information presented (orally and/or visually) and explain how the information helps them better understand the short story, a central idea, and the development of the plot. (SL.6.2)

Wrap Up Check understanding as you guide students to briefly share what they have learned and produced today

Gather students to discuss their experience once the discussions have concluded. Here are some questions to guide your conversation:

- Was the discussion guide helpful in shaping your conversation about the short story?
- Describe the experience of participating in or leading a discussion group. How did the experience enhance the reading experience?
- What did you discover about the short story through the comments of others in the group?
- Which types of questions initiated the best conversations—those close to the text or general questions?
- How did your thoughts about the story change as a result of this conversation?

Writing Lessons

The Core I.D.E.A. / Daily Writing Instruction at a Glance table highlights the teaching objectives and standards alignment for all 10 lessons across the four stages of the lesson set (Introduce, Define, Extend, and Assess). It also indicates which lessons contain special features to support English language learners, technology, speaking and listening, close reading opportunities, and formative ("Milestone") assessments.

The Core I.D.E.A. / Daily Writing Instruction at a Glance

Grade 6 Packing a Punch: The Art and Craft of Short Stories

Instructional Stage	Lesson	Teaching Objective	Core Standards	Special Features
Introduce: *notice, explore, collect, note, immerse, surround, record, share*	1	Writers choose their words wisely.	W.6.4 • W.6.6 • W.6.10 • SL.6.1 • SL.6.6 • L.6.1 • L.6.2 • L.6.3 • L.6.6	ELL Tech
	2	Writers share their thoughts on their reading with others.	RL.6.1 • RL.6.10 • W.6.4 • W.6.6 • W.6.9 • W.6.10 • SL.6.1 • SL.6.6 • L.6.1 • L.6.2 • L.6.3 • L.6.6	ELL Tech Close Reading Opportunity Milestone Assessment
Define: *name, identify, outline, clarify, select, plan*	3	Writers reflect on key components of their reading through literary commentary.	RL.6.1 • RL.6.3 • RL.6.10 • W.6.4 • W.6.9 • W.6.10 • SL.6.1 • SL.6.6 • L.6.1 • L.6.2 • L.6.3 • L.6.6	ELL Close Reading Opportunity
Extend: *try, experiment, attempt, approximate, practice, explain, revise, refine*	4	Writers include quotations from the text to support and strengthen their written literary commentaries.	RL.6.1 • RL.6.3 • RL.6.10 • W.6.4 • W.6.9 • W.6.10 • SL.6.1 • SL.6.4 • SL.6.6 • L.6.1 • L.6.2 • L.6.3 • L.6.6	ELL S&L Close Reading Opportunity
	5	Writers revise and edit literary commentaries for strength and clarity.	W.6.4 • W.6.5 • W.6.9 • W.6.10 • SL.6.1 • SL.6.4 • SL.6.6 • L.6.1 • L.6.2 • L.6.3 • L.6.6	ELL S&L Milestone Assessment
	6	Writers compose a strong written literary commentary of their reading in a single sitting.	RL.6.1 • RL.6.10 • W.6.4 • W.6.5 • W.6.6 • W.6.9 • W.6.10 • SL.6.1 • L.6.1 • L.6.2 • L.6.3 • L.6.6	ELL Close Reading Opportunity
	7	Writers use their reading and analysis of short stories to inspire their own writing.	RL.6.1 • RL.6.10 • W.6.3 • W.6.4 • W.6.5 • W.6.10 • SL.6.1 • SL.6.4 • SL.6.6 • L.6.1 • L.6.2 • L.6.3 • L.6.6	ELL S&L Close Reading Opportunity
	8	Writers purposefully incorporate specific narrative techniques to enhance their short stories.	RL.6.1 • RL.6.10 • W.6.3 • W.6.4 • W.6.5 • W.6.10 • SL.6.1 • SL.6.6 • L.6.1 • L.6.2 • L.6.3 • L.6.6	ELL Close Reading Opportunity
	9	Writers revise and edit their short stories with a peer.	W.6.3 • W.6.4 • W.6.5 • W.6.10 • SL.6.1 • SL.6.4 • SL.6.6 • L.6.1 • L.6.2 • L.6.3 • L.6.6	ELL S&L Milestone Assessment
Assess: *reflect, conclude, connect, share, recognize, respond*	10	Writers share their short stories in authentic ways.	W.6.3 • W.6.4 • W.6.6 • W.6.10 • SL.6.1 • SL.6.2 • SL.6.4 • SL.6.6 • L.6.1 • L.6.2 • L.6.3 • L.6.6	ELL Tech S&L

Writing Lesson 1

▼ **Teaching Objective**

Writers choose their words wisely.

▼ **Standards Alignment**

W.6.4, W.6.6, W.6.10, SL.6.1, SL.6.6, L.6.1, L.6.2, L.6.3, L.6.6

▼ **Materials**

- Examples of six-word memoirs (some samples in the sidebar of this lesson, others easily available online)
- Writing samples for each stage of the six-word memoir writing process (either your own or the provided sample)
- Charting supplies or interactive whiteboard to jot a quick list of steps to writing a six-word memoir

▼ **To the Teacher**

We begin this writing lesson set by asking students to write a six-word memoir. Six-word memoirs restrict writers to sharing an important aspect of their own life in only six words, forcing students to choose their words wisely and recognize the power and weight of each word, much like short story writers must do. The process of composing a six-word memoir, however, is more thoughtful than it may first appear: Students begin by freewriting about themselves, then select key words or ideas to highlight, choose one particular idea to develop, and, finally, compose a six-word memoir.

▼ **Procedure**

Warm Up Gather the class to set the stage for today's learning

Engage the class in a discussion of the importance of word choice.

> Which is harder for you when you write: writing a long piece or a very short piece? Why?

Many students find writing a lot is challenging, but some students have trouble keeping their writing short and clear. Briefly discuss thoughts about these different types of writing challenges. **ELL** Frontload the Lesson—Activate Prior Knowledge. Discussions such as these help ELLs orient themselves to the lesson by grounding what they are about to learn in familiar experiences.

Emphasize the importance of word choice in the creation of short stories.

> As readers and writers, we are going to be studying the art and craft of writing a short story. In a short story, every choice the author makes, right down to the specific word he or she uses to describe a moment in time, matters. In today's lesson, we are going to try our hands at a writing form that requires very careful word choice!

Teach Model what students need to learn and do

Sample Six-Word Memoirs
Braved storms, grateful for the rainbows
Refining the content of my character
Making music got me through it
Good life, great family, outstanding dog
My clothes aren't who I am
Why did you have to leave?
Set up. Eye contact. Kick. *Score!*

Introduce the six-word memoir by defining this genre of writing for the class.

> A six-word memoir is a very short way of sharing the story of your life with others. Talk about a short short story! In a six-word memoir, authors have exactly six words to make a statement about their own lives. I thought we could play around with the importance of word choice by giving six-word memoirs a try ourselves.

Show the class your chosen examples of six-word memoirs. Read through the memoirs together, allowing students the time and space to react to and comment on those you decide to share. Here are some guiding questions:

- What do you notice about this form of writing?
- What seems to be the purpose of this form of writing?
- What do you think a writer has to do to create this type of writing?

ELL Enable Language Production—Reading and Writing. Notice that the six-word memoir works in part because its writers assume they share certain background knowledge with their readers. For example, the author of "Refining the content of my character" is subtly referencing Dr. King's "I Have a Dream" speech. Students from immigrant families may have a different set of experiences that makes it harder to interpret these texts. At the same time, some memoirs they compose might be hard for *you* to understand if you do not share your students' backgrounds. Be on the lookout for moments when you might need to explain something extra or when you might need to ask for more explanation from your ELLs.

Make the point that writing less sometimes means beginning by writing more. Outline the following process for crafting a six-word memoir. Jot each step in the process on a chart for your students to refer to while engaging in their own work. In addition, as you outline the process for students, show students examples of your own writing at each step along the way. **ELL** Provide Comprehensible Input—Models. This is a linguistically demanding task! ELLs will be better able to tackle it if they can watch you wade through a sea of ideas and get them down to six core words. If you feel uncomfortable about sharing this sort of writing with your students, you can rely on the samples of each stage in the process provided below as your model of what a writer might do.

Six-Word Memoir Process

- **Begin by freewriting a list of words/phrases to describe yourself.** This list can include but should not be limited to: topics, memories, personality traits, what you like to do, favorite possessions, places you like to visit, and feelings. Encourage students to write for three full minutes and/or to fill an entire page.

- **Circle the words/phrases that stand out as most important.** Select and circle two or three words or phrases that you feel as if you can say more about or that truly capture the story of your life that you want to tell.

- **Pick one word/phrase and freewrite about that.** Do not worry about length or editing. Rather, write whatever comes to mind when you think of that word or phrase in relation to who you are and your own life.

- **Synthesize your writing.** Reread your freewriting, and try to decide what it is that you are really trying to say. What is the gist or message that drives your writing around this word or phrase? Try to capture that in an understandable six words.

Sample of a Six-Word Memoir Process

1 **Begin by freewriting a list of words/phrases to describe yourself.**
Loving and caring daughter and friend. Fostering dogs, especially pit bulls with brindle coats. Going to the beach, especially in the evening. Traveling to Great Smoky Mountains National Park and living in Florida. Writing, books, reading. *I Capture the Castle* and *101 Dalmatians* and *The Princess Bride*. Loves mysteries, especially ones set in small English towns, especially ones where a woman solves the crime. Very good worrier. Empathetic. A special ring that my mom wore on her

---

finger. The mustard seed necklace my grandmother wore. The raspberry bushes behind my house. The train to the city, again and again and again, past the same green hills. My stuffed black bear and the wooden blocks. Coffee and sweet tea, pasta with butter. Romantic. Curious, especially about: London, outer space, other people's lives, other people on trains. Gets *super angry* in traffic. Impatient, especially on line in a grocery store. Frightened of many things, including the boogey man and, while camping, mountain lions. Also, when camping, bears. But also brave. Likes skeet shooting. Wants to do one million things. Including: travel to Europe, sail on the ocean, have children, watch the sun set on a beach in Mexico.

2 **Circle the words and phrases that stand out as most important.**

loving, writing, wants to do one million things

3 **Pick one word or phrase and freewrite about that.**

Writing

Is like dreaming over and over again. It's like reliving every single book I loved and getting to live inside it again. It's the tiny pen-and-ink map on the front pages of *Winnie-the-Pooh* and the word *incarnadine* from Macbeth (which apparently means "red") and the way when I read about Elizabeth McCracken's loss I immediately started to cry, as if I'd been punched. It's the descriptions of meals in Redwall and the Turkish Delight in *The Lion, the Witch, and the Wardrobe,* and the buttermead in Harry Potter. It's the fear that kept me from getting up to turn off the light when reading R. L. Stine, and it's lying on a couch and devouring the entire Sweet Valley High series while eating chocolate. It's desire to do one million things and how there's never enough time. But in a book you can. You can train as a knight and live on a farm and you can sail alone around the world and you can have a family of twelve siblings. And then it's taking all of those things—all of those things that you love, all of those things that make you ache—and creating something new. Something that belongs only to you. That you have written, which wouldn't have existed at all otherwise. And it's taking every fear and impatience and loneliness and worry—all the things you dislike about yourself and all the things you love about yourself—and hammering them into something new.

4 **Synthesize your writing.**
Do one million things, then write.
Other samples: She created something new from nothing. Loved the world, so she wrote. Writer who wanted to do everything.

Try Guide students to quickly rehearse what they need to learn and do in preparation for practice

Distribute supplies so that students can engage in a quick freewrite about themselves. Then allow students to try the first step in this process.

> Let's get started now. Take three minutes to freewrite about yourself. For a quick write like this, it is OK to write in phrases and jot notes. I want you to focus on getting down the words and phrases that best capture who you are and what you would like to share about your life story.

Provide students with three minutes to freewrite about themselves. **ELL** Enable Language Production—Reading and Writing. If you have ELLs who are literate in their home language, encourage them to use that language in their freewrite if it would help them get their ideas out. Then offer students the opportunity to share and discuss their freewrite with a partner. However, due to the potential sensitivity of these freewrites, students should also be granted the ability to opt out of sharing their writing with a partner.

Clarify Briefly restate today's teaching objective and explain the practice task(s)

Pearson Education

Briefly review the process for writing a six-word memoir with your class.

> Now that you have a freewrite about yourself, take a moment to circle the two or three words or phrases that stand out the most to you or that you feel you can say more about. Then freewrite about those words or phrases alone. Finally, try to capture the gist or message that underlies your freewrite in just six words.

Then connect this work back to the idea of the power of word choice.

> Remember that our work today is intended to give you insight into the importance of word choice and how carefully authors work to choose the exact word or phrase that suits their purposes in their own writing.

Practice Students work independently and/or in small groups to apply today's teaching objective

Students compose their own six-word memoir(s) using the six-word memoir process as a guide. Provide students with the opportunity to occasionally check in with a writing partner in order to bounce ideas off one another if they feel they need support. **ELL** Enable Language Production—Increasing Interaction. ELLs are defined as students who lack sufficient English to be successful in an all-English school setting. Students may be "reclassified" as fluent in English as they reach the requirements set by their district, which usually involve both oral and written proficiency. Many students reach this bar at some point in elementary school and are then not considered ELLs. By middle school, ELLs tend to fall into one of two groups: recent arrivals with prior schooling in their home language or students who have lived in the United States for many years and have high oral proficiency but who struggle with literacy. (Of course, your ELLs may fall somewhere in between or be entirely different!) Both types of students may benefit from adding some conversation to their freewrite process. Circulate to support students in this writing process as necessary. Have a few students share orally at this point as you encounter those who are ready to do so.

Wrap Up Check understanding as you guide students to briefly share what they have learned and produced today

After students complete their memoirs, ask each student to compose a brief paragraph that describes or elaborates upon his or her six-word memoir. This paragraph should explain how the six chosen words capture an important central idea in the author's life. In addition, ask students to select or create an image to work alongside their memoir. Some high-tech and low-tech suggestions for sharing this work with an audience follow.

Goal	Low-Tech	High-Tech
Students share their six-word memoirs.	• Students post their six-word memoirs, explanatory paragraphs, and images on a classroom bulletin board. • Students create a class anthology that includes their six-word memoirs, explanatory paragraphs, and chosen images.	• Students create a class slideshow of their six-word memoirs and images (using an application such as Prezi, PowerPoint, or Keynote). As a class, students select music to accompany the slideshow. • Students post their six-word memoirs, explanatory paragraphs, and images to a classroom blog for others to read and comment upon.

Writing Lesson 2

▼ Teaching Objective

Writers share their thoughts on their reading with others.

Close Reading Opportunity

▼ Standards Alignment

RL.6.1, RL.6.10, W.6.4, W.6.6, W.6.9, W.6.10, SL.6.1, SL.6.6, L.6.1, L.6.2, L.6.3, L.6.6

▼ Materials

- "A Bad Road for Cats" found in *Every Living Thing* by Cynthia Rylant
- Microblog Paper (Appendix 6.5)

▼ To the Teacher

In this lesson, we introduce students to the idea of informally sharing their thoughts about their reading with more than just their classmates. Using Twitter as a platform, students share their initial thoughts on their reading of short stories.

Goal	Low-Tech	High-Tech
Students use microblogging to share their thoughts on recently read short stories with others.	Students compose tweets using pencil and paper. Tweets are posted in a central location to promote conversation and replies from classmates.	Students compose tweets using Twitter, posting and responding to one another using a common hashtag.

ELL Enable Language Production—Reading and Writing. By sixth grade, all children (barring disability or extreme neglect) are highly proficient in the language of their home communities and often use language in very sophisticated ways. Young people of this generation are additionally often very skilled at communicating through multimedia. A microblog can help form a bridge between the conventions of short stories (valued in academic realms) and the multilingual, nonmainstream ways that many ELL middle school students communicate with their peers and families by showing them how both forms require them to choose words carefully in order to "pack a punch."

▼ Procedure

Gather the class to set the stage for today's learning

Build enthusiasm for and/or an understanding of how and why readers share their thoughts about specific texts with others. Share moments from your own life in which you shared thoughts on your reading with others, taking care to also articulate *how* you shared your thoughts with others. Also highlight real-world places where people express their opinions about reading such as book reviews in newspapers and magazines, book clubs, Facebook, bookseller site reviews, and Twitter. Here is one way your conversation might unfold, but please customize the story to fit your own experiences.

> My mother and I love to share books and book recommendations with one another. Sometimes, when I am in the middle of a really good book, I pick up the phone and call my mother to tell her about it and to encourage her to get started reading it too. Other times, I read a really interesting book about teaching and want to share my thoughts on it with other teachers. I might talk to some teachers over lunch, or I might turn to technology and use Twitter to share my thinking with teachers in my network. Whether it's over the phone, in person, or online, when readers have thoughts, strong feelings, or questions about their reading, they share them with other readers as a way to start a conversation.

Invite students to share their experiences with talking about or sharing their reading lives with others. Make sure to ask students to be clear about *how* they shared thoughts about their reading. **ELL** Frontload the Lesson—Make Connections. This Warm Up asks your students to bring together two probably familiar experiences: communicating with friends and family and reading interesting books. As students learn new things, they need to connect them to something they already understand; these connections help ELLs in particular orient themselves to and get excited about a new lesson.

Model what students need to learn and do

Introduce the concept of *microblogging* using a platform such as Twitter. Microblogging is similar to blogging; however, writers are limited to short sentences and brief statements. For example, when using Twitter, writers are limited to 140 characters. Regardless, authors are able to include a variety of media such as hyperlinks, photographs, voice threads, and videos into their microblogs.

Explain Twitter and describe its purpose as well as the opportunities for readers using this sort of form of connecting with others.

> Twitter is a form of microblogging that lets users communicate with one another using 140 or fewer characters. Hashtags are used as a way to label or tag a conversation so that you can participate in or follow a conversation via Twitter.

Take a closer look at the anatomy of a tweet. A tweet, or a single post on Twitter, is limited to 140 characters. The "@" symbol is used to indicate a particular user. The # symbol is used to label or tag a conversation so that all comments about that particular comment can be easily gathered or followed. Users can simply follow various hashtags (#) or participate in or follow a specific conversation. For example, you can follow (or read) a conversation on Twitter by searching a specific hashtag (such as #childrenslit) and read or add to the Twitter conversation about children's literature. By searching for a specific hashtag, you weed out any other unrelated tweets in your Twitter feed. Users also use condensed hyperlinks to link to other web pages, photographs, videos, or voice threads. A hyperlink is a link (which may look like a highlighted word or phrase or an entire web address) that takes you to a specific location on the Internet. Interested users can click on a hyperlink to visit the related online material. Show the class several examples of tweets to support this conversation. For example, you may wish to follow Goodreads (@goodreads) or Penguin Publishers (@penguinusa) to generate some interesting examples of book-related conversations happening on Twitter. **ELL** Provide Comprehensible Input—Visuals. If some of your ELLs are new to Twitter, they will understand it much better if they can watch you actually navigate the site than they could if they only heard you talk about it.

Share the types of discussions being had on Twitter, including conversations among readers.

> People are discussing everything on Twitter—from their personal lives to their interests. You can follow tweets about current events, about celebrities, or about a topic you are interested in learning more about. I think Twitter could be a great platform for us to share our thinking about our reading.

Model composing a tweet about the story you shared with the class during Reading Lesson 1. Here is one way your modeling could unfold, though your modeled tweet should emulate your own writing style and opinions of the text shared. (Note: If you have selected the low-tech version of this lesson, model composing your tweet using the Microblog Paper in Appendix 6.5, which has 140 blank spaces.)

Microblog Paper

Directions: Use the following paper to plan a tweet with up to 140 spaces. One character per box, including spaces.

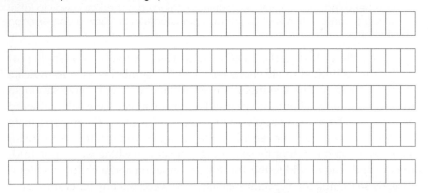

I want to share my opinion about "A Bad Road for Cats" on Twitter. Remember that I have only 140 characters, so I have to choose my words carefully and make my ideas clear. I will begin by thinking about my opinion in general. Reading this story really made me rethink my feelings toward some of the people I've encountered in my life. There have been moments where I have been angry at or frustrated with people and never really considered their personal situation and how that might affect their behavior. This story really resonated with me and challenged my sometimes quick judgments about people. How can I express that in a tweet?

Now type or write as you think aloud.

I could write: "Important lesson learned in this short story: Rethinking quick decisions about others. Lesson learned. #abadroadforcats #cynthiarylant #compassion" But that is a few characters too long. How can I revise this tweet to shave a few characters off? I could change the word *important* to *key* to make it shorter. Using a synonym for a longer word is a good strategy for shortening up tweets that are too long.

Rewrite your tweet to read: "Key lesson learned in this short story: Rethinking quick decisions about others. Lesson learned. #abadroadforcats #cynthiarylant #compassion"

Did you notice how I used hashtags to label this tweet as being about a specific short story, a particular author, and a particular central idea? Using these hashtags, I am adding my own voice to related conversations and am able to read what other people might have to say about these topics as well.

After modeling composing a tweet for the class, take a moment to reiterate the process you used. First, you considered your general opinion of the short story, without the restrictions of the 140-character limit. Then you worked to express your ideas clearly, including topic hashtags, in 140 or fewer characters. Finally, you checked to be certain that your tweet was strong and fit into the 140-character limit. **ELL** Provide Comprehensible

Input—Repeat. ELLs benefit from hearing your directions multiple times, particularly if the repetition focuses on the most important information they need to remember.

Try Guide students to quickly rehearse what they need to learn and do in preparation for practice

Direct students to reflect on their own opinions of the text shared in Reading Lesson 1. Then ask students to attempt to compose their own tweet that shares their opinion in 140 or fewer characters. Circulate as students work, supporting their word choices and guiding them to writing clearly in a limited amount of space. (Note: If doing this with pencil and paper, provide students with the Microblog Paper in Appendix 6.5 so they can focus on the composition of the tweet itself rather than on counting characters.)

Now, ask students to share their tweets with a partner.

As students collaborate, remind them of the importance of staying on topic and expressing themselves clearly. (SL.6.1a, SL.6.1b) **ELL** Enable Language Production—Reading and Writing. Some of your ELLs may find this task more difficult because they have a limited range of alternative words and structures in English. Help them find concise ways to express themselves by presenting them with some new language where appropriate.

Clarify Briefly restate today's teaching objective and explain the practice task(s)

Connect the idea of sharing one's thoughts on reading with the platform of microblogging.

While it is nice to share your thoughts on a text with the person sitting next to you, it is also exciting to think about the possibility of opening up that conversation to a much larger and diverse community. By using a platform such as microblogging on Twitter, we can share our thoughts with others quickly and be a part of a larger, more dynamic conversation about books and our reading. Because of the limited number of characters allowed, Twitter also pushes us to choose our words wisely without sacrificing clarity.

Direct students to compose tweets that share their thoughts on their recent reading of short stories. Create a common hashtag for students to use that allows you to track their work as well as students to comment on and reply to the tweets of their classmates.

Practice Students work independently and/or in small groups to apply today's teaching objective

Students compose tweets that reflect their thoughts on the various short stories they have read thus far, focusing on careful word choice, correct spelling, and rereading their work to make sure their tweets make sense. Emphasize the importance of making specific references to the short story itself and the elements that appealed most as they were reading. Students should use a common hashtag (such as your room number, #class229) to aggregate their work as a class. Students should also be expected to respond to the tweets of several of their classmates. **ELL** Enable Language Production—Increasing Interaction. ELLs will benefit from seeing many examples of concise writing from their peers.

Wrap Up Check understanding as you guide students to briefly share what they have learned and produced today

Gather the class, and read through the thread of tweets collected using your common hashtag. Highlight several particularly successful or interesting tweets. Begin to notice and note the various types of comments that were made about the reading: Did students focus on central idea, word choice, mood, character, imagery?

Milestone Performance Assessment

Practicing Concise Writing PD TOOLKIT™

Collect and analyze students' six-word memoirs and tweets as a performance-based assessment to determine if students need additional instruction or support as a whole class, in small groups, or one on one. **ELL** Assess for Content and Language Understanding—Formative Assessment. Study your ELLs' work closely to see where their strengths and gaps lie. While English learners may grasp the purpose of concise writing, they may struggle to compose concisely in English. Notice what kinds of

language supports—vocabulary? sentence structure? composing with audience in mind?—you might need going forward in this lesson set.

Use this checklist to assess student work on their six-word memoirs and tweets.

Standards Alignment: RL.6.1, W.6.4, W.6.6, W.6.9, W.6.10

Task	Achieved	Notes
Craft a six-word memoir that effectively captures a central idea of the writer's life.		
Write a reflection paragraph and include an image that clearly elaborates on the words chosen for the memoir.		
Concisely articulate thinking about the short story using the microblogging format.		

Writing Lesson 3

▼ **Teaching Objective**

Writers reflect on key components of their reading through literary commentary.

Close Reading Opportunity

▼ **Standards Alignment**

RL.6.1, RL.6.3, RL.6.10, W.6.4, W.6.9, W.6.10, SL.6.1, SL.6.6, L.6.1, L.6.2, L.6.3, L.6.6

▼ **Materials**

- "The Last Leaf" by O. Henry or another short story that is a class favorite
- Completed Elements of a Short Story Graphic Organizer (first used by students during Reading Lesson 2)
- Short stories students selected for independent reading in reading lessons

▼ To the Teacher

In alignment with the Common Core State Standards, sixth-grade students must be able to clearly and articulately express their understanding of a text in writing by responding to a specific prompt or question. In this lesson, we ask students to transition from the more informal tone of microblogging and Twitter to take on a more formal tone in their writing as they work to answer a specific prompt about their reading. In this lesson, we model writing a response to a specific prompt or question using "The Last Leaf" by O. Henry. Read aloud the model story prior to teaching the lesson.

▼ Procedure

Warm Up Gather the class to set the stage for today's learning

Transition your students from the idea of informally sharing their thoughts on their reading to composing a more formal written literary commentary of their reading.

> While it is fun to share your thoughts about your reading with your friends, it is also important that you know how to formally put those ideas into writing as well. Think of it as changing the way that you talk to fit a situation. Sometimes you can be relaxed and casual—like after school with your friends or at home with your family. You might not speak in complete sentences, and you might use words or slang that you would not usually put into writing. Other times, you need to speak more formally—like when you are talking with an adult at school or trying to make a good impression on someone. Then you want to use complete sentences, standard grammar, and academic vocabulary. This sends a message that you can be taken seriously.

This is a good opportunity to reinforce how we adapt speech to a variety of contexts and tasks, demonstrating command of formal English when indicated or appropriate. (SL.6.6)

ELL Frontload the Lesson—Activate Prior Knowledge. Students construct their knowledge by building on what they already know. ELLs in particular will likely find it easier to understand what you want them to do in this lesson when you explicitly connect it to the familiar idea of communicating with different people in different ways.

Teach Model what students need to learn and do

Introduce the idea of responding thoughtfully in writing to questions that ask you to closely read and analyze a text.

> Many times as readers we are asked to demonstrate our understanding of a text by sharing our thoughts aloud. Other times, you must share your thoughts in writing in a clear and formal manner.

ELL Enable Language Production—Reading and Writing. Be very aware when discussing this idea of formal tone that you maintain awareness that many of your students may speak nonstandard varieties of English with grammatical rules that may differ from the grammar of standard English. (It can be difficult to tell if an ELL's nonstandard usage is a learner error or a feature of the dialect learned from peers.) At the same time, different uses of English carry different social weight, and all speakers adjust their language according to the demands of the social context. Emphasize for your students the idea of *situational appropriateness* and that they need to be informed about different sorts of language so that they can choose how to present themselves.

Present students with a specific question that asks them to analyze a text and present their knowledge clearly in writing. For the purposes of this lesson, we will rely on the following prompt that asks students to draw on their work from Reading Lesson 2: Describe how a story's plot unfolds through a series of episodes and how the characters respond to those key episodes. *Episode* means "related events, or scenes, that make up the plot of a story."

Take out the Elements of a Short Story Graphic Organizer that you modeled filling in with the class during Reading Lessons 2 and 3. Clarify for students that this graphic organizer can and should help them to jumpstart their thinking and aid them in responding to this prompt in writing.

> When we filled in the Elements of a Short Story Graphic Organizer during our reading work, we did a great deal of the close reading necessary to answer this prompt. We can use the notes we recorded here to support and organize our writing today.

Model for students how to use the notes to formulate a coherent response that reflects a more formal tone. Here is one way your modeling could unfold. **ELL** Provide Comprehensible Input—Models. It is very helpful for ELLs if you explicitly demonstrate how to use language to create a formal tone, as the different connotations of particular words or structures may be unfamiliar to students just learning English.

> It is important to clearly address each aspect of the question or prompt when responding in writing. Let's take a closer look at the prompt. It reads, "Describe how a story's plot unfolds through a series of episodes and how the characters respond to those key episodes." So, first, I want to make sure I clearly name the short story that I will be writing about and summarize the main episodes that make up the plot of the story.

Now write or type the following as the class watches or share with the class a first draft of your response that you completed in advance. For your convenience, you can rely upon the drafted response to this prompt included here. (Note: This draft is purposefully lacking components of a strong response and does not address all parts of the given prompt. Students will work with the teacher in the Try portion of this lesson to resolve this.)

Describe how a story's plot unfolds through a series of episodes and how the characters respond to those key episodes.

In "The Last Leaf" by O. Henry, the story unfolds through a series of key episodes. However, the most interesting aspects of the story unfold through the reaction of the main characters to those episodes. At first, Johnsy, a young artist, is convinced that she will die when the last leaf falls from the tree, but after it mysteriously fails to fall, she regains hope along with her desire to live.

 In the beginning of the story, Johnsy develops pneumonia and is waiting to die. Johnsy's roommate, Sue, is devastated by what is happening to Johnsy, but she tries to hide it and convince Johnsy to find the will to get better. Sue tells Mr. Behrman, an artist who lives nearby, about Johnsy. Later, when the last leaf continues to remain on the tree, Johnsy's feelings change about dying and she begins to get better. Finally, Sue and Johnsy discover that Mr. Berhman died of pneumonia from staying outside to paint the last leaf on the tree, sacrificing his life in order to save Johnsy.

Notice how I began by clearly stating the short story I was going to write about. Then I summarized the gist of my response in a few words as an introduction. Next, because the prompt asked me to describe how the plot unfolded through a series of key episodes, I wrote about each of the key episodes in the story in the order they occurred. The prompt also asked me to describe how the character(s) reacted to these key episodes to advance the plot.

Try Guide students to quickly rehearse what they need to learn and do in preparation for practice

Now ask students to participate in this work. Return to the writing question or prompt to determine if your answer is complete.

> Now that I have written the first part of my response, I want to return to the question or prompt to make sure I replied to all of its parts in my writing. This prompt reads, "Describe how a story's plot unfolds through a series of episodes and how the characters respond to those key episodes." We named the series of episodes but have not yet addressed how the characters respond to each of these episodes. Let me go back into my writing and add that in.

Demonstrate returning to your response and identifying where you wrote about the first key episode. Reread this section aloud to the class. It is included here.

In the beginning of the story, Johnsy develops pneumonia and is waiting to die.

Ask students to think about both parts of the prompt.

Did I name the first episode in the story clearly? Did I describe how the characters responded to this first episode?

Now, ask students to consider how you might revise your writing to address both parts of the question. As volunteers share their thinking, ask them to formulate this part of your writing. Record student responses in your draft, modeling how to revise to include how characters respond to the events of the text by inserting additional details using carets or another relevant method for revision.

Here is how your draft might look at this point:

In the beginning of the story, Johnsy develops pneumonia and is waiting to die. She lays looking out the window near her bed. The doctor has little expectation his care will help Johnsy due to her lack of hope. He says she would have a better chance if she has something to look forward to. Johnsy, however, is convinced she will die when the last leaf falls from the tree outside her window.

If desired, show your class a second version of your initial response, which is complete with textual evidence to support each of your claims. Remark that each aspect of your response addresses both parts of the prompt: the episode and the character's reaction to the episode. For your convenience, the revised draft is included here.

Describe how a story's plot unfolds through a series of episodes and how the characters respond to those key episodes.

In "The Last Leaf" by O. Henry, the story unfolds through a series of key episodes. However, the most interesting aspects of the story unfold through the reaction of the main characters to those episodes. At first, Johnsy, a young artist, is convinced that she will die when the last leaf falls from the tree, but after it mysteriously fails to fall, she regains hope along with her desire to live.

 In the beginning of the story, Johnsy develops pneumonia and is waiting to die. She lays looking out the window near her bed. The doctor has little expectation his care will help Johnsy due to her lack of hope. He says she would have a better chance if she has something to look forward to. Johnsy, however, is convinced she will die when the last leaf falls from the tree outside her window.

Johnsy's roommate, Sue, is devastated by what is happening to Johnsy, but she tries to hide it and convince Johnsy to find the will to get better. She lies about the odds that the doctor gave Johnsy, saying she had a ten to one chance of living rather than dying. Johnsy, however, just wants to die.

Sue tells Mr. Behrman, an artist who lives nearby, about Johnsy. He dismisses Johnsy's feelings about the leaf as foolishness, but his concern for Johnsy is evident as he and Sue look with fear at the ivy vine losing its leaves outside. Mr. Behrman decides to help Johnsy, but the author does not reveal this to the reader until later. As the last leaf clings to the tree, Johnsy still wants to die.

Later, when the last leaf continues to remain on the tree, Johnsy's feelings change about dying and she begins to get better. She starts eating and sitting up. She speaks of painting in the future again.

Finally, Sue and Johnsy discover that Mr. Berhman died of pneumonia from staying outside to paint the last leaf on the tree, sacrificing his life in order to save Johnsy.

Clarify Briefly restate today's teaching objective and explain the practice task(s)

Reiterate the importance of clearly articulating understanding of a text through writing.

As you grow older, it becomes essential to be able to express yourself and share your knowledge clearly orally as well as in your writing. Today we are responding to a specific prompt in writing as a way to demonstrate our deep understanding of our short story reading.

Recap for students the process you used to ensure that you addressed each component of the question or prompt and included your thoughts in a logical sequence. A clear response both addresses all parts of the question and unfolds in a clear and logical fashion.

Often, the questions or prompts that we are given to demonstrate our understanding of our reading are complicated and have many parts. Therefore, it is

necessary that you take the time to read and reread the question or prompt several times. Remember how I began drafting my response by reading the prompt and taking care that I clearly addressed the first part. Then I went back to the prompt for a second time and realized that it was necessary to go back in and add in more details about the characters' responses in the order they occurred in the story. An effective piece addresses all parts of the question and unfolds in a clear and logical fashion.

ELL Enable Language Production—Reading and Writing. By reiterating your process one more time, you make it clearer for your ELLs how they, too, can successfully compose an answer to a written prompt.

Direct students to select a short story from their own reading to write about. Remind students to rely on their Elements of a Short Story Graphic Organizers as they respond to the prompt in writing: Describe how a story's plot unfolds through a series of episodes and how the characters respond to those key episodes.

Practice Students work independently and/or in small groups to apply today's teaching objective

Students work independently to answer the prompt: Describe how a story's plot unfolds through a series of episodes and how the characters respond to those key episodes.

Students can and should rely on the close reading work they completed and recorded on the Elements of a Short Story Graphic Organizer during Reading Lesson 2.

Allow students ample time to complete this written response before moving on. Identify one student to share his or her work with the class during the Wrap Up portion of this lesson. Select a student whose writing clearly illustrates the qualities of a strong response.

Wrap Up Check understanding as you guide students to briefly share what they have learned and produced today

Gather the class, and review the qualities of a strong written response. A strong written response should discuss each of the components mentioned in the question or prompt and be written clearly and in a logical order. Share the work of the student you preselected during the Practice portion of this lesson. Identify where and how the student met these criteria.

The next lesson will focus on how to strengthen a response even more by incorporating specific evidence from the text.

Writing Lesson 4

▼ Teaching Objective

Writers include quotations from the text to support and strengthen their written literary commentaries.

Close Reading Opportunity

▼ Standards Alignment

RL.6.1, RL.6.3, RL.6.10, W.6.4, W.6.9, W.6.10, SL.6.1, SL.6.4, SL.6.6, L.6.1, L.6.2, L.6.3, L.6.6

▼ Materials

- Student written responses drafted during Writing Lesson 3
- Teacher modeled response drafted during Writing Lesson 3

▼ To the Teacher

Today we ask students to refine their written literary commentary of a text by considering when to use direct quotations from the text. Students return to the writing they completed during Writing Lesson 3 and insert direct quotations and related explanation as textual evidence to support their thinking when appropriate.

▼ Procedure

Warm Up Gather the class to set the stage for today's learning

Review the work of Writing Lesson 3 in which students practiced clearly sharing their analysis of their reading through writing. Ask one student to share his or her piece and receive feedback from the class based on the criteria established in Writing Lesson 3. **ELL** Enable Language Production— Increasing Interaction. It is important to create an atmosphere of supportive sharing in your classroom so that your ELLs feel comfortable discussing their struggles with their peers and can benefit from others' suggestions.

Teach Model what students need to learn and do

Remind the class of the importance of relying upon specific textual evidence to support one's thinking.

> As readers, we work to provide specific evidence from the text to support what we are saying or what we think about a given text. As writers working to show our understanding of our reading, it is equally important to include textual evidence in our written literary commentaries of a text.

Define and discuss the difference between a direct quotation and paraphrasing a specific portion of the text. Up to this point, students have relied on paraphrasing what happens in the text as they wrote about the key episodes and the characters' reactions to those episodes. In a direct quotation, writers use the text exactly as it is presented by the original author, using quotation marks and a page number to clearly indicate this to a reader. When paraphrasing a specific portion of a text, a reader refers to and briefly recaps a specific episode or event from the text but does not copy the text directly. Give examples of both a direct quotation and how to paraphrase a specific moment from a text using a short story familiar to the class.

Now, move on to discuss when to use a direct quotation and one's own explanation of the significance of the quotation as textual evidence to support a written literary commentary.

> In general, you want to use a direct quotation from the text when the specific words the author used are an essential piece of the evidence. For example, if you are writing about a specific image the author created within his or her writing, you may wish to use the author's words directly because that word choice matters. Using quotations can strengthen one's commentary because a quotation provides direct evidence from a text.

> When inserting a quotation as evidence of your points, it is usually a good idea to add your own thinking about why the quotation is significant. We will look at what I mean by this in a few moments.

> In general, it is not appropriate to directly quote entire paragraphs. Rather, direct quotations typically consist of a word, a phrase, or a couple of sentences.

Revisit the written literary commentary you drafted during Writing Lesson 3, displaying a copy for the class to view. Reread the response, thinking aloud about the inclusion of quotations with explanations as textual evidence to support your analysis. Here is one way your modeling could unfold using the sample draft included in Writing Lesson 2, which is copied below for your convenience.

Describe how a story's plot unfolds through a series of episodes and how the characters respond to those key episodes.

In "The Last Leaf" by O. Henry, the story unfolds through a series of key episodes. However, the most interesting aspects of the story unfold through the reaction of the main characters to those episodes. At first, Johnsy, a young artist, is convinced that she will die when the last leaf falls from the tree, but after it mysteriously fails to fall, she regains hope along with her desire to live.

In the beginning of the story, Johnsy develops pneumonia and is waiting to die. She lays looking out the window near her bed. The doctor

---

has little expectation his care will help Johnsy due to her lack of hope. He says she would have a better chance if she has something to look forward to. Johnsy, however, is convinced she will die when the last leaf falls from the tree outside her window.

Johnsy's roommate, Sue, is devastated by what is happening to Johnsy, but she tries to hide it and convince Johnsy to find the will to get better. Sue lies about the odds that the doctor gave Johnsy, saying she had a ten to one chance of living rather than dying. Johnsy, however, just wants to die.

Sue tells Mr. Behrman, an artist who lives nearby, about Johnsy. He dismisses Johnsy's feelings about the leaf as foolishness, but his concern for Johnsy is evident as he and Sue look with fear at the ivy vine losing its leaves outside. Mr. Behrman decides to help Johnsy, but the author does not reveal this to the reader until later. As the last leaf clings to the tree, Johnsy still wants to die.

Later, when the last leaf continues to remain on the tree, Johnsy's feelings change about dying and she begins to get better. She starts eating and sitting up. She speaks of painting in the future again.

Finally, Sue and Johnsy discover that Mr. Berhman died of pneumonia from staying outside to paint the last leaf on the tree, sacrificing his life in order to save Johnsy.

> I need to add some specific evidence from the text in the form of direct quotations. Adding direct quotations from the text adds some authority and reliability to my writing. This prompt asks me to name each key episode in the story as well as the character's response to these episodes in order to describe how the plot unfolds. Listen as I go back to the first episode and find quotes from the text that provide evidence of my thinking.

Return to the text and scan the beginning to identify a specific quote from the text to support your claim about the character. Then model for the class inserting that quotation and your explanation of why the quote is significant into your writing. Take care to emphasize the use of quotation marks and copying carefully from the original text. An example of the revised draft is included below with the quotations in **bold** and the explanations in *italics*.

> In the beginning of the story, Johnsy develops pneumonia and is waiting to die. She lays **"scarcely moving"** looking out the window near her bed. The doctor has little expectation his care will help Johnsy due to her lack of hope. **". . . whenever my patient begins to count the carriages in her funeral procession I subtract 50 per cent from the curative power of medicines. If you will get her to ask one question about the new winter styles in cloak sleeves I will promise you a one-in-five chance for her, instead of one in ten."** *The doctor's experience has taught him that a patient*

with nothing to look forward to will respond poorly to medicine compared to a patient with a vision of the future. A positive outlook is as powerful as medicine. Johnsy insists she will die when the last leaf falls from the tree outside her window. **"Leaves. On the ivy vine. When the last one falls I must go, too. I've known that for three days."** *The falling ivy leaves symbolize the life draining out of Johnsy. As each one falls, her strength and desire to live decrease.*

Highlight the process you used to include specific textual evidence in your writing.

> First, I returned to my writing and reread it. Stopping after each point I made in my writing, I thought about whether a quotation would be useful as textual evidence to support my thinking. Once I identified places that would benefit from a quotation as evidence, I went back and added them to my writing. Then I added explanation of how the quotation is significant to the meaning of the story. Then I continued to read on through the next point in my response.

Try Guide students to quickly rehearse what they need to learn and do in preparation for practice

Return to the draft you created during Writing Lesson 2. Read the next section of your written literary commentary. Then stop to ask the class to consider where quotations with explanations would help support the point. Emphasize the pattern:

1. make a point
2. include a quotation to support point
3. explain the significance of the quotation

For your convenience, a completed draft is included. While this draft represents a strong written response, your revised draft should mirror the suggestions of your class. It is not necessary that students select these exact same quotations to support their writing. Rather, it is important that students practice the process of returning to the text, noticing moments that need specific textual evidence, finding relevant evidence, and revising their work accordingly.

> **Describe how a story's plot unfolds through a series of episodes and how the characters respond to those key episodes.**
>
> In "The Last Leaf" by O. Henry, the story unfolds through a series of key episodes. However, the most interesting aspects of the story unfold through the reaction of the main characters to those episodes. At first,

Johnsy, a young artist, is convinced that she will die when the last leaf falls from the tree, but after it mysteriously fails to fall, she regains hope along with her desire to live.

In the beginning of the story, Johnsy develops pneumonia and is waiting to die. She lays looking out the window near her bed. The doctor has little expectation his care will help Johnsy due to her lack of hope. He says she would have a better chance if she has something to look forward to. **". . . whenever my patient begins to count the carriages in her funeral procession I subtract 50 per cent from the curative power of medicines. If you will get her to ask one question about the new winter styles in cloak sleeves I will promise you a one-in-five chance for her, instead of one in ten."** *The doctor's experience has taught him that a patient with nothing to look forward to will respond poorly to medicine compared to a patient with a vision of the future. A positive outlook is as powerful as* Johnsy, however, is convinced she will die when the last leaf falls from the tree outside her window. **"Leaves. On the ivy vine. When the last one falls I must go, too. I've known that for three days."** *The falling ivy leaves symbolize the life draining out of Johnsy. As each one falls, her strength and desire to live decrease.*

Johnsy's roommate, Sue, is devastated by what is happening to Johnsy, but she tries to hide it and convince Johnsy to find the will to get better. She . . . **"cried a Japanese napkin to a pulp. Then she swaggered into Johnsy's room with her drawing board, whistling ragtime."** *Sue tries to influence Johnsy's outlook, remaining steadfastly positive.* Sue lies about the odds that the doctor gave Johnsy, saying she had a ten to one chance of living rather than dying. Johnsy, however, just wants to die, **stating "I want to turn loose my hold on everything, and go sailing down, down, just like one of those poor, tired leaves."** *Johnsy personifies the leaves, connecting them to her own tiredness and desire to let go of life.*

Sue tells Mr. Behrman, an artist who lives nearby, about Johnsy. He dismisses Johnsy's feelings about the leaf as foolishness, but his concern for Johnsy is evident as he and Sue look with fear at the ivy vine losing its leaves outside. Mr. Behrman decides to help Johnsy, but the author does not reveal this to the reader until later. As the last leaf clings to the tree, Johnsy still wants to die. **"The lonesomest thing in all the world is a soul when it is making ready to go on its mysterious, far journey. The fancy seemed to possess her more strongly as one by one the ties that bound her to friendship and to earth were loosed."** *Even Johnsy's relationship with Sue does not change her feelings and make her want to live. It seems that her soul is ready to leave Earth and pass to the other side.*

Later, when the last leaf continues to remain on the tree, Johnsy's feelings change about dying and she begins to get better. **"Something has**

made that last leaf stay there to show me how wicked I was. It is a sin to want to die. You may bring a me a little broth now, and some milk with a little port in it, and—no; bring me a hand-mirror first, and then pack some pillows about me, and I will sit up and watch you cook." *Johnsy believes that the leaf clinging to the tree is a sign saying she should not want to die. She regains her hope and desire to live.* She starts eating and sitting up. She speaks of painting in the future again.

Finally, Sue and Johnsy discover that Mr. Berhman died of pneumonia from staying outside to paint the last leaf on the tree, sacrificing his life in order to save Johnsy. **Sue tells Johnsy to "look out the window, dear, at the last ivy leaf on the wall. Didn't you wonder why it never fluttered or moved when the wind blew?"** *Mr Berhman painted the leaf so well, it fooled Johnsy into thinking it was real. Sue calls Behrman's painting his masterpiece because in an incredible act of kindness, he gave his life for the life of another person. Through his sacrifice, Johnsy regains the hope that rekindles her will to live. This reveals the prominent central idea of the story—the importance of hope when facing life's challenges.*

BOLD = added quotation   *ITALICS* = explanation of quotation

Clarify Briefly restate today's teaching objective and explain the practice task(s)

Take a moment to clearly underscore the importance of using specific textual evidence in composing a strong written literary commentary.

Direct students to return to their writing from Writing Lesson 3 and revise it to include quotations with explanations as specific textual evidence throughout.

Practice Students work independently and/or in small groups to apply today's teaching objective

Students revise their written literary commentary of a short story to include specific text evidence in the form of a direct quotations with explanations.

Wrap Up Check understanding as you guide students to briefly share what they have learned and produced today

Gather the class, and ask students to share examples of where they used quotations as textual evidence in their written literary commentary.

 Remind students to use appropriate eye contact, adequate volume, and clear pronunciation as they share their textual evidence. (SL.6.4)

Writing Lesson 5

▼ **Teaching Objective**

Writers revise and edit literary commentaries for strength and clarity.

▼ **Standards Alignment**

W.6.4, W.6.5, W.6.9, W.6.10, SL.6.1, SL.6.4, SL.6.6, L.6.1, L.6.2, L.6.3, L.6.6

▼ **Materials**

- Written Literary Commentary Checklist (Appendix 6.6)
- Completed student writing

▼ **To the Teacher**

Throughout this lesson set, you have emphasized the importance of reading and rereading the work of short stories to develop and strengthen students' understanding of a text and ability to write an analysis of it. Today we ask students to return once again to their own work to revise and edit their writing for clarity with a peer. **ELL** Enable Language Production—Reading and Writing. Make sure your ELLs understand that revision is a normal part of the writing process and that it is good to go through multiple attempts before settling on the best one.

▼ **Procedure**

Warm Up Gather the class to set the stage for today's learning

Emphasize the importance of reading and rereading your own writing to develop and strengthen it. Connect this practice to the work students have done in the reading portion of this lesson set.

> As readers, we have read and reread various short stories to develop an understanding of how an author can create a strong impact in a limited space. As writers, we have read and reread these stories in order to craft a clear written literary commentary of our reading. Reading and rereading are always critical pieces of our work as readers and as writers. Today we are going to reread our written analyses. Writers frequently read and reread their own work. Each time they read their work it is with a different purpose or eye. Today you will reread your written analyses for two purposes: to determine if you have clearly addressed the question being asked and to think about the conventions of standard English with an editor's eye. This is an important last step to ensure that our writing is easy for a reader to engage with and understand.

Teach Model what students need to learn and do

Written Literary Commentary Checklist

	Yes/No
Revising	
Did I answer all components of the question/prompt?	
Are my ideas in a logical sequence?	
Did I include sufficient text evidence by using direct quotations and/or paraphrasing?	
COPS Editing	
Did I check and correct my **c**apitalization?	
Did I check and correct my **o**rder and usage of words?	
Did I check and correct my **p**unctuation?	
Did I check and correct my **s**pelling?	

Orient students to the Written Literary Commentary Checklist. **ELL** Provide Comprehensible Input—Organizers. The checklist will help all your students, but your ELLs in particular, understand how to revise their writing. The checklist provides an anchor students can carry with them after the lesson to support their independent work. Distribute copies of the Written Literary Commentary Checklist (Appendix 6.6) to your students. Then take time to discuss each item on the checklist.

Try Guide students to quickly rehearse what they need to learn and do in preparation for practice

Allow students a moment to form partnerships. Give writing partnerships a moment to get organized. **ELL** Enable Language Production—Increasing Interaction. Revising in pairs will help your ELLs make sure that their writing makes sense to English-proficient readers. Partnerships should organize as follows:

- Take out the draft of the written literary commentary they completed during this lesson set.
- Decide on a process: Will the authors read and edit their own work independently and then share with their partner or complete the entire checklist collaboratively?

It is essential to allow sixth graders the ability and independence to set their own goals and determine roles when collaborating with a partner. It is not necessary that each writing partnership use the same process. It is necessary that all students engage thoughtfully in the revising and editing process, not that all partnerships follow the same path toward this goal.

 Highlight for students the importance of thoughtful collaboration including setting specific goals and deadlines and defining individual roles as needed. (SL.6.1b)

Clarify Briefly restate today's teaching objective and explain the practice task(s)

Remind students that they should collaborate with and support their writing partners. Partners should not only help each other analyze a particular piece of writing; they should help to revise and edit sections as necessary.

> Rereading your own writing to revise and edit can be difficult. Often we read our own writing too quickly and miss places where we could be clearer or have made a grammar error. Rely on your partner to help you slow down and identify places for improvement. Take care to focus on each item included on the Written Literary Commentary Checklist. It may feel redundant, but this last step is just as important to the writing process as all the others.

Practice Students work independently and/or in small groups to apply today's teaching objective

Students work collaboratively with a partner to use the Written Literary Commentary Checklist to revise at least one piece of written literary commentary, though each partnership may outline and use a different process for addressing the items on this list. If time allows, students should continue to select other pieces of written literary commentary from their collection of writing to revise and edit with their partners.

Tips for Effective Editing

1. Leave time between drafting and editing for the brain to "reset" to see the piece with fresh eyes. Consider doing a "quick edit" at the start of every writing period as opposed to the more commonly assigned end of the period.

2. Encourage students, even those working alone, to read their piece aloud. The brain tends to "hear" more errors that way.

3. Some students will hear more order and usage errors when listening to their writing read "as is" by another student or the teacher.

---

4. To check spelling, read the text backward, one word at a time. Removing context helps errors stand out.

5. To check sentences, read the text backward, one sentence at a time. Removing context helps errors stand out.

6. Reading with exaggerated expression helps emphasize where punctuation is needed (pauses, questions, exclamation points, etc.).

7. Provide students with extensive errors with a "short list" of one or two achievable items on which to focus for a limited amount of time. Model editing for these specific skills with them first, then have them continue on their own. Hold them accountable for catching all or most of the targeted errors. Repeat again at a later time.

Wrap Up Check understanding as you guide students to briefly share what they have learned and produced today

Gather the class, and ask students to share one specific revision or edit they made to their written literary commentary today and how the checklist helped them reread with a careful eye. Students should also detail how their partner contributed to their revising and editing process in specific, concrete ways.

Collect and analyze student writing as a performance-based assessment to determine if students need additional instruction or support as a whole class, in small groups, or one on one. **ELL** Assess for Content and Language Understanding—Formative Assessment. This is an opportunity for you to assess your ELLs' language and content needs, especially revising and editing strategies. Notice where their gaps are: Have they misunderstood something about the characteristics of literary commentary? Or do they struggle with the language they need to express those characteristics? Do they need support on written conventions (spelling, punctuation)? Are they able to make controlled choices about which varieties of English to use? Use this information to plan upcoming lessons.

Milestone Performance Assessment

Revising Written Literary
Commentaries

 Use this checklist to assess student revisions.

Standards Alignment: W.6.4, W.6.5, W.6.9, W.6.10, L.6.1, L.6.2, L.6.3, L.6.6

Task	Achieved	Notes
Revising		
Craft a strong written literary commentary that answers all components of the question/prompt.		
Compose ideas in a logical sequence		
Include text evidence with effective use of direct quotations and/or paraphrasing.		

Task	Achieved	Notes
COPS Editing*		
Capitalization.		
Order and usage of words		
Punctuation.		
Spelling.		

* We recommend that you focus your assessment lens in these areas. Select and assess a few skills that you have previously taught or that have emerged as areas of need in your ongoing assessment of student writing.

Writing Lesson 6

▼ Teaching Objective

Writers compose a strong written literary commentary of their reading in a single sitting.

Close Reading Opportunity

▼ Standards Alignment

RL.6.1, RL.6.10, W.6.4, W.6.5, W.6.6, W.6.9, W.6.10, SL.6.1a, SL.6.1, L.6.1, L.6.2, L.6.3, L.6.6

▼ Materials

- Charting supplies or interactive whiteboard to outline the steps to completing a strong written literary commentary
- Written Literary Commentary Checklist (Appendix 6.6)
- Writing Prompts for Written Literary Commentaries (Appendix 6.7)

▼ To the Teacher

Over the past few lessons, students have engaged with the process of composing a clear piece of written literary commentary to demonstrate their understanding of a piece of short text. However, it is also essential that we prepare students to complete this entire process in a single sitting in order to develop students' stamina and capacity to succeed in various test-taking situations. Today students will work to complete a typed, three-page written literary commentary of a familiar short story in a single sitting by selecting a prompt or question to respond to in writing. Therefore, it is essential to provide students with ample time but to also set clear limits so that they may plan their work accordingly.

If your students have access to technology that would allow them to draft, revise, publish, and share their writing on the computer, they will be working toward fulfilling Common Core State Standard W.6.6: *Use technology, including the Internet, to produce and publish writing as well as to interact and collaborate with others; demonstrate sufficient command of keyboarding skills to type a minimum of three pages in a single sitting.** Several suggestions for how to use technology to meet this standard are provided in the tech boxes across the lesson set. While the length of a "sitting" is not defined in the standards, the page requirement (three pages in a single sitting) clearly suggests that students need to have both the writing stamina and keyboard fluency needed to focus and produce a fairly large volume of writing in a short period of time. This capacity will develop if students are increasingly accountable for quantity as well as quality (with your guidance and encouragement) and are provided repeated opportunities to build and practice these skills through authentic writing experiences. **ELL** Enable Language Production—Reading and Writing. If you have newcomer students in your classroom, consider how you might adapt this assignment so it is both challenging and attainable. If you are working with students who are only just beginning to learn English but who are literate in their home language, you might have them complete their analysis in that language. This allows beginning ELLs to work on many other goals of the lesson (stamina, speed, keyboarding, literary analysis) without getting stuck by the one that will take them longer to attain: English proficiency. Then you can show them how to put their essays through an online translator so you may review them.

▼ Procedure

Warm Up Gather the class to set the stage for today's learning

Recap the work students have done thus far to formally share their analysis of a short story in writing.

> As writers, we have worked to clearly share our analysis of short stories through our writing by completely addressing each aspect of the question or prompt. We have also taken care to thoughtfully include textual evidence in the form of direct quotations or by paraphrasing a specific moment from the text as appropriate. Finally, we worked with a partner to revise and edit our written analyses for clarity. Each step of this process is important.

Take a moment to briefly lay out the process students have relied upon to complete their written literary commentary over a series of lessons or days. Record these steps on a quick process chart titled "Writing a Strong Analysis of Your Reading." The steps utilized throughout this lesson set are included in the sample chart.

Writing a Strong Analysis of Your Reading

1. Select a familiar short story.
2. Closely read the prompt or question.
3. Return to your short story to closely read with the prompt or question in mind, jotting notes as necessary.
4. Draft a written literary commentary.
5. Use the Written Literary Commentary Checklist to revise and edit.

ELL Provide Comprehensible Input—Organizers. This stable, concise, visual representation of what students have been learning will support your ELLs as they go through this process in a condensed period of time.

Teach Model what students need to learn and do

Inform students that it is sometimes necessary to be able to complete this type of writing in a single sitting, especially in a testing setting.

> Completing a clear piece of writing in a single sitting is an important skill, particularly when it comes to answering a question that shows your understanding

of a text. Today you will work with a familiar short story to think about, draft, revise, and edit a written literary commentary of your reading in a single sitting.

Introduce the Writing Prompts for Written Literacy Commentaries (Appendix 6.7) from which students will be able to choose to complete their written literary commentary. Read each prompt carefully, taking time to examine its parts and open up the conversation to address any student questions. For your convenience, the prompts are reproduced here. You may wish to display them for the class to view or to distribute a copy of the entire list of questions for students to refer to.

Writing Prompts for Written Literary Commentaries

- Determine a central idea of the short story, explain what the author's message is about the central idea, and discuss how the author conveys that message. Include specific evidence from the text.
- Choose an important character in a short story whose point of view changes as the story unfolds. Explain how the point of view changes and why. Explain how this change connects to a central idea of the story.
- Name the narrative techniques used by the author to enhance the experience of reading the short story. How does the use of these narrative techniques work to contribute to the meaning, tone, and/or mood of the text?
- Choose one key episode or event from the short story. Why is this significant? How does it contribute to your understanding of a central idea or how is it important to the development of the plot?

Try Guide students to quickly rehearse what they need to learn and do in preparation for practice

Give students a moment to consider which short story they would like to analyze as well as which question they would like to address in writing. Ask several students to share their choices.

Now outline the time limits for today's work. Prompt students to create a plan.

> How will you use this time to thoughtfully work through the process outlined in your Warm Up? What are your goals for completing this task?

Once you have given students time to create a plan on their own, direct them to share their initial thoughts with a partner. **ELL** Enable Language Production—Increasing Interaction. ELLs of all proficiency levels will benefit from the opportunity to get their ideas out before they start writing independently. Encourage ELLs to discuss their ideas in their home language if they like.

Clarify Briefly restate today's teaching objective and explain the practice task(s)

Reiterate the importance of being able to express yourself clearly in writing in a single sitting.

> There are many situations in which you will not have the time or ability to return to your writing over several days to make sure it is clear and engaging. Perhaps you are taking a test, composing an email at work, or sharing your thoughts with classmates. Today we are going to practice working through each of the steps of composing a strong written response in a single sitting. Working through a process in a single sitting like this takes discipline and stamina, which we can develop only with practice.

Practice Students work independently and/or in small groups to apply today's teaching objective

Each student selects a familiar short story and a question or prompt to respond to in writing. Then students work independently to compose a strong three-page written literary commentary of their reading.

Wrap Up Check understanding as you guide students to briefly share what they have learned and produced today

Gather the class. Ask students to share their experiences by responding to some or all of the following questions:

- How did you organize your time?
- How did creating a plan of attack in advance help you to complete this assignment? Did you have to modify your plan? How?
- What parts of the process felt challenging?
- When, if ever, did you feel your focus or stamina was beginning to fall apart? What can you do to refocus or reenergize in that situation?

Writing Lesson 7

▼ Teaching Objective

Writers use their reading and analysis of short stories to inspire their own writing.

Close Reading Opportunity

▼ Standards Alignment

RL.6.1, RL.6.10, W.6.3, W.6.4, W.6.5, W.6.10, SL.6.1, SL.6.4, SL.6.6, L.6.1, L.6.2, L.6.3, L.6.6

▼ Materials

- Elements of a Short Story Graphic Organizer (Appendix 6.1)
- Common Central Ideas in Middle School Literature (Appendix 6.2)

▼ To the Teacher

Writers are often avid readers. It is by reading often and widely that many writers improve upon their craft and are inspired to take on new projects. It is time to shift gears and allow our students to compose engaging central idea–driven short stories inspired by their reading and analysis of mentor short stories. We provide the Elements of a Short Story Graphic Organizer to support students' planning if needed.

▼ Procedure

Warm Up Gather the class to set the stage for today's learning

Revisit the Common Central Ideas in Middle School literature list. Ask students:

- Which central idea feels the most inspirational to them and might inspire their own original story?
- Which stories from their reading were the most compelling to them? Why?
- How did the author address the central idea in your favorite stories?
- Which of these have emerged so far in the stories we have read in the reading lessons?

Teach Model what students need to learn and do

Introduce the idea of writing a short story.

> For the past few days, we have closely read and discussed the craft and power of the short story. Today we are going to shift gears and use what we have learned about short stories to craft our own. Each of you will choose a central idea that inspires you and work to craft your own short story around that central idea.

Enable students to view the Elements of a Short Story Graphic Organizer included in Appendix 6.1. Take time to review and discuss each section of the planner. Remind students of the basic elements of a short story.

Now, move on to discuss some of the more practical guidelines and understandings of short stories students have acquired or observed through their reading in this lesson set. You may wish to list and post these guidelines for student reference. Begin with this question to the class: What do we know about the format and structure of a short story?

As your discussion unfolds, be sure to highlight and record the following guidelines for writing a powerful short story.

Guidelines for Writing a Short Story

- Short stories can be read in one sitting and are typically only a few pages in total.
- Short story settings often span a short amount of time.
- Short stories often happen in one location.
- Short stories include only a few important characters.
- Short stories use vivid, descriptive language to paint a clear picture in a small amount of space.
- Short stories usually convey one or more central ideas (themes).

ELL Provide Comprehensible Input—Organizers. Charts can help ELLs access the content you are teaching by turning the oral discussion, which may be moving fast, into stable, written bullet points that highlight key takeaway information. The chart will give ELLs something concrete to refer back to during independent work.

Try Guide students to quickly rehearse what they need to learn and do in preparation for practice

Distribute copies of the Elements of a Short Story Graphic Organizer (Appendix 6.1) to the class. Direct students to use the planner as a reference while they begin discussing writing plans with a partner.

Circulate as students discuss their plans with a partner. Support students as they think through both the guidelines of writing a short story as well as the elements of a short story included in the Elements of a Short Story Graphic Organizer.

Encourage students to stay on topic, speak clearly, listen carefully to their partner, and ask thoughtful and relevant questions when necessary. (SL.6.1a, SL.6.1b, SL.6.1c, SL.6.1d) Once students have had ample time to discuss their ideas with a partner, ask one or two volunteers to share their plans with the entire class.

Clarify Briefly restate today's teaching objective and explain the practice task(s)

Encourage students to apply what they have learned from the short story genre in reading to what they are going to produce in writing.

Generally, authors are avid readers. They read the work of other authors closely, studying the genre and styles they wish to incorporate into their own work. Now that we have spent several days digging into the work of other authors, it is time to use what we have learned to craft our own powerful short stories.

Direct students to use the Elements of a Short Story Graphic Organizer (Appendix 6.1), if desired, to develop their short stories and then to move directly into drafting.

Practice Students work independently and/or in small groups to apply today's teaching objective

Christian Schwier/Fotolia

Students work independently to plan and begin drafting their short stories. Therefore, this lesson may be best taught across more than one day. Ideally, students should have fairly complete drafts of at least one short story before moving on to Writing Lesson 8. However, if students complete an entire draft within your given time frame, they may work to plan and draft additional short stories.

ELL Enable Language Production—Reading and Writing. Newcomer ELLs may be better able to show what they know about the craft of short stories if they are allowed to write in their home language. You could encourage them to try composing two versions, one in their strong language and one in their emergent language, using a bilingual dictionary and bilingual peers as resources. Orally proficient ELLs who struggle with literacy may benefit from discussing their ideas with you first before putting pen to paper.

Once students have completed drafts of their narratives, they should work in partnerships to read, review, and work through any trouble spots.

Writing Lesson 8 ·

▼ Teaching Objective

Writers purposefully incorporate specific narrative techniques to enhance their short stories.

Close Reading Opportunity

▼ Standards Alignment

RL.6.1, RL.6.10, W.6.3, W.6.4, W.6.5, W.6.10, SL.6.1, SL.6.6, L.6.1, L.6.2, L.6.3, L.6.6

▼ Materials

- Helping Our Short Stories Pack a Punch chart (content this lesson)
- Sample Short Story Version #1 and Version #2: *The London Eye* (Appendix 6.8)

▼ To the Teacher

In this lesson, we introduce a list of techniques that the Common Core State Standards require students to employ in narrative writing. We have included two drafts of a sample short story in Appendix 6.8 for you to use during the Teach portion of this lesson, one that employs many techniques and one that does not. Alternately, you might use your own writing or a favorite short story as a model of strong narrative techniques.

▼ Procedure

Warm Up Gather the class to set the stage for today's learning

This chart outlines key techniques required in student narratives by the Common Core State Standards for writing. Review the content with the class, explaining each element as needed. Students should be quite familiar with most of the items on the chart because of the work they did in Reading Lesson 5. We have consolidated precise words and phrases, sensory imagery, and figurative language under a single heading: word choice. The term *pacing* may be new to students. We explain pacing as an author's decision to

slow down the pace of how an important part of a story unfolds through the addition of dialogue, relevant descriptive detail, and careful word choice. In contrast, an author may speed up parts that are not central to the story by minimizing these elements.

Helping Our Short Stories Pack a Punch
Character dialogue: Advances the story in an engaging way and/or reveals important information
Detailed description: Provides details about events, experiences, setting, and characters
Word choice: Makes description more powerful through precise words and phrases and sensory language
Pacing: When the author slows down the parts that matter most by adding dialogue, description, and careful word choice

Teach Model what students need to learn and do

Remind students of the importance and purpose of the use of narrative techniques in the writing of short stories.

> Short stories have to pack a punch in a limited amount of space. Authors must choose their words carefully to create images and scenes in the minds of readers. In order to make their writing sharp and dynamic, many authors rely on the narrative techniques we included on this chart. We have already studied and identified most of these devices as readers. Today it is time to work with them as writers of our own short stories.

Display a short story you have crafted that intentionally lacks any use of narrative techniques. Or, for your convenience, you may use our sample short story: *The London Eye* (Appendix 6.8) for this modeling work. You will notice that this short story is included twice—the first version contains fewer narrative techniques than the second. The second draft includes several examples of dialogue, description, and careful word choice. It also demonstrates control of pacing by slowing down key parts with the addition of detail through various narrative techniques.

Provide students with copies of both drafts. Tell them that Version #1 was revised to include narrative techniques to enhance the story. Version #2 is the revised story. Give them several minutes to read both versions. They should then compare the two versions and highlight in Version #2 where they have found revisions. Ask students to find at least one example of each technique in the list (dialogue, detailed description, word choice, and control of pacing) and articulate how the use of the technique enhanced the story. **ELL** Enable Language Production—Increasing Interaction. ELLs may be more successful with this task if they are allowed to collaborate with bilingual peers.

Have students come together to share their findings on each technique. **ELL** Provide Comprehensible Input—Models. ELLs will benefit from seeing many examples of strong narrative writing so they can develop the necessary language to make these techniques work in their own writing.

Try Guide students to quickly rehearse what they need to learn and do in preparation for practice

Ask students to turn to their own drafts and mark a few places that would benefit from the addition of one or more of these techniques. Remind them to stretch the parts that feel most important to the central idea of the story with dialogue, description, and careful word choice. This is what the last technique of pacing is all about.

Clarify Briefly restate today's teaching objective and explain the practice task(s)

Using the two drafts of a short story as a concrete reference, reiterate the impact of using these narrative techniques.

> The narrative techniques we discussed as readers represent some of the techniques and tools authors rely on to craft an experience for the reader. Authors

of short stories in particular use these narrative techniques to ensure that their work truly packs a punch in a short amount of space. Today, as writers, your job is to find places within your own work to test out the use of these narrative techniques.

Direct students to revise their current drafted short stories to include various narrative techniques. If students complete their revisions, they should move on to crafting a new short story, thinking about the inclusion of narrative techniques from the original drafting stage.

Practice Students work independently and/or in small groups to apply today's teaching objective

Students work independently to revise their writing to thoughtfully include the use of several narrative techniques. **ELL** Enable Language Production—Reading and Writing. Your on-the-spot coaching helps your ELLs understand how to apply these powerful techniques to their own writing.

Wrap Up Check understanding as you guide students to briefly share what they have learned and produced today

Gather the class, asking students to have their revised drafts handy. Then ask students to share their work with a partner. Direct partners to highlight at least one place within their work in which they added the use of a specific narrative technique. Then ask several volunteers to share their inclusion of various narrative techniques in front of the entire class. You may wish to post these examples for the class, thereby elevating the work of your students to mentor status. **ELL** Enable Language Production—Increasing Interaction. Peer sharing is a valuable way for ELLs to get feedback on their work from English-proficient peers. They can find out whether their efforts at developing a central theme are having the intended effect, and they can hear how others have applied the writing techniques you have taught.

Writing Lesson 9

▼ **Teaching Objective**

Writers revise and edit their short stories with a peer.

▼ **Standards Alignment**

W.6.3, W.6.4, W.6.5, W.6.10, SL.6.1, SL.6.4, SL.6.6, L.6.1, L.6.2, L.6.3, L.6.6

▼ **Materials**

- Short Story Checklist (Appendix 6.9)
- Completed student short stories

▼ To the Teacher

Today's lesson is similar to Writing Lesson 5 in which we asked students to revise and edit their written literary commentary of a text with a partner. However, in alignment with the Common Core State Standards, it is essential to drive home the importance of this step of the process for any piece of writing as well as to emphasize how partners can support one another through specific suggestions of revisions.

▼ Procedure

Warm Up Gather the class to set the stage for today's learning

Emphasize the importance of reading and rereading your own writing to develop and strengthen it. Highlight the role of a peer to help suggest specific revisions and to look at writing with "fresh eyes."

> During this lesson set, we have already engaged with the process of revising and editing our written literary commentary of short stories. Today we are going to again revise and edit our work to improve our short stories and to make sure they really pack a punch. To do this, you will work with a partner. Take the role of being someone's partner seriously. As a writing partner, it is your job to look at a piece of writing with fresh eyes, to help your partner slow down and thoughtfully consider his or her own writing, and to suggest specific ways to improve that piece of writing. A strong writing partner contributes meaningfully to the revising and editing process and does not merely sit by and check each item off a checklist.

Teach Model what students need to learn and do

	Yes/No
Revising	
Is my short story inspired by at least one clear central idea (theme)?	
Did I establish a narrator?	
Did I include only a few important characters?	
Did I include a clearly defined setting?	
Did I include a problem or complication?	
Did I use several narrative techniques to enhance the short story? • Character dialogue • Detailed description • Word choice • Pacing	

	Yes/No
Did I include a conclusion that reveals a message or truth about the central idea?	
COPS Editing	
Did I check and correct my **c**apitalization?	
Did I check and correct my **o**rder and usage of words?	
Did I check and correct my **p**unctuation?	
Did I check and correct my **s**pelling?	

Orient students to the Short Story Checklist (Appendix 6.9). Distribute copies to your students. Then take time to discuss each item on the checklist.

Try Guide students to quickly rehearse what they need to learn and do in preparation for practice

Allow students a moment to organize themselves into partnerships. Give writing partnerships a moment to get organized. Partnerships should get organized by addressing the following:

- Take out the short story that they have completed during this lesson set.
- Decide on a process: Will the authors read and edit their own work independently and then share with their partners or complete the entire checklist collaboratively?

As stated previously in Writing Lesson 5, it is essential to allow sixth graders the ability and independence to set their own goals and determine roles when collaborating with a partner. It is not necessary that each writing partnership utilize the same process. It is necessary that all students engage thoughtfully in the revising and editing process, not that all partnerships follow the same path toward this goal.

Highlight for students the importance of thoughtful collaboration including setting specific goals and deadlines and defining individual roles as needed. (SL.6.1b)

Clarify Briefly restate today's teaching objective and explain the practice task(s)

Remind students that they should collaborate with and support their writing partners. Partners should not only help each other analyze a particular piece of writing; they should also help to correct sections as necessary.

Practice Students work independently and/or in small groups to apply today's teaching objective

Students work collaboratively with a partner to use the Short Story Checklist (Appendix 6.9) to revise at least one piece of written literary commentary, though each partnership may outline and utilize a different process for addressing the items on this list. **ELL** Enable Language Production—Increasing Interaction. Peer discussion gives your ELLs a low-pressure environment to hear examples of how to revise and to practice the language they need to express their own ideas about revision. Working with English-proficient peers can also help ELLs learn new techniques for accomplishing their goals with their stories.

If time allows, students should continue to select other short stories from their collection of writing to revise and edit with their partners.

Wrap Up Check understanding as you guide students to briefly share what they have learned and produced today

Gather the class, and ask students to share one specific edit they made to their short story and how the checklist helped them reread with a careful eye. Students should also detail how their writing partner contributed to their editing process in specific, concrete ways.

Milestone Performance Assessment

Revising Short Stories   PD **pd** TOOLKIT™

Collect and analyze student writing as a performance-based assessment to determine if students need additional instruction or support as a whole class, in small groups, or one on one. **ELL** Assess for Content and Language Understanding—Formative Assessment. If you notice that some of your ELLs are missing aspects of the checklist, plan how you will support them. Help them to figure out *how* to add what is missing: Was it an oversight, or are they not sure how to make their meaning clear in English?

 Use this checklist to assess student revisions.

Standards Alignment: W.6.3, W.6.4, W.6.5, W.6.10, L.6.1, L.6.2, L.6.3, L.6.6

Task	Achieved	Notes
Revising		
Short story inspired by at least one clear central idea (theme).		
Establish a narrator.		
Include only a few important characters.		
Include a clearly defined setting.		
Include conflict or resolution.		
Use several narrative techniques to enhance the short story. • Character dialogue • Detailed description • Word choice • Pacing		
Include a conclusion that reveals a message or truth about the central idea.		
COPS Editing*		
Capitalization.		
Order and usage of words.		
Punctuation.		
Spelling.		

* We recommend that you focus your assessment lens in these areas. Select and assess a few skills you have previously taught or that have emerged as areas of need in your ongoing assessment of student writing.

Writing Lesson 10

▼ Teaching Objective

Writers share their short stories in authentic ways.

▼ Standards Alignment

W.6.3, W.6.4, W.6.6, W.6.10, SL.6.1, SL.6.1d, SL.6.2, SL.6.4, SL.6.6, L.6.1, L.6.2, L.6.3, L.6.6

▼ Materials

- Students' competed short stories
- Common Central Ideas in Middle School Literature (Appendix 6.2)

▼ To the Teacher

In this lesson, students' short stories are recognized through purposeful sharing. Prior to teaching this lesson, select one of the methods suggested for sharing your students' work with an authentic audience.

Goal	Low-Tech	High-Tech
Students share their short stories with an authentic audience.	Students share their stories by: • hosting an authors' event in which students share their work aloud. • publishing their short stories in a literary magazine and distributing them to families and other classrooms.	Students share their stories by: • creating a VoiceThread for other students to link to and listen to. • posting their writing on a classroom blog for peers to read and respond to via the comments function. • creating multimedia presentations of their work using iMovie. Students select images to be shown as their story is read aloud.

ELL Enable Language Production—Listening and Speaking, Reading and Writing. Consider that if you have many ELLs with the same home language who are only beginning to learn English, they may benefit from working in a group that reads its stories in their shared language. These students may be able to engage in more complex thinking and conversation in their home language than in English. Also, consider that if you are sharing stories with your ELLs' family members, it is important to find a way to include them in the celebration by giving them access to their children's works. Could part of the literary magazine be bilingual, with translations of some of the stories? Could students record bilingual versions to post online? Multilingual practices show students and their families that your school is a place for people from all different backgrounds.

Depending on your selection, this lesson may be best taught across several days to allow for adequate student preparation.

▼ Procedure

Warm Up Gather the class to set the stage for today's learning

Lead students in a discussion of the hard work they put into their final short stories. Use the following questions as a guide:

- How did the experience of writing a short story differ from writing a longer text?
- What inspired you to write your particular short story?
- What narrative techniques did you select to use in your work, and why?

Teach Model what students need to learn and do

Share with students the methods you have selected for sharing their short stories with an authentic larger audience. In general, consider and address the following concerns:

- How will students be sharing their work with a larger audience?
- What will students need to do to prepare their work to be shared with a larger audience?
- What is the time frame for completing this work?

Try Guide students to quickly rehearse what they need to learn and do in preparation for practice

Ask students to discuss rules and etiquette for sharing their work with one another. For example, students should talk about how to be a good audience and/or how to leave constructive criticism and how to share specific compliments that are grounded within the text.

Here are some rules your students may outline for their group discussions:

- We will do the required work before the discussion takes place so we are prepared for a group conversation.
- We will treat each other with respect and kindness, we will speak one at a time, and we will not interrupt each other or speak negatively about each other's opinions or ideas.
- We will listen closely when another group member is talking and use evidence from the text to talk more about his or her point or to explain why we have a different opinion.
- We will set goals for our discussion, and each person in the group will have a special job to do to keep the discussion on track.

Clarify Briefly restate today's teaching objective and explain the practice task(s)

Take a moment to briefly review the process for sharing student work. Remind students of the importance of sharing their writing with an audience.

> When writers craft stories to share a message about a central idea, it is important that they get their work out into the world. As they begin to think about how and where they share their work, authors must consider the audience they would like to read their work.

Practice Students work independently and/or in small groups to apply today's teaching objective

Students share their writing with classmates, responding to the work of one another as appropriate and outlined in the Teach portion of this lesson. Then students work to share their short stories with an authentic larger audience.

As students share their stories, remind them to speak clearly and use appropriate eye contact, adequate volume, clear pronunciation, and standard English when appropriate. Support audience members as they carefully listen to the short stories and consider how each text reflects the class study of short stories. (SL.6.2, SL.6.4, SL.6.6)

Wrap Up Check understanding as you guide students to briefly share what they have learned and produced today

Gather the class, and reflect on the central ideas that were addressed in students' writing. Use the Common Central Ideas in Middle School Literature (Appendix 6.2) to help guide this conversation. Work with students to recognize any patterns across the class: Were some central ideas more popular than others? Ask students to hypothesize about these patterns.

Finally, work with students to determine how their growth as writers over the course of this lesson set can and should influence their other narrative writing work, regardless of genre.

GLOSSARY

antagonist: character(s) who oppose or come into conflict with the main character.

central idea: the terms *central idea* and *theme* both describe the unifying idea or subject of the story. A well-developed central idea often suggests a universal truth about life or human behavior.

conflict: the problem or issue that arises in a story.

connotation: the associations and emotional connections we make to a work beyond the literal meaning

denotation: the literal meaning of a word

dialogue: a conversation between two or more people in a narrative.

episode: related events, or scenes, that make up the plot of a story, including the conflict and resolution.

figurative language: when the usual (literal) meaning of a word or phrase is changed in order to compare, emphasize, or provide a clear image

first-person narrator: a story told from the point of view of a character who participates in the action of the story.

literary commentary: an analysis of a literary text.

memoir: a text that describes a person's past experiences.

metaphor: when one object is described as being the same as another, seemingly dissimilar object (Example: *I am feeling a roller coaster of emotions.*)

mood: the effect of the author's words on the reader, how the piece makes the *reader* feel.

narrator: the person telling the story.

narrative mode: the method the writer uses to tell, or narrate, the plot of a story.

narrative technique: the way a story is told.

personification: when inanimate objects are given human qualities (Example: *The sunlight danced across the floor.*)

point of view: how a character views a particular situation. In other words, the attitude or feelings a character has toward key events or individuals in a story.

protagonist: the main character in a work of fiction.

resolution: the way the conflict or problem was solved or the ending of a story.

secondary characters: characters in addition to the main characters who may or may not be essential to the story.

second-person narrator: a story told from the point of view of one character telling the story to another character.

setting: the time and place in which the story is set.

short story: a narrative text that often has characters, a narrator, a setting, key plot episodes, and a clear central idea but is shorter than a novel. Often defined as a story that may be read in one sitting, but the length of a sitting is debatable.

simile: when two unlike things are compared directly using the words *like* or *as* (Example: *She is as pretty as a rose.*)

third-person narrator: story told from the point of view of someone who is not a character and does not participate in the action. Tells the story as an outside observer. Can be a limited narrator whose knowledge is limited to the thoughts and feelings of only one character or an omniscient narrator who knows all of the thoughts and feelings of every character in the story.

theme (i.e., central idea): the terms *central idea* and *theme* can both be used to describe the unifying idea or subject of the story. A well-developed central idea, or theme, often suggests a universal truth about life or human behavior.

tone: the attitude or feelings the *author* or *narrator* seems to have toward the material or the reader.

PD TOOLKIT™

Accompanying *Core Ready for Grades K–2*, there is an online resource site with media tools that, together with the text, provides you with the tools you need to implement the lesson sets.

The PDToolkit for Pam Allyn's *Core Ready* Series is available free for 12 months after you use the password that comes with the box set for each grade band. After that, you can purchase access for an additional 12 months. If you did not purchase the box set, you can purchase a 12-month subscription at **http://pdtoolkit.pearson** **.com.** Be sure to explore and download the resources available at the website. Currently the following resources are available:

- Pearson Children's and Young Adult Literature Database
- Videos
- PowerPoint Presentations
- Student Artifacts
- Photos and Visual Media

- Handouts, Forms, and Posters to supplement your Core-aligned lesson plans
- Lessons and Homework Assignments
- Close Reading Guides and Samples
- Children's Core Literature Recommendations

In the future, we will continue to add additional resources. To learn more, please visit **http://pdtoolkit.pearson.com.**

Grade 7

Examining Past Perspectives: Historical Fact and Fiction

Introduction

Historical fiction enables readers to take a voyage on a print-driven time machine. Who doesn't love to imagine themselves alive during a distant time? A knight at King Arthur's court? A newly minted soldier encountering the French battlefields of World War II? A nurse tending to soldiers at Gettysburg? A woman, recently freed from slavery, leading others north to freedom? When we read these stories we can't help but place ourselves at the center of the story and wonder, "How would I react if I had been there? Would I rise to the challenge?" The genre of historical fiction allows the reader to get up close and personal with characters who lived through a significant historical event. Writers of these stories prompt the reader to consider what it might be like to be a witness to history or even an agent of change. After all, despite the fact that we learn about the famous names in history, the truth is that history is made not only by the famous, but by the countless everyday people who witness and become a part, however small, of the important events of their time period.

In this lesson set, we will take seventh graders on this journey through time. Through the magic of historical fiction, students will experience settings and cultures that are unlike their own. In reading, they will view the events of a given time period from the perspective of characters who are imagined but realistic. In

Why This Lesson Set?

In this lesson set, students will:

- Read historical fiction closely to determine a writer's point of view
- Analyze the ways a character's perspective shapes story
- Consider how historical context informs plot
- Compare and contrast a fictional portrayal of a true-life event with a historical account
- Analyze what is real and what is imagined in a piece of historical fiction
- Engage in class discussions about the themes and issues rooted in the text
- Compare and contrast a work of historical fiction with a film of the same story
- Read and analyze informational text to gain a better understanding of a historical time period
- Read informational text to tease out the point of view of actual historical figures
- Research a historical time period in order to bring historical fiction pieces to life
- Create characters within a historical and cultural background
- Consider the ways in which historical context shapes the point of view of characters
- Craft both narrative and informational text with a focus on an era of historical significance

writing, they will thoughtfully create their own characters and imagine how their life experiences might influence the unique point of view of each. Hopefully, these learning experiences will serve to broaden the perspective of our students and foster an appreciation of others who differ from themselves

Although our reading and writing will be grounded in the civil rights period during the 20th century, students will also be immersed in other historical fiction stories representing a variety of times and places. They will endeavor to answer such questions as: Whose story is it, and why does that matter? As writers, they will have the opportunity to create their own short works of historical fiction. Writers will learn the importance of research and the need to balance true facts with the author's imagination. In addition, they will craft short informational pieces, "author's notes," in which they will explain why they decided to choose both the historical era and a particular character and point of view. They will consider the following questions: What makes this a story worth telling? How does the historical context of the writer influence the perspective of the story? Why was the story told from this point of view? What does this perspective offer the reader in terms of a deeper understanding of the historical context?

Common Core State Standards Alignment

Reading Standards

RL.7.1 Cite several pieces of textual evidence to support analysis of what the text says explicitly as well as inferences drawn from the text.

RL.7.2 Determine a theme or central idea of a text and analyze its development over the course of the text; provide an objective summary of the text.

RL.7.3 Analyze how particular elements of a story or drama interact (e.g., how setting shapes the characters or plot).

RL.7.6 Analyze how an author develops and contrasts the points of view of different characters or narrators in a text.

RL.7.7 Compare and contrast a written story, drama, or poem to its audio, filmed, staged, or multimedia version, analyzing the effects of techniques unique to each medium (e.g., lighting, sound, color, or camera focus and angles in a film).

RL.7.9 Compare and contrast a fictional portrayal of a time, place, or character and a historical account of the same period as a means of understanding how authors of fiction use or alter history.

RL.7.10 By the end of the year, read and comprehend literature, including stories, dramas, and poems, in the grades 6–8 text complexity band proficiently, with scaffolding as needed at the high end of the range.

RI.7.1 Cite several pieces of textual evidence to support analysis of what the text says explicitly as well as inferences drawn from the text.

RI.7.2 Determine two or more central ideas in a text and analyze their development over the course of the text; provide an objective summary of the text.

RI.7.3 Analyze the interactions between individuals, events, and ideas in a text (e.g., how ideas influence individuals or events, or how individuals influence ideas or events).

RI.7.5 Analyze the structure an author uses to organize a text, including how the major sections contribute to the whole and to the development of the ideas.

RI.7.6 Determine an author's point of view or purpose in a text and analyze how the author distinguishes his or her position from that of others.

RI.7.8 Trace and evaluate the argument and specific claims in a text, assessing whether the reasoning is sound and the evidence is relevant and sufficient to support the claims.

RI.7.9 Analyze how two or more authors writing about the same topic shape their presentations of key information by emphasizing different evidence or advancing different interpretations of facts.

RI.7.10 By the end of the year, read and comprehend literary nonfiction in the grades 6–8 text complexity band proficiently, with scaffolding as needed at the high end of the range.

Writing Standards

W.7.3 Write narratives to develop real or imagined experiences or events using effective technique, relevant descriptive details, and well-structured event sequences.

a. Engage and orient the reader by establishing a context and point of view and introducing a narrator and/or characters; organize an event sequence that unfolds naturally and logically.

b. Use narrative techniques, such as dialogue, pacing, and description, to develop experiences, events, and/or characters.

c. Use a variety of transition words, phrases, and clauses to convey sequence and signal shifts from one time frame or setting to another.

d. Use precise words and phrases, relevant descriptive details, and sensory language to capture the action and convey experiences and events.

e. Provide a conclusion that follows from and reflects on the narrated experiences or events.

W.7.4 Produce clear and coherent writing in which the development, organization, and style are appropriate to task, purpose, and audience. (Grade-specific expectations for writing types are defined in standards 1–3 above.)

W.7.5 With some guidance and support from peers and adults, develop and strengthen writing as needed by planning, revising, editing, rewriting, or trying a new approach, focusing on how well purpose and audience have been addressed. (Editing for conventions should demonstrate command of Language standards 1–3 up to and including grade 7 here.)

W.7.6 Use technology, including the Internet, to produce and publish writing and link to and cite sources as well as to interact and collaborate with others, including linking to and citing sources.

W.7.7 Conduct short research projects to answer a question, drawing on several sources and generating additional related, focused questions for further research and investigation.

W.7.9 Draw evidence from literary or informational texts to support analysis, reflection, and research

a. Apply *grade 7 Reading standards* to literature (e.g., "Compare and contrast a fictional portrayal of a time, place, or character and a historical account of the same period as a means of understanding how authors of fiction use or alter history").

W.7.10 Write routinely over extended time frames (time for research, reflection, and revision) and shorter time frames (a single sitting or a day or two) for a range of discipline-specific tasks, purposes, and audiences.

Speaking and Listening Standards

SL.7.1 Engage effectively in a range of collaborative discussions (one-on-one, in groups, and teacher-led) with diverse partners on grade 7 topics, texts, and issues, building on others' ideas and expressing their own clearly.

SL.7.2 Analyze the main ideas and supporting details presented in diverse media and formats (e.g., visually, quantitatively, orally) and explain how the ideas clarify a topic, text, or issue under study.

SL.7.4 Present claims and findings, emphasizing salient points in a focused, coherent manner with pertinent descriptions, facts, details, and examples; use appropriate eye contact, adequate volume, and clear pronunciation.

SL.7.6 Adapt speech to a variety of contexts and tasks, demonstrating command of formal English when indicated or appropriate. (See grade 7 Language standards 1 and 3 for specific expectations.)

Language Standards

L.7.1 Demonstrate command of the conventions of standard English grammar and usage when writing or speaking.

L.7.2 Demonstrate command of the conventions of standard English capitalization, punctuation, and spelling when writing.

L.7.3. Use knowledge of language and its conventions when writing, speaking, reading, or listening.

L.7.6 Acquire and use accurately grade-appropriate general academic and domain-specific words and phrases; gather vocabulary knowledge when considering a word or phrase important to comprehension or expression.

Core Questions

Before getting started with the day-to-day lessons, it's important to consider the core questions that drive this lesson set. Each lesson should come back to these overarching ideas:

- How is historical fiction different from other genres?
- What is more powerful for a reader—fact or fiction?
- Why do authors choose to tell true stories with imaginary elements?
- How is the time period important to a story?
- How might historical context influence a character's perspective?
- How might a character's background influence his or her perspective?
- What are the most important tools of an author of written text? What are the most important tools of a filmmaker?
- What's better—the book or the movie?
- What events are worth telling stories about?

Lesson Set Goals

Within this lesson set, there are many goals we as teachers want to help our students reach.

Reading Goals

- Examine how the historical setting shapes the plot of the story. (RI.7.1, RL.7.1, RL.7.3, RI.7.3, RI.7.10, RL.7.10, W.7.4, W.7.10, SL.7.1, SL.7.4, SL.7.6, L.7.1, L.7.3, L.7.6)
- Identify the narrator of a story and analyze the point of view the narrator conveys. (RL.7.1, RL.7.3, RL7.6, RL.7.10, W.7.4, W.7.9, W.7.10, SL.7.1, SL.7.6, L7.1, L.7.2, L.7.3, L.7.6)
- Compare and contrast a written story to its filmed version and analyze the effects of techniques unique to each medium. (RL.7.1, RL.7.2, RL.7.7, R.7.10, W.7.4, W.7.9, W.7.10, SL.7.1, SL.7.2, SL.7.4, SL.7.6, L.7.1, L.7.3, L.7.6)
- Compare and contrast how stories in both film and print examine the way the cultural background influences point of view. (RL.7.1, RL.7.3, RL.7.6, RL.7.7, RL.7.10, W.7.4, W.7.9, W.7.10, SL.7.1, SL.7.2, SL.7.4, SL.7.6, L.7.1, L7.3, L.7.6)
- Compare and contrast a fictional portrayal and a historical account of the same period. (RL.7.1, RI.7.1, RI.7.2, RI.7.3, RL.7.9, RL.7.10, RI.7.10, W.7.4, W.7.9, W.7.10, SL.7.1, SL.7.2, SL.7.4, SL.7.6, L.7.1, L.7.3, L.7.6)
- Examine the balance of historical fact and imagined elements in a historical fiction text. (RL.7.1, RI.7.1, RI.7.2, RI.7.3, RL.7.9, RL.7.10, RI.7.10, W.7.4, W.7.9, W.7.10, SL.7.1, SL.7.2, SL.7.4, SL.7.6, L.7.1, L.7.3, L.7.6)

- Examine the development of point of view across historical accounts. (RI.7.1, RI.7.2, RI.7.5, RI.7.6, RI.7.8, RI.7.9, RI.7.10, SL.7.1, SL.7.2, SL.7.4, SL.7.6, L.7.1, L.7.3, L.7.6)

- By the end of the year, read and comprehend literature, including stories, dramas, and poems, in the grades 6–8 text complexity band proficiently, with scaffolding as needed at the high end of the range. (RL.7.10)

- By the end of the year, read and comprehend literary nonfiction in the grades 6–8 text complexity band proficiently, with scaffolding as needed at the high end of the range. (RI.7.10)

- In collaborative discussions, demonstrate evidence of preparation and exhibit responsibility for the rules and roles and purpose of conversation. (SL.7.1)

- In collaborative discussions, share and develop ideas in a manner that enhances understanding of a topic and contribute and respond to the content of the conversation in a productive and focused manner. (SL.7.1)

- Adapt speech to a variety of contexts and tasks, demonstrating command of formal English when indicated or appropriate. (SL.7.6)

- Demonstrate command of standard English and its conventions and use the knowledge when writing, speaking, reading, and listening. (L.7.1, L.7.2, L.7.3)

- Acquire and use accurately grade-appropriate general academic and domain-specific words and phrases, strategically building vocabulary knowledge when needed. (L.7.6)

Writing Goals

- Write historical fiction narrative that includes key elements of historical fiction. (W.7.3, W.7.4, W.7.5, W.7.10)

- Conduct research to craft a realistic setting with authentic details in the narrative. (RI.7.1, RI.7.2, RI.7.3, RI.7.10, W.7.3, W.7.4, W.7.5, W.7.6, W.7.7, W.7.10, SL.7.1, SL.7.2, SL.7.6, L.7.1, L.7.2, L.7.3, L.7.6)

- Articulate a character/narrator's background and illustrate its influence on his or her perspective. (W.7.3, W.7.4, W.7.5, W.7.10)

- Employ dialogue to reinforce characters' point of view. (RL.7.1, RL.7.6, RL.7.10, W.7.3, W.7.4, W.7.5, W.7.10)

- Write a reflective author's note to explain their thinking and writing process. (W.7.4, W.7.5, W.7.10)

- By the end of the year, read and comprehend literary nonfiction in the grades 6–8 text complexity band proficiently, with scaffolding as needed at the high end of the range. (RI.7.10)

- With some guidance and support from peers and adults, develop and strengthen writing as needed by planning, revising, editing, rewriting, or trying a new approach, focusing on how well purpose and audience have been addressed. (W.7.5)

- Use technology, including the Internet, to complete required tasks: to produce and publish writing, link to and cite sources, and interact and collaborate with others. (W.7.6)

- In collaborative discussions, demonstrate evidence of preparation and exhibit responsibility for the rules and roles and purpose of conversation. (SL.7.1)

- In collaborative discussions, share and develop ideas in a manner that enhances understanding of a topic and contribute and respond to the content of the conversation in a productive and focused manner. (SL.7.1)

- Adapt speech to a variety of contexts and tasks, demonstrating command of formal English when indicated or appropriate. (SL.7.6)

- Demonstrate command of standard English and its conventions and use the knowledge when writing, speaking, reading, and listening. (L.7.1, L.7.2, L.7.3)

- Acquire and use accurately grade-appropriate general academic and domain-specific words and phrases, strategically building vocabulary knowledge when needed. (L.7.6)

Choosing Core Texts

The shelves of our middle school libraries are brimming with myriad wonderful historical fiction stories. Each offers insight into past events and is filled with characters who meet adversity and grow from the experience. In this lesson set, we have chosen to focus on civil rights developments of the 20th century, and we have selected the wonderful novel *Roll of Thunder, Hear My Cry* by Mildred B. Taylor. The strategies presented in this lesson set, however, will lend themselves to any historical fiction text, so feel free to choose a different time period and model texts to suit your class interests or local curriculum. In addition to working with this historical fiction text, we will also use multimedia and various nonfiction sources as we explore the place in our collective psyche where history, experience, and perspective collide.

Core Texts Used Within the Lesson Set

- "Civil Rights Bill Passed, 73-27; Johnson Urges All to Comply; Dirksen Berates Goldwater" by E. W. Kenworthy in *The New York Times* (July 2, 1964

- George Wallace's 1963 Inaugural Address ("Segregation Now, Segregation Forever")

- John Lewis's 1963 Speech at the March on Washington

- *Roll of Thunder, Hear My Cry* by Mildred B. Taylor

- Excerpts from *The Watsons Go to Birmingham—1963* by Christopher Paul Curtis

Fiction

- *Above All Things* by Tanis Rideout
- *Freedom on the Menu* by Carole Boston
- *Freedom Summer* by Deborah Wiles
- *Short Stories of the Civil Rights Movement* edited by Margaret Earley Whitt

Historical Fiction Book Club Selections by Historical Era *America in Early 20th Century (Immigration, Labor Movement, Jim Crow, etc.)*

- *Bread and Roses Too* by Katherine Paterson
- *Brooklyn Bridge* by Karen Hesse
- *Esperanza Rising* by Pam Munoz Ryan
- *Roll of Thunder, Hear My Cry* by Mildred D. Taylor
- *Uprising* by Margaret Peterson Haddix
- *The Watch That Ends the Night: Voices from the Titanic* by Allan Wolff

Civil War/Slavery

- *Copper Sun* by Sharon Draper
- *Girl in Blue* by Ann Rinaldi
- *How I Found the Strong* by Margaret McMullan
- *The Middle Passage* by Charles Johnson
- *Nightjohn* by Gary Paulsen
- *Sarny* by Gary Paulsen
- *Soldier's Heart: A Novel of the Civil War* by Gary Paulsen

Colonial America

- *Fever* by Laurie Halse Anderson
- *My Brother Sam Is Dead* by James Lincoln Collier
- *Witch of Blackbird Pond* by Elizabeth Speare

World War II

- *Between Shades of Gray* by Ruta Sepetys
- *The Book Thief* by Markus Zusak
- *Code Name Verity* by Elizabeth Wein
- *Milkweed* by Jerry Spinelli
- *Number the Stars* by Lois Lowry
- *Sarah's Key* by Tatiana Rosnay
- *Saving Private Ryan* by Max Allan Collins
- *The Year of Impossible Goodbyes* by Sook Nyul Choi

Nonfiction

- *In My Eyes* by Ruby Bridges
- *Freedom's Children: Young Civil Rights Activists Tell Their Own Stories* by Ellen Levine
- *Travels with Charley* by John Steinbeck

Speeches (text and audio can be found online)

- George Wallace's 1963 "Schoolhouse Door Speech"
- President Kennedy's Civil Rights Address, June 11, 1963

Film *Feature Films*

- *42*
- *Roll of Thunder, Hear My Cry*
- *Watsons Go to Birmingham: 1963*
- *The Butler*

Documentary

- *Eyes on the Prize* (produced by PBS)
- *Four Little Girls* (produced by 40 Acres & A Mule Filmworks)
- *Riding to Freedom* (found at www.Smithsonianmag.com)

Websites

- http://photos.state.gov/galleries/usinfo-photo/39/civil_rights_07/ (for photos and text)
- www.pbs.org
- www.teachingamericanhistory.org

Teacher's Notes

This lesson set will be grounded in an anchor text, *Roll of Thunder, Hear My Cry* by Mildred B. Taylor. In addition, your students will participate in Historical Fiction Book Clubs. There are many ways to structure the book clubs. These kinds of learning groups present a great opportunity to place readers with "just right" books—books on their reading level. In addition, book clubs allow for a certain amount of student choice at a time in the their lives when they are striving for autonomy. It is possible to marry both of these needs: student reading level and student choice. We suggest teachers create text sets that allow a teacher to offer each student several selections on their reading level. We have provided many potential titles from which to choose. It is important to balance student choice with the need to put each child in the right book club for his or her reading level. Plan your groups and have them choose their books in advance of teaching the Reading Lessons.

Roll of Thunder, Hear My Cry by Mildred B. Taylor takes place in rural Mississippi during the Great Depression and presents a particular picture of life in the American South during that time. The main characters of the story are poor due not only to the Depression, but also due to the severe racial inequalities of the time period. Some of the content is sensitive in nature as it tackles racism head on. The novel also tackles questions of what happens when individuals seek to change the culture and customs into which they were born. It is wise to be cognizant of students' background and comfort level as these issues are explored. We have selected a variety of informational texts to complement and support students' study.

Questions for Close Reading

The Core Ready lessons include many rich opportunities to engage students in close reading of text that require them to ask and answer questions, draw conclusions, and use specific text evidence to support their thinking (Reading Anchor Standard 1). These opportunities are marked with a close reading icon. You may wish to extend these experiences using our recommended Core Texts or with texts of your choosing. Use the following questions as a resource to guide students through close reading experiences in historical fiction and viewing film versions of familiar stories.

Genre Questions

- What makes this text part of the historical fiction genre?
- What is the historical setting of the story?
- How does the historical setting shape the plot?
- How does the historical setting affect the characters?
- How do historical events contribute to this story? Set the scene?
- What parts of the story are factual? What parts are imaginary?
- Why do you think the author chose to tell this story?

Point of View Questions

- Is there a clearly defined narrator? If so, whose story is this?
- What information in the text helps the reader to understand a character's point of view?
- What shared beliefs and experiences from his or her cultural group or time period affect the character's point of view?
- Why do you think the author chose to tell the story from the point of view of this particular character or group?
- How do the perspectives of two characters differ? Why do they see things differently?

- In what ways would a character's point of view change if he or she found himself or herself on the other side of an event?
- What societal issue(s) is(are) the focus of the writing (e.g., slavery, segregation, human rights, war, etc.)? What is the author's point of view about it(them)?
- How does the writer address the focus issue(s) through the story?
- What is the author suggesting should be done about the focus issue(s)? What challenges will this bring to people involved? (Consider all sides of the issue.)

Media Comparisons

- How does the multimedia version compare to the written text? What tools does the multimedia creator use that are not available to the author of writing alone? How does the creator use them to affect the story?
- What effect does the multimedia presentation have on the viewer that is different from simply reading the words?

Building Academic Language

A list of academic language to build your students' comprehension of the focus of this lesson set and facilitate their ability to talk and write about what they learn follows. There are words and phrases listed. Rather than introduce all the words at once, slowly add them to a learning wall as your teaching unfolds. See the glossary at the end of this chapter for definitions of the words. Also listed are sentence frames that may be included on a sentence wall (Carrier & Tatum, 2006), a research-proven strategy for English language learners (Lewis, 1993; Nattinger, 1980), or as a handout to scaffold student use of the content words. Some students, especially English language learners, may need explicit practice in using the sentence frames. Encourage all students to regularly use these words and phrases in their conversations and writing.

Recognition

At the conclusion of this lesson set, it is important to celebrate and share all that your students have accomplished. Upon completion of the reading lessons, your students will engage in a Socratic seminar in which they will discuss the ways historical fiction can connect us to actual historical events and to our own lives. In the writing lesson set, your students will become writers of their own historical fiction stories. In addition, they will craft personal author's notes in which they will reflect on their writing process and their reasons for selecting a particular historical event. There are many ways to accomplish this recognition.

Core Words

camera angles and focus	first-person narrator	perspective
central idea	historical context	point of view
color	historical fiction	second-person narrator
conflict	lighting	sound
culture	narrator	third-person narrator
episode	narrative mode	

Core Phrases

- *To identify the genre:* I know that this text is historical fiction because _____.

- *To express author's purpose:* The author probably chose to write about this time period because_____.

- *To expand on author's purpose:* The message the author is trying to convey about _____[time period/issue]_____ is _____. This message is conveyed by _____[text evidence]_____.

- *To articulate an experience that changed a character:* After _____ [experience]_____, _____[Character]_____ changes. [Explain how.]

- *To identify a key line in the text:* The most powerful line in this text is _____. [Explain why.]

- *To identify strong imagery:* This line conveys a very powerful image of the historical time period: _____. [Explain how.]

- *To identify strong character description:* The sentence that best characterizes _____[Character]_____'s perspective on the historical event is: _____. [Explain why.]

- *To identify a sentence that conveys an idea:* The sentence that best reveals this is: _____. [Explain how.]

- *To identify the narrative point of view:* This scene/story uses _____ narration. [Explain.]

- *To articulate the point of view of the narrator in the story:* In this scene/story, the narrator is _____ [name narrator]_____. The narrator's point of view toward _____ [time period/issue]_____ is _____.

Students may create an author's website, you may host a reading, students might create podcasts, or they may dress up as a character from their own story. You may opt to share within the classroom, across the grade level, or with the entire school community.

Complementary Core Methods

Read Aloud

Use this structure to share additional selected works of historical fiction, excerpts from longer works, or complex informational text with your students in order to provide a model for students as they consider how writers create works of fiction that are grounded in historical fact. Read-aloud texts support both readers and writers. They provide an opportunity for teachers to share how readers tackle complex text as well as how writers create their own historical narratives. Select a variety of texts in order to expose students to multiple genres and to engage them with the work of thinking across texts. Be sure to highlight and include pieces of writing that center on a historical focus event, incorporate a clear point of view, and highlight realistic settings and interesting characters. Consider closely reading the text, using multiple reads of these pieces to emphasize the importance of returning to key readings to discover new elements. In your first read, you are providing a foundation for the content of the piece as a whole, and your students may benefit from a read-aloud without repeated interruption. In your second read-aloud of the text, you may prompt students to notice a writer's choice of particular words and phrases as well as structure. Finally, return again to the text to contemplate its connection to other texts and events. The read-aloud structure allows for the modeling and practice of the way readers make meaning that allows for deeper understanding of the text.

When appropriate, use your read-aloud as another chance for students to practice one or two of the following skills:

- Identify elements of historical fiction.
- Analyze how historical context influences point of view
- Identify the way point of view develops across the text.
- Analyze the use, purpose, and power of specific narrative techniques.
- Consider the way historical fiction connects us to real-life events.

Shared Reading

Shared reading provides a wonderful opportunity to look closely at excerpts from grade-level appropriate read-alouds or short texts for close reading. Shared reading is a large or small group reading experience where everyone has a clear view or individual copy of the text to read closely and discuss with the group.

In this lesson set in particular, use shared reading of excerpts of historical fiction stories or short informational texts to help students develop the ability to analyze the way historical context influences point of view and historical fact influences fiction.

Here are some prompts you may want to use in your conversations about these texts:

- Identify the point of view of the narrator and other characters.
- Analyze how historical fact informs historical fiction.
- Compare and contrast informational text with its fictional representation.
- Identify key scenes or moments related to the focus event.

Shared Writing

During shared writing, the teacher collaborates with the students to create a piece of writing. While the teacher is in control and does the actual writing, he or she also guides students through the process they will need to ultimately use independently. The content for the writing is facilitated by the teacher yet reflective of students' ideas. In this lesson set, shared writing can be viewed as an opportunity to provide additional practice or scaffolding with the following:

- Crafting believable characters and accurate settings.
- Responding with evidence to a shared reading or read-aloud.

- Planning for writing.
- Practicing a particular narrative technique, such as dialogue or descriptive detail.

Core Connections at Home

Consider asking relatives or community members who experienced or are experts in the Civil Rights Movement or other historical time periods in their books to speak to the class about the time period and their impression of how society has changed since that time.

With any book/movie pairing that they may have experienced, encourage family members to share their responses to the question: What's better—the book or the movie? Why? Do they prefer to read poems or hear them spoken? Which resonates more deeply for them, gives them more of a feeling of meaningfulness?

Families serve as an educator's partner in a child's education. Whenever possible, it is important to keep lines of communication open. It is always helpful to provide students with project checklists and timelines so that families at home are aware of expectations. Keep families informed regarding what is happening in school. In addition, encourage families to talk to their kids about what they are reading and studying in your class. Finally, welcome families into your classroom to celebrate your students' hard work.

Reading Lessons

The Core I.D.E.A. / Daily Reading Instruction at a Glance table highlights the teaching objectives and standards alignment for all 10 lessons across the four stages of the lesson set (Introduce, Define, Extend, and Assess). It also indicates which lessons contain special features to support English language learners, technology, speaking and listening, close reading opportunities, and formative ("Milestone") assessments.

The Core I.D.E.A. / Daily Reading Instruction at a Glance

Grade 7 Examining Past Perspectives: Historical Fact and Fiction				
Instructional Stage	**Lesson**	**Teaching Objective**	**Core Standards**	**Special Features**
Introduce: *notice, explore, collect, note, immerse, surround, record, share*	1	Readers build background knowledge on a time period by examining historical photographs.	RI.7.1 · RI.7.3 · RI.7.10 · W.7.4 · W.7.10 · SL.7.1 · SL.7.4 · SL.7.6 · L.7.1 · L.7.3 · L.7.6	S&L ELL Close Reading Opportunity
	2	Readers identify the elements of historical fiction in a model text.	RL.7.1 · RL.7.2 · RL.7.3 · RL.7.9 · RL.7.10 · W.7.4 · W.7.9 · W.7.10 · SL.7.1 · SL.7.2 · SL.7.4 · SL.7.6 · L.7.1 · L.7.3 · L.7.6	S&L ELL Milestone Assessment Close Reading Opportunity
Define: *name, identify, outline, clarify, select, plan*	3	Readers identify the narrative mode of a story and analyze how the author develops characters' points of view.	RL.7.1 · RL.7.2 · RL.7.3 · RL.7.6 · RL.7.10 · W.7.4 · W.7.9 · W.7.10 · SL.7.1 · SL.7.2 · SL.7.4 · SL.7.6 · L7.1 · L7.3 · L.7.6	S&L ELL Close Reading Opportunity
	4	Readers compare and contrast a fictional portrayal and a historical account of the same period to examine how historical fiction authors use history in their writing	RL.7.1 · RI.7.1 · RL.7.2 · RI.7.2 · RL.7.3 · RI.7.3 · RL.7.9 · RL.7.10 · RI.7.10 · W.7.4 · W.7.9 · W.7.10 · SL.7.1 · SL.7.2 · SL.7.4 · SL.7.6 · L.7.1 · L.7.3 · L.7.6	S&L ELL Close Reading Opportunity
	5	Readers analyze how an author uses the historical setting to shape character and plot.	RL.7.1 · RI.7.1 · RL.7.2 · RI.7.2 · RI.7.3 · RL.7.3 · RL.7.9 · RL.7.10 · RI.7.10 · W.7.4 · W.7.9 · W.7.10 · SL.7.1 · SL.7.2 · SL.7.4 · SL.7.6 · L.7.1 · L.7.3 · L.7.6	Tech ELL Milestone Assessment Close Reading Opportunity
Extend: *try, experiment, attempt, approximate, practice, explain, revise, refine*	6	Readers compare and contrast point of view in a print version of a historical fiction text to a film version.	RL.7.1 · RL.7.2 · RL.7.3 · RL.7.6 · RL.7.7 · RL. 7.10 · W.7.4 · W.7.9 · W.7.10 · SL.7.1 · SL.7.2 · SL.7.4 · SL.7.6 · L.7.1 · L.7.3 · L.7.6	S&L ELL Close Reading Opportunity
	7	Readers evaluate the effect filmmaking techniques have on a story.	RL.7.7 · W.7.4 · W.7.10 · SL.7.1 · SL.7.2 · SL.7.4 · SL.7.6 · L.7.1 · L7.3 · L.7.6	Tech ELL Milestone Assessment
	8	Readers determine point of view in historical accounts and analyze its development over the course of the text.	RI.7.1 · RI.7.2 · RI.7.3 · RI.7.5 · RI.7.6 · RI.7.8 · RI.7.9 · RI.7.10 · SL.7.1 · SL.7.2 · SL.7.4 · SL.7.6 · L.7.1 · L.7.3 · L.7.6	S&L ELL Close Reading Opportunity
	9	Readers consider how authors shape an argument to their advantage.	RI.7.1 · RL.7.1 · RI.7.3 · RL.7.3 · RI.7.6 · RL.7.6 · RI.7.8 · RI.7.9 · RI.7.10 · RL.7.10 · W.7.4 · W.7.9 · W.7.10 · SL.7.1 · L.7.1 · L.7.2 · L.7.6	Tech ELL Milestone Assessment Close Reading Opportunity
Assess: *reflect, conclude, connect, share, recognize, respond*	10	Readers reflect on the ways historical fiction can connect us to real-life events.	RI.7.1 · RI.7.2 · RI.7.10 · RL.7.1 · RL.7.2 · RL.7.3 · RL.7.10 · W.7.4 · W.7.9 · W.7.10 · SL.7.1 · SL.7.4 · SL.7.6 · L.7.1 · L.7.2 · L.7.3 · L.7.6	S&L ELL Close Reading Opportunity

Reading Lesson 1

▼ Teaching Objective

Readers build background knowledge on a time period by examining historical photographs.

Close Reading Opportunity

▼ Standards Alignment

RI.7.1, RI.7.3, RI.7.10, W.7.4, W.7.10, SL.7.1, SL.7.4, SL.7.6, L.7.1, L.7.3, L.7.6

▼ Materials

- A selection of photographs that depict different events related to American civil rights in the 20th century and Southern farm life in the early 20th century.
- Photograph 7 of the "Washington Freedom Riders Committee" and its accompanying text from http://photos.state .gov/galleries/usinfo-photo/39/civil_rights_07/.
- Analyzing a Photo graphic organizer (Appendix 7.1)
- Charting supplies or interactive whiteboard
- Sticky notes

▼ To the Teacher

In this lesson, we want to set the stage for the lesson set through the introduction of the historical context for our core novel, *Roll of Thunder, Hear My Cry* by Mildred B. Taylor, while at the same time prompting students to begin thinking about the genre of historical fiction. Photos play an important role in this lesson set, and we suggest they be presented as text as they are essential primary source documents. Through the act of viewing a photograph or painting, readers can learn a great deal about the importance of noticing details while at the same time learning about a historical event. We want students to observe the photographs as anthropologists observe communities, to draw inferences about a particular time, place, and people. There are many places to find powerful photographs on any modern time period. Although less common, paintings and drawings of time periods prior to photography are also available. A simple Internet search will yield many. It is important to select images that engage readers and make them think and wonder about what it might have been like to be present at this moment in history. In short, we want them to feel something, react to what they're seeing, and begin to understand the perspectives of the people in the photos.

If you are using the model texts we use in this lesson set, one website with a large collection of images is http://photos.state.gov/galleries/usinfo-photo/39/civil_rights_07/. This website pairs short informational text with each photograph. The text provides background information. Photos related to Southern farming in the 1920s and 1930s may be found at www.livinghistoryfarm.org in the farm life section. An Internet search of "Great Depression sharecroppers" will also yield many images that provide context for *Roll of Thunder, Hear My Cry*. We suggest you also try searching the following events or topics: school integration, school segregation, Great Depression, sharecropping, Jim Crow laws, Ruby Bridges, the Little Rock Nine, lunch counter sit-ins, Freedom Riders, Birmingham church bombings, right-to-vote demonstrations, and John Lewis and the march from Selma to Montgomery. **ELL** Provide Comprehensible Input—Visuals. A lesson focused on images will allow your ELLs to learn a great deal without having to rely solely on text. This helps all your students begin this lesson set on equal footing.

Prior to teaching the lesson, preselect one photo that captures important events from the focus time period.

▼ Procedure

Warm Up Gather the class to set the stage for today's learning

Inform your students that you are beginning a new lesson set: Together and independently, students will read and write historical fiction narratives. In addition, they will become immersed in the reading and writing of nonfiction text.

> Today we begin a lesson set grounded in the genre of historical fiction. We will read and discuss historical fiction as a class, and you will also tackle a novel on your own.
>
> In addition, we will be immersed in informational text related to our core texts and in your independent books. Through these, we will examine the time periods that provide the backdrop for the stories and look at individuals and events that shaped that part of history. Finally, you will become authors of historical fiction as you create your own characters and craft your own narratives. Much of what we read will be about a chapter of American history where many Americans experienced discrimination because of their race. Today we are going to be doing some talking and writing about this notion that history influences the stories we tell.
>
> Before we begin, please turn and talk with your neighbor about these questions: Can you think of an event that has taken place in our world recently that might make for a good story or novel? What about this event would make it a worthwhile story?

Chart student responses. Ask students to justify the events they choose for the first question. They may say that the events tell an exciting story, evoke strong emotion, changed history, demonstrate the good in humanity, and so forth.

Teach Model what students need to learn and do

For this teaching model, we will use photograph 7 of the "Washington Freedom Riders Committee" and the accompanying text from this website: http://photos .state.gov/galleries/usinfo-photo/39/civil_rights_07/7.html. The accompanying text provides some background information that may come in handy during the initial writing lesson. If this photo is not available to you, use another historical photo that presents a powerful image about which the following questions would elicit a quality discussion.

> Today we are going to have a look at a few photographs taken during the 20th century. Photographs provide a window into what actually happened during different periods of history. As readers, we will be looking for details that give us information about what was taking place when the photo was taken. We will consider what stories might come from these images. When we begin to read our Historical Fiction Book Club texts, we will also look for those important details in the text, the ones that give us clues and help us to imagine and understand a particular moment in time.

Using the Freedom Riders photo, model for your students the way you 'read' this type of text for details and clues. Model how to complete the Analyzing a Photo graphic organizer (Appendix 7.1), focusing on the first three questions for your model. We provide a sample of what your graphic organizer might look like. Responses would vary by individual or group, but we want to encourage keeping thoughts grounded in evidence from the photo. **ELL** Provide Comprehensible Input—Organizers. This tool will make the process of analyzing a photograph more transparent for your ELLs. They can see clearly what process they are meant to go through.

Analyzing a Photo graphic organizer

Describe the photo What do you notice?	• This is a photo of a silver bus in a parking lot. • I notice that there are people leaning out of the bus windows. • I see large buildings in the background. • They are holding signs; the signs are about freedom and ending segregation. • Two of the signs make reference to a law. • One of the signs says "Enforce Constitution 13th, 14th, 15th amendments." • The people I can see in the windows are white. • The bus is different than buses we see today—the windows open, and it is rounder somehow. • The name of the bus company (Orange & Black Bus Lines Inc.) plus some letters and numbers are written on the bottom edge of the bus (ICCMC 66582 NJPUC 21484).

What might these details tell you about this historical time period?	These details tell me that the people on the bus want an end to segregation. They are probably traveling to protest segregation and to uphold Amendments 13, 14, and 15 of the Constitution.
How are the individuals in your photo affected by the events taking place?	I think I can infer that the individuals on the bus have been inspired to help put an end to segregation. They believe that the Constitution needs to be upheld—they have been motivated to act. They're trying to change the culture of segregation—their beliefs conflict with that system.
What conclusions might you draw?	
What questions might you ask?	

ELL Frontload the Lesson—Build Background. Keep in mind that students raised partially outside the United States or whose parents grew up in another country may not yet be familiar with this part of history and therefore might not be able to immediately interpret the photograph as representing a protest against segregation. All students can notice details and ask questions about them, but you may need to explicitly instruct students about the era represented in the photographs or direct them to other sources so they can answer their own questions.

Try Guide students to quickly rehearse what they need to learn and do in preparation for practice

Have students turn and talk with a partner to discuss the last two questions on the graphic organizer. Have students share their ideas and chart them. Possible responses:

What conclusions might you draw?	Because most of the people that I can see on the bus are white, one conclusion that I can draw is that some white people also fought for civil rights. Because I see that the Freedom Riders were traveling by bus, I can guess that maybe people were coming to the South from other parts of the country. Maybe they are from another area? I will need to learn some more before I can say that this is a fact.
What questions might you ask?	What laws are the riders referring to on their signs? How were they organized? What happened on their trip? Were they successful? What prompts someone to step outside of his or her own life and comfort zone to seek change?

Ask the class: Is there anything that we missed? and/or Do you have anything else to add? Always bring students back to the photo, keeping them grounded in what the photo contains explicitly.

Clarify Briefly restate today's teaching objective and explain the practice task(s)

Provide students with a selection of photographs that they can analyze collaboratively or independently using the Analyzing a Photo graphic organizer (Appendix 7.1). Coach students as needed and ask at least one group to share as a model for the rest of the class.

> Your task today is to analyze a historical photograph. Remember that we are looking for details in the photo that might give us some insight into the event taking place and the point of view of the people in the photo. Always stay grounded in the photo; use the details as evidence to stretch your thinking. You will use the Analyzing a Photo graphic organizer to record your findings.

Practice Students work independently and/or in small groups to apply today's teaching objective

Distribute photos and the Analyzing a Photo graphic organizer to students. Students may work in pairs to analyze the photographs. Be sure to circulate among your students to check in and support where needed.

Use this opportunity to support students with important speaking and listening skills such as staying on topic, asking and answering thoughtful questions, and referring to textual evidence. (SL.7.1a, SL.7.1b)

ELL Enable Language Production—Listening and Speaking. Bear in mind that while your ELLs probably notice many interesting things about their photographs, they may not have the words to explain in English what they are seeing or what they think it means. If you pair your ELLs with English-proficient students, they can work together to find the language to describe the pictures.

Wrap Up Check understanding as you guide students to briefly share what they have learned and produced today

Collect students' photographs and graphic organizers and hang their work around the room as a gallery exhibit. Provide students with sticky notes and instruct them to circulate with sticky notes and comment on one another's photos and observations.

> As you circulate among the photos, I'd like you to think about which one jumps out at you. Which one do you consider to be the most powerful? On your sticky note, write a few words about why you think this photo is the most powerful. What details in the photo contribute to its overall impact?

Bring students back together for a class discussion.

As students share their findings, remind them to emphasize salient points in a focused, coherent manner with pertinent descriptions, facts, details, and examples. (SL.7.4)

> Let's wrap up for today with a conversation about these photographs. Using the information in your graphic organizer and the photos themselves, let's consider the following questions:

- What do you imagine the people depicted in these photographs are thinking or feeling? How did you come to this conclusion?
- Is there a potential story in any of these photos?
- What might that story be?

Students will likely respond to the more obvious examples of racism in these particular photos. They may wonder about the story behind the motives of the people depicted in the images. Another story might be told about how it felt to be in the moment shown in the pictures. They may also wonder about the story of what happened after the photo was taken: What was the end result of whatever action was taking place?

Reading Lesson 2 ·····················

▼ Teaching Objective

Readers identify the elements of historical fiction in a model text.

Close Reading Opportunity

▼ Standards Alignment

RL.7.1, RL.7.2, RL.7.3, RL.7.9, RL.7.10, W.7.4, W.7.9, W.7.10, SL.7.1, SL.7.2, SL.7.4, SL.7.6, L.7.1, L.7.3, L.7.6

▼ Materials

- *Roll of Thunder, Hear My Cry* by Mildred B. Taylor (Chapter 1)
- Selection of texts for the Historical Fiction Book Clubs (see Choosing Core Texts list for suggestions)
- Elements of Historical Fiction graphic organizer (Appendix 7.2)

- Charting supplies or interactive whiteboard to create the Elements of Historical Fiction chart
- Sticky notes

▼ To the Teacher

Today we will begin to read excerpts from *Roll of Thunder, Hear My Cry* by Mildred B. Taylor. This book will be our anchor novel, and we will use it as a model for how readers make sense of historical fiction. Although we model using *Roll of Thunder, Hear My Cry,* you can use an excerpt from any historical fiction text you would like. This lesson is designed expose your students to the general elements of historical fiction.

In this lesson, they will begin to read their own Historical Fiction Book Club texts and will use these books in the Practice segment of upcoming lessons. Plan these groups in advance of the lesson. See the Teacher's Notes and Choosing Core Texts in the introduction for more information. We provide you with the Elements of Historical Fiction graphic organizer (Appendix 7.2) for modeling and student use with their independent reading. Students may not be able to identify all the elements in their own reading every day, but encourage them to identify as many as they can as they read their Historical Fiction Book Club texts. In order to address all of the elements of the lesson, plan for two or more days of instruction.

▼ Procedure

Warm Up Gather the class to set the stage for today's learning

Review the definition of *historical fiction*. Historical fiction tells a tale that happens during a recognizable time period in history, often through the eyes of fictional characters who are part of the story. Factual events, settings, and people are often intermingled with fictional story elements.

Ask students:

- How does historical fiction differ from other kinds of fiction?
- What are we looking for/noticing when we read historical fiction?

Chart your students' responses. Possible student responses: takes place in the past, is about an important historical event and/or time period, is often told through the eyes of fictional characters who are part of the story. **ELL** Frontload the Lesson—Activate Prior Knowledge. This brief discussion ensures that all your students begin this lesson on the same page. Explicit connections between prior learning and new learning are very helpful for ELLs trying to orient themselves to a lesson.

Present students with the Elements of Historical Fiction graphic organizer (Appendix 7.2). Quickly review the elements of this genre and then move on to the Teach portion of the lesson.

Teach Model what students need to learn and do

Elements of Historical Fiction Graphic Organizer

Name _____ Date _____

Title and Author _____

Directions: Use these graphic organizers to record observations and thoughts about the elements of historical fiction.

Historical Fiction Element: Characters	Evidence from the Text (include page number)	Describe what you are thinking at this point.
-Characters are realistic. They may include fictional people created by the author, real people who lived at the time, or both.		
-Fictional or real, all characters' actions, words, thoughts and experiences are consistent with people of the time period. What are we learning about the characters in general? What about the characters is realistic to the historical time period and place?		

Historical Fiction Element: Setting	Evidence from the Text (include page number)	Describe what you are thinking at this point. (e.g., your background knowledge, questions, conclusions, predictions)
Setting is an authentic historical time period and location. The setting is very important in historical fiction because it influences all other elements. -What historical time period and location are represented in the book?		

Historical Fiction Element: Key Plot Events	Evidence from the Text (include page number)	Describe what you are thinking at this point.
-Events may be fictional, real, or both. The problems and experiences faced by the characters are realistic to the historical setting. -What plot details are representative of the time period and place? -What, if any, real events are part of the plot?		

Historical Fiction Element: Description	Evidence from the Text (include page number)	Describe what you are thinking at this point.
What descriptive language does the writer use to bring the time period alive?		

Historical Fiction Element: Dialogue	Evidence from the Text (include page number)	Describe what you are thinking at this point.
Is there dialogue? If so, how does it help show thoughts/perspectives of the time period? Is the language/slang typical of the time period?		

Inform students that they will be listening to an excerpt from a historical fiction text in order to identify the various elements. Today students will also begin their reading journeys with their own Historical Fiction Book Clubs. In this lesson, we model reading the first chapter from *Roll of Thunder, Hear My Cry* by Mildred B. Taylor. In these pages, we are introduced to Cassie Logan and her brothers, Little Man, Christopher John, and Stacey. Through her words, we begin to understand her background and the time period in which she lives. Model for students how to note the elements of historical fiction with sticky notes or taking notes so they can continue this practice in their independent reading.

Prior to reading aloud, remind students to carefully listen for the elements of historical fiction and any supporting details they can identify. (SL.7.2) **ELL** Frontload the Lesson—Set a Purpose for Reading. When you give your students a specific listening task, you help your ELLs to zero in on the most important information in the text.

Historical fiction tells a tale that takes place during a recognizable time period in history, often through the eyes of fictional characters who are part of the story. Factual events, settings, and people are often intermingled with fictional story elements. Today we will begin reading *Roll of Thunder, Hear My Cry*, a historical fiction novel by a writer named Mildred B. Taylor. Set in Mississippi during the Great Depression in around 1933 to 1934. It is the story of an African American family who struggles to live with the economical and civil rights challenges of the time period. As we read, we will be noticing those details that give us information about the time period, and these will fall into the historical fiction element categories we discussed earlier. I have given each of you a packet of sticky notes—use these to mark places in the text that you think are interesting or important or related to what our focus is for the day. Ready to get started?

Read Chapter 1, pages 1 to 13, or up until just after the bus incident and Stacey's statement, "Ask Mama." Create a chart titled "Elements of Historical Fiction." Together with the class, fill in the chart with the information you have about the text thus far. At this point, some of the "thinking aloud" prompted by the chart for *Roll of Thunder, Hear My Cry* might look like this. In order to keep the work with the chart from becoming tedious, you don't have to write every conversation point down word for word— you might take abbreviated notes or just chart part of the conversation as a model for students' work in practice.

Historical Fiction Elements	Evidence from the Text (include page number or percentage—may vary with edition)	Describe what you are thinking at this point. (e.g., your background knowledge, questions, conclusions, predictions)
Characters -Characters are realistic. They may include fictional people created by the author, real people who lived at the time, or both. -Fictional or real, all characters' actions, words, thoughts and experiences are consistent with people of the time period. What are we learning about the characters in general? What about the characters is realistic to the historical time period and place?	• Narrator, Cassie Logan, has three brothers: Little Man, 6, Stacey, 12, and Christopher John, 7. They live in the country on their family farm. (pp. 3–4) They are African-American. • They go to school together. • Christopher John: quiet, cheerful, sensitive (p. 5) • Little Man: neat and looking forward to school (pp. 3–4) • Stacey: moody, upset his mother is not his teacher this year • Cassie: tomboy, hates dresses and shoes (p. 5). • T.J. Avery: a neighbor who also comes from a farming family, poor, outspoken, tricky (pp. 7–12) The characters' reactions to the first day of school, the story of the burning, and the bus incident seem typical of their age and experience. They seem surprised by the burning story, but the bus incident seems like something that has happened to them before.	Even though she is not the oldest, Cassie seems strong and like she won't put up with nonsense based on the way she speaks to her brothers and TJ. I am curious to learn more about Cassie's relationships with her brothers and father. It seems like she has a close relationship with her father. I wonder if that will be important later in the story.

Historical Fiction Elements	Evidence from the Text (include page number or percentage—may vary with edition)	Describe what you are thinking at this point. (e.g., your background knowledge, questions, conclusions, predictions)
Setting Setting is an authentic historical time period and location. The setting is very important in historical fiction because it influences all other elements. -What historical time period and location are represented in the book?	October, 1933, in the countryside of Mississippi (pp. 3—6)	I know that this is during the Great Depression. The economy was very bad, and many people struggled tremendously to make ends meet. Cassie indicates this when she describes how her father needs to work on the railroad to pay bills. I also know that race relations in Mississippi were very bad, and African Americans were the victims of discrimination and violence due to racism. We see this through the description of the burning of the Berrys and the mean kids on the bus who enjoy getting the Logan children dirty.
Key Plot Events -Events may be fictional, real, or both. The problems and experiences faced by the characters are realistic to the historical setting. -What plot details are representative of the time period and place?	The first 13 pages depict the children walking together to school. The author also provides background information about the children's ages and personalities. Then, Cassie explains that her family owns their own land but that her father must work far away on the railroad and her mother and grandmother also work to pay for it. The family is poor, but their taxes and mortgage are paid. (pp. 6—7)	I am pretty sure that the fact that Cassie's family owns their own land is going to be important in the story because Cassie talks about it so much. I bet that a lot of poor families, black or white, could not afford land at that time. The family's land is clearly very important to them based on the amount of attention the author pays to this. Will they have trouble keeping up with the bills and lose their land?

Historical Fiction Elements	Evidence from the Text (include page number or percentage—may vary with edition)	Describe what you are thinking at this point. (e.g., your background knowledge, questions, conclusions, predictions)
-What, if any, real events are part of the plot?	When TJ joins the group, we hear about some of the terrible racism and violence black people in the community experience. He tells the Logans that neighbors have been burned by some white men. He also mentions getting his brother in trouble for going to a store dancing room (pp. 8–11) Suddenly, a bus carrying white children speeds up to the kids and covers Little Man in dust. The passengers laugh. Stacey tells Little Man that the people on the bus like to see them run and that there is no bus for them. (p. 13)	The Logan children seemed shocked to hear about the burning, like they have never heard of this type of thing before. Their mother and grandmother chose not to tell them about it, probably to protect them from being scared. I wonder how common that kind of violence was at the time. Why is going to the dancing room a problem? The older children seem to expect the behavior of the bus and passengers. This kind of thing may have happened a lot. Poor treatment of black people was very common at the time. The fact that the black children have to walk when the white children have a bus is not fair. What other injustices do the Logans live with?

Continue reading the remainder of the chapter with the class. An important text feature to highlight for your students is the way the writer includes breaks in the chapter marked by asterisks. These breaks mark the passage of time. It is also important for students to keep track of what is happening in the "present time" in the story and what is description of past events. For example, Cassie provides important background information about their family's land and their father's need to work on the railroad to keep the bills paid. These devices are important because they allow the writer to build in background via flashbacks and scene changes while helping the reader to follow along. Young readers may not see this on their own and may get lost and frustrated. **ELL** Enable Language Production—Reading and Writing. Your ELLs in particular may have a harder time following along as a story shifts back and forth across times, places, and ideas. By showing them the conventions that authors use to indicate scene changes, you are helping them gain access to the world of complex literature.

Try Guide students to quickly rehearse what they need to learn and do in preparation for practice

When the chapter is completed, address Description and Dialogue. Ask students to share the descriptive details and speech that they notice and any information they learn about the time period. Record what they notice on the Elements of Historical Fiction Chart. These two sections lend themselves to the use of quotations as direct evidence of these elements. Guide students to select powerful examples from the text. Discuss new information from the chapter to add to previous sections of the chart as well. Record in writing, if desired.

Description		
Description reveals details about the historical setting that help the reader make sense of the other elements of the text. -What descriptive language does the writer use to bring the time period alive? What background information helped you better understand the story?		
Dialogue		
Dialogue reveals the understandings, thoughts and perspectives of people of the historical time period and place. -Is there dialogue? If so, how does it help show thoughts and perspectives of the time period? Is there dialect, vocabulary or slang typical of the time period?		

Clarify Briefly restate today's teaching objective and explain the practice task(s)

Reiterate the importance of identifying the elements of historical fiction and supporting details as students read their own Historical Fiction Book Club texts. Distribute copies of the Elements of Historical Fiction graphic organizer (Appendix 7.2). Direct students to record their thinking on the graphic organizer as they read independently.

> Today you will begin reading your Historical Fiction Book Club texts. As you read, record what you notice onto your Elements of Historical Fiction graphic organizer. Keep in mind that because you are just beginning your books, you may not find evidence of all of the elements. They will continue to appear as we progress further into our stories. Remember that we'll be continuing to add

to our understanding as we read further. I will be circulating to check in with you as you dive into these books!

Practice Students work independently and/or in small groups to apply today's teaching objective

Students read independently with their Historical Fiction Book Club texts using the Elements of Historical Fiction graphic organizer to record their observations and thinking. This may take more than one class period. Over the course of the lesson set, students will work with two Elements of Historical Fiction graphic organizers, one for *Roll of Thunder, Hear My Cry* and one for their Historical Fiction Book Club texts. **ELL** Enable Language Production—Reading and Writing. By middle school, ELLs tend to fall into one of two groups: students who have been in the country for many years and have high oral English proficiency but who struggle with reading and writing and students who are relatively recent arrivals to the country and are in the beginning years of learning English. Be sure to consider your ELLs' individual language and literacy needs when creating book clubs. Orally proficient students may be able to tackle a more cognitively complex text than they can read independently—could they listen to part of the book using a recording? Newcomer students may have high literacy skills in their home language—could they read a translated novel and work in a bilingual group?

Wrap Up Check understanding as you guide students to briefly share what they have learned and produced today

Gather your class, and ask several students to share the elements and supporting details they identified in their own independent reading. Then pose new questions to students that they can answer either in partnerships or independently: What do you think it might have been like to live during the particular time and place in their books? How does the place one grows up and lives in shape his or her beliefs and actions? Instruct students to record their answers in writing. Remind students to use information from the text to support their answers.

Milestone Performance Assessment

Identifying the Elements of Historical Fiction   PD **pd** TOOLKIT™

Collect and analyze students' Elements of Historical Fiction graphic organizers as a performance-based assessment to determine if students need additional instruction or support as a whole class, in small groups, or one on one. **ELL** Assess for Content and Language Understanding—Formative Assessment. Bear in mind that ELLs often understand more than they can say in standard English. Study ELLs' work closely to determine the source of any gaps you notice: Are they confused about the elements of historical fiction? Is the language of the particular text over their heads? Do they have the necessary background knowledge to make sense of their text? Do they comprehend but struggle to clearly express their meaning in writing?

 Use this checklist to assess student work on their Elements of Historical Fiction graphic organizers.

Standards Alignment: RL.7.1, RL.7.3, W.7.4, W.7.10

Task	Achieved	Notes
Identify as many elements of historical fiction as possible at this point in their reading.		
Use information from the text to draw conclusions about the historical time period.		

Reading Lesson 3

▼ Teaching Objective

Readers identify the narrative mode of a story and analyze how the author develops characters' points of view.

Close Reading Opportunity

▼ Standards Alignment

RL.7.1, RL.7.2, RL.7.3, RL.7.6, RL.7.10, W.7.4, W.7.9, W.7.10, SL.7.1, SL.7.2, SL.7.4, SL.7.6, L7.1, L 7.3, L.7.6

▼ Materials

- *Roll of Thunder, Hear My Cry* by Mildred B. Taylor. (Chapter 1, when Cassie and Little Man receive books at school)
- Elements of Historical Fiction graphic organizer (Appendix 7.2)
- Narrative Mode Definitions (Appendix 7.3)
- Historical Fiction Book Club texts
- Charting supplies or interactive whiteboard

▼ To the Teacher

In today's lesson, we teach students to identify the literary point of view (or narrative mode) of a text and analyze the point of view of characters as conveyed by the narrator. In literature, there are two common meanings for the term *point of view*. The first type of point of view is called the literary point of view, or narrative mode, and refers to how the author chooses to narrate the story. Is the voice telling the story part of the action? Is the narrator addressing another character or action directly? Is the narrator an outside observer who is not part of the action? The answer to these questions will determine the literary point of view or narrative mode. There are three possible narrative modes: first person, second person, and third person. This will be explained more in depth. We will rely mainly on the term *narrative mode* to reduce confusion between this meaning for point of view and the other common meaning. The second meaning refers to how a particular character, who may or may not be the narrator, sees a situation—his or her attitude or way of looking at a particular set of circumstances. It is helpful for your students to understand these sometimes confusing terms and the difference between them. Both are important pieces in literary analysis and discussion.

Students will read a portion of the text and analyze the point of view of the narrator. One of the reasons *Roll of Thunder, Hear My Cry* is such a compelling story is because the author uses the voice of Cassie Logan as the narrator and therefore offers us the ability to understand the complexities of her thoughts and emotions. The story is not only told from her perspective, but it also is told in the past tense. This implies that Cassie is being reflective about the events and is telling them as they had happened to her in the past.

Note that the page numbers we provide may vary depending on edition. After this lesson, you may continue to read *Roll of Thunder, Hear My Cry* with the class at your own pace. While the following lessons don't require reading beyond this point, it's a wonderful story, and any of the concepts taught here may be extended through the remainder of the text.

▼ Procedure

Warm Up Gather the class to set the stage for today's learning

Gather your class. Have students refer back to their Elements of Historical Fiction graphic organizers (Appendix 7.2) to share their thinking about what they have learned so far about the characters and the setting in their texts. Have some students summarize the events that have happened thus far in the novel. How are the events reflective of the atmosphere of the time period? Be mindful that not all students will have information about all of the elements yet, but they can discuss the ones they have identified thus far.

> In Reading Lesson 2, we started reading the first chapter of *Roll of Thunder, Hear My Cry*, a story about a young African American girl in the South during the 1930s. We also began our Historical Fiction Book Club texts. Now, spend a few minutes telling each other about the characters you've met so far from *Roll of Thunder, Hear My Cry*. Please refer to your Elements of Historical Fiction chart to refresh your memory.

Teach Model what students need to learn and do

Your students may or may not be familiar with the concept of *narrative mode*. In either circumstance, it is worthwhile to take the time to review or introduce the Narrative Mode Definitions (Appendix 7.3). If your students are proficient at identifying narrative mode, keep the instruction swift to move on to character point of view quickly. If your students need a lot of work on this concept, you may wish to split the Teach portion into two days of instruction. **ELL** Identify and Communicate Content and Language Objectives—Key Content Vocabulary. Make sure your ELLs are comfortable with these terms so that they can dive right into working with them in the rest of the lesson.

Narrative Mode Definitions

Narrative Mode	Explanation
First-Person	The narrator reveals the plot through a character, usually the protagonist, who is a participant in the story and relates the events through his or her eyes. Uses the pronouns *I, me*, or *we* to refer to himself or herself.
Second-Person	The narrator reveals the plot by telling the story to another character, usually the protagonist, or directly addressing the reader. Refers to the addressee as "you." Also known as the imperative point of view. This perspective is found very seldom in fiction. A writer would be more likely to use second person in a nonfiction piece.

Narrative Mode	Explanation
Third-Person	The narrator does not participate in the action and is not a character in the story. Tells the story as an outside observer. Uses the pronouns *he, she*, and *they*. There are three types of third-person point of view. They are: • Third-person omniscient: This narrator is all-knowing and shares thoughts, feelings, and opinions of any and all characters in the story or event. • Third-person limited: This narrator shares only the thoughts, feelings, and opinions of a single character in the story or event. • Third-person objective: When writing from this perspective, the writer does not share any thoughts, feelings, or opinions. It is left to the reader to interpret these things from information given (dialogue, action, setting, and so forth).

Discuss the various narrative modes. Cite examples of each from books and stories you have shared with your students over the course of the school year. Ask them to chime in with other examples.

Start by rereading the beginning of the first chapter of *Roll of Thunder, Hear My Cry*. Ask students to look for clues to determine who is telling the story and which narrative mode the author uses. Immediately there are plenty of pronoun references (e.g. *I* and *my*) to reveal the mode, and the narrator's name, Cassie, is revealed in the dialogue by the second page.

Students should be able to recognize Cassie as the narrator and to select first-person point of view from the chart. (SL.7.1a, SL.7.2) **ELL** Identify and Communicate Content and Language Objectives—Language Form and Function. Authors make heavy use of pronouns to communicate narrative mode, and your ELLs may have a harder time interpreting the significance of these words than your English-proficient students do. Be explicit with ELLs about how words like *I, me*, and *my* form a natural class that means the speaker is talking about herself.

The first-person narrator in a work of historical fiction is particularly interesting because the narrator is generally on one side of the historical record or the other (rarely, in a work of fiction, does one meet a neutral narrator). The writer makes a deliberate decision to represent a certain point of view. Mildred B. Taylor, the author of *Roll of Thunder, Hear My Cry* chooses to show the challenges of the 1930s in the South through the eyes of a young African American girl.

Now, shift the conversation from narrative mode (literary point of view) to character point of view, or perspective. Reinforce the concepts of *perspective* and *point of view*. Ask students to share their understanding of each term. Explain, if needed, that the two terms have the exact same meaning.

The definition might be: a character's point of view or perspective is how he or she sees or interprets a particular situation. In other words, the attitudes or feelings a character has toward key events or individuals in the story.

Discuss the way that the author expresses his or her point of view by revealing details about a character. Here is the way your modeling could unfold if using *Roll of Thunder, Hear My Cry*.

Let's think about what shared beliefs and experiences from the character's environment affect his or her point of view. We can learn about a character and her point of view by looking at clues such as her actions, the words she speaks, her thoughts, her background, the problems she has, and the way other characters interact with her. For example, in *Roll of Thunder, Hear My Cry*, there is a first-person narrator who tells the story to us. Because the story is written through her voice, we become aware of her specific point of view or perspective—even when she is talking about another character. We are able to see how she reacts to, feels about, and behaves in certain situations she has experienced. As we read, let's pay close attention to how the author brings Cassie's voice to life. How does the author let us know what Cassie is thinking? How she is feeling? How she is reacting? And why? We can learn via her actions, the words she speaks, her thoughts, her background, the problems she has, and the way other characters interact with her.

Return to the second half of Chapter 1 of *Roll of Thunder, Hear My Cry*. We recommend the scene at the school that begins when Miss Crocker announces that the children will have books for the school year on page 20 until the asterisks on page 26. Ask students to identify the characteristics of the narrator, to provide evidence from the text, and to analyze what they learned about the narrator's perspective, or point of view. Results might look like the chart on the following page.

Try Guide students to quickly rehearse what they need to learn and do in preparation for practice

Direct students to focus on how the author develops another character's point of view toward the same scene. If using *Roll of Thunder, Hear My Cry*, we suggest you focus on Little Man's point of view toward the same situation. Although the story is not told from his perspective in terms of narrative mode, there is plenty of evidence that reveals his point of view toward the book conflict. Continue the work focusing on how the author develops Miss Crocker's point of view, which is quite different from that of Cassie and Little Man.

Clarify Briefly restate today's teaching objective and explain the practice task(s)

Review the three narrative modes as well as the clues an author uses to reveal a character's point of view. Explain to students that they will focus on identifying the narrative mode as well as analyzing the point of view of two

Character Point of View

Character/ Title/ Narrative Mode	Summary of important event or situation in text	Evidence from the Text (include page number— may vary with edition) Clues include character's actions, words, thoughts, background, problems, the way other characters interact with him/her.	Point of View
Cassie *Roll of Thunder, Hear My Cry* Written in first person	The children receive books for the first time in school. The books are soiled and marred, handed down after being used for over 10 years in the white school.	Cassie calls the announcement "startling" and admits she felt excited initially. She had never had her own book. (p. 20) She sees how damaged the books are and describes her sinking disappointment. She looks to see how Little Man, who likes cleanliness, will react to the books. He complains and is about to get whipped. (pp. 21–23) Cassie steps in when Little Man is about to get whipped and explains why he is disappointed. She points out to Miss Crocker the list of white names and the term used to describe the children in her school. She gives back her book and accepts the consequence of getting whipped with the switch also. (pp. 26–27)	Cassie is surprised and excited at first, but then she feels disappointed, offended, and defiant at the way her school has been treated as she realizes the books were discarded by the white school for use at her school.

or more characters toward an important event or situation in their Historical Fiction Book Club texts. They will recreate the Character Point of View chart on chart paper to share.

Your task is to keep reading and marking the text in the places where you are learning about your characters and their points of view toward what is happening in your stories. Remember that we learn about characters via their actions, the words they speak, their thoughts, their background and life experience, the problems they have, and the way other characters interact with them. Take all of these things into consideration as you read the text. Be prepared to back up your thinking about these characters with evidence from the text as you gather content for our chart.

Practice Students work independently and/or in small groups to apply today's teaching objective

Students will be working with their Historical Fiction Book Club texts for the Practice portion of today's lesson. They may read independently and mark or make notes on the text and then come together in small groups or pairs to discuss their texts. You will want to take this opportunity to circulate in order to check informally for understanding or to conference with individuals. Also, this is a perfect time to bring together a few students who may need more support with their novel for some small-group instruction. **ELL** Enable Language Production—Increasing Interaction. ELLs are simultaneously learning literary analysis skills and English skills, and language must develop through interaction with proficient speakers. When you have your ELLs work with English-proficient peers, you give them the chance to develop their English and help them successfully analyze their characters' perspectives. ELLs may be working hard to just understand what the words mean; their peers can help them go one step further to understanding the implications of what the characters say and do.

Provide each group with a sheet of chart paper. Ask that they recreate the Character Point of View chart and record their thinking about the points of view of two or more characters in their Historical Fiction Book Club texts toward the same event or situation.

Wrap Up Check understanding as you guide students to briefly share what they have learned and produced today

Ask groups to display and share their charts. As they share, use the questions above to lead a conversation about what your students are noticing about their novels' narrators and the clues that reveal point of view.

In advance of Reading Lesson 4, ask students to find one or two short pieces of informational text containing information connected to the historical event(s) they are reading about in their Historical Fiction Book Club texts. **ELL** Frontload the Lesson—Build Background. This assignment ensures that your students will be ready to make connections between their book club novels and real-life historical events in the next lesson.

Reading Lesson 4

▼ Teaching Objective

Readers compare and contrast a fictional portrayal and a historical account of the same period to examine how historical fiction authors use history in their writing.

Close Reading Opportunity

▼ Standards Alignment

RL.7.1, RI.7.1, RL.7.2, RI.7.2, RL.7.3, RI.7.3, RL.7.9, RL.7.10, RI.7.10, W.7.4, W.7.9, W.7.10, SL.7.1, SL.7.2, SL.7.4, SL.7.6, L.7.1, L.7.3, L.7.6

▼ Materials

- "Public Schools in the Great Depression" from www.ncpedia.org (http://ncpedia.org/public-schools-great-depression#tab3), audio file included (or any historical account of the same time period as the model text you are using)
- *Roll of Thunder, Hear My Cry* by Mildred B. Taylor
- Charting supplies or interactive whiteboard
- Close Reading Protocol (downloadable PDF in the Core Ready PDToolkit)

- Informational Text and Its Influence on Historical Fiction (Appendix 7.4)
- Informational texts with information connected to historical events in Historical Fiction Book Club text
- Historical Fiction Book Club texts

▼ To the Teacher

At this point in the lesson set, students should be fairly immersed in their Historical Fiction Book Clubs. They may be getting curious about the fact behind the fiction. During this lesson and the following one, we will use an online encyclopedia article on the schools during the Great Depression in the American South as a means of understanding how Mildred B. Taylor used and altered history to shape her story. Students will be comparing the information in this text to the fictional work of *Roll of Thunder, Hear My Cry*. They will also seek out nonfiction text about the time period they are reading about in their Historical Fiction Book Club texts. Using information from these sources, they will follow the same close reading and comparison procedure with their Book Club texts. Due to the depth of this exercise, this lesson may be extended to more than one class session.

▼ Procedure

Warm Up Gather the class to set the stage for today's learning

Write the words "Fact vs. Fiction" on the board for students. Ask, "Now that you are well into your historical fiction reading, what do you think is more important in historical fiction: the *facts* or the *fiction* in the story?" Take a vote and ask students to discuss what they voted for and why.

Teach Model what students need to learn and do

Next, take your students through a close reading of a historical account from the time period of the core text. For the purpose of modeling, we use "Public Schools in the Great Depression" by Anita Price Davis from www.ncpedia.org. Although this article focuses on North Carolina, the descriptions are closely aligned to the conditions in schools in Mississippi during this time period. The close reading process supports students in their quest to become thoughtful, critical, and independent readers because it offers a process for reading any text as opposed to a set of questions that apply to this text and this text only.

As you read the text out loud, remind students to listen for the central ideas and supporting details of the text. (SL.7.2) **ELL** Frontload the Lesson—Activate Prior Knowledge. The work students have done with *Roll of Thunder, Hear My Cry* will enable them to understand *The New York Times* article more easily. When you explicitly make connections between texts, you help your ELLs to see how experience they already have can help them understand something new.

Model your thinking as you cycle through the levels of the close reading protocol. Use the following questions to guide the reading and analysis of the text. When we ask students to do a "close read" of a text, we are developing an awareness of the multiple ways that we read a text. This type of analysis asks that readers visit a text more than one time and hone in on a different aspect of the text during each encounter. **ELL** Enable Language Production—Reading and Writing. This close reading protocol will help all your students, but it is an especially powerful scaffold for your ELLs. The different emphases at each level help your ELLs to wade through the complex academic language of the text and find the most important ideas.

Close Reading Protocol

Level one: Preview. Examine the overall form and features of the text.

Level two: Read for *what* the text says. Try to summarize what the text is mainly about. Clarify unknown words.

Level three: Read for *how* the text is written. Analyze the author's choices of structure, words, and phrases to deepen your understanding of the text.

Level four: Read for *why* the text is written. Determine the purpose and central ideas of the text.

Level one: Preview: Examine the overall form and features of the text.

Preview the text of the informational article to examine the form and features of the text. In this case the article contains several paragraphs with headings, an audio option, and a photograph. Read the headings to preview the central idea of each section of the text.

Level two: Read for what the text says: Try to summarize what the text is mainly about. Clarify unknown words.

Read the article and ask students to summarize, or articulate the "what," of each section of the article.

Level three: Read for how the text is written. Analyze the author's choices of structure, words, and phrases to deepen your understanding of the text.

Notice elements of how the text is written such as structure, style, and word choice. Some items to notice: how related information is clustered together and the formal, relatively objective style characteristic of many encyclopedia articles. Narrative techniques such as dialogue, dialect, and figurative language are rarely found in this type of writing, which pays careful attention to English language conventions and avoids slang and conversational language. Colloquial terms such as "frills" and "store-bought bread" are presented with quotes.

ELL Identify and Communicate Content and Language Objectives—Language Form and Function. Explicit attention to the linguistic choices that authors make is an important way to demystify complex text for your ELLs. Recognize that students who are relative newcomers to English may not initially be able to identify the connotations or implications of the author's word choice—be clear about how you make connections across terms to uncover themes and the text's mood.

Level four: Read for why the text is written: Determine the purpose and central ideas of the text.

After the analysis of the author's choice of words and structure, it is time to get to the heart of the text—this is our level-four read.

Finally, after readers have determined the central idea of a text and then analyzed its word choice and structure, we begin to tease out the deeper message of the text. We ask ourselves: What does the author want us to understand? Give the article one last quick read, and then let's discuss our thinking. As always, use evidence from the text to support your thinking.

Possible response: The main purpose of this article is to describe the conditions and challenges that North Carolinae schools faced during the Great Depression. There is an underlying message of pride, however, that the schools rose above many of these challenges, perhaps better than some other states did, and made progress in spite of the obstacles. The remarks from the governor in paragraph one and the author in the final paragraph reveal this message.

Try Guide students to quickly rehearse what they need to learn and do in preparation for practice

Comparing both the article and the novel, students work in pairs or small groups to complete the first column in the Informational Text and Its Influence on Historical Fiction graphic organizer (Appendix 7.4) to consider how the author used historical fact to shape the details of the novel based on what they have read so far. Share results. The chart contains possible student responses. **ELL** Enable Language Production—Reading and Writing. ELLs may be more successful at expressing their interpretations if they can bounce ideas off peers before writing them down. If you have students who are relatively new to English, consider grouping them with bilingual students (if possible) so they can hold their discussion in both languages.

Informational Text and Its Influence on Historical Fiction

Historical Fiction Text: *Roll of Thunder, Hear My Cry*
Informational Source: "Public Schools in the Great Depression" from www .ncpedia.org

Historical facts that the author uses in the historical fiction story	Elements and details in the historical fiction story that were imagined by the author
The Great Depression caused a lack of money. Schools were segregated. Schools for black students and schools for white students were not equal. Less money went to schools for black students.	

Historical facts that the author uses in the historical fiction story	Elements and details in the historical fiction story that were imagined by the author
Schools for white students discarded materials and gave them to schools for black students. Many families were sharecroppers. Children had to help work the farm. Many children walked very long distances on dirt roads to schools. Some children had buses. The school year was shorter than it is now.	

Clarify Briefly restate today's teaching objective and explain the practice task(s)

Reiterate how historical fiction authors weave a great deal of historical facts in to their stories, often doing a great deal of research in preparation to write. Sometimes as readers, building background knowledge on the time period helps us tease out what is fact and what is fiction in a novel.

Explain that in Practice, the Book Clubs will repeat the close reading and fact-finding process using informational text related to their club novels.

Practice Students work independently and/or in small groups to apply today's teaching objective

Students use the Close Reading Protocol to examine an informational text related to their club novels. They should complete the first column in the Informational Text and Its Influence on Historical Fiction graphic organizer (Appendix 7.4) to consider how the author used historical fact to shape the details of the novel based on what they have read so far.

Wrap Up Check understanding as you guide students to briefly share what they have learned and produced today

Ask volunteers to share some of the historical facts they have found their authors used in their historical fiction texts. Ask: Are you finding that your novels are mostly fact or mostly fiction? Explain.

Reading Lesson 5 ·····················

▼ **Teaching Objective**

Readers analyze how an author uses the historical setting to shape character and plot.

Close Reading Opportunity

▼ **Standards Alignment**

RL.7.1, RI.7.1, RL.7.2, RI.7.2, RI.7.3, RL.7.3, RL.7.9, RL.7.10, RI.7.10, W.7.4, W.7.9, W.7.10, SL.7.1, SL.7.2, SL.7.4, SL.7.6, L.7.1, L.7.3, L.7.6

▼ Materials

- "Public Schools in the Great Depression" from www.ncpedia.org (http://ncpedia.org/public-schools-great-depression#tab3), audio file included (or any historical account of the same time period as the model text you are using)
- *Roll of Thunder, Hear My Cry* by Mildred B. Taylor
- Charting supplies or interactive whiteboard
- Close Reading Protocol (downloadable PDF in the Core Ready PDToolkit)
- Informational Text and Its Influence on Historical Fiction (from Reading Lesson 4)
- Informational texts with information connected to historical events in Historical Fiction Book Club text
- Historical Fiction Book Club texts
- Access to www.easel.ly or drawing paper and other art supplies to create infographics

▼ To the Teacher

As an optional extension and culmination of Reading Lessons 4 and 5, we suggest a creative way of comparing a fictional portrayal and a historical account of the same period; see the tech box with high- and low-tech options. Infographics are graphic visual representations of data or knowledge. Infographics have the power to present complex topics "at a glance," breaking down a large amount of information in succinct ways.

Goal	Low-Tech	High-Tech
Students compare and contrast a fictional portrayal and a historical account of the same period.	Students write a compare/contrast essay *or* Students hand-draw an infographic using large drawing paper and various art supplies.	Students use an online resource such as www.easel.ly to create infographics. Prior to teaching the lesson, it might be helpful to do an online search of infographics that compare and contrast information to use as examples.

ELL Identify and Communicate Content and Language Objectives—Check for Understanding. When choosing how your students will show their understanding of this lesson, consider that your ELLs may be more effective at communicating through a combination of text and graphics rather than through the written word alone. At the same time, if you do have students write an essay, remember that you will need to scaffold the language and structures of a compare/contrast text so that your ELLs are able to make their meaning clear and to compose an effective argument. Scaffolding ensures that your assessment really lets you check your students' understanding of content so meaning does not get lost because students are bogged down in language.

▼ Procedure

Warm Up Gather the class to set the stage for today's learning

As in Reading Lesson 4, begin by writing "Fact vs. Fiction" on the board. Today's warm-up discussion will be focused on this question: "What do you enjoy reading more—informational text (facts) or historical fiction? Why?"

Teach Model what students need to learn and do

Emphasize the importance of setting in historical fiction and how historical fiction authors use setting to shape the other elements and details of the story in order to make the time period come alive for the reader.

> Reading Lesson 2 emphasized the importance of setting in historical fiction. The setting of a historical fiction text is a realistic time and place on which all of the other elements are based. While some details in historical fiction are historically factual, other elements and details are imagined by the author to fit into the setting. Even when imagined, the characters are people who could have existed at that time and think, act, and view the world as some people of the time really did. Likewise, the events are things that might actually have happened during that time period, even if they did not. By creating imaginary characters and situations, the author immerses the reader in the inner thoughts and experiences of the characters, allowing the reader to "experience" the time period in powerful ways that rarely can be achieved in informational text. It is also important to note, however, that sometimes an author takes the license to alter the facts of history to enhance the story in some way. This is sometimes revealed in the introduction or author's note of a novel.

The class has used the informational text "Public Schools in the Great Depression" as a reference to determine which details in the story were factual. Now you will consider which important elements were imagined by the author for narrative effect. Together with the students, list characters, events, and other details that appear to have come from the imagination of the author. This list need not be exhaustive, but do try to choose elements that seem to be important to the overall impact of the story.

Informational Text and Its Influence on Historical Fiction

Historical Fiction Text: *Roll of Thunder, Hear My Cry*

Informational Source: "Public Schools in the Great Depression" from www.ncpedia.org

Historical facts that the author uses in the historical fiction story	Elements and details in the historical fiction story that were imagined by the author
The Great Depression caused a lack of money. People had to work extra hard to make up for this. Schools were segregated. Schools for black students and schools for white students were not equal. Less money went to schools for black students. Schools for white students discarded materials and gave them to schools for black students. Many families were sharecroppers. Children had to help work the farm. Many children walked very long distances on dirt roads to schools. Some children had buses. The school year was shorter than it is now.	The Logan family and all its members. The details about how the Logans came to own the land. The boy who got in trouble for walking with the Logans. The school bus incident where Little Man was splashed. The character's reactions to receiving hand-me-down books. The scene of working in the cotton fields as a family. Father feeling the need to have a man protect the family.

As you fill in the chart, it is likely that students will feel the gray area between fact and fiction in the novel. As they list "imaginary" elements, they may even be saying, "Yes, but that could have happened!" or "But that really did happen to people!" And that's the point! The job of a good historical fiction author is to create characters and situations that are shaped by what really did happen during the time period of the story. Ironically, this is what brings the reader closer to what it was *really* like to live at that time.

Try Guide students to quickly rehearse what they need to learn and do in preparation for practice

Have students talk in partnerships to discuss the following questions:

- How did the inclusion of imaginary characters and events in *Roll of Thunder, Hear My Cry* help you to better understand what life was like at the time of the novel?
- Which characters, events or details best made the time period come alive for you?

Clarify Briefly restate today's teaching objective and explain the practice task(s)

Have students share the results of their discussion during the Try. Explain that in Practice, they will fill in the imagined elements of their Historical Fiction Book Club books on the graphic organizer Informational Text and Its Influence on Historical Fiction (Appendix 7.4)

Practice Students work independently and/or in small groups to apply today's teaching objective

Students complete the second column of the graphic organizer Informational Text and Its Influence on Historical Fiction (Appendix 7.4) and answer the questions in writing:

- How did the inclusion of imaginary characters and events in your story help you to better understand what life was like at the time of the novel?
- Which characters, events or details best made the time period come alive for you?

Wrap Up Check understanding as you guide students to briefly share what they have learned and produced today

Conduct a brief discussion of the students' results from Practice today. Use the following question to guide the conversation: Why do authors tell factual stories through fictional characters?

If desired, plan for time to complete the extension activity described in the To the Teacher segment of the lesson.

Milestone Performance Assessment

Comparing and Contrasting Historical Fiction and Nonfiction

 PD TOOLKIT™

Collect and analyze students' work as a performance-based assessment to determine if students need additional instruction or support as a whole class, in small groups, or one on one. **ELL** Assess for Content and Language Understanding—Formative Assessment. Look for the source of any gaps you see in your ELLs' work. Have they completely understood the assignment? Was the text at an appropriate level of difficulty? Did they have sufficient background knowledge to interpret their texts? Or have they perhaps entirely understood and completed the assignment but used nonstandard language? Each will require a different instructional response from you.

 Use this checklist to assess student short essays or infographics.

Standards Alignment: RL.7.1, RI.7.1, RL.7.2, RI.7.2, RI.7.3, RL.7.3, RL.7.9, W.7.4, W.7.9, W.7.10

Task	Achieved	Notes
Compare and contrast the depiction of a historical period in a fictional source and in an informational source.		
Provide sufficient textual evidence to support thinking.		

Reading Lesson 6 . . . .

▼ Teaching Objective

Readers compare and contrast point of view in a print version of a historical fiction text to a film version.

Close Reading Opportunity

▼ Standards Alignment

RL.7.1, RL.7.2, RL.7.3, RL.7.6, RL.7.7, RL.7.10, W.7.4, W.7.9, W.7.10, SL.7.1, SL.7.2, SL.7.4, SL.7.6, L.7.1, L.7.3, L.7.6

▼ Materials

- Film: *The Watsons Go to Birmingham—1963* (the scene of the Alabama church bombing)
- Excerpt of novel: *The Watsons Go to Birmingham—1963* (from the beginning of Chapter 14 to when Kenny runs home to Grandma Sand's house)
- Charting supplies or interactive whiteboard to create Comparing a Written Text to a Film chart
- Index cards or exit slips

▼ To the Teacher

In this reading lesson, we will launch a comparison of a text version and a film version of the same text. Over the course of the next four lessons we will move forward in time to the period of the Civil Rights movement of the 1960s. This movement arose in protest to the unjust treatment of African Americans described in *Roll of Thunder, Hear My Cry*. We suggest that you use both the text and movie versions of *The Watsons Go to Birmingham,* but the lesson structure here may be applied to any text and film combination. Although *The Watsons Go to Birmingham* is below seventh grade level, it allows students to have the experience of comparing a historical fiction text focusing on African American civil rights to an age-appropriate film version of the same text.

The Watsons Go to Birmingham—1963 is a novel that revolves around the life of a young boy named Kenny Watson. Kenny Watson is a fourth grade African-American boy growing up in Michigan. The novel introduces us to his interactions with his family members and his insecurities growing up. Toward the end of the novel, he and his family travel down to Birmingham, Alabama, to visit his grandmother. While in Birmingham, the family is confronted with a different racial culture and climate than what it is accustomed to in Michigan. The 1963 Birmingham church bombing occurs during their stay in Birmingham. We see the traumatic reaction Kenny faces after this event—questioning the hate and racism that plague this historical time period. Today students will read an excerpt from the story *The Watsons Go to Birmingham—1963*. Afterward, they will watch the same scene in its movie version. They will compare how literary elements are conveyed in the film with how they are conveyed in the novel. Because of its historical context, this excerpt in both the novel and the film portrays acts of racial violence. Explain that this disturbing scene is included to show the racial climate during that time in history. Also, let students know that this excerpt from both the novel and the film is based on a real event, a defining characteristic of historical fiction. Students may wish to explore this event further to learn more about the historical facts surrounding it. As with any text, please be sure to preview it thoroughly before introducing it to your students and choose what is appropriate for your audience.

▼ Procedure

Warm Up Gather the class to set the stage for today's learning

Today we will begin by prompting students to imagine film as a visual form of text. Adolescents are extremely visual, but that does not necessarily mean that they are always actively engaged with what they are watching on the screen. Often they are passive consumers of movies: the action washes over them, and they miss details and nuances. Just as we strive to encourage active readers, we also wish for our students to become active, critical consumers of film, so Reading Lessons 6 and 7 will endeavor to help with that. **ELL** Provide Comprehensible Input—Audiovisual Aids. ELLs who are highly orally proficient but who are behind in reading and writing can usually tackle difficult concepts and abstract ideas. However, when nearly all their classwork and assessments are based on reading and writing, it can be hard for a teacher to infer what they really understand about the content of the lesson set. This lesson allows you to see what kind of critical thinking your ELLs can do because it is based on a film and therefore is accessible even to struggling readers. Even newcomer ELLs who are not strong in oral English yet will be able to get a lot out of the movie, as it provides substantial visual support.

Many of you have enjoyed movies that have taken their inspiration from a novel. Can we name a few? Which did you like better—the film or the book? Let's discuss!

Students might mention such films as *The Lord of the Rings*, *The Hobbit*, *Percy Jackson*, *Diary of a Wimpy Kid*, *Holes*, and *The Hunger Games*.

Now, using the examples we just listed, think about all the decisions the filmmaker needed to weigh in order to transform these stories from print to a

medium that completely engages us via sound and sight. There are many factors to consider: how to reveal a character's thoughts, how to bring a story like *The Lord of the Rings* to life using only the words written decades ago as a guide, and how to create a setting that is either realistic like the schoolyard in *Diary of a Wimpy Kid* or out-of-this-world fantastic as in *Percy Jackson* or *The Hunger Games*.

Discuss the many choices a filmmaker must make when translating a book into a film. Possible elements: casting, costumes, lighting, scenery, music and sound, what to keep and discard from the original text, adding details that are not in the book, and so on.

Teach Model what students need to learn and do

Read the excerpt from *The Watsons Go to Birmingham—1963* (see Materials). Ask students to think like filmmakers. As you read the passage aloud, have students jot down notes on key elements (and the details that reveal them) that they would include in a film version of *The Watsons Go to Birmingham—1963*, focusing on:

- The narrator
- Characters
- Setting
- Key event(s)
- Point of view of main characters

I am going to read aloud a passage from another civil rights book called *The Watsons Go to Birmingham—1963*. It is the story of a young boy named Kenny Watson. He is a fourth grader from Michigan. The passage we will read today happens toward the end of the novel and is based on a real historical event. In this passage, he and his family are in Birmingham, Alabama, visiting his grandmother. I want you to jot notes about the key elements of the story and the text details that describe them.

Select several students to share their thinking.

As they share, remind them to speak clearly and provide relevant details and examples from the text. (SL.7.4) Chart their findings on the Comparing a Written Text to a Film chart.

A sampling of the modeling and discussion might reveal:

So far, I have been introduced to Kenny and some of his family members. I notice that the text is written in his voice, using first-person narrative mode. This is particularly interesting in this scene because it shows what Kenny thinks and how he feels during this traumatic event of the bombing. It seems like he is in shock and does not quite know how to process what he observes. Although he does not quite know how to articulate his feelings, he still gives a lot of details about what he sees. Let's list some of them.

Try Guide students to quickly rehearse what they need to learn and do in preparation for practice

View the film excerpt that shows the Alabama church bombing. This is toward the end of the film. In this scene, we witness the confusion and fear of the characters. As you work with the film, you will treat it as you would any other text. Together with students, think aloud about the same key elements and details in the film that you noticed in the written text. Record observations on the Comparing a Written Text to a Film chart in the film column.

ELL Provide Comprehensible Input—Models. Your ELLs will better understand how to compare the book and the movie if they can watch you first go through the structured process represented in the chart below.

Comparing a Written Text to a Film

Observations from the Written Text	Observations from the Film	Conclusions
• Narrator • Characters • Setting • Key event(s) • Point of view of main characters toward key elements • Mood	• Narrator • Characters • Setting • Key event(s) • Point of view of main characters toward key elements • Mood	• What similarities did you notice? • What differences? • If there are differences between the film and the novel, why do you think the filmmaker made these changes? • Do you agree with the choices the filmmaker made? Why or why not?

Clarify Briefly restate today's teaching objective and explain the practice task(s)

Reiterate the focus of today's lesson, which is to compare and contrast two scenes from different texts. During Practice, students will draw conclusions about their observations of both versions of this story. How does the medium of film as text demonstrate the same concept or idea as a novel? Is it as successful?

ELL Provide Comprehensible Input—Repeat. When you state your expectations one more time, you ensure that your ELLs know exactly what to do as they watch the movie.

Practice Students work independently and/or in small groups to apply today's teaching objective

Students will work with a partner to discuss their conclusions about how the literary elements in the novel compare with those in the film.

As needed, direct them to comparing key elements and the details that revealed them. They should record their responses in writing. Later, you will chart conclusions in the third column of the Comparing a Written Text to a Film chart.

For example, pay close attention to how the film portrays Kenny's perspective and reaction to the event. How does the film demonstrate this scene in comparison with the novel? Why do you think the filmmaker made these choices? Did the filmmaker do a good job? Would you have done something differently? Why or why not?

Students will analyze key elements presented in diverse media and formats (text and film) and explain their significance to the overall story being told. (SL.7.2)

Wrap Up Check understanding as you guide students to briefly share what they have learned and produced today

Bring your students back together to share their findings.

Encourage them to support their ideas with examples and supporting details. Remind them to use appropriate eye contact, adequate volume, and clear pronunciation. (SL.7.4)

Let's share what we have seen.

- What major similarities and differences did you notice between the film and the novel?
- If you noticed differences, why do you think the filmmaker made such decisions?
- Do you think the film did a good job translating this scene from the novel? Would you have done it differently? If so, how and why?
- What are we learning about the characters and their perspectives toward the events of this time period?
- What clues in the film support your thinking?

At the conclusion of today's lesson, you will use an exit slip or index card to hear back from your students. An exit slip is a short written response conducted at the end of a day's learning. Exit slips present an opportunity for students to reflect on what they've gleaned from the lesson. In addition, they allow teachers to gain some insight into the age-old question: Did they get it?

Ask your students to respond to today's exit slip question: Which version of *The Watsons Go to Birmingham—1963* did you prefer—the novel or the film? Why? Use evidence of literary elements from both the text and the film to support your thinking.

Reading Lesson 7 ·

▼ Teaching Objective

Readers evaluate the effect filmmaking techniques have on a story.

▼ Standards Alignment

RL.7.7, W.7.4, W.7.10, SL.7.1, SL.7.2, SL.7.4, SL.7.6, L.7.1, L7.3, L.7.6

▼ Materials

- Film: *The Watsons Go to Birmingham—1963* (the scene of the Alabama church bombing)
- Novel: *The Watsons Go to Birmingham—1963* (from the beginning of Chapter 14 to when Kenny runs home to Grandma Sand's house)
- Comparing a Written Text to a Film chart (from Reading Lesson 6)
- Charting supplies or interactive whiteboard to create Evaluating Filmmaking Techniques chart
- www.socrative.com, index cards, or exit slips

▼ To the Teacher

The previous lesson focused on comparing the elements in a written version of a story with a film version. This lesson focuses on how these elements are revealed in film. Today you will have students examine the same excerpt from *The Watsons Go to Birmingham—1963* to focus in more depth on specific film techniques and the impact they have on the story being told. Written texts use words, punctuation, and specific writing structure to tell a story, while film has its own unique techniques to reveal the narrator, characters, key events, setting, point of view, and mood. Again, the structure of this lesson may be used to study film techniques in practically any film.

Have students create a double-entry chart titled "Evaluating Filmmaking Techniques" with "Film Observations" on one side and "My Thinking About the Film" on the other side to record their thinking. They will use that information to respond, in writing, at the conclusion of the lesson. In addition, we suggest a high-tech alternative or addition to this lesson. You may elect to use www.socrative.com as a means of response via mobile phones, tablets, or laptops.

▼ Procedure

Warm Up **Gather the class to set the stage for today's learning**

Discuss with your students the unique tools a filmmaker uses to reveal character, key events, setting, point of view, and mood.

> In Reading Lesson 6, we read and watched a portion of *The Watsons Go to Birmingham—1963*. Our focus was primarily on literary elements and how a filmmaker makes choices about including elements that are originally created in novel form. Authors of books use words, punctuation, and writing structure to tell stories, but how do filmmakers portray similar elements such as how a character is thinking or feeling in a film? Films rely heavily on what is seen and heard by the viewer to transmit both the plot of the story as well as more subtle elements such as character point of view and mood. They use techniques such as lighting, camera angles and focus, sound, and color to bring a story to life. Today we will be looking at these elements.

Teach **Model what students need to learn and do**

Inform your students that as they watch the same excerpt of the film today they will be looking for the ways the filmmaker uses specific techniques (lighting, camera angles and focus, sound, color) to illustrate the narrator, characters, events, setting, point of view, and mood.

> Today we will rewatch the excerpt from the film. We will process our thinking using a double-entry note-taking chart. Today as we watch the film we will be looking for evidence of the use of lighting, camera angles and focus, sound, and color. Let's discuss what each of these techniques is and might achieve.

Define each technique and explain how it might be used with general examples to have an impact on literary elements.

- **Lighting:** Filmmakers may vary the amount of light in a scene for dramatic effect. For instance, filmmakers might use darkened lighting to create a serious or sad feeling.
- **Camera angles and focus:** Filmmakers frequently adjust the direction, scope, or focus of the camera lens. Filmmakers may widen or narrow the frame of a scene. Example: A close-up on a character's face might emphasize strong emotions. A wide angle might show many things happening at once to suggest a situation is very complicated or important. Filmmakers may use the camera angle to show what's happening from a particular direction or from the narrator's point of view. They might also choose to show something happening from a selected character's point of view. Seeing an event from a particular character's eyes helps the viewer identify with that character or "read

his mind." Filmmakers may also vary the focus from sharp to blurry. Example: Blurring images as scenes transition may suggest a setting change such as time passing or location shifting. Dull focus may suggest sadness or confusion.

- **Sound:** Filmmakers may adjust volume, use sound effects, and add music to establish the setting, paint strong images, and affect mood. Example: Music might be used to create a happy or somber mood. Increasing volume might make a scene more exciting or suspenseful. Voice-overs may allow the viewer to hear the narrator's inner thoughts.
- **Color:** Filmmakers adjust color to establish setting, emphasize something, or suggest a mood. Example: An important character may wear a contrasting color that stands out from others. Dark, dull colors in a scene may suggest sadness while light, bright ones may convey joy. Black and white may suggest a setting in the past. Sharp or saturated color might suggest a departure from reality.

Try Guide students to quickly rehearse what they need to learn and do in preparation for practice

Review the findings from Reading Lesson 6's Comparing a Written Text to a Film chart. Together with the class, share a few examples of how the author used techniques in the written text such as word choice, punctuation, or text structure to help develop literary elements. **ELL** Enable Language Production—Listening and Speaking. Group conversation gives your ELLs a chance to hear how others express their interpretations of the novel's intentions and allows them to get some practice voicing their own ideas before switching to viewing the film.

Now view the film excerpt in search of the use of film techniques. Have students create a double-entry chart titled "Evaluating Filmmaking Techniques" with "Film Observations" on one side and "My Thinking About the Film" on the other side to record their thinking. Fill in the left column only of the Evaluating Filmmaking Techniques chart.

Evaluating Filmmaking Techniques

Film Observations What filmmaking techniques (lighting, camera angles and focus, sound, and color) are used?	My Thinking About the Film How do these techniques affect the development of the narrator, characters, setting, key events, point of view, or mood of the story?

Clarify Briefly restate today's teaching objective and explain the practice task(s)

Reiterate the focus of today's lesson. Remind students that filmmakers use many techniques to bring their stories to life on the screen just as authors do in written texts. In Practice, students will fill in the "My Thinking About the Film" side of the Evaluating Film Techniques chart.

> Remember that today we are evaluating this film as a piece of text. We are paying close attention to the techniques used by filmmakers to translate the story to film, establishing a narrator and developing characters, setting, key events, point of view, and mood.

Practice Students work independently and/or in small groups to apply today's teaching objective

In small groups, students will discuss the impact of each film technique they observe on the development of one or more literary elements in the film (narrator, characters, setting, key events, point of view, or mood). Each group should record the details of the conversation to share at the end of the work session. Have volunteers share their findings. Chart them in the right column of the Evaluating Film Techniques chart.

Wrap Up Check understanding as you guide students to briefly share what they have learned and produced today

As an exit slip, provide students with the following prompt and have them reply to the questions in writing. We provide several high-tech and low-tech options.

- What do you consider to be the most significant part of this scene? Why was it significant?
- What technique did the filmmakers use that you believe was the most effective? Use evidence from the film to support your thinking.
- Which medium do you think did the most powerful job telling this story—the novel or the film? Provide specific examples to justify your thinking.

Goal	Low-Tech	High-Tech
Students respond to an exit slip prompt and use evidence from the text to support their thinking.	Students respond to an exit slip prompt on index cards or exit slips.	Students respond to an exit slip prompt using www.socrative.com and submit their responses via mobile phones, tablets, or laptops.

Milestone Performance Assessment

Identifying and Analyzing Filmmakers' Techniques

 PD **pd** TOOLKIT™

Collect and analyze students' work as a performance-based assessment to determine if students need additional instruction or support as a whole class, in small groups, or one on one. **ELL** Assess for Content and Language Understanding—Formative Assessment. Be thoughtful when examining your ELLs' work. Consider that they may package thorough content understanding in nonstandard language. Look for places where you might need to reteach content and for opportunities to teach students about more conventional ways to explain their thinking.

 Use this checklist to assess student exit slips and Evaluating Filmmaking Techniques charts.

Standards Alignment: RL.7.7, W.7.4, W. 7.9, W.7.10

Task	Achieved	Notes
Identify techniques such as lighting, camera angle and focus, sound, and color.		
Analyze the way the use of these techniques contributes to the overall effect of the film and the development of literary elements.		
Articulate and evaluate similarities and differences between the book and the film.		
Provide sufficient textual evidence to support thinking.		

Reading Lesson 8 ....

▼ Teaching Objective

Readers determine point of view in historical accounts and analyze its development over the course of the text.

Close Reading Opportunity

▼ Standards Alignment

RI.7.1, RI.7.2, RI.7.3, RI.7.5, RI.7.6, RI.7.8, RI.7.9, RI.7.10, SL.7.1, SL.7.2, SL.7.4, SL.7.6, L.7.1, L.7.3, L.7.6

▼ Materials

- John Lewis's "Speech at the March on Washington"
- Charting supplies or interactive whiteboard

▼ To the Teacher

In the next two lessons, we will be looking at two speeches from 1963. Segregation was still the law of the land in many areas and remained a hotly debated issue at this time, which is exemplified in the speeches. In Reading Lesson 8, we ask students to closely read John Lewis's "Speech at the March on Washington," and in Reading Lesson 9 students will read Governor George Wallace's inaugural address. The speeches are very different from the other genres encountered in the lesson set thus far. Examining them will allow students to trace opposing arguments on the same topic and compare how the speakers each shape their presentations of information and reasoning to support their own point of view. If you are studying a different historical time period, seek two informational texts on the topic with opposing points of view.

The perspective of someone like George Wallace may seem very outdated in our time. However, it is appropriate to hear him because he spoke for many people at that moment in history. He represents the beliefs of seg-regationists, while Lewis represents the people who were no longer willing to accept it. It is undeniable that each man has played an important role in this country's conversation around civil rights. Both of these speeches are available online if you would like to have your students hear them spoken in the actual voices of Wallace and Lewis. **ELL** Provide Comprehensible Input—Audio. Combining the written and spoken versions of these speeches will give your ELLs multiple points of access to the text.

John Lewis returned to the Washington Mall during the summer of 2013 to commemorate the 50th anniversary of that summer. At the conclusion of this lesson, it would be worthwhile to consider sharing this speech with your students. It is readily available online as both a visual and written text.

▼ Procedure

Warm Up Gather the class to set the stage for today's learning

Prompt your students to think about speeches and what sets them apart from other kinds of texts.

> Turn and talk with your neighbor about speeches. Think of examples of speeches you have heard or read. Use these questions to guide your conversation:
>
> - What are the characteristics of a speech?
> - How are speeches different from other forms of text?
> - Who gives speeches? To whom?
> - Why do people give speeches?

Teach Model what students need to learn and do

Before you begin to read the speech, provide students with a little back-ground information about John Lewis.

> Today we will be reading a speech that was given more than 50 years ago during the historic March on Washington in 1963. We are probably all aware of the event's most famous speech, Dr. Martin Luther King Jr.'s "I Have a Dream" speech, but many other inspiring and dedicated civil rights leaders also took to the podium on that day. The youngest man to speak was just 23 years old. His name is John Lewis, and he is currently a congressman from the state of Georgia. Let's see what he had to say. As we read, we will be analyzing his words to determine his point of view, and we will follow it over the course of the speech.

Explain that you will be reading two speeches by two different histori-cal figures and comparing how they convey their points of view. Create a triple-column note page on chart paper, and have your students to do the same in their notebooks. The left column should be labeled "Speech #1: John Lewis," the middle column should be labeled "Compare and Contrast

Both Speeches: Lewis and Wallace," and the third column should be labeled "Speech #2: George Wallace." This will help students organize their thoughts. **ELL** Provide Comprehensible Input—Organizers. Visual layouts like this three-column chart help your ELLs understand how to sort information to support analysis. Next, read aloud the first piece of the speech, and think aloud about what you are learning about John Lewis's point of view as you proceed through the text. Take notes on your triple-column note page as you record students' thinking.

Speech #1: John Lewis	Compare and Contrast Both Speeches: Lewis and Wallace	Speech #2: George Wallace

> As I read, I want to be thinking about the following questions:
>
> - What is the speaker's point of view on the issue of integration?
> - Who is his audience? To whom is he speaking?
> - How does he convey his perspective to this audience?

Lewis's first sentence proclaims the intent of the march: Marchers were seeking jobs and freedom. The word that jumps out at me is the word *but*. He says: "We march for jobs and freedom, but we have nothing to be proud of." He goes on to list details of the state of African Americans living in the South. He wants the public to know that the situation is dire and that while the March is important, it is not enough. The first paragraph grabs the audience's attention by person-alizing his message. He says he is fighting for the sharecropper in the field, the students and activists in jail.

He goes on, in the next couple of paragraphs, to talk about the Civil Rights Act. He claims that it is not enough when he states, "We support it with great reservations, however." The word *however* serves a similar purpose as the word *but* in the previous paragraph. He is using those words to emphasize that the United States has not done enough to end segregation. I am also noticing that he is putting forth this idea that it is the government's responsibility to protect its citizens. He repeats the phrases "will not protect" and "nothing to protect"—the bill as it stood at that time was simply not strong enough to keep people safe.

In the fourth paragraph, he uses repetition again to drive his point home. He repeats the phrase "we need a bill" and links it to the plight of African Americans who are not getting their fair share.

At this point I want to stop because I have a pretty good understanding of Lewis's point of view—he is a passionate advocate for civil rights, but he is frustrated by the lack of progress and feels that the government's attempts have not gone far enough to promote freedom and equality. **ELL** Identify and Communicate Content and Language Objectives—Language Form and

Function. It is important to draw students' attention to how particular verbal choices clue you in to Lewis's message. ELLs in particular benefit from the explicit attention to how certain words and techniques allow authors to drive their meaning home to readers.

Try Guide students to quickly rehearse what they need to learn and do in preparation for practice

Pause here to invite your students to offer input regarding how Lewis conveys his point of view across the piece thus far. Encourage students to list what they notice about the speech, and chart those observations:

- He uses very specific situations (citizens of Danville, Virginia, sharecroppers, James Farmer, the SNCC field secretaries etc.). This creates a personal connection between the audience and the people in the American South.

- He repeats certain phrases ("nothing to protect," "will not protect," "we need a bill," etc.) to emphasize his points.

  It is likely that we will learn more about Lewis's perspective as we continue to read the speech. We may also find other examples of how he conveys his point of view, so let's keep our eyes open. Also, I think Lewis is building toward a call to action, a point in the speech where he will ask his audience to join his fight. Let's be looking for that as well.

Clarify Briefly restate today's teaching objective and explain the practice task(s)

Remind your students of today's objective, which is to analyze John Lewis's speech in order to determine the piece's point of view and its development over the course of the text.

Practice Students work independently and/or in small groups to apply today's teaching objective

Students will work in pairs to read and mark the text as they trace the development of Lewis's speech. They should continue reading the speech and be on the lookout for Lewis's point of view toward civil rights legislation and how he conveys it.

Direct students to answer these questions as they read:

- What is the speaker's point of view on the issue of integration?
- Who is his audience? To whom is he speaking?
- How does he convey his perspective to this audience?

As students progress through the text, they should answer these questions:

- Is there a call to action? If so, what is it?
- Is this an effective speech? Why or why not?

ELL Identify and Communicate Content and Language Objectives— Check for Understanding. Check in with your ELLs as they work to make sure they understand how to look for the way Lewis uses language to convey his perspective. If students are struggling, you might need to provide additional modeling ("When I see this, it makes me think . . ."), scaffolding ("Here's an important word. Why do you think he used it?"), or peer support (Can bilingual peers translate key words?).

As students read, they should mark the text so they can easily reference it during later discussion. When finished, they should skim back over the text one more time independently. Then they should select one line that they think is the most powerful or important. Each person will share his or her line out loud in Wrap Up.

Wrap Up Check understanding as you guide students to briefly share what they have learned and produced today

Students will share the line they selected from the speech that they feel is the most powerful point. (SL.7.4) If possible, arrange students in a circle or even standing in a line around the classroom. Ask that they read their chosen line aloud, proceeding from one student to the next without pause or discussion. Let them know that it is OK to repeat a line— there may be several lines that resonate with multiple readers, which speaks to the effect Lewis's rhetoric has on his audience. Emphasize the need to read loudly and clearly so that each voice is heard by everyone in the room. The point here is simply to hear and appreciate these powerful words.

Reading Lesson 9 . . . .

▼ **Teaching Objective**

Readers consider how authors shape an argument to their advantage.

Close Reading
Opportunity

▼ **Standards Alignment**

RI.7.1, RL.7.1, RI.7.3, RL.7.3, RI.7.6, RL.7.6, RI.7.8, RI.7.9, RI.7.10, RL.7.10, W.7.4, W.7.9, W.7.10, SL.7.1, L.7.1, L.7.2, L.7.6

▼ Materials

- George Wallace's 1963 inaugural address ("Segregation Now, Segregation Forever")
- John Lewis's "Speech at the March on Washington"
- List of speech elements generated during Reading Lesson 8
- Students' triple-column notes begun in Reading Lesson 8

▼ To the Teacher

This lesson will look at how different authors shape or manipulate information to their argumentative advantage. Writers pick and choose what information they'd like to shine a light on or bring to the forefront. Students will analyze how two or more authors, writing about the same topic, shape their presentation of key information by emphasizing different information or advancing different interpretations of fact. Although it can be difficult for readers in the 21st century to understand the thinking of someone like George Wallace at that point in American history, it is important to expose students to those whose beliefs are different from their own and encourage them to try to understand the historical context of those beliefs. Wallace's speech is lengthy and difficult. Because it was his inaugural address, it discusses many issues other than segregation and integration. We suggest chunking it or excerpting it in this way:

- Begin your model with paragraph 6, which begins, "I want to assure every child that this State government is not afraid to invest in their future through education."
- Model your think-aloud with paragraphs 6, 7, and 8.
- Continue to read through paragraph 12 in a shared fashion as the Try part of the lesson.
- Finally, ask students to work on paragraphs 21, 22, and 23 in which Wallace articulates his philosophy regarding race and segregation.

Students will write a response to the speech in the form of a journal or blog from one of two perspectives. We provide low-tech and high-tech options below. Select the option you will use prior to your teaching.

Goal	Low-Tech	High-Tech
Students create a journal or blog response to a speech.	Students write a journal entry.	Students create a blog post using such sites as: www.edublogs.org www.education.weebly.com www.classpress.com www.kidblog.org

▼ Procedure

Warm Up Gather the class to set the stage for today's learning

To prompt your students for today's lesson, ask students to free-write on a topic:

Think of a time you had an argument with someone over something you felt strongly about. What was that argument about? What was your point of view? What was the other person's point of view? Why did you take the stance you did? Why did the other person feel the way they did? How did the argument turn out? Did sound reasoning shape the outcome of the argument or did other factors influence how it turned out?

Use these follow-up questions to guide your discussion:

- Why might it be helpful for a reader to consider multiple points of view?
- In our everyday lives, is it important for us to think about other people's points of view? Why or why not?

ELL Frontload the Lesson—Make Connections. This opening exercise helps students see the value in looking at multiple points of view. This is especially useful for your ELLs, who, as they work out the meaning of Wallace's words, may initially be confused about why the class is reading the speech of such a prejudiced man. By giving them hands-on practice with articulating two views in a familiar situation, you give them context for the new reading.

Teach Model what students need to learn and do

Explain to your students that you will be reading aloud a portion of George Wallace's inaugural address from 1963. It is possible that your students may not know what an inaugural address is, so you should be prepared to give them that information. In addition, you may decide to provide a little background information about what role Wallace played during the Civil Rights era. Remind your students to continue taking notes on the triple-column note page they created during Reading Lesson 8. Also, refer students to the list of speech elements you created in Reading Lesson 8.

Speech #1: John Lewis	Compare and Contrast Both Speeches: Lewis and Wallace	Speech #2: George Wallace

Let's read a portion of a speech given by George Wallace, the governor of Alabama in 1963. It is his inaugural address, which is the speech an elected official gives upon taking office after an election. This speech offers the opposite point of view of John Lewis. Governor Wallace wanted very much to maintain the institution of segregation in Alabama. He was a part of segregationist culture and wanted that culture to stay in place for all Southerners, African-American and white. So, our task is twofold. First, we will read the speech in much the same way we read John Lewis's. We will be determining Wallace's point of view, and we'll be looking for those elements of speeches that we discussed in our previous lesson. In addition, we will be comparing the arguments put forth by both men. We will need to consider their audiences as well as whom each man is trying to convince. The speech is lengthy so we will only read a portion of it in which he addresses the issue of segregation. Let's get started!

I am going to read a portion of the speech aloud. The first part of the speech, which I won't share today, is essentially a "thank you" to the people of Alabama for voting Wallace into office. I am going to begin with paragraph 6 because this is where he begins to address the issue of segregation.

Read the text aloud and discuss it with students. Emphasize details that reveal Wallace's purpose and point of view on segregation. Highlight details that support his point of view. Compare his interpretation of the issue to Lewis's.

This first paragraph is very short, but he talks about children and education—he appeals to families in this way because the integration of schools is imminent. In fact, at this point, the U.S. government had intervened and was using everything in its power to ensure that Alabama allowed black students to integrate historically all-white schools. Because we have that background information, we can conclude that this mention of children is deliberate on Wallace's part. The inclusion of children strengthens his argument because he is appealing to a society's most precious resource.

In the next paragraph, Wallace appeals to the spirit of the people of Alabama. In fact, he references "his people" and speaks about the "Cradle of the Confederacy" and "Heart of the Great Anglo-Saxon Southland" as if to create a strong group identity—to remind his audience that Alabama is the cradle or beginning and also the actual heart, which to me means life force, of the South. Because *Anglo-Saxon* basically means "white," I'm starting to think that his audience—the people he's trying to talk to—is white Alabamans, not all Alabamans. I am going to circle these terms and jot my thinking about their meaning in the margins. His use of certain words is also important here. He deliberately and repeatedly mentions both freedom and tyranny multiple times. I think he wants the state of Alabama to be free to live without what he calls the tyranny of the federal government. I am going to underline these words because I bet we'll see them again. This is really important because the Civil Rights Movement also talks about those two words but in the opposite way—it wants African American people to be free to live without the tyranny of racism and segregation. Isn't it amazing that speakers on both sides of this issue would choose the same language? Each speaker uses language with this imagery to strengthen his argument. Let's be thinking about which man uses it more effectively.

This paragraph concludes with Wallace's cry for "segregation today . . . segregation tomorrow . . . segregation forever." He is vehemently in support of segregation—this is his perspective and his point of view. With these words he sets the white people of Alabama apart as the "greatest people that have ever trod this earth"—he calls them to rally around this cause.

In the next paragraph, Wallace goes on to discuss the schools of Washington, D.C., as an example of what he calls a failing integrated system. He is appealing, again, to families and children. He is using fear as a motivator to resist integration.

As I come to the end of this first chunk of the speech, I am thinking that Wallace wants to create unity among the white people of Alabama and considers them his audience, the only people he is trying to convince. He uses language to indicate that he views the white people of Alabama as a family or even as one body. I wonder if he views himself as the father of the state of Alabama. The use of this image asks that his people stay dependent on him and look to him as their leader in all things. In addition, by accusing the federal government of tyranny, he is telling the people of Alabama that they should fear and distrust the government. They should place their trust in him, their protector. His tactics differ here from those used by Lewis in that Wallace seeks to motivate people through fear whereas Lewis seeks to empower. Also, even though Lewis is speaking to the general public, his message is also to the politicians who he feels have not done enough to advance integration. Wallace, on the other hand, is speaking directly to individual white citizens of Alabama; his approach is more grassroots and less about public policy and the rule of law. Lewis's speech is about looking forward and change, while Wallace wants his audience to fight to keep things the same as they have always been. Ultimately, it is the image of family and Wallace as the protector from perceived tyranny that makes his speech a strong one for this particular audience.

Try Guide students to quickly rehearse what they need to learn and do in preparation for practice

At this point, you can bring your students into the process of thinking aloud through Wallace's speech. Read the next four paragraphs aloud, pausing after each to allow time for your students to process what they are reading. Remind them to record their thinking on the triple-column note page.

I am now going to read the next four paragraphs aloud. I will pause after each one to give you a chance to mark the text. You may circle or highlight words and phrases that are significant as well as make notes in the margin. We'll have a quick conversation about what we're finding before we go on to the Practice portion of our lesson. Remember that we are noticing the ways in which Wallace tries to achieve his purpose and convey his point of view, or perspective, toward segregation: "segregation today, segregation tomorrow, segregation forever." Ultimately, we are comparing Wallace's words and view of integration with those of John Lewis. As you read, keep this in mind and consider the arguments put forth in each speech.

When you reach the end of paragraph 12, take a few minutes to share and write their observations of the Wallace speech as it compares to the Lewis speech. Ask your students to begin to compare this speech with that of John Lewis. Ask them especially to think about the groups each man was addressing: Whom was Lewis trying to convince? What about Wallace? If students don't realize this on their own, point out that Wallace's speech was probably not effective at convincing African-American Southerners to support segregation, but that was not his goal. Rather, he wanted to rally the white citizens of Alabama to fight for segregationist views—was his speech effective for that audience and purpose?

Clarify Briefly restate today's teaching objective and explain the practice task(s)

Remind students of today's goal, which is to read Wallace's speech and to compare his view of segregation and integration with that of John Lewis.

Practice Students work independently and/or in small groups to apply today's teaching objective

Have students complete their reading and analysis of Wallace's speech. In addition, have them compare his speech with the words of John Lewis. Remind students to use their triple-column notes for this work.

> Today you will read this final excerpt independently. As always, mark the text. Remember that we are analyzing what Wallace is saying as well as how he is saying it. We are paying very close attention to the words he chooses and the images he creates as he advances his argument.
>
> When you have completed your reading, have a discussion with your partner about the strengths of each speech. Use these questions to guide your conversation:

- What argument is each man trying to make in his speech?
- Who is the audience for each speech, both literally standing in front of the speaker and hearing or reading the text later? Whom is each man trying to convince?
- What techniques do the speakers use to make these speeches effective? Why are these techniques effective? Would they be equally effective for a different audience with a different perspective? Use evidence from the text.
- How does each man shape his argument? Use evidence from the text.
- What is each man's perspective? Use evidence from the text.
- How does Lewis see the South? How does Wallace?
- Is it helpful to hear both sides of the argument? Why or why not?

ELL Enable Language Production—Reading and Writing, Listening and Speaking. Guiding questions can help your ELLs focus their reading, writing, and conversation. This can provide an important scaffold for students who are learning academic English.

Wrap Up Check understanding as you guide students to briefly share what they have learned and produced today

Students will work in partnerships to articulate their observations in writing. Each partner will create a short written response in the form of a journal or blog entry. To consider the role of audience in shaping a speech, one student will write as an audience member who was present for John Lewis's speech and the other will write as someone who has had the opportunity to hear the words of George Wallace.

Students will include:

- Analysis of the focus speaker's point of view/perspective.
- Evidence of the focus speaker's point of view/perspective's development across the text.
- Comparison of how the speaker shaped his argument by emphasizing different interpretations and evidence than the other speaker did.
- Reflection on the feelings of the audience that each speaker was trying to connect with.

Share a sampling of entries from both perspectives. Finally, this lesson teaches the extremely important skill of being able to critically analyze and understand both a speaker's words and the semantic tricks of the trade that can be used to sway, persuade, and manipulate listeners. It is critical to reaffirm at the end of the lesson that some behaviors are simply wrong no matter how eloquently the speaker may present them, making sure students leave understanding that segregation is never a morally defensible practice and that even Wallace, in later years, apologized for his racist beliefs and asked for forgiveness for his actions as governor. Words have enormous power, and students need to understand that they can (and are) often used for unkind and dangerous purposes.

Milestone Performance Assessment

Written Response to a Speech

Collect and analyze students' journals or blog entries as a performance-based assessment to determine if students need additional instruction or support as a whole class, in small groups, or one on one. **ELL** Assess for Content and Language Understanding—Formative Assessment. Keep in mind that these objectives are heavily linguistic. Students need to muster all their academic language skills to convey that they have analyzed the speaker's point of view, how they are comparing and contrasting the two speakers, and what evidence supports their reasoning. ELLs may struggle to convey their understanding effectively, even if they *do* grasp the content objectives. Examine their work thoughtfully to find strengths, and consider how you might teach them conventional strategies for explaining their thinking in writing.

 Use this checklist to assess student written responses.

Standards Alignment: RI.7.1, RI.7.3, RI.7.6, RI.7.8, RI.7.9, RI.7.10, W.7.4, W.7.9, W.7.10

Task	Achieved	Notes
Analyze the focus speaker's point of view/perspective.		
Include evidence from the text to trace the development of the POV/perspective of the focus speaker across the text.		

Task	Achieved	Notes
Compare how the two speakers shape their argument through differing interpretations and evidence.		
Reflect on the experience of hearing the opposition's point of view.		
Use evidence from the text to support analysis and reflection.		

Reading Lesson 10

▼ Teaching Objective

Readers reflect on the ways historical fiction can connect us to real-life events.

Close Reading Opportunity

▼ Standards Alignment

RI.7.1, RI.7.2, RI.7.10, RL.7.1, RL.7.2, RL.7.3, RL.7.10, W.7.4, W.7.9, W.7.10, SL.7.1, SL.7.4, SL.7.6, L.7.1, L.7.2, L.7.3, L.7.6

▼ Materials

- Historical Fiction Book Club texts
- Charting supplies or interactive whiteboard
- *Roll of Thunder, Hear My Cry* by Mildred B. Taylor
- Nonfiction texts with information connected to historical events in Historical Fiction Book Club texts
- Class Discussion Notes (downloadable PDF in the PDToolkit)

▼ To the Teacher

This lesson concludes the reading portion of this lesson set. The culminating activity will be a large group discussion or Socratic seminar. We suggest using this Sydney Smith quote from Lecture XIX : On the Conduct of the Understanding, Part II, "It is the greatest of all mistakes to do nothing because you can only do little" to inspire and guide the discussion. It is likely that the conversation may grow beyond the quote, and that is a good thing! The one factor to remain true to is to keep the talk grounded in the text while at the same time encouraging students to make connections to other texts and historical events as well as current happenings. We want students to see the larger picture here and to understand the ways in which historical fiction illuminates the human condition.

To facilitate the conversation, if it is possible, arrange the seating in your room either in a U shape or a circle so everyone is able to see one another.

▼ Procedure

Warm Up Gather the class to set the stage for today's learning

Present the Sydney Smith quote to your students. Ask them to reflect on the quote in preparation for today's Socratic seminar. They will record their thinking in the Class Discussion Notes (PDToolkit).

> Today we will be having a class discussion as a culminating activity. We have done so much reading, writing, and thinking about the genre of historical fiction; now it's time we talked about it. We will use a quote as a guide for our conversation. Please respond to this quote: What does it mean to you? Do you agree? Disagree? What other stories, films, historical events, or current happenings come to mind as you reflect on the accuracy or inaccuracy of Sydney Smith's words? We have learned that historical fiction is based on true historical events, but it uses imaginary characters and scenarios to help us connect to the human truths of the story. Be thinking about how reading these stories prompts us to think about real-life events and the human lessons to be learned from them. Remember to use all of our source material to support your ideas.

Class Discussion Notes

Respond to the following quote::

"It is the greatest of all mistakes to do nothing because you can only do little."
—Sydney Smith, Lecture XIX: On the Conduct of the Understanding, Part II
What does it mean to you? Do you agree or disagree? Explain.

Before the Discussion:

Find several pieces of evidence from our texts (fiction and nonfiction) to support your ideas about the quote (reference text, author, and page or paragraph number).

Think of connections you might make beyond our texts. You can connect these ideas to another historical event, another book, or something that is going on in our world right now.

Before the discussion

Ask questions! Think of a discussion question or two you might pose to the class. Try to ask questions that begin with *why* or *how*; these kinds of questions generate the best conversations!

During the discussion:

Take notes here. Jot down comments that interest you, that you wonder about, or even that you disagree with.

After the discussion:

Reflect.
How do you think the discussion went?
How do you feel about your participation?
What is something you might do differently next time?

ELL Enable Language Production—Listening and Speaking. This discussion guide will help your ELLs come to the conversation prepared, clear about exactly what is expected of them and what qualifies as a sound contribution.

Teach Model what students need to learn and do

Once you have completed the Before the Discussion portion of the graphic organizer, review the important conversation guidelines here. (SL.7.1a, SL.7.1b, SL.7.c, SL.7.d, SL.7.4)

- We come to the discussion prepared with ideas, text, and discussion graphic organizer.
- One person speaks at a time.
- Everybody participates.
- We show respect for our peers by making eye contact.
- We work to build and grow our understanding.

ELL Enable Language Production—Listening and Speaking. Keep in mind that even these apparently basic speaking conventions are culturally specific and may vary even among subcultures within the United States. For example, what is considered appropriate eye contact varies broadly across human societies. Look for behaviors that may indicate your students have been socialized in ways that are not part of the U.S. mainstream, and think about how to encourage them to be culturally flexible depending on the demands of the context.

Try Guide students to quickly rehearse what they need to learn and do in preparation for practice

Allow a few minutes for a practice run here. Ask students to turn and talk with a neighbor about their interpretation of the quote as well as some of the discussion ideas they have recorded on their graphic organizers.

Clarify Briefly restate today's teaching objective and explain the practice task(s)

Remind students of today's objective, which is to discuss their study of historical fiction and the ways in which this genre helps to connect us to real-life events.

> Today we are conducting a class discussion. The inspiration for today's conversation is our study of historical fiction and the ways in which it allows us to understand and connect to real-life events. We are using Sydney Smith's quote as a jumping-off point for our conversation.

Practice Students work independently and/or in small groups to apply today's teaching objective

Your role during this discussion is that of conversation starter, and depending on the facility of your students, you may need to jump in to troubleshoot or redirect from time to time. During the conversation, you should take note of any interesting comments, the number of times each student participates, and anything else worth noting. The goal, ultimately, is to fade into the background in order to allow your students to truly take ownership of the seminar. At some point, you may even want to film the seminar so students can see themselves in action. Participating in this type of discussion takes time and practice!

If everyone is ready, we will get started. I am going to read the quote and then I'll turn the discussion over to you!

Wrap Up Check understanding as you guide students to briefly share what they have learned and produced today

When the conversation has been completed, allow time for students to reflect on the discussion as a whole as well as their participation in it. Collect their Class Discussion Notes.

Grade 7

Writing Lessons

The Core I.D.E.A. / Daily Writing Instruction at a Glance table highlights the teaching objectives and standards alignment for all 10 lessons across the four stages of the lesson set (Introduce, Define, Extend, and Assess). It also indicates which lessons contain special features to support English language learners, technology, speaking and listening, close reading opportunities, and formative ("Milestone") assessments.

The Core I.D.E.A. / Daily Writing Instruction at a Glance

Grade 7 Examining Past Perspectives: Historical Fact and Fiction

Instructional Stage	Lesson	Teaching Objective	Core Standards	Special Features
Introduce: *notice, explore, collect, note, immerse, surround, record, share*	1	Writers craft questions to focus their topic and guide their research.	RI.7.1 • RI.7.2 • RI.7.3 • RI.7.10 • W.7.3 • W.7.4 • W.7.5 • W.7.9 • W.7.10 • SL.7.1 • SL.7.2 • SL.7.6 • L.7.1 • L.7.2 • L.7.3 • L.7.6	ELL Milestone Assessment Close Reading Opportunity
	2	Writers of historical fiction conduct research to prepare to write.	RI.7.1 • RI.7.2 • RI.7.3 • RI.7.10 • W.7.3 • W.7.4 • W.7.5 • W.7.7 • W.7.9 • W.7.10 • SL.7.1 • SL.7.6 • L.7.1 • L.7.2 • L.7.3 • L.7.6	S&L ELL Tech Close Reading Opportunity
Define: *name, identify, outline, clarify, select, plan*	3	Writers research factual details to create accurate historical settings.	RI.7.1 • RI.7.2 • RI.7.3 • RI.7.10 • W.7.3 • W.7.4 • W.7.5 • W.7.6 • W.7.7 • W.7.10 • SL.7.1 • SL.7.2 • SL.7.6 • L.7.1 • L.7.2 • L.7.3 • L.7.6	ELL Close Reading Opportunity
Extend: *try, experiment, attempt, approximate, practice, explain, revise, refine*	4	Writers choose characters whose perspectives offer the most powerful story.	RI.7.1 • RI.7.2 • RI.7.3 • RI.7.10 • W.7.3 • W.7.4 • W.7.5 • W.7.10 • SL.7.1 • SL.7.4 • SL.7.6 • L.7.1 • L.7.2 • L.7.3 • L.7.6	ELL Close Reading Opportunity Milestone Assessment
	5	Writers compose a story from three different perspectives.	RI.7.1 • RI.7.2 • RI.7.3 • RI.7.10 • W.7.3 • W.7.4 • W.7.5 • W.7.6 • W.7.10 • SL.7.2 • SL.7.1 • SL.7.6 • L.7.1 • L.7.2 • L.7.3 • L.7.6	ELL S&L Close Reading Opportunity
	6	Writers use dialogue to emphasize point of view.	RL.7.1 • RL.7.6 • RL.7.10 • W.7.3 • W.7.4 • W.7.5 • W.7.10 • SL.7.1 • SL.7.2 • SL.7.6 • L.7.1 • L.7.2 • L.7.3 • L.7.6	ELL Close Reading Opportunity
	7	Writers plan author's notes to describe and reflect on their historical fiction writing experience.	RI.7.1 • RI.7.5 • RI.7.10 • W.7.3 • W.7.4 • W.7.5 • W.7.10 • SL.7.1 • SL.7.6 • L.7.1 • L.7.2 • L.7.3 • L.7.6	ELL Close Reading Opportunity
	8	Writers compose author's notes to describe and reflect on their historical fiction writing experience.	W.7.3 • W.7.4 • W.7.5 • W.7.6 • W.7.10 • SL.7.1 • SL.7.4 • SL.7.6 • L.7.1 • L.7.2 • L.7.3 • L.7.6	ELL Milestone Assessment
	9	Writers collaborate on revision and editing.	W.7.3 • W.7.4 • W.7.5 • W.7.6 • W.7.10 • SL.7.1 • SL.7.6 • L.7.1 • L.7.2 • L.7.3 • L.7.6	S&L ELL Milestone Assessment
Assess: *reflect, conclude, connect, share, recognize, respond*	10	Writers share and celebrate their work.	W.7.6 • SL.7.1 • SL.7.2 • SL.7.4 • SL.7.6 • L.7.1 • L.7.2 • L.7.3 • L.7.6	S&L ELL Tech

Writing Lesson 1

▼ **Teaching Objective**

Writers craft questions to focus their topic and guide their research.

Close Reading Opportunity

▼ **Standards Alignment**

RI.7.1, RI.7.2, RI.7.3, RI.7.10, W.7.3, W.7.4, W.7.5, W.7.9, W.7.10, SL.7.1, SL.7.2, SL.7.6, L.7.1, L.7.2, L.7.3, L.7.6

▼ **Materials**

- Photo of Freedom Riders
- Sample Informational Text: *The Freedom Riders* (Appendix 7.5)
- *Roll of Thunder, Hear My Cry* by Mildred B. Taylor
- Charting supplies or interactive whiteboard
- A selection of photographs that depict different events from the Civil Rights Movement. One website with a large collection is http://photos.state.gov/galleries/usinfo-photo/39/civil _rights_07/. This website pairs short informational text with each photograph. The text provides background information.
- A collection of informational articles and documents for students to use for research
- Selecting a Topic graphic organizer (Appendix 7.6)

▼ **To the Teacher**

In order to ensure your students' comfort and facility with the genre of historical fiction, we suggest you begin the writing lessons after Reading Lesson 3. Over the course of these writing lessons, students will craft a short historical fiction story. They will consider point of view while pondering how to create characters who come alive. For the purpose of this lesson set, we will ask that students write historical fiction stories based on one of several moments, which we will refer to as focus events, that occurred during the Civil Rights era. Possible focus events under consideration might be school integration, lunch counter sit-ins, the Birmingham church bombing, and the voter-rights demonstration march from Selma to Montgomery, Alabama. You may provide the research materials, require your students to find sources independently, or decide on a combination of these two approaches. Please refer to the Choosing Core texts list for potential resources. Your writers will model their pieces on our core novel, *Roll of Thunder, Hear My Cry*. In addition, while your students are writing their historical fiction stories, you, too, will be crafting your own to use as a model. We suggest you use the Freedom Riders as your focus event. We have provided a sample story to use as your model. It is also possible to meet the lesson set goals by focusing on a different historical time period that aligns with your local curriculum. **ELL** Identify and Communicate Content and Language Objectives—Language Form and Function. By seventh grade, all children (barring disability or severe neglect) are highly proficient in the language of their home communities and often use language in very sophisticated ways. Some of your ELLs may be proficient in a language other than English; others may be skilled users of a nonstandard variety of English. Throughout this lesson set, be on the lookout for opportunities to build on what your ELLs already know about communication. Teach them standard alternatives to their nonstandard language uses, and engage them in discussion about situational appropriateness. This set's combination of narrative and expository writing lends itself very well to multiple styles of writing used for distinct purposes.

▼ **Procedure**

Warm Up Gather the class to set the stage for today's learning

Ask that students refer back to the collection of photos used in Reading Lesson 1. These will serve as inspiration for the focus event of their historical fiction stories. The website we suggest in the Materials section partners each photo with a short piece of informational text. Students may use this short text to glean more background information about the photos. **ELL** Provide Comprehensible Input—Visuals. Familiar pictures will help ELLs orient themselves to this lesson and will enable even students who are just beginning to learn English to gather information about this historical time period.

> Have a look at the civil rights information and photos in our collection. What major events in the Civil Rights era do they illustrate? What conflicts do they show between the dominant group and minority groups or between the dominant group and individual perspectives? Which is most interesting to you? Why? Take a few minutes to review them and be prepared to share your thoughts.

Have students share their thoughts, and record them on a chart. Possible responses: school integration, lunch counter sit-ins, the Birmingham church bombing, and the voter-rights demonstration march from Selma to Montgomery, Alabama. Fill in gaps in your chart as needed.

Teach   Model what students need to learn and do

Today your students will settle on a focus event for their historical fiction stories. Provide students with the questions below to help generate ideas as they plan their stories.

- Why is it important to tell the story of _____, your area of interest/topic?
- What can we learn from the actions of people involved in this event?
- What were the consequences of the event?

Think aloud as you articulate your thinking around topic selection.

Today we are going to begin the process of writing short historical fiction pieces. Our first challenge is to select the focus of our story. We have been reading about the Civil Rights era both in *Roll of Thunder, Hear My Cry* as well as in several nonfiction pieces. Today we will do two things: First, we will select an event from this time period to inspire our historical fiction stories, and second, we will articulate what it is about this particular event that makes for good storytelling.

I am thinking that I might write about the Freedom Riders. You probably remember that we learned about them during Reading Lesson 1. Let's have a look again at the Freedom Riders photograph and informational text.

Read the Sample Informational Text: *The Freedom Riders* (Appendix 7.5) aloud. Model marking the details that help to shape your selection of a topic. Then think aloud about how the article inspired a possible historical fiction writing focus.

I am interested in what makes a person help someone who is not a part of their everyday lives. The Freedom Riders are inspiring because they risked personal injury in order to push for change. These people were clearly thinking about a bigger issue and recognized that civil rights were meant for all Americans, not just African Americans.

Now that I think I have narrowed down my topic, I am going to answer these questions. Thinking about these questions will help me shape the characters and central ideas (themes) of the story I will write.

Complete the Selecting a Topic graphic organizer (Appendix 7.6) in front of students.   **ELL**   Provide Comprehensible Input—Models. When you physically demonstrate how to choose and write about a topic, you help your ELLs understand both what is expected of them and how to successfully complete the assignment. If you have students who are literate in their home language, they can complete the graphic organizer in that language, but they will still benefit from watching you do the same exercise in English.

Selecting a Topic

Focus event: The Freedom Riders' bus rides

Why is it important to tell the story of the Freedom Riders?   This is an important story to tell because it provides another example of the ways people fought for integration and equality during the Civil Rights era.

What can we learn from the actions of people involved in this event?   Their actions teach us that there are some things important enough to motivate people to use their time and get on a bus to go somewhere and state their belief about something. Even though the problem they were trying to solve was a very big one and had been a big problem for a long time, they believed that taking a simple yet thoughtful and active step could lead to a big change.

What were the consequences of this event?   One of the consequences of the Freedom Rides was that they gave the issue of integration a wider audience. This particular event brought attention to the fight for civil rights because it was mobile and because the people on the buses were from a variety of racial backgrounds and from different parts of the country. The concept of the Freedom Rides was new and different. The Freedom Riders helped shape the discussion and understanding of the issue by the American people.

Try   Guide students to quickly rehearse what they need to learn and do in preparation for practice

Prompt your students to give the text a quick review to see if there is anything else they might want to add to the notes. Remind students that we often reread text to clarify a point or to make sure that we haven't missed any important information.

Readers often reread portions of text. We might reread to clarify a point or to make sure that we haven't missed any important or interesting information. Before we move on today, skim back over the information for the Freedom Riders. Is there anything you think I should add to my responses?

Clarify   Briefly restate today's teaching objective and explain the practice task(s)

Remind students of today's focus, which is to use questions to generate ideas for the writing of historical fiction stories.

We've done a lot of reading about the Civil Rights Movement. Today we're going to do some thinking about which event is the most interesting to you and about which you will write your historical fiction story. You will use the questions we discussed earlier to help you to articulate your reasons for writing this particular story about this particular focus event.

You may select from any of the events we listed earlier. If you have something else in mind, please meet with me during the work period. When you have focused your topic, complete the Selecting a Topic graphic organizer. Be prepared to share.

Practice Students work independently and/or in small groups to apply today's teaching objective

Students should work independently to select their focus event and complete the Selecting a Topic graphic organizer. They will use the Civil Rights–era photographs and the Sample Informational Text: *The Freedom Riders* (Appendix 7.5) as well as any other information you have gathered as inspiration for their Historical Fiction stories. They will use these resources to answer the guiding questions in the graphic organizer as they reflect on the event's importance and relevance. **ELL** Enable Language Production—Reading and Writing. If you have students who are new to English, they may benefit from working with a bilingual peer, if possible. This will allow them to ask questions about the content and share their ideas with someone who understands their home language.

Wrap Up Check understanding as you guide students to briefly share what they have learned and produced today

Ask students to share their writing topics with a partner. Today you will collect the Selecting a Topic graphic organizers. Take this opportunity to check in with your students on their topic selections.

Explain to students that in advance of Writing Lesson 2, they will need to collect two nonfiction sources related to their selected time period. They will be working with them in class.

Milestone Performance Assessment

Selecting a Topic

PD TOOLKIT™

Collect and analyze students' Selecting a Topic graphic organizers as a performance-based assessment to determine if students need additional instruction or support as a whole class, in small groups,

or one on one. **ELL** Assess for Content and Language Understanding—Formative Assessment. Remember that your ELLs might understand the content very well but have written their notes in nonstandard English. At this point in the writing process, focus on their ideas, but also consider how you can scaffold students' language production as form becomes more important later in the lesson set.

Use this checklist to assess student Selecting a Topic graphic organizers.

Standards Alignment: RI.7.1, RI.7.2, RI.7.3, RI.7.10, W.7.3, W.7.4, W.7.5, W.7.9, W.7.10

Task	Achieved	Notes
Select a focus event and explain its importance.		
Articulate what might be learned through the example put forth by the people involved in this focus event.		
Explain the consequences of this focus event.		

Writing Lesson 2

▼ Teaching Objective

Writers of historical fiction conduct research to prepare to write.

Close Reading Opportunity

▼ Standards Alignment

RL.7.1, RI.7.2, RI.7.3, RI.7.10, W.7.3, W.7.4, W.7.5, W.7.7, W.7.9, W.7.10, SL.7.1, SL.7.6, L.7.1, L.7.2, L.7.3, L.7.6

▼ Materials

- A collection of informational articles and documents for students to use for research
- Charting supplies or interactive whiteboard
- Note-taking supplies (See tech box)
- Sample Informational Text: *The Freedom Riders* (Appendix 7.5)
- Historical Fiction Planning Chart (downloadable PDF in the PDToolkit)
- Informational sources related to selected topic from Writing Lesson 1

▼ To the Teacher

In this lesson, students will begin the research process in preparation for the writing of their historical fiction stories. Emphasize for your students that in order to create historically accurate stories that come across to the reader as true, the writer must engage in research. **ELL** Enable Language Production—Reading and Writing. A lesson focused on research strategies will ensure that your ELLs have enough background knowledge to compose strong pieces of historical fiction.

▼ Procedure

Warm Up Gather the class to set the stage for today's learning

Explain the importance of research as preparation for writing historical fiction stories. Students should explore the time period in search of key facts and details to embed in their stories.

Today we are going to begin the research for our historical fiction stories. During Writing Lesson 1, we narrowed our topic and thought about why it was important to tell the stories we intend to write. Because we want to write stories based on real facts, it will be important to find those interesting and important details that will help you as writers create vibrant settings and characters that ring true. During this lesson, each one of you will be asked to think about this question: What are the really important details about this time period that I want to make sure I include in my story?

Writers often look at other works and use them as mentors, which means that writers learn from other writers by reading their stories and noticing their techniques. Let's think for a minute about *Roll of Thunder, Hear My Cry.* What knowledge have we gained about the lives, thoughts, and perspectives of both African Americans and White Americans in the United States, especially in the

South, during the time period of the story? What message or lesson is Taylor addressing in her writing? What techniques does she use? Have a look back at the excerpts we have read to find some examples. Turn and talk.

 Prompt students to return from discussion prepared to share aloud. (SL.7.1a) Record student responses.

You may hear observations such as:

- Separate was not equal during this time period.
- African Americans and White Americans were expected to live and socialize separately. Even people who didn't believe in those ideas had to live by them.
- Some White Americans considered themselves superior to African Americans and acted cruelly and violently toward them.
- Owning land was a form of status and security.
- Possible messages: Human emotions are universal. Hope can guide people through even the worst challenges. The notion of family was very important. Old traditions should be questioned and confronted when they unfairly and negatively affect people's lives.
- Some techniques students might name or you might point out: first-person narrator, flashbacks, strong imagery, and the inclusion of historical facts.

Mildred B. Taylor was able to include these elements in her story because she did very careful research in order to be sure her writing was an accurate reflection of the time period. In addition, she believed in her story and that her story had something to teach us. Occasionally we might find authors of historical fiction who change parts of history in their stories—these will be good moments to think about the importance of thorough research and perhaps why an author may twist historical events to better fit a fictional story.

Teach Model what students need to learn and do

Using the Sample Informational Text: *The Freedom Riders* (Appendix 7.5), or a nonfiction informational piece of your choice, model for students the way we find information in a nonfiction text to inspire and draw from in historical fiction stories.

One of the key characteristics of historical fiction writing is that the characters and events are placed in a realistic setting. Therefore, writers of historical fiction need to develop an understanding of the time period about which they are writing. In the case of Mildred B. Taylor, she used actual family stories as the basis of *Roll of Thunder, Hear My Cry.* Not all authors have such a direct link to the time period of their writing, so in order to create vivid characters and realistic scenes, they often conduct research to learn more about the time period they are writing about. Today we will begin our own research. Specifically we will be looking for information and details that we will want to include in our own writing. To help us along, I am going to show you how I work with nonfiction text to find important information. Listen as I read aloud the first section of a nonfiction text on which I plan to base a fictional piece of writing.

In 1961, the American South was deeply segregated. Buses, trains, schools, libraries, restaurants, and movie theaters—even water fountains—had separate areas for African Americans and White Americans. In 1960, the Supreme Court had ruled in *Boynton v. Virginia* that segregation was illegal in public transportation.

Nevertheless, public transportation in the South was still segregated. A group named, the Congress of Racial Equality (CORE), decided to do something about it. On May 4, 1961, thirteen riders—ten men and three women, seven of whom were black and six of whom were white—boarded two buses in Washington, D.C., and headed south. Instead of dividing the bus along color lines, the riders sat together. That was all.

Use the Historical Fiction Planning Chart (PD Toolkit) to record your thinking. At this point, the chart might look like this:

Focus Event: The Freedom Riders' bus rides

Source: Sample Informational Text: *The Freedom Riders*

Information from the Source	What story might I tell?
• In 1960, segregation on all forms of transportation was declared illegal by the Supreme Court. • The South did not recognize this ruling and continued to enforce segregation on trains and buses. • CORE (Congress of Racial Equality) decided to organize the ride as a protest. • The ride took place on May 4, 1961, and departed from Washington, D.C. • The group was composed of men and women, black and white.	I think I will tell a story about the Freedom Riders. I will probably focus less on the actual ride and more on an event that might take place once the bus reaches the South. I would like to create a situation where the riders come into direct contact with Southern White Americans. I am curious about how that interaction might play out. How would their two different perspectives affect their interaction with each other?

Try Guide students to quickly rehearse what they need to learn and do in preparation for practice

Ask students to look at the next paragraph. Instruct them to mark the text to highlight information that might inform your research. Have them share their thinking.

I'd like you to give this a go with the next couple of paragraphs. Take a couple of minutes to read and mark the text. You will help me add information about the Freedom Riders to my chart. Then we'll share what we're finding.

Ask students to read the following section from the Sample Informational Text: *The Freedom Riders*.

But by riding an integrated bus across the Deep South, the Freedom Riders were making one of the most dramatic and courageous stands against segregation in the entire Civil Rights Movement. Their route would take them through towns and cities that supported segregation, places where they faced tremendous danger.

Maybe the most amazing thing about the Freedom Riders is that the riders were, in a way, completely ordinary. A lot of them were college students. No one pushed them to sign up—many of their families actually tried to stop them from going. They could have carried on with their lives as regular students, studying, seeing their friends. But they decided to take a stand, and the nation and the world watched.

As your students share the facts they've found, add their findings to your chart. Now that you have gathered some information, model the way you might begin to focus in on the story you want to tell. Jot your ideas in the last column on the chart.

I am beginning to gather some really interesting information about the Freedom Riders. Here's what I'm thinking about the story I want to tell: I think I will tell the story of the Freedom Riders. I will probably focus less on the actual ride and more on an event that might take place once the bus reaches the South. I would like to create a situation where the riders come into direct contact with some people once they arrive in the South. I am curious about how that interaction might play out.

Clarify Briefly restate today's teaching objective and explain the practice task(s)

Reiterate the importance of research when writing historical fiction. Explain that in the Practice section, students will begin to read informational sources in order to find information about the historical event they have selected. Instruct your students to record their notes on their Historical Fiction Planning Chart (PD Toolkit). Emphasize the importance of paraphrasing and citing sources.

Practice Students work independently and/or in small groups to apply today's teaching objectives

Students work with their informational texts on their chosen topics. As they take notes on their focus event and historical time period, circulate to check for understanding. Students will add information to their columned notes, index cards, or Evernote (see high-tech and low-tech suggestions). Some students may need to acquire additional pieces to round out their research.

Sepy/Fotolia

Wrap Up Check understanding as you guide students to briefly share what they have learned and produced today

As an exit slip, ask students to share, in writing, one interesting piece of historical information that they found during their research today. In addition, ask that they explain the role this information will play in their historical fiction stories.

Goal	Low-Tech	High-Tech
Students take notes and track their sources.	Students use graphic organizers or take notes on categorized index cards.	Students take notes in Evernote: http://evernote.com/schools/ or any other digital note taking application.

Writing Lesson 3

▼ Teaching Objective

Writers research factual details to create accurate historical settings.

Close Reading Opportunity

▼ Standards Alignment

RI.7.1, RI.7.2, RI.7.3, RI.7.10, W.7.3, W.7.4, W.7.5, W.7.6, W.7.7, W.7.10, SL.7.1, SL.7.2, SL.7.6, L.7.1, L.7.2, L.7.3, L.7.6

▼ Materials

- Note-taking supplies
- Historical Fiction Planning Chart (from Writing Lesson 2)

- Charting supplies or interactive whiteboard
- Google Drive or another collaborative writing site
- A collection of informational articles and documents for students to use for research
- Sample Informational Text: *The Freedom Riders* (Appendix 7.5)
- Sticky notes

▼ To the Teacher

In this lesson, students will use research materials to create accurate historical settings. It is important to stress the importance of adhering to historical accuracy while crafting a setting for the historical fiction stories. You will model your thinking using our sample informational text: *The Freedom Riders*.

▼ Procedure

Warm Up Gather the class to set the stage for today's learning

Direct students to review the informational sources they are using to research their stories.

> Today you will think about the setting for your story. Writers of historical fiction are careful to place their stories in accurate settings. Before we begin, have a look at your sources to find information about where this event took place.

Teach Model what students need to learn and do

For the modeling portion of this lesson, we'll use the Sample Informational Text: *The Freedom Riders* (Appendix 7.5) to look for helpful details and information regarding setting.

> I am going to refer back to my source about the Freedom Riders. Here's what I will be looking for today to help me develop an accurate setting in my fiction piece:

- Where and when the story takes place.
- Words and phrases that will give me more details about the setting.

> Read the text aloud. Mark the text as you notice information about the setting. Your annotated text may look like this:

> But by riding an integrated bus across the <u>Deep South,</u> the Freedom Riders were making one of the most dramatic and courageous stands against segregation in the entire Civil Rights Movement. <u>Their route would take them through towns and cities where segregation was the law, places where they faced tremendous danger.</u>

> Maybe the most amazing thing about the Freedom Riders is that the riders were, in a way, completely ordinary. A lot of them were college students. No one pushed them to sign up—many of their families actually tried to stop them from going. They could have carried on with their lives as regular students, studying, seeing their friends. But they decided to take a stand, and the nation and the world watched.

> <u>In Alabama, one of the buses was firebombed. In Montgomery, more than a thousand people attacked the bus after it pulled into the station.</u> The riders were beaten very badly. But they practiced nonviolence. No matter what they faced from the angry crowd, they wouldn't fight back.

List the details in the text that tell the reader something about the setting.

Here are a few details I found in the text that will help me to create a setting:

- Deep South: This must be the part of the American South that is both geographically very far south and philosophically very tied to Southern ideals and customs.
- "places where they faced tremendous danger": This tells me the mood of the places where they'd be traveling, but I wonder what "tremendous danger" looks like to someone riding one of the buses? How might I show my reader what this kind of danger looks and feels like? I need to think about that.
- The last paragraph gives me what I need—"buses were firebombed" and "more than a thousand people attacked the bus after it pulled into the station"—ah ha! Here is what I was looking for—the danger is in the form of angry mobs of people and firebombings. This really helps me get a picture in my mind of what the Freedom Riders experienced or were scared they would experience.

Try Guide students to quickly rehearse what they need to learn and do in preparation for practice

Ask students to refer back to their informational resources. Have them mark their texts where they find information that tells them something about the setting. Prompt them to turn and talk with a neighbor about the information they are finding.

> Today you will gather information about where and when your historical event took place in order to create a realistic setting and include accurate details to your story. Refer back to one of your sources to find information about the setting. Mark the text and share your thoughts with a partner.

Clarify Briefly restate today's teaching objective and explain the practice task(s)

Remind students that even though the stories they are writing are fiction, they are based on true events, and the goal is to make them as realistic as possible. Including accurate information about the setting is an important part of this process. Encourage students to use the questions below as they research their setting.

> Remember that even though we are writing fictional stories, they are based on true events, and it is important to make them as accurate as possible. One way to do this is to include real, historical details about where and when the events took place.

As you refer back to your sources, think about the following questions.

- Where and when does your story take place?
- What words and phrases can you find that tell you something about the setting?
- What does your setting look like? Sound like?
- What things might we find in your setting?

Mark the text for words and phrases that tell you something about the setting. Then you'll begin to craft the setting for your own story.

Practice Students work independently and/or in small groups to apply today's teaching objective

Students will work independently to find information that will help them create a realistic setting. Remind them to consider what the setting looks like and what they might see or hear. Refer back to the preceding questions. Circulate among them as they write. You may want to take time to conference with your students during this lesson in order to get an idea of their plans thus far. **ELL** Identify and Communicate Content and Language Objectives—Check for Understanding. Check in with your ELLs to make sure that they understand both the concept of setting and how to find words in a text that give information about the setting.

Wrap Up Check understanding as you guide students to briefly share what they have learned and produced today

Have students share their setting ideas with a partner. Each pair will swap papers. Instruct partners to note, on sticky notes, the details that they think will make for an accurate setting. Explain that students should hold on to this work and draw from it when creating settings for their stories.

Writing Lesson 4

▼ Teaching Objective

Writers choose characters whose perspectives offer the most powerful story.

Close Reading Opportunity

▼ Standards Alignment

RI.7.1, RI.7.2, RI.7.3, RI.7.10, W.7.3, W.7.4, W.7.5, W.7.10, SL.7.1, SL.7.4, SL.7.6, L.7.1, L.7.2, L.7.3, L.7.6

▼ Materials

- *Roll of Thunder, Hear My Cry* by Mildred B. Taylor
- Sample Informational Text: *The Freedom Riders* (Appendix 7.5)
- Historical Fiction Planning Chart (From Writing Lessons 2 and 3)
- A collection of informational articles and documents for students to use for research
- Charting supplies or interactive whiteboard
- Character Planning graphic organizer (downloadable PDF in the PDToolkit)
- Exit slip (see content below)

▼ To the Teacher

Today your writers will develop characters with clear points of view and choose narrators. Their historical fiction stories will mimic the *Roll of Thunder, Hear My Cry* format in that they will employ a narrator in first-person narrative mode. However, your students should write in that mode from three different narrator perspectives. We want students to practice writing from different points of view. By using three narrators, your students will need to develop the perspectives of three characters who may have different interpretations or ideas about the same historical event or setting. You may use Sample Informational Text: *The Freedom Riders* (Appendix 7.5) as a model for your thinking about point of view.

▼ Procedure

Warm Up Gather the class to set the stage for today's learning

Writers experiment with a variety of character perspectives and consider which might tell a powerful story. Remind students of all they have learned through their reading of historical fiction and research. History often changes because regular, everyday people make the decision to stand up against adversity in ways large and small. Also, sometimes stories are told from the perspective of a witness to history, someone on the edges of the actual event. This, too, can be an interesting way to tell a story. Keeping this in mind, ask students to think about the narrator in *Roll of Thunder, Hear My Cry* and their Historical Fiction Book Club texts: Whom do they consider to be strong narrators? Why? What qualities do strong narrators bring to the telling of the story?

> Before we get started today, I'd like you to think about all of the narrators you've met over the course of this lesson set, either from *Roll of Thunder, Hear My Cry* or from your Historical Fiction Book Club texts. Turn to a partner and talk about the narrators that you consider to be the strongest, the ones that tell the best story. Who are they, and what makes them so effective?

Conduct a quick discussion. Chart student responses.

Teach Model what students need to learn and do

In preparation for this portion of the lesson, list several potential characters for your model historical fiction story about the Freedom Riders on the left side of the Character Planning graphic organizer (PDToolkit). Inform your students that they will be writing stories that are told from multiple perspectives. Each story will have three narrators. Circle your choice of narrators, and then model for your students what you are thinking about in terms of their cultural backgrounds and life experiences and how these might influence their perspectives or points of view toward your focus event. Also think aloud about what perspectives might be most challenging for you to write, given your own cultural background and individual experiences. Where will you need to do more research? The chart on the following page includes samples of what your modeling might look like and samples of how students might contribute during the Try segment of the lesson.

> I have listed a few potential characters here on the left side of my chart. I need to evaluate the possibilities in order to select my narrators. I am going to select a couple of Freedom Riders and a Southerner as my narrators. I like the idea of using the perspective of a Southerner who may not be actively involved in anti-integration activities but who is also not willing to embrace integration out of fear of reprisal. The narrative mode for my story, and for your stories, too, will be first person. Now I will do some thinking about my narrators and characters. I need to use what I know about their cultures, backgrounds, and possible life experiences to articulate their points of view. I need to imagine the mind-set of someone living in the South in the early 1960s. I will have to think carefully about how to treat this character thoughtfully because I think he or she might be more complicated than some of the other characters in my story. I might need to do some extra research to show that person's perspective well.

Character Planning graphic organizer

Character	Historical Context	Point of View
Teach segment of the lesson One of the Freedom Riders	**Teach segment of the lesson** This character could be a person from a Northern state, free of a life of overt, legally mandated segregation, who is very concerned about the unfairness of segregation. *or* This character could be an African-American college student who knows that his or her options have been limited by racism.	**Teach segment of the lesson** This character would be passionate about civil rights and specifically interested in the Freedom Rides. Perhaps he or she may be a little idealistic. Willing to put himself or herself at risk to effect change.
The bus driver	Perhaps a Northerner? Someone who is nonpolitical but just can't imagine segregation?	This character is likely to be pro-civil rights as well because he or she is willing to put himself or herself on the line for this cause.
Try segment of the lesson (possible responses) One of the people the Riders meet along the way	**Try segment of the lesson** (possible responses) Someone like this would likely come from a more extreme background. Or perhaps he or she is threatened by African Americans rising in the social/economic sphere. Racist family background?	**Try segment of the lesson** (possible responses) This character is not looking to change the way things are—he or she is afraid of change.
Potential bystanders, maybe at the bus station? Perhaps a Southern person who is not directly involved in the conflict	This person is a product of his or her environment. He or she has lived in this one way (segregated) and knows no other way. There is family and community expectation and pressure to believe that this way is the best way.	This person could go either way. He or she may not feel strongly one way or the other. Or he or she may know that segregation is wrong but be afraid to stand up for what's right. I wonder if many people in the South were confused by the events going on around them.

Try Guide students to quickly rehearse what they need to learn and do in preparation for practice

Ask your students to work in pairs to complete columns two and three for the remaining characters. Remind them to consider the cultural background of each character and to use those ideas to articulate the point of view of that person. Remind students to stretch their thinking about characters with whom they do not personally identify and to make sure they are not stereotyping but are staying rooted in historical fact. Ask them to share their responses, and chart them.

> I could really use your input. Please help me do some more thinking about my characters and narrators. Working with a partner, complete the second and third columns for my remaining characters. Remember to consider the characters' backgrounds and how they might influence their perspectives on the focus event.

After students have shared their thinking, select your narrators. Circle them on your chart, and explain why you have selected these narrators.

> After evaluating all of the potential characters and narrators, I have decided to narrate my story from the point of view of two Freedom Riders and someone who works in the bus station, a shoeshine man. I want these characters to come into contact with one another, and I am excited to see how it will all play out!

Clarify Briefly restate today's teaching objective and explain the practice task(s)

Ask your students to list several possible narrators on the left side of their own blank Character Planning graphic organizer. Their task today will be to evaluate their options and to select three narrators. Emphasize that this is an opportunity to help their readers "see" their focus event from multiple points of view. This is a good place to remind students that when we are trying to see others' points of view, we are always coming from our own perspective, and we have to be on guard against stereotypes creeping into the voices that we write. We need to be honest about what we *don't* know about people in other places and times and use research to improve our writing.

Before moving on to the Practice portion of the lesson, ask students to turn and talk with a neighbor about the first person on their list. **ELL** Enable Language Production—Reading and Writing. Oral language development usually runs ahead of written language development. When you give your ELLs a chance to discuss their ideas, you prepare them to be more successful when they start to write.

> We have been reading *Roll of Thunder, Hear My Cry*, a story written from the perspective of Cassie, a 9-year-old African American girl in the 1930s. As we've discussed, this construct offers the reader insight into one view of that historical time period. It is a powerful way to tell a story. Today we are going to think about what characters we might like to explore in our historical fiction stories. We will also decide who will tell the story. Because we are playing around with perspective, I want us to write a story that has three separate narrators. These narrators can all be written in first person so we can explore the various points of view

of these narrator choices. On the left side of the Character Planning graphic organizer, list the various characters who might have taken part in or witnessed the focus event you have selected. You may want to use the photograph you were inspired by from Writing Lesson 1 to help you think about this task.

> Please turn to a partner to discuss the first person you have listed on the left side of your graphic organizer. Talk about how the historical context may influence his or her perspective on your focus event, and write your thoughts on the right side of your graphic organizer.

Practice Students work independently and/or in small groups to apply today's teaching objective

Students work independently to create realistic characters and select three narrators. Ask your students to work with their character list. Their task is to consider how the place where each character grew up and his or her life experiences might shape his or her point of view toward the focus event of the story. Much of the work in this lesson set has focused on cultural upbringing and perspective; remind your students to consider how characters' beliefs and actions might be shaped by the environment they were raised and live in and where characters might hold individual perspectives that disagree with others and result in conflict. From this conflict grows historical and societal change. Remind your students to consider the perspectives of each character as well as that person's ability to tell a powerful story. Finally, they need to select their narrators. Remind your students that other characters from their list may appear in the story even if they are not one of the narrators.

> Each of you will work with your character list to select each potential narrator's point of view. Continue to work with your character list. Your task is to articulate the perspectives of your narrators.

Wrap Up Check understanding as you guide students to briefly share what they have learned and produced today

At this point in the process it is wise to check in with your writers. You'll want to determine where they are in order to plan interventions for those who might need more support. Ask that students describe their setting and their narrators, including their perspectives, on an exit slip. Collect the exit slip as an assessment.

Exit Slip

What focus event have you selected for your story?

Where will your story take place? Is this a realistic setting? Provide a few details.

What characters have you selected?

Who will your story's three narrators be? What are their points of view or perspectives regarding the event?

Are your characters realistic? Write a brief description here.

Milestone Performance Assessment

Selecting and Establishing Character, Narrator, and Setting

 PD TOOLKIT™

Collect and analyze students' exit slips as a performance-based assessment to determine if students need additional instruction or support as a whole class, in small groups, or one on one. **ELL** Assess for Content and Language Understanding—Formative Assessment. Notice both your ELLs' progress in the content objective and where they might need support and scaffolding with their developing English skills.

 Use this checklist to assess student writing plans.

Standards Alignment: W.7.3, W.7.4, W.7.5, W.7.10

Task	Achieved	Notes
Select and describe a realistic setting.		
Select three narrators.		
Articulate point of view/ perspective of each narrator.		
Create realistic characters.		
Provide a brief character description.		

Writing Lesson 5

▼ Teaching Objective

Writers compose a story from three different perspectives.

Close Reading Opportunity

▼ Standards Alignment

RI.7.1, RI.7.2, RI.7.3, RI.7.10, W.7.3, W.7.4, W.7.5, W.7.6, W.7.10, SL.7.1, SL.7.2, SL.7.6, L.7.1, L.7.2, L.7.3, L.7.6

▼ Materials

- Sample Informational Text: *The Freedom Riders* (Appendix 7.5)
- Sample Historical Fiction Text: *Riding for Freedom* (Appendix 7.7)
- Historical Fiction Planning Chart (from Writing Lesson 2)
- Character Planning graphic organizer (from Writing Lesson 4)
- List of Transitional Words and Phrases (Appendix 7.8)

- Charting supplies or interactive whiteboard
- A collection of informational articles and documents for students to use for research

▼ To the Teacher

In this lesson, students will begin to draft their stories in earnest. We suggest using Google Drive as a drafting tool. Google Drive allows writers to share their work, readers to comment, and teachers to conference electronically. Ultimately, your students' stories could be published as online books via such websites as www.epubbud.com where they can be read and shared.

We have provided a Sample Historical Fiction Text: *Riding for Freedom* (Appendix 7.7) for you to use as a model. You may choose to write your own model text instead. We suggest that students model their stories on *Roll of Thunder, Hear My Cry* in that they will use first-person narrative mode. However, we also suggest that students create multiple narrators in order to practice using various perspectives. Therefore, each student's story will be told in three parts from the perspectives of multiple narrators. Students will use their planning materials to write their stories. In addition you will discuss the use of transitions and the way transitions help to move the plot from one stage to another.

The goals of this lesson will take more than one class period to accomplish, so plan accordingly.

▼ Procedure

`Warm Up` Gather the class to set the stage for today's learning

Prompt your students to work with a neighbor to list the elements of historical fiction that they will want to include in their stories. These elements will be represented on a checklist they will use to keep track of the project's requirements. **ELL** Enable Language Production—Reading and Writing. A checklist of requirements will help your ELLs stay organized and zero in on what the most important components of historical fiction are. This focus demystifies the genre for students.

> The time has come to pull all of the pieces together to craft your historical fiction stories! Before we get started, please turn to your neighbor and quickly list all the elements that we will want to include in our stories. Let's share our responses to make sure we are clear about our expectations.

List your students' responses, and be sure to fill in any gaps. Note that a lesson on dialogue follows this one. Your list should look something like this:

Elements of Our Historical Fiction Stories:

- Stories are based on a true event from a real time period in history.
- The narrative mode is first person.
- The story is written in three parts and uses three narrators.
- The main characters are realistic with clear points of view toward the focus event that reflect their background experiences.
- The historical setting is realistic and includes details based on researched facts about the event and time period.
- Dialogue enhances the development of character point of view.
- The writer uses transitions to move the story from one idea to the next.
- There is a logical conclusion to each of the three parts.

`Teach` Model what students need to learn and do

During today's model, you will use the Sample Historical Fiction Text: *Riding for Freedom* (Appendix 7.7) to show your students how you have included the elements from the list in the crafting of your story. Explain that as students plot their own stories, they should pay close attention to transitions. In order for a plot to progress logically, writers use transition words to move the reader from one idea to the next. For your convenience, we include a List of Transitional Words and Phrases (Appendix 7.8) that students can use

to help guide them. **ELL** Identify and Communicate Content and Language Objectives—Language Form and Function. This is a very important lesson for your ELLs as it explicitly teaches them how authors signal key information about time to their readers. This will support both their reading comprehension and their written composition of text. You may want to distribute this list prior to jumping in today so students are able to reference this list as you read aloud.

As you read the Sample Historical Fiction Text: *Riding for Freedom* aloud, charge your students with the task of listening for the presence of transition words as well as identifying the elements in the text. (SL.7.2)

> As I read my draft aloud, listen for evidence of the elements from our list so you can get an idea of the types of things you need to include in your stories. In addition, notice the transition words and phrases that I used to move from one idea to the next. I will stop after the first narrator's story so we can discuss what we are noticing.

Here is a sampling of items your students might notice from Narrator 1: Charles Person

- Narrative mode is first person; Charles is telling the story using the pronoun *I*.
- Information about Charles's educational background is included; he was not allowed to apply to Georgia Institute of Technology because of his race.
- Inclusion of the date of the Freedom Riders' departure: May 4, 1961
- Mention of the *Freedom 7* space flight: a historical event that actually took place.
- More character background: He spent 16 days in jail—this has probably influenced him to take more action.
- Nice descriptive passage about lunch counters—helps the reader to picture the feel or vibe of the overall setting, the American South, at this time.
- The bus pulls into Charlotte, North Carolina, a state in the American South. This is where the action of this particular focus event takes place.
- Description of the inside of the bus station: Both the waiting room and the shoeshine counter have signs that read "Whites Only." This is historically accurate and also sets the scene for the event—the riders are clearly not welcome at this bus station.
- Introduction of the shoeshine man and the interaction between him and Charles.
- Transitions: paragraph 3: *This all started for me . . .*; paragraph 4: *Sometimes, outside the lunch counter, on the sidewalk . . .*; paragraph 6: *When at last we pulled into Charlotte . . .*

Try Guide students to quickly rehearse what they need to learn and do in preparation for practice

Sepy/Fotolia

Ask that students work in their historical fiction groups to read the rest of the Sample Historical Fiction Text: *Riding for Freedom*. They will mark the text in the places where they find evidence of the elements of historical fiction. In addition, they will notice where the writer uses transition words or phrases. Bring students back together to share their findings. Chart and name what students notice.

Clarify Briefly restate today's teaching objective and explain the practice task(s)

Often it is helpful for writers, or anyone who is embarking on a project, to share ideas orally in order to talk through their thinking. In the spirit of this

idea, encourage students to turn to a neighbor to share their story ideas: the event, the setting, and the narrators. Ask them to consider how each narrator will view the event. Also, refer students to their transition list. Ask that they mark several transition words and phrases they might try to incorporate into their historical fiction stories.

Practice Students work independently and/or in small groups to apply today's teaching objective

Have students work independently to draft their stories. Have them use their planning materials from Writing Lessons 1 to 5 to guide them as they write. Remind them to be mindful of transitions as they move from one idea to the next. They should refer to the list of transitional words and phrases they selected to help them. As students write their multiview stories, they should be sure to include the elements listed during the Warm Up. **ELL** Identify and Communicate Content and Language Objectives—Check for Understanding. Make sure your ELLs are making good use of the transitional words and phrases. Help them see that these are tools for communicating more clearly with readers and that skilled writers use transitions so their audience can follow the train of their writing.

Wrap Up Check understanding as you guide students to briefly share what they have learned and produced today

As you circulate among your students, take note of students who are making smart decisions. Perhaps they are using their transition charts or looking at mentor texts for ideas or referring back to their nonfiction sources. Identify these best practices, and share them at the end of class.

Writing Lesson 6 ·

▼ **Teaching Objective**

Writers use dialogue to emphasize point of view

Close Reading Opportunity

▼ **Standards Alignment**

RL.7.1, RL.7.6, RL.7.10, W.7.3, W.7.4, W.7.5, W.7.10, SL.7.1, SL.7.2, SL.7.6, L.7.1, L.7.2, L.7.3, L.7.6

▼ **Materials**

- *Roll of Thunder, Hear My Cry* by Mildred B. Taylor
- Historical Fiction Book Club texts
- Sample Historical Fiction Text: *Riding for Freedom* (Appendix 7.7)
- Student drafts

▼ To the Teacher

In this lesson, you will be exploring the power of dialogue. Middle school students typically love to write with dialogue. The problem is that many of them forget to make the dialogue important to the story and instead compose a string of conversation that means little and goes nowhere— "Hi . . . How are you? . . . I'm fine . . . What's new? . . . Not much . . ." and so on—uneventful and doing little to add to the story or connect to the central idea. Dialogue, when used well, is an entertaining way to move the story forward as characters describe setting and events through speech. A focus of this lesson set is perspective. Dialogue should be used to reveal important information about the characters and their points of view. Sometimes dialogue is valuable in what it doesn't say. Characters can be very chatty, revealing a lot when they speak, but we should also pay attention when characters say very little to one another. A scarcity of words can actually speak volumes.

For this lesson, you will initially direct your students to find passages in *Roll of Thunder, Hear My Cry* and their Historical Fiction Book Club texts that include dialogue that develops experiences, events, and/or characters. The model text for this lesson will be the Sample Historical Fiction Text: *Riding for Freedom* (Appendix 7.7). Students will then go back into their drafts to find places to either include dialogue or to revise existing dialogue. We want to stress the importance of meaningful conversation among our characters. **ELL** Provide Comprehensible Input—Models. ELLs will need to see many examples of how you, their peers, and published authors incorporate dialogue to advance stories. This is a difficult skill that requires sophisticated and specialized uses of language.

▼ Procedure

Warm Up Gather the class to set the stage for today's learning

Ask your students to take a moment to reflect on the stories they've been reading to consider how dialogue helps authors develop experience, events, and characters. Use this opportunity to make sure students understand dialogue, how it works, and why it is important.

> Can you think of a few examples in your reading when an author has used dialogue to help us learn about the event taking place or the character's point of view? Skim back over your books to find some examples of strong dialogue. Mark the text with a sticky note. Do you find the use of dialogue in this instance helpful to you as a reader? Why or why not?

Allow students time to discuss the use of dialogue in their own reading.

Teach Model what students need to learn and do

During this portion of the lesson, you will model your thinking about the inclusion of dialogue in the model piece about the Freedom Riders. There is not a great deal of dialogue in this piece, but the dialogue that is included matters because it illustrates the way two people, one white and one black, might have communicated with each other in the 1960s.

> Today I want to refer back to the Sample Historical Fiction Text: *Riding for Freedom*. This time we will be looking specifically at the dialogue that is included. Here's a snippet from the first narrator in the story, Charles Person.

Read the text aloud.

> In one corner of the station was a shoeshine counter with a wooden sign that read "Whites Only." A man sat on a stool with a rag over his shoulder and jars of open polish beside him. I handed him the correct change and settled into a chair. Nothing happened; he didn't move.
>
> "May I have a shoeshine?" I asked.
>
> "No," he said. He wouldn't look me in the eye. "Please leave."
>
> I have made a deliberate choice to keep the dialogue in this story very simple because it would not have been realistic for these two characters to have a long, involved conversation. This is an awkward and difficult moment for both men, and I wanted the reader to feel that discomfort.
>
> Here's another piece from the perspective of my second narrator, Frank, the shoeshine man at the bus station.
>
> "May I have a shoeshine?" he asked.
>
> "No," I said. I couldn't look him in the eye. "Please leave."
>
> The young man stayed very still, waiting for me to say more. I tried to swallow, but my mouth had gone dry. I wanted to tell him I was sorry. I admired how brave he was.
>
> But I didn't say that. Instead, I simply repeated, "Please leave."
>
> After what felt like a very long time, he nodded, stood up, and walked away.
>
> In this part, you'll notice I added another short piece of dialogue, repeating the words "Please leave" spoken by Frank. I wanted the reader to know that Frank does have some realization that this situation is not fair and that he should probably shine Charles's shoes, but he feels so much pressure and fear that he can only say the words that reflect his desire to keep his job.

Dialogue also plays an important role in emphasizing a character's point of view in *Roll of Thunder, Hear My Cry*. For additional practice, we suggest the short exchange as the white children's school bus passes the Logans in Chapter 1. The dialogue clearly reveals Little Man's frustration and bewilderment about how they are treated by the riders on the bus and the fact that the black school does not have a bus. It also conveys his siblings' sympathy for his view in contrast to the less sensitive T.J.

Try Guide students to quickly rehearse what they need to learn and do in preparation for practice

Have students work with a partner to look closely at their drafts with a focus on adding thoughtful and effective dialogue. Explain that they should identify places where adding dialogue would enhance their piece. Collaboratively, students should orally rehearse their ideas and make notes on their drafts about their plans to incorporate dialogue.

Ask students to particularly consider where dialogue would strengthen the story by emphasizing the character's point of view.

Identify places in your draft where you might include or revise dialogue. Work with a partner to discuss your ideas. You may read the dialogue you have and talk about the ways that you might make it stronger.

Have a quick discussion here. **ELL** Enable Language Production— Increasing Interaction. Hearing their peers' examples and getting feedback on their own will help ELLs compose more effective dialogue.

Clarify Briefly restate today's teaching objective and explain the practice task(s)

Reiterate that dialogue is an effective technique that writers use to bring a character to life and to reinforce his or her point of view. Direct students to add dialogue to their stories that conveys the characters' feelings and points of view.

Practice Students work independently and/or in small groups to apply today's teaching objective

Writers will add new dialogue or revise existing dialogue. Students should be wrapping up the rough drafts of their historical fiction stories.

Wrap Up Check understanding as you guide students to briefly share what they have learned and produced today

Ask students to share what they accomplished today. Encourage them to share their process or a snippet of their dialogue. This will be the last lesson devoted to the writing of their Historical Fiction stories. At this point, students should finish writing their drafts before they engage in writing author's notes, introduced in the next lesson.

Writing Lesson 7

▼ **Teaching Objective**

Writers plan author's notes to describe and reflect on their historical fiction writing experience.

Close Reading Opportunity

▼ **Standards Alignment**

RI.7.1, RI.7.5, RI.7.10, W.7.3, W.7.4, W.7.5, W.7.10, SL.7.1, SL.7.6, L.7.1, L.7.2, L.7.3, L.7.6

▼ **Materials**

- Author's Note from *Roll of Thunder, Hear My Cry*
- Author's note from *The Watsons Go to Birmingham—1963* by Christopher Paul Curtis
- Author's notes or epilogues from Historical Fiction Book Club texts
- Historical Fiction Book Club texts
- Charting supplies or interactive whiteboard

▼ **To the Teacher**

At this point, your students will have completed their historical fiction stories. Today students will begin to write their author's notes. There is no single correct format for this kind of writing, so we suggest that students have a look at several versions. For purposes of a model, we will read the author's note at the start of *Roll of Thunder, Hear My Cry* in which she discusses her inspiration from her father's storytelling. Afterwards, students will also read the epilogue to *The Watsons Go to Birmingham—1963* by Christopher Paul Curtis as well as samples from their own Historical Fiction Book Club texts. This inquiry into other authors' techniques will help them build the big picture of what may be included in an author's note and prompt them to think about how they plan to craft their own notes.

▼ **Procedure**

Warm Up Gather the class set the stage for today's learning

Ask students if they have noticed the author's notes or epilogues (explain that these terms are often interchangeable) in the back of their Historical

Fiction Book Club texts. Explain that writers often include this short essay at the conclusion of a book as a way to share their thinking and to give context for the story they have written. Historical fiction writers tend to explain such things as why they selected this topic, why they decided on a particular character's point of view, how they did their research, what they found as they conducted the research, and what they learned from the process. In addition to providing background information to stories, "author's notes" will seek to answer this question: Why is this an important story to tell? This is an authentic informational essay, a perfect example of how this kind of essay writing exists in the "real" world. Then explain that students will begin to write their own author's notes for their historical fiction stories.

> You are now writers of historical fiction, and it is time to write your author's note! But first, let's look closely at the author's note at the start of *Roll of Thunder, Hear My Cry.*

Teach Model what students need to learn and do

As you read aloud Mildred B. Taylor's author's note, highlight the various parts or elements of the text. Identify the information that provides important personal background about the author and her purpose in writing the book.

Begin a running list of parts or elements that *may* be included in the author's note to a historical fiction story. In this case, Mildred B. Taylor provides:

- Explanation of why the she chose to write about the events/time period: She wished to preserve the legacy of her father's storytelling.
- Her background: She grew up in the South, like the characters in the book.

Try Guide students to quickly rehearse what they need to learn and do in preparation for practice

Read aloud the epilogue to *The Watsons Go to Birmingham—1963.* Also read aloud another sample or two, perhaps from the students' Historical Fiction Book Club texts. Discuss additional elements that may be found in historical fiction author's notes. Add to the list of author's note elements. Students may find the following:

- Information on sources used for research
- Reflection on the process of research and/or writing
- Brief historical information about the event/time period
- Opinion about the event(s) that took place during the time period
- Explanation of why this is a topic worth remembering and honoring

ELL Provide Comprehensible Input—Models. Here you are breaking down the structure and content of a strong author's note. This will help all your students, but particularly ELLs, to understand what characterizes a good author's note so they can incorporate aspects of the model into their own work.

Clarify Briefly restate today's teaching objective and explain the practice task(s)

Lisa F. Young/Fotolia

Review the author's note elements discovered and listed in the Teach and Try. Explain that Practice will be spent planning their personal author's notes.

Practice Students work independently and/or in small groups to apply today's teaching objective

Now that students have read several examples of "author's notes," they should jot some notes of key items they would like to include in their own author's notes. Direct them to address the bullets listed in the Teach and Try. Have them share their thinking with a partner.

Wrap Up Check understanding as you guide students to briefly share what they have learned and produced today

Ask several volunteers to share their ideas thus far. Notice and illuminate where students have successfully addressed the required elements.

Writing Lesson 8

▼ Teaching Objective

Writers compose author's notes to describe and reflect on their historical fiction writing experience.

▼ Standards Alignment

W.7.3, W.7.4, W.7.5, W.7.6, W.7.10, SL.7.1, SL.7.4, SL.7.6, L.7.1, L.7.2, L.7.3, L.7.6

▼ Materials

- Author's notes from a variety of historical fiction texts
- Charting supplies or interactive whiteboard
- Resource materials
- Students' drafts

▼ To the Teacher

In this lesson, students will use your feedback to continue drafting their author's notes by adding details to support their ideas and strengthen their writing. Distribute the drafts with your feedback. If you have noticed any particular patterns of need, use this time to address those needs. If the issue is pervasive, address it in a whole-class mini-lesson. Otherwise tackle the needs one on one or in small groups. **ELL** Identify and Communicate Content and Language Objectives—Language Form and Function. This is a good opportunity to discuss with your ELLs how the different purposes of the story and the author's notes might require different uses of language. Talk about some formal alternatives to any informal features you have noticed in their plans, and discuss why an author might choose to change his or her language when shifting from narrative to expository mode. Talk about this in terms of purpose, convention, and audience—not in terms of correctness. Each form is "correct" only in its particular context for the author's specific purpose.

▼ Procedure

Warm Up Gather the class to set the stage for today's learning

During this lesson, students will continue to draft their author's notes. Their specific task will be to incorporate details into their writing. Ask that they review the list you created in Writing Lesson 7.

> During our last writing session, you organized your thinking in preparation for writing your author's notes. Today you will be writing, and as you do so, you will want to include interesting details to support your ideas. Let's take a few minutes to revisit the various elements we've identified so that you'll be ready to go when we sit down to write.

> When we explored examples of author's notes, we found that each one included at least some of these elements:

- Explanation of why the author chose to write about the time period
- The author's background
- Brief historical information about the focus event/time period
- Opinion about the event(s) that took place during the time period
- Explanation of why this is a topic worth remembering and honoring
- Information on sources used for research
- Reflection on the process of research and/or writing

Teach Model what students need to learn

Model for your students the way you might think through the details of your writing.

> Today you will begin to write your author's notes. You will refer back to your notes and your sources for details to support your ideas. For example, if I were writing an author's note about why it is important to remember and write about the Freedom Riders, I would want to recognize the riders for their commitment to the cause of civil rights. To support that idea, I would be sure to include details like how some of the riders weren't Southerners and most were college students who stepped away from their everyday lives to protest segregation. I might even find information about a particular rider and share an anecdote about that person.

> I would also want to include some details about my own background and how it has influenced me to write my story about the Freedom Riders. I grew up in a Northern state in New England. Fighting for civil rights was not a part of my life because I was not born until the last half of the 1960s. My parents were open-minded and engaged with what was happening during that time, but they were by no means politically involved. They were not activists. I guess a part of me wonders why they weren't moved to act. I wonder if I would have been moved to do something. Would I have been too scared? Or too removed from what was going on in the Southern states? I hope I would have stepped up like the Freedom Riders did, but, truthfully, I am not sure. The riders have my admiration. This is why I write about them today. My own experiences also meant I had an extra challenge in trying to represent perspectives that are different from my own. I wanted to identify with the Freedom Rider in my story, so it felt easy to write in his voice, but I had a very hard time understanding the Southern narrator in my story. I had to think hard about the factors that might have shaped his behavior.

> These are the kinds of details you will be using in your own writing.

Try Guide students to quickly rehearse what they need to learn and do in preparation for practice

Have students work with a partner to discuss the details they might want to include to support their thinking. Circulate as students discuss and offer support where needed. **ELL** Enable Language Production—Increasing Interaction. Planning their author's notes with their peers will help ELLs get their ideas ready to write.

> Let's take a few minutes to discuss the details you might want to include in your author's note. Share with a partner and talk about the kinds of details you might use to support your thinking. Let's quickly share some of your ideas.

Clarify Briefly restate today's teaching objective and explain the practice task(s)

Reiterate the importance of including supporting details in an author's note. Have several students share where they intend to add details to their notes.

> Writers support their ideas with interesting details. We want to create interesting pieces, and we also want our readers to learn about our thinking process! Let's share.

Practice Students work independently and/or in small groups to apply today's teaching objective

Students draft their author's notes taking care to include supporting details where appropriate.

Wrap Up Check understanding as you guide students to briefly share what they have learned and produced today

Prompt your students to discuss their process. Use the following questions as a guide:

- How are we feeling about our author's notes?
- Would anyone like to share what he or she learned today about this writing process?
- Might some people like to share an interesting detail they are using to support their ideas?

Milestone Performance Assessment

Author's Notes   PD **pd** TOOLKIT™

Collect and analyze students' author's notes as a performance-based assessment to determine if students need additional instruction or support as a whole class, in small groups, or one on one. **ELL** Assess

for Content and Language Understanding—Formative Assessment. Check to make sure your ELLs are on the right track with both the content of their author's notes and the linguistic forms they use to explain that content.

 Use this checklist to assess student work on author's notes.

Standards Alignment: W.7.3, W.7.4, W.7.5, W.7.6, W.7.10, L.7.1, L.7.2, L.7.3

Task	Achieved	Notes
Include explanation of why the author chose to write about the events/time period.		
Provide brief historical information about the events/time period.		
Include opinion about the events that took place during the time period.		
Provide information on sources used for research.		
Include a reflection on the process of research and/or writing.		
Include an explanation of why this is a topic worth remembering and honoring.		

Writing Lesson 9

▼ Teaching Objective

Writers collaborate on revision and editing.

▼ Standards Alignment

W.7.3, W.7.4, W.7.5, W.7.6, W.7.10, SL.7.1, SL.7.6, L.7.1, L.7.2, L.7.3, L.7.6

▼ Materials

- Peer Revision Planner (downloadable PDF in the PDToolkit)
- Revising and Editing Checklist (Appendix 7.9)
- Charting supplies or interactive whiteboard to create What are our responsibilities during a peer conferencing session? chart
- Student drafts of historical fiction stories and author's notes

▼ To the Teacher

Today students will work in pairs to revise both their historical fiction stories and their author's notes. When they have completed the revision and editing process, they will be ready to publish their pieces. We provide both low-tech and high-tech options for publishing and sharing their writing in Writing Lesson 10. **ELL** Enable Language Production—Increasing Interaction. Peer discussion gives your ELLs a low-pressure environment to hear examples of how to revise and to practice the language they need to express their own ideas about revision. Working with English-proficient peers can also help ELLs learn new techniques for accomplishing their goals with their stories.

▼ Procedure

Warm Up Gather the class to set the stage for today's learning

On chart paper or on your interactive whiteboard, create a chart with this question at the top: What are our responsibilities during a peer conferencing session? Create two columns, "Writer" and "Reviewer."

> Today you will work with a partner to revise your writing. Remember that revision literally means "seeing again," so we'll be giving these pieces a very thorough read. It is important to make this a productive time for each partner. Take a minute to think about the job you will do both as a writer and as the reviewer of someone else's work. What are our responsibilities during a peer

conferencing session? Let's make a list that we can use as a guide while we're conferencing.

Chart responses. Students should chime in with suggestions such as be prepared, be respectful, give the text your full attention, and remember that our focus at this point is revision, not editing.

> Each of you will play two roles today: writer and reviewer, and we want everyone to have equal time, so I will be keeping us on a schedule as we work.

Teach Model what students need to learn and do

Encourage your writers to take the lead during these peer conferences. Using their Revising and Editing Checklist (Appendix 7.9) as a reference, ask that they read through their work in order to identify places in their pieces where they could use some support. **ELL** Provide Comprehensible Input—Models. You are continuing to bring your ELLs into the world of English writers by showing them how revision works and demystifying the process of collaborative exchange among writers.

> Also, I want you as the writer to be in control of this conversation, so we will take a few minutes to work with our own texts to decide where we want feedback. Before we proceed, please read through your work, and as you do so, use your checklist to find places in both your story and your author's note where you need some support. Record your thoughts on your Peer Revision Planner. Each one of you must come to your peer revision conversation with something concrete to talk about with your partner. Use the Revising and Editing Checklist to help you and your partner focus your critiquing.

 Remind your students of the importance of engaging in effective collaborative discussions during this peer revision process. (SL.7.1)

> Here are our agreed-upon guidelines:

- Each person comes prepared to work with their graphic organizers complete.
- Each person reads their partner's piece.
- Each writer is in control of their writer's conference—their questions and concerns guide the conversation.
- Each reviewer offers real, positive, and constructive feedback so that the writer leaves the conference feeling clear about next steps.
- Each writer commits to a revision and follows through with that revision.

Peer Revision Planner

Writer: What piece will you be considering for revision today?
Writer: Which part of your piece or aspect of your writing would you like to talk about today?
Writer: What are your questions or concerns? Be specific! The more specific you are, the better feedback you'll get!
Reviewer: What advice can you give the writer regarding his or her concerns? How can the writer strengthen this piece? What else did you notice about this piece of writing? Start with the positive, and be constructive!
Writer: Make a note here about any changes you intend to make to your draft as a result of this revision process.

ELL Provide Comprehensible Input—Organizers. This planner can scaffold the revising and editing process for your ELLs.

Try Guide students to quickly rehearse what they need to learn and do in preparation for practice

Revising and Editing Checklist

Task	Yes/No
Revising	
Historical Fiction Narrative	
Is my story based on a true event?	
Did I use a consistent first-person narrative mode?	
Does my narrative contain three sections, each with its own narrator?	
Are my main characters (narrators) realistic with clear points of view toward the focus event that reflect their background experiences?	
Did I include a realistic historical setting with details based on researched facts?	
Does my dialogue enhance development of character point of view?	

Task	Yes/No
Did I use transitions to move the story from one idea to the next?	
Did I include a logical conclusion to each of the three parts?	
Author's Note	
Did I include my own personal reasons for writing about this particular historical event/time period?	
Did I provide brief historical information about the event(s)/time period?	
Did I share my opinion about the event(s) that took place during the time period?	
Did I provide information on sources used for research?	
Did I reflect on the process of research and/or writing?	
Did I include an explanation of why this is a topic worth writing about?	
COPS Editing	
Did I check and correct my **c**apitalization?	
Did I check and correct my **o**rder and usage of words?	
Did I check and correct my **p**unctuation?	
Did I check and correct my **s**pelling?	

Ask that students work in pairs to revise their drafts using the Revising and Editing Checklist (Appendix 7.9) as a guide. **ELL** Enable Language Production—Reading and Writing. It can be difficult to tell if an ELL's nonstandard usage is a learner error or a feature of the dialect he or she is learning from their peers. Different uses of English carry different social weight, and all speakers adjust their language according to the demands of the social context. Emphasize for your students the idea of *situational appropriateness* and that they need to be informed about different sorts of language so they can choose how to present themselves.

> Let's get started! All writers revise and edit their writing. There is no such thing as a perfect first draft, so I urge you to consider this an opportunity to gain another writer's perspective and to improve your piece.

Clarify Briefly restate today's teaching objective and explain the practice task(s)

Students are now ready to revise their drafts based on the feedback they received during their peer revision session. During a class discussion, prompt your students to share one piece of advice that they received from their peer reviser. If some of your students still seem unsure as to their next steps, note their names and either conference with them one on one or gather them as a group during the Practice portion of the lesson. Remind students to use the notes from their revision session to do this work.

> Please make sure you have committed to making changes to your draft, and note these on your Peer Revision Planner. Before we begin the work of revision, let's have a quick discussion. What is the most helpful piece of advice you were given today?

Practice Students work independently and/or in small groups to apply today's teaching objective

Students will revise and edit their pieces using the Revising and Editing Checklist (Appendix 7.9) as a guide. Use this time to conference with those students who remain unsure of their next steps. You may decide to work with students one on one or gather them into a small group. **ELL** Enable Language Production-Reading and Writing. Make sure your ELLs understand that revision is a normal part of writing and that it's good to find areas to improve. Then help them to figure out *how* to add what is missing: Was it an oversight, or are they not sure how to make their meaning clear in English?

Wrap Up Check understanding as you guide students to briefly share what they have learned and produced today

Check student progress. They should be ready to publish their pieces. Ask students to share which items on the checklist were most challenging and how they solved problems they found.

Milestone Performance Assessment

Revising and Editing Writing   PD TOOLKIT™

Collect and analyze students' writing as a performance-based assessment to determine if students need additional instruction or support as a whole class, in small groups, or one on one. **ELL** Assess for Content and Language Understanding—Summative Assessment. This is an opportunity for you to assess your ELLs' language and content needs, especially revising and editing strategies. Notice where their gaps are:

Have they misunderstood something about the characteristics of historical fiction? Or do they struggle with the language they need to express those characteristics? Do they need support on written conventions (spelling, punctuation)? Are they able to make conscious choices about which varieties of English to use? Use this information to plan upcoming lessons.

  Use this checklist to assess student revisions and editing.

Standards Alignment: W.7.4, W.7.5, W.7.10, L.7.1, L.7.2, L.7.3

Task	Achieved	Notes
Revising		
Historical Fiction Narrative		
Story based on a true event.		
Use consistent first-person narrative mode.		
Contains three sections, each with its own narrator.		
Main characters (narrators) are realistic with clear points of view toward the focus events that reflect their background experiences.		
Include realistic historical setting with details based on researched facts.		
Dialogue enhances development of character point of view.		
Use transitions to move story from one idea to the next.		
Logical conclusion to each of the three parts.		

Task	Achieved	Notes
Author's Note		
Include own personal reasons for writing about this particular historical event/time period.		
Provide brief historical information about the event(s)/time period.		
Share opinion about the event(s) that took place during the time period.		
Provide information on sources used for research.		

Task	Achieved	Notes
Reflect on the process of research and/or writing.		
Include an explanation of why this topic is worth writing about.		
COPS Editing*		
Capitalization.		
Order and usage of words.		
Punctuation.		
Spelling.		

*We recommend that you focus your assessment lens in these areas. Select and assess a few skills that you have previously taught or that have emerged as areas of need in your ongoing assessment of student writing.

Writing Lesson 10

▼ Teaching Objective

Writers share and celebrate their work.

▼ Standards Alignment

W.7.6, SL.7.1, SL.7.2, SL.7.4, SL.7.6, L.7.1, L.7.2, L.7.3, L.7.6

▼ Materials

- Published historical fiction stories including author's notes

▼ To the Teacher

Now that we have arrived at the final lesson of this set, it is time to share and celebrate the work of your writers. It is a triumph to have worked through the process of reading, researching, writing, and revising, and we want to recognize it as such. There are two points worth driving home here. The first is that it is crucial to create a safe atmosphere in which to recognize and celebrate our students' work. Secondly, it is equally important to encourage all students to be accountable by supporting and commenting on the work of their peers. At this point in the process, peer-generated questions and comments should be supportive and positive. Having said that, there are many, many ways to achieve these two goals. For this particular lesson set, we have suggested several options, both low- and high-tech (on the next page). Once you have selected the means of sharing and celebration, you may need to allow a class period or two for preparation. This is all worth the time spent as it speaks to the ways in which "real" writers authentically share their work with the public.

▼ Procedure

Warm Up Gather the class to set the stage for today's learning

Congratulate students for all of their hard work.

> Bravo! Today you are published authors of historical fiction! When professional authors have completed their books, they consider a variety of ways to present their work to the public. Now that you have worked through this whole process of reading, researching, writing, and revising, it is time to share your published stories with the world.

Goal	Low-Tech	High-Tech
Students will publish their historical fiction narratives and author's notes.	• Students dress as their main character and perform a dramatic reading of a critical portion of their story. Perhaps this is done in your school's performance space and shared with the larger school community. Classmates would respond in writing to a prompt regarding the ways in which the writers brought the Civil Rights–era to life, citing examples from a designated selection of stories. • Writers stage a reading of their work. Peers are expected to pose thoughtful questions regarding their classmates' stories.	• Writers create their own author's website in which they include an excerpt from their work or the work in its entirety. Peers read a designated selection of their classmates' stories and respond via a comments section on the site. • Writers share their stories via www.epubbud.com/. Peers act as book reviewers and write short "blurbs" about each story.

Teach Model what students need to learn and do

Explain to your students the chosen method for sharing and celebrating their stories. As always, it is helpful to provide a model. You may model with your own work, or you may use samples of authors' websites, online videos of authors reading their work, or excerpts of book reviews (the short ones often found on the back covers of books).

Try Guide students to quickly rehearse what they need to learn and do in preparation for practice

Provide students with clear expectations regarding the respectful sharing of their work. Remind them to be respectful of one another and constructive with their comments. Ask them to remember that this is a celebration of all of their hard work. Check in with students to ascertain whether they want to add anything to the expectations. Allow them time to prepare their presentations.

Clarify Briefly restate today's teaching objective and explain the practice task(s)

Remind your students that the focus is both sharing and celebrating. Your writers have a responsibility to present their work clearly and neatly, following the guidelines you have created and shared. In addition, their peers have a responsibility to be respectful and supportive of the writers.

We are both sharing our historical fiction stories as writers and experiencing them as listeners or readers. We are a community of learners, and we each have a responsibility during this celebration period. You have all worked very hard, and each of you deserves our attention and support.

Practice Students work independently and/or in small groups to apply today's teaching objective

Students share their historical fiction stories. Peers respond to the stories.

As they respond to one another's stories, remind students to explain how the ideas in the text clarify the topic. (SL.7.1, SL.7.2)

Wrap Up Check understanding as you guide students to briefly share what they have learned and produced today

Allow some time for students to respond to one another's stories. As a final wrap-up, conduct a class discussion about the process of reading, researching, and writing historical fiction.

Remind students as they speak in a class discussion that it is important to be aware of contexts and tasks and to speak accordingly. (SL.7.6) **ELL** Enable Language Production—Listening and Speaking. Remember that some students might not use what you consider formal English because they don't know that particular register of the language. Newcomer ELLs may still be acquiring the mechanics of English; orally proficient ELLs may be accustomed to a nonstandard variety of English. It is important to notice how students use language and to give them the tools to make conscious choices about what style of language they will use in different settings. At the same time, take great care in clarifying points of mechanics and usage with ELLs using nonstandard language so that you do so in a way that does not make them reluctant to contribute their ideas in the future.

Use the following questions as a guide:

- Having worked through the process of writing these stories, can you describe your experience?
- What was positive about the experience? What was challenging?
- What was the most important or interesting information you learned through your research?
- How did that information influence the story you wrote?
- As a writer, what do you think you did well?
- What will you do differently the next time you write?

Ask students to use the information from this conversation to write a short piece about what they learned through the process of researching and writing their historical fiction stories and author's notes.

GLOSSARY

camera angles and focus: filmmakers frequently adjust the direction, scope, or focus of the camera lens. Filmmakers may widen or narrow the frame of a scene.

central idea: the terms *central idea* and *theme* both can be used to describe the unifying idea or subject of the story. A well-developed central idea often suggests a universal truth about life or human behavior.

color: filmmakers adjust color to establish setting, emphasize something, or suggest a mood.

conflict: the problem or issue that arises in a story.

culture: the beliefs and customs of a particular society or group of people.

episode: related events, or scenes, that make up the plot of a story, including the conflict and resolution.

first-person narrator: a story told from the point of view of a character who participates in the action of the story.

historical context: the setting or conditions in which an event occurs.

historical fiction: tells a tale that happens during a recognizable time period in history, often through the eyes of fictional characters who are part of the story. Factual events, settings, and people are often intermingled with fictional story elements.

lighting: filmmakers may vary the amount of light in a scene for dramatic effect. For instance, filmmakers might use darkened lighting to create a serious or sad feeling.

narrator: the person telling the story.

narrative mode: the method the writer uses to tell, or narrate, the plot of a story.

perspective: how a character views a particular situation. In other words, the attitude or feelings a character has toward key events or individuals in a story.

point of view: how a character views a particular situation. In other words, the attitude or feelings a character has toward key events or individuals in a story. (Synonymous with *perspective*.)

second-person narrator: a story told from the point of view of one character telling the story to another character.

sound: filmmakers may adjust volume, use sound effects, and add music to establish the setting, paint strong images, and affect mood.

third-person narrator: story told from the point of view of someone who is not a character and does not participate in the action. Tells the story as an outside observer. Can be a limited narrator whose knowledge is limited to the thoughts and feelings of only one character or an omniscient narrator who knows all of the thoughts and feelings of every character in the story.

Accompanying *Core Ready for Grades 6–8*, there is an online resource site with media tools that, together with the text, provides you with the tools you need to implement the lesson sets.

The PDToolkit for Pam Allyn's *Core Ready* Series is available free for 12 months after you use the password that comes with the box set for each grade band. After that, you can purchase access for an additional 12 months. If you did not purchase the box set, you can purchase a 12-month subscription at **http://pdtoolkit.pearson.com.**

Be sure to explore and download the resources available at the website. Currently the following resources are available:

- Pearson Children's and Young Adult Literature Database
- Videos
- PowerPoint Presentations
- Student Artifacts
- Photos and Visual Media

- Handouts, Forms, and Posters to supplement your Core-aligned lesson plans
- Lessons and Homework Assignments
- Close Reading Guides and Samples
- Children's Core Literature Recommendations

In the future, we will continue to add additional resources. To learn more, please visit **http://pdtoolkit.pearson.com.**

Grade 8

Revealing Character: The Hero's Journey

Introduction

Everybody loves a hero. They are the courageous, self-sacrificing people setting examples for all of us. Throughout history, people have looked to heroes to guide their ideas of right and wrong. From the stories performed in the amphitheaters by the Ancient Greeks to the Star Wars fans lining up for midnight shows, we all look to the hero to exemplify the values our culture holds dear.

Most eighth graders have learned how to understand characters in the literature they read. They have examined how the setting and plot shape the characters and how particular points of view elicit emotions from the reader. Now they are challenged with analyzing how characters are revealed and how and why decisions are made. The decision by the hero to fight darkness in its myriad shapes is perhaps one of the most common and complex in all of literature. With a deep understanding of the development of the literary character

Why This Lesson Set?

In this lesson set, students will:

- Examine the theme of heroism and analyze its development as it relates to character, setting, and plot over the course of the text

- Analyze how incidents in mythological and fantasy texts propel the action, reveal aspects of a character, or provoke a decision

- Analyze how a modern work of fantasy fiction draws on themes, patterns of events, and character types from traditional literature

- Analyze the extent to which a filmed production of a story stays faithful to or departs from the text

- Develop a literary essay that draws on evidence from a literary text to support analysis

of the hero as well as the examination of the hero's dilemma, students will begin to recognize the commonalities and archetypes in mythology, classic literature, modern literature, and drama.

In this lesson set, students will explore both how a hero shapes a culture and how cultures have shaped the idea of a hero as the key character in a text. We will explore how the heroes of mythology and modern-day literature reveal similar characteristics of innocence and naïveté and then take themselves on a journey that reveals their best qualities: strength, courage, and selflessness. These heroes understand evil and hardship, and they work, along with allies, to make sure good triumphs and the world, real or imagined, is a better place. The students will also be introduced to the genre of mythology and will connect these myths to film and fantasy texts in contemporary culture.

Common Core State Standards Alignment

Reading Standards

RL.8.1 Cite the textual evidence that most strongly supports an analysis of what the text says explicitly as well as inferences drawn from the text.

RL.8.2 Determine a theme or central idea of a text and analyze its development over the course of the text, including its relationship to the characters, setting, and plot; provide an objective summary of the text.

RL.8.3 Analyze how particular lines of dialogue or incidents in a story or drama propel the action, reveal aspects of a character, or provoke a decision.

RL.8.7 Analyze the extent to which a filmed or live production of a story or drama stays faithful to or departs from the text or script, evaluating the choices made by the director or actors.

RL.8.9 Analyze how a modern work of fiction draws on themes, patterns of events, or character types from myths, traditional stories, or religious works such as the Bible, including describing how the material is rendered new.

RL.8.10 By the end of the year, read and comprehend literature, including stories, dramas, and poems, at the high end of grades 6-8 text complexity band independently and proficiently.

RI.8.1 Cite the textual evidence that most strongly supports an analysis of

what the text says explicitly as well as inferences drawn from the text.

RI.8.2 Determine a central idea of a text and analyze its development over the course of the text, including its relationship to supporting ideas; provide an objective summary of the text.

RI.8.10 By the end of the year, read and comprehend literary nonfiction at the high end of the grades 6-8 text complexity band independently and proficiently.

Writing Standards

W.8.2 Write informative/explanatory texts to examine a topic and convey ideas, concepts, and information through the selection, organization, and analysis of relevant content.

a. Introduce a topic clearly, previewing what is to follow; organize ideas, concepts, and information into broader categories; include formatting (e.g., headings), graphics (e.g., charts, tables), and multimedia when useful to aiding comprehension.

b. Develop the topic with relevant, well-chosen facts, definitions, concrete details, quotations, or other information and examples.

c. Use appropriate and varied transitions to create cohesion and clarify the relationships among ideas and concepts.

d. Use precise language and domain-specific vocabulary to inform about or explain the topic.

e. Establish and maintain a formal style.

f. Provide a concluding statement or section that follows from and supports the information or explanation presented.

W.8.4 Produce clear and coherent writing in which the development, organization, and style are appropriate to task, purpose, and audience. (Grade-specific expectations for writing types are defined in standards 1-3 above.)

W.8.5 With some guidance and support from peers and adults, develop and strengthen writing as needed by planning, revising, editing, rewriting, or trying a new approach, focusing on how well purpose and audience have been addressed. (Editing for conventions should demonstrate command of Language standards 1-3 up to and including grade 8 here.)

W.8.6 Use technology, including the Internet, to produce and publish writing and present the relationships between information and ideas efficiently as well as to interact and collaborate with others.

W.8.9 Draw evidence from literary or informational texts to support analysis, reflection, and research.

a. Apply grade 8 Reading standards to literature (e.g., "Analyze how a modern work of fiction draws on themes, patterns of events, or character types from myths, traditional stories, or religious works such as the Bible, including describing how the material is rendered new").

W.8.10 Write routinely over extended time frames (time for research, reflection, and revision) and shorter time frames (a single sitting or a day or two) for a range of discipline-specific tasks, purposes, and audiences.

Speaking and Listening Standards

SL.8.1 Engage effectively in a range of collaborative discussions (one-on-one, in groups, and teacher-led) with diverse partners on grade 8 topics, texts, and issues, building on others' ideas and expressing their own clearly.

SL.8.4 Present claims and findings, emphasizing salient points in a focused, coherent manner with relevant evidence, sound valid reasoning, and well-chosen details; use appropriate eye contact, adequate volume, and clear pronunciation.

SL.8.5 Integrate multimedia and visual displays into presentations to clarify information, strengthen claims and evidence, and add interest.

SL.8.6 Adapt speech to a variety of contexts and tasks, demonstrating command of formal English when indicated or appropriate. (See grade 8 Language standards 1 and 3 <u>here</u> for specific expectations.)

Language Standards

L.8.1 Demonstrate command of the conventions of standard English grammar and usage when writing or speaking.

L.8.2 Demonstrate command of the conventions of standard English

capitalization, punctuation, and spelling when writing.

L.8.3 Use knowledge of language and its conventions when writing, speaking, reading, or listening.

L.8.6 Acquire and use accurately grade-appropriate general academic and domain-specific words and

phrases; gather vocabulary knowledge when considering a word or phrase important to comprehension or expression.

Core Questions

- What is a hero?
- Have there always been heroes?
- Do we need heroes in real life? In literature?
- Do we all have the potential to be a hero?
- What circumstances enable people to display heroic attributes?
- How do heroes help to define a culture?
- What do literary heroes have in common across time?
- How does an author reveal a character to a reader or viewer?

Lesson Set Goals

Within this lesson set, there are many goals we as teachers want to help our students reach.

Reading Goals

- Examine and analyze the elements of the genre of myth. (RL.8.1, RL.8.2, RL.8.3, RL.8.10, W.8.4, W.8.9, W.8.10)
- Examine and analyze the elements of the genre of fantasy. (RL.8.1, RL.8.2, RL.8.3, RL.8.10, W.8.4, W.8.9, W.8.10)
- Identify and describe the theme of heroism in a myth and analyze its development over the course of the text, including its relationship to the characters, setting, and plot; provide an objective summary of the text. (RL.8.1, RL.8.2, RL.8.10, W.8.4, W.8.9, W.8.10, SL.8.1, SL.8.4, SL.8.6, L.8.1, L.8.3, L.8.6)
- Identify and describe the theme of heroism in a fantasy text and analyze its development over the course of the text, including its relationship to the characters, setting, and plot; provide an objective summary of the text.

(RL.8.1, RL.8.2, RL.8.10, W.8.4, W.8.9, W.8.10, SL.8.1, SL.8.4, SL.8.6, L.8.1, L.8.3, L.8.6)

- Identify the character traits of a hero and, through an exploration of heroism, develop a deep understanding of how real people are heroic. (RI.8.1, RI.8.2, RI.8.10, W.8.4, W.8.10, SL.8.1, SL.8.6, L.8.1, L.8.3, L.8.6)
- Identify the character traits of a hero and, through an exploration of heroism, develop a deep understanding of how literary figures are heroic. (RL.8.1, RL.8.2, RL.8.3, RL.8.10, W.8.4, W.8.9, W.8.10, SL.8.1, SL.8.4, SL.8.6, L.8.1, L.8.3, L.8.6)
- Identify and analyze how their modern fantasy texts draw on and renew the themes (heroism), pattern of events (the hero's journey), and character types (the hero) from myths. (RL.8.1, RL.8.2, RL.8.3, RL.8.9, RL.8.10, W.8.4, W.8.9, W.8.10, SL.8.1, SL.8.4, SL.8.6, L.8.1, L.8.3, L.8.6)
- Analyze the extent to which a filmed version of a fantasy text stays faithful to or departs from the written text and evaluate the choices made by the filmmaker. (RL.8.7)
- Create and present to the class a visual display (either digitally or by hand) comparing a fantasy hero with one from Greek mythology. (RL.8.1, RL.8.2, RL.8.3, RL.8.9, RL.8.10, W.8.4, W.8.6, W.8.9, W.8.10, SL.8.1, SL.8.4, SL.8.5, SL.8.6, L.8.1, L.8.2, L.8.3, L.8.6)
- By the end of the year, independently and proficiently read and comprehend a variety of literature at the high end of the grades 6–8 text complexity band. (RL.8.10)
- In collaborative discussions, demonstrate evidence of preparation and exhibit responsibility for the rules and roles and purpose of conversation. (SL.8.1a, SL.8.1b)
- In collaborative discussions, share and develop ideas in a manner that enhances understanding of a topic and contribute and respond to the content of the conversation in a productive and focused manner. (SL.8.1c, SL.8.1d)

- Adapt speech to a variety of contexts and tasks, demonstrating command of formal English when indicated or appropriate. (SL.8.6)
- Demonstrate command of standard English and its conventions and use the knowledge when writing, speaking, reading, and listening. (L.8.1, L.8.2, L.8.3)
- Acquire and use accurately grade-appropriate general academic and domain-specific words and phrases, strategically building vocabulary knowledge when needed. (L.8.6)

Writing Goals

- Write a literary essay that analyzes the theme of heroism. (W.8.2, W.8.4, W.8.5, W.8.9, W.8.10, RL.8.1, RL.8.2, RL.8.3, RL.8.9, RL.8.10)
- Prove thesis with explicit textual evidence and/or quotations. (W.8.2, W.8.4, W.8.10, RL.8.1, RL.8.2, RL.8.3, RL.8.9, RL.8.10)
- By the end of the year, independently and proficiently read and comprehend a variety of literature at the high end of the grades 6–8 text complexity band. (RL.8.10)
- With some guidance and support from peers and adults, develop and strengthen writing as needed by planning, revising, editing, rewriting, or trying a new approach, focusing on how well purpose and audience have been addressed. (W.8.5)
- Use technology, including the Internet, to produce and publish writing and present the relationships between information and ideas efficiently as well as to interact and collaborate with others. (W.8.6)
- In collaborative discussions, demonstrate evidence of preparation and exhibit responsibility for the rules and roles and purpose of conversation. (SL.8.1a, SL.8.1b)
- In collaborative discussions, share and develop ideas in a manner that enhances understanding of a topic and contribute and respond to the content of the conversation in a productive and focused manner. (SL.8.1c, SL.8.1d)
- Adapt speech to a variety of contexts and tasks, demonstrating command of formal English when indicated or appropriate. (SL.8.6)
- Demonstrate command of standard English and its conventions and use the knowledge when writing, speaking, reading, and listening. (L.8.1, L.8.2, L.8.3)
- Acquire and use accurately grade-appropriate general academic and domain-specific words and phrases, strategically building vocabulary knowledge when needed. (L.8.6)

Choosing Core Texts

The following books are used as examples in this lesson set:

- *D'Aulaires' Book of Greek Myths* by Ingri d'Aulaire and Edgar Parin d'Aulaire
- *The Lightning Thief* by Rick Riordan

Additional Text Suggestions

Fantasy Texts

- *Coraline* by Neil Gaiman
- *The Graveyard Book* by Neil Gaiman
- *Hero.com* by Andy Briggs
- *Just Ella* by Margaret P. Haddix

Series

- *Artemis Fowl* by Eoin Colfer
- *Cirque Du Freak* by Darren Shan
- *Eragon* by Christopher Paolini
- *Everlost* by Neal Shusterman
- *Graceling* by Kristin Cashore
- *Harry Potter* by J. K. Rowling
- *The Hunger Games* by Suzanne Collins
- *Keys to the Kingdom* by Garth Nix
- *The Last Apprentice* by Joseph Delaney
- *Leviathan* by Scott Westerfeld
- *The Lord of the Rings* by J. R. R. Tolkien
- *The Ranger's Apprentice* by John Flanagan
- *The Secrets of the Immortal Nicholas Flamel* by Michael Scott

Teacher's Notes

This lesson set takes on a sophisticated, and important, goal of the Common Core State Standards. Students are expected to be able to analyze how a modern work of fiction draws on themes, patterns of events, or character types from myths, traditional stories, or religious works. We have chosen to focus on plot patterns and character and to use fantasy and mythology as the comparative contemporary versus traditional forms.

Sometimes it is pedagogically effective to use a below grade level text to model complex literary concepts. For some of the lessons in this set, we use *The Lightning Thief* by Rick Riordan, a popular book from a series for intermediate to middle grade students, to model finding evidence of the hero archetype. The text will likely be easy to comprehend for most, allowing students to grasp the modeling and transfer it to their book group texts, which may be differentiated by reading level.

We suggest you begin reading *The Lightning Thief* aloud to the class while working on Reading Lessons 1 to 5 so that you are up to Chapter 6 by Reading Lesson 7.

In order for students to read both myth and fantasy and given that fantasy novels are by nature quite long, allow students sufficient time to delve into their texts using a book group calendar. The 10 lessons will stretch over more than 10 days as you take opportunities to revisit and reinforce various teaching objectives and provide time for students to engage in independent reading.

Questions for Close Reading

The Core Ready lessons include many rich opportunities to engage students in close reading of text requiring them to ask and answer questions, draw conclusions, and use specific text evidence to support their thinking (Reading Anchor Standard 1). These opportunities are marked with a close reading icon. You may wish to extend these experiences using our recommended Core Texts or with texts of your choosing. Use the following questions as a resource to guide students through close reading experiences in Revealing Character: The Hero's Journey.

- What do we learn about this character from what he or she says?
- What do the character's actions reveal about him or her?
- What did the character do in this situation? Why do you think the character behaved this way?
- Who is the hero here? Why do you think so? What text evidence backs up this thinking?
- What characteristics describe this character? What text evidence backs up this thinking?
- How does _____ (a modern work of fiction) draw upon _____ (a myth or traditional story)? What does the author do to modernize the material? Use examples from both works to support your analysis.
- In what ways does the main character resemble the archetypal hero?
- In what ways does the main character experience anything similar to the archetypal hero's journey?

Core Words

allies	quest	theme
archetype	hero	threshold
central idea	journey	traditional literature
enemies	monomyth	trials
fantasy text	myth	
	mythology	

Core Phrases

- *To connect a character's beliefs to actions:* _____[Character's name]_____ beliefs caused him/her to _____.

- *To compare a character to the archetypal hero:* _____[Character's name]_____ is similar to an archetypal hero because _____[text evidence of classic heroic traits]_____.

- *To compare a character's journey to the archetypal hero's journey:* The journey of _____[Character's name]_____ is similar to the archetypal hero's journey because _____[text evidence]_____.

- *To describe character change:* _____[Character's name]_____ changed throughout the story from _____ to _____ as demonstrated by _____[text evidence]_____.

- *To describe character traits:* I would describe _____[Character's name]_____ as _____[trait]_____. I think this because _____[text evidence]_____.

- *To compare a modern version of a story to a classic one:* In the classic version of _____[title]_____, the author _____. In the modern version, the author _____.

- *To articulate central idea/theme:* The story's central idea (or theme) is _____. Evidence of this central idea (or theme) can be found _____.

Building Academic Language

On the prior page is a list of academic language to build your students' comprehension of the focus of this lesson set and facilitate their ability to talk and write about what they learn. Rather than introducing all the words at once, slowly add them to a learning wall as your teaching unfolds. See the glossary at the end of this chapter for definitions of the words. Also listed there are sentence frames that may be included on a sentence wall (Carrier & Tatum, 2006), a research-proven strategy for English language learners (Lewis, 1993; Nattinger, 1980), or as a handout to support student use of the content words. Some students, especially English language learners, may need explicit practice in using the sentence frames. Encourage all students to regularly use these words and phrases in their conversations and writing.

Recognition

As students encounter heroic characters in mythology, modern literature, and film, discuss which of these heroes appeal to them and why. Develop a "Hallway of Heroes" that showcases these heroes with a picture (drawn or printed) and a description of the characteristics of the hero and how the hero embodies the archetypes studied as well as why the student is drawn to the hero.

Thoughtful writing about reading is a difficult task, and it should be celebrated. At the end of the literary essay writing lesson set, allow students to share their writing in a gallery that focuses on the positive aspects of one another's writing. This activity builds peer relationships and writer identity and allows time for the writers to pause and reflect on their own writing.

Complementary Core Methods

Read Aloud

This is an opportunity to share complex texts with your students. They will watch as you grapple with complex vocabulary and analyze the content of a text. With the goal that students be able to make comparisons between characters and events in mythology and modern literature, the more actual myths read to and by the students, the better. This knowledge will provide students with a trove of characters to reference as they read their fantasy texts. Use your read-aloud to teach and reinforce the following skills:

- Determining theme
- Analyzing character (dialogue, actions, thoughts)
- Determining archetypes
- Analyzing plot
- Determining the meaning of unknown words
- Analyzing the impact specific words have on meaning and tone

Shared Reading

Shared reading is yet another opportunity for students to be exposed to increasingly complex literature. Excerpts from read-alouds can be used for close reading. Model how to choose meaningful and important pieces from the text. Below are some prompts you can use for close reading:

- How do the character's words or actions propel the action of the story?
- How do these particular words reveal aspects of the character?
- How does the author reiterate the theme throughout the course of the text?
- How does the author use language to allude to another text?

Core Connections at Home

Provide students with copies of short myths to bring home and share with their families. For homework, ask students to read and discuss a myth with family members. What central message do they think the myth is meant to convey? Is there a hero? What characteristics do they notice in the hero?

Do a community myth search. Send home a letter asking students and family members to find and bring to class ads, pictures, and signs of mythology in their community (for example, Atlas Gym, Nike, Midas Car Service, Apollo Theater, Hermes Messenger Service).

Have a fantasy movie night and invite families to share in a discussion about the role of the hero and the genre of fantasy and how it connects to mythology.

Have students share their final writing pieces and "Hallway of Heroes" with their families. Invite parents to the classroom for a writing celebration. Another option is to have students electronically post their literary essays and ask parents to respond with celebratory comments:

- The part of your essay I found most interesting was . . .
- The character you wrote about in your essay reminds me of . . .

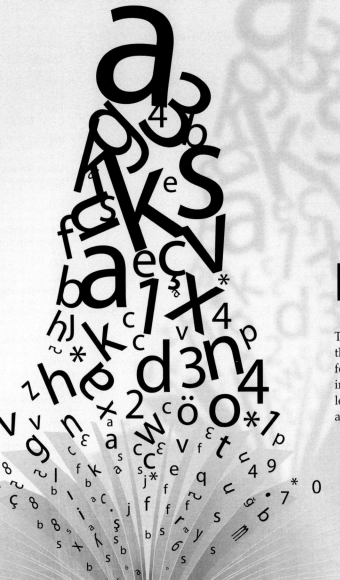

Grade 8

Reading Lessons

The Core I.D.E.A. / Daily Reading Instruction at a Glance table highlights the teaching objectives and standards alignment for all 10 lessons across the four stages of the lesson set (Introduce, Define, Extend, and Assess). It also indicates which lessons contain special features to support English language learners, technology, speaking and listening, close reading opportunities, and formative ("Milestone") assessments.

The Core I.D.E.A. / Daily Reading Instruction at a Glance

	Grade 8	Revealing Character: The Hero's Journey		
Instructional Stage	**Lesson**	**Teaching Objective**	**Core Standards**	**Special Features**
Introduce: *notice, explore, collect, note, immerse, surround, record, share*	1	Readers define and describe the meaning of "hero."	RI.8.1 • RI.8.2 • RI.8.10 • W.8.4 • W.8.10 • SL.8.1 • SL.8.6 • L.8.1 • L.8.3 • L.8.6	S&L ELL Tech Close Reading Opportunity
	2	Readers discover key events and characters in Greek mythology.	RL.8.1 • RL.8.3 • RL.8.10 • W.8.4 • W.8.9 • W.8.10 • SL.8.1 • SL.8.4 • SL.8.6 • L.8.1 • L.8.3 • L.8.6	S&L ELL Close Reading Opportunity Milestone Assessment
Define: *name, identify, outline, clarify, select, plan*	3	Readers search for the archetypal hero's characteristics in mythological texts.	RL.8.1 • RL.8.2 • RL.8.3 • RL.8.10 • W.8.4 • W.8.9 • W.8.10 • SL.8.1 • SL.8.4 • SL.8.6 • L.8.1 • L.8.3 • L.8.6	S&L ELL Close Reading Opportunity Milestone Assessment
	4	Readers search for the archetypal hero's journey in mythological texts.	RL.8.1 • RL.8.2 • RL.8.3 • RL.8.10 • W.8.4 • W.8.9 • W.8.10 • SL.8.1 • SL.8.4 • SL.8.6 • L.8.1 • L.8.3 • L.8.6	S&L ELL Close Reading Opportunity
	5	Readers develop understandings about the characteristics of Greek heroes through collaborative discussion.	RL.8.1 • RL.8.2 • RL.8.3 • RL.8.10 • SL.8.1 • SL.8.4 • SL.8.6 • L.8.1 • L.8.3 • L.8.6	S&L ELL Close Reading Opportunity
Extend: *try, experiment, attempt, approximate, practice, explain, revise, refine*	6	Readers preview contemporary novels to search for evidence of the archetypal hero and the monomyth structure.	RL.8.1 • RL.8.2 • RL.8.3 • RL.8.9 • RL.8.10 • SL.8.1 • SL.8.4 • SL.8.6 • L.8.1 • L.8.3 • L.8.6	S&L ELL Tech Close Reading Opportunity
	7	Readers search for the archetypal hero's characteristics in independent novels.	RL.8.1 • RL.8.2 • RL.8.3 • RL.8.9 • RL.8.10 • W.8.4 • W.8.9 • W.8.10 • SL.8.1 • SL.8.4 • SL.8.6 • L.8.1 • L.8.3 • L.8.6	S&L ELL Close Reading Opportunity Milestone Assessment
	8	Readers search for the archetypal hero's journey in independent novels.	RL.8.1 • RL.8.2 • RL.8.3 • RL.8.9 • RL.8.10 • W.8.4 • W.8.9 • W.8.10 • SL.8.1 • SL.8.4 • SL.8.6 • L.8.1 • L.8.3 • L.8.6	ELL Close Reading Opportunity Milestone Assessment
	9	Readers recognize the importance of secondary characters in fantasy novels.	RL.8.1 • RL.8.2 • RL.8.3 • RL.8.10 • W.8.4 • W.8.6 • W.8.9 • W.8.10 • SL.8.1 • SL.8.4 • SL.8.5 • SL.8.6 • L.8.1 • L.8.2 • L.8.3 • L.8.6	S&L ELL Tech Close Reading Opportunity Milestone Assessment
Assess: *reflect, conclude, connect, share, recognize, respond*	10	Readers reflect on connections between mythology and modern literature by comparing and contrasting a novel to the filmed version.	RL.8.1 • RL.8.2 • RL.8.3 • RL.8.7 • RL.8.9 • RL.8.10 • W.8.4 • W.8.9 • W.8.10 • SL.8.1 • SL.8.4 • SL.8.6 • L.8.1 • L.8.3 • L.8.6	ELL Close Reading Opportunity Milestone Assessment

Reading Lesson 1

Close Reading Opportunity

▼ Teaching Objective

Readers define and describe the meaning of "hero."

▼ Standards Alignment

RI.8.1, RI.8.2, RI.8.10, W.8.4, W.8.10, SL.8.1, SL.8.6, L.8.1, L.8.3, L.8.6

▼ Materials

- Charting supplies or interactive whiteboard to create Carnegie Award Heroes chart
- "I Need a Hero" podcast: www.radiolab.org
- Carnegie Award Heroes Graphic Organizer (downloadable PDF in the Core Ready PDTookit)
- Printouts or Internet access to descriptions of awardees from the Carnegie Hero Fund Commission (http://carnegiehero.org)

▼ To the Teacher

In this lesson, the class will collaboratively define the word hero and name the characteristics of someone we designate with that title. Although this lesson focuses on real-life acts of heroism, we can (and ultimately will) easily translate the character traits from real people to fictional characters. To help students develop a clear collaborative definition of the word *hero*, they will be listening to and reading firsthand accounts of recipients of awards given by the Carnegie Hero Commission. These awards are presented to individuals who risk their lives to save others. The website for the commission provides written descriptions of the recipients and their stories.

If the capacity to listen to this radio show is not available to you, provide students with access to the descriptions of the accomplishments of these people (available at http://carnegiehero.org) or any people who have been recognized for heroic acts, available online at many sites. **ELL** Provide Comprehensible Input—Audiovisual Aids. This media-based introduction to real-life heroes will help your ELLs gain access to the concept that they will be studying mostly through texts.

We provide low-tech and high-tech options for how students can learn about the individuals who received the Carnegie Hero Award. Make this choice prior to teaching this lesson.

During the Wrap Up of this lesson, you will want to introduce the term *archetype* to students. An archetype is a pattern of character traits, behaviors, or events that recurs in stories again and again, most often in folklore and mythology.

Note on advance preparation for upcoming reading lessons: We suggest you begin reading *The Lightning Thief* aloud to the class while working on Reading Lessons 1 to 5 so that you are up to Chapter 6 by Reading Lesson 7.

▼ Procedure

Warm Up Gather the class to set the stage for today's learning

Engage students in a brief conversation to tap into their thinking about the term *hero*. Ask them to define *hero* and write down key words and phrases they share. **ELL** Frontload the Lesson—Activate Prior Knowledge. Asking students to generate examples will help your ELLs orient themselves to the lesson by allowing them to work with familiar information; they will also develop their vocabulary for discussing heroes by hearing and seeing their peers' ideas.

Teach Model what students need to learn and do

We read and listen better when we do so with a purpose. Explain how students will listen to a radio show called RadioLab. You can access the broadcast at www.radiolab.org/story/104009-i-need-a-hero/. The show segment explores real-life heroes who have won an award from the Carnegie Foundation for their bravery. Recipients of the Carnegie Medal put their lives at extreme risk while saving (or trying to save) the lives of others (http://carnegiehero.org).

As you and students listen to the selection, record notes about William David Pennell using the format of the Carnegie Award Heroes graphic organizer (PDToolkit). Students may follow along with their own copies of the organizer. **ELL** Provide Comprehensible Input—Organizers. The chart helps ELLs follow the audio recording and provides a visual anchor for them to refer back to during discussion.

Carnegie Award Heroes

Carnegie Award Recipient	Is This Person a Hero?	Evidence
William David Pennell	Yes	• Runs toward the burning car when others stand by and watch. • Has deep empathy for families with children, which prompts his heroic action. • Dives into a burning car multiple times to get survivors.

Your job while we continue to listen is to capture the show's working definition of a hero, specifically for Lora Shrake. You should be listening to Lora's heroic story and thinking about how to decide whether you find the speaker's reasoning relevant and sound. Summarize the content of the selection about Lora, and then record your thoughts on the Carnegie Award Heroes graphic organizer. Use the following questions to guide your listening and thinking:

- What do the speakers claim about heroism?
- What does each person do that is heroic?
- Do the actions of the individual meet the criteria of the speakers for heroism?

ELL Frontload the Lesson—Set a Purpose for Reading. This gives your ELLs a focus for their listening and helps them avoid getting bogged down in unfamiliar language.

Try Guide students to quickly rehearse what they need to learn and do in preparation for practice

Have students share their insights and notes from the Carnegie Award Heroes graphic organizer with a partner. **ELL** Enable Language Production—Increasing Interaction. In order to develop their language skills, ELLs must use language: talking with their peers gives them a chance to articulate their own ideas and allows them to hear someone else's take on the recording. If they did not fully understand what they listened to, their peers' contributions can help.

What did you hear that helps you refine your own definition of a hero? Turn and share your ideas with a classmate. Add to your list if you want after talking to your partner.

As students analyze the information they gathered while listening to the radio segment and share their thinking, remind them of the importance of coming to discussions prepared, staying on task, building on each other's ideas and expressing their own ideas clearly. (SL.8.1a, SL.8.1b, SL.8.1c, SL.8.1d)

Possible student response on the graphic organizer:

Carnegie Award Recipient	Is This Person a Hero?	Evidence
Lora Shrake	Yes	• Saw woman being mauled by a bull. • Separated from woman by electric fence. • Climbed fence and hit the bull with pipe to save the woman. • Says if nobody came to this woman's rescue, she would have died.

Clarify Briefly restate today's teaching objective and explain the independent task(s)

Using the Carnegie Award Heroes graphic organizer and the notes garnered during the opening discussion, create a class definition of a hero and record it. This definition will be referenced later in the lesson set as students analyze the characteristics of characters in various cultures and media.

Here is a sample of what your class definition might look like at this point:

Class Definition of Hero

Heroes are people who put the well-being of others before their own, placing themselves at risk in the process. They feel compelled to perform extraordinary acts of courage and kindness for others because they feel it is the right thing to do.

Your challenge is to examine the descriptions of some of the other Carnegie Award winners from the Carnegie web page. I want you to look for similarities and differences across individuals. For each profile, determine if you feel that this person fits our class definition of hero.

Practice Students work independently and/or in small groups to apply today's teaching objective

Pearson Education

Students listen to or read hero summaries and compare and contrast to see if each candidate fits the class definition of hero. Students should first summarize the text and then use the Carnegie Award Heroes graphic organizer (PDToolkit) to record their thinking.

Carnegie Award Recipient	Is This Person a Hero?	Evidence

We have provided low-tech and high-tech options for how students can learn about the accomplishments of the individuals recognized for heroism.

Goal	Low-Tech	High-Tech
Students explore the accomplishments of individuals recognized for heroism.	Students read specific stories of the heroes who received the Carnegie Award for heroism.	Students listen to Carnegie Award recipients at http://carnegiehero.org (search for the Audio Archives under Resources).

Wrap Up Check understanding as you guide students to briefly share what they have learned and produced today

After this lesson, students will use the generated class definition of a hero to push their thinking to the next level and connect it to traditional and contemporary literature. They will consider the motivations of heroes and notice the characteristics that seem to be common to them. These may include personal injustice, injustice against a loved one or friend, empathy elicited from stories or images, strongly empathetic response to the suffering or distress of others, and obligations and allegiances to social, political, or cultural ideals.

Now that you have read some descriptions of the lives of heroes and we have determined our class definition, let us consider this question: Why would an ordinary person act in heroic ways?

We will be seeing this pattern of behavior in characters throughout this lesson set.

Reading Lesson 2

▼ Teaching Objective

Readers discover key events and characters in Greek mythology.

Close Reading Opportunity

▼ Standards Alignment

RL.8.1, RL.8.3, RL.8.10, W.8.4, W.8.10, SL.8.1, SL.8.4, SL.8.6, L.8.1, L.8.3, L.8.6

▼ Materials

- *D'Aulaires' Book of Greek Myths* by Ingri d'Aulaire and Edgar Parin d'Aulaire
- Charting supplies or interactive whiteboard to create Greek Myths chart
- Greek Gods and Goddesses graphic organizer (Appendix 8.1)

▼ To the Teacher

In this lesson, students will develop a foundational understanding of the genre of mythology. The segments of this lesson probably will need to be taught over more than one day. In this lesson, students will look closely at the character traits of the gods and goddesses of Greek mythology. They will develop an understanding of how these gods and goddesses often provide support and obstacles to the Greek heroes.

▼ Procedure

Warm Up Gather the class to set the stage for today's learning

Explain how some of the world's first literary heroes came from myths. Ask students:

What are myths?

Define *mythology*. One definition is:

Mythology is a collection of ancient stories, passed down first by oral storytelling, that a culture uses to help explain its world. Thousands of years ago there were few scientific explanations for the weather or volcanoes or any other natural phenomena. Myths tried to explain these things. Myths are found in all parts of the world and come from many different cultures. Is anyone familiar with any myths from this country or other countries?

ELL Identify and Communicate Content and Language Objectives—Academic Vocabulary. Knowing common genres and their characteristics is part of participating in an academic community. By explicitly teaching this information, you are demystifying the genre of mythology for your ELLs.

Teach Model what students need to learn and do

Greek Myths

How did the world begin?	What do you notice about the gods and goddesses?

Explain to students that in the case of the Greeks, their myths not only focused on how the world was formed, but they also taught the listener about the Greek gods. **ELL** Frontload the Lesson—Build Background. Consider that some of your ELLs might come from cultures where Ancient Greece does not loom as large as it does in traditions rooted in Western Europe. Even students raised in the United States might not know much about Ancient Greece or why we will spend all this time studying very old stories from a small country that is very far away. Spend some time orienting students to the idea of Ancient Greece. You need not tell them everything—perhaps you can give your students a sense of time and place and then charge them with the task of figuring out *why* these stories have remained so important for so long.

Now we are going to read to learn more about the Greek gods and the belief system in Ancient Greece. We will be reading selections from *D'Aulaires' Book of Greek Myths.*

Instruct students to read along with you as you gather information about the Ancient Greeks' mythology. Tell them to set up their notes in the same format as the chart you will be modeling. They will continue to take notes during Practice.

Listen and read along as I read aloud the section called "In Olden Times." Your job as a listener is to analyze the information presented: Listen for information that would present the Greeks' interpretation of the beginning of the world and the history of the gods.

- According to Greek mythology, how did the world begin? What conflicts arose in early times?
- What do you notice about the gods and goddesses you encounter?

Jot your findings. I will think alongside you and share my thinking as we move through the text.

Chart your observations of Ancient Greek beliefs as presented in the text in the following chart.

On this first page, I read that there was good and bad in the world. Good was represented by the gods and Bad by beasts and monsters. It was the job of good to defeat evil, and the heroes were there to help the gods accomplish this. This sounds like the premise for every superhero story I have ever read!

ELL Provide Comprehensible Input—Models. Your ELLs will find it easier to process what they are hearing and take notes if they can watch you do these same things as they practice.

Greek Myths

How did the world begin?	What do you notice about the gods and goddesses?
• Good and bad forces • Good defeats evil • Sounds like superhero stories	• They manipulate events in the lives of people to obtain their own goals • Heroes defeat beasts and monsters • Gods give heroes their tasks

ELL Enable Language Production—Listening and Speaking. This lesson is an opportunity to give students practice at determining the meanings of unknown words using context. Instead of trying to teach ELLs all the words they might not know in this text, encourage them to speak up when a word is disrupting their comprehension, and lead the class in some problem solving about what the word might mean. You need not stop at every word, and over time, you will want to teach your students to be increasingly independent in using word-solving strategies (like context clues and reference materials).

Try Guide students to quickly rehearse what they need to learn and do in preparation for practice

Read the *D'Aulaires' Book of Greek Myths* Gaea page with students. Remind them to continue taking notes.

What do you think we need to analyze or interpret on this second page?

After listening to the Gaea page from *D'Aulaires' Book of Greek Myths,* have students share their interpretations with one another. **ELL** Enable Language Production—Increasing Interaction. When ELLs share with peers, they can check and refine their understanding of what they have heard, listen to strong examples of proficient English, and practice sharing their own thinking aloud in English.

 As students share, direct them to acknowledge any new information presented by other students and how that new information

may have altered or supported their thinking. (SL.8.1d) Some possible observations:

How did the world begin?	What do you notice about the gods goddesses?
• Family conflict	• Power struggles • Influence humans' actions, thoughts, and feelings

Clarify Briefly restate today's teaching objective and explain the independent task(s)

Explain that students will read myths about the Titans and the origin of Zeus and the gods on Mount Olympus. Other texts that provide these myths can also be used to support students as they gather information about the Ancient Greek belief system.

> Now you will read the next two chapters of *D'Aulaires' Book of Greek Myths*: "The Titans" and "Zeus and His Family." In these two chapters, you will continue to gather basic information about the names and roles of the Greek gods and goddesses. As you read, analyze, and interpret what you have learned from the text about the Greek gods and their origins and structure, use the following questions to guide you:

- What are the names and roles of the Greek gods and goddesses?
- How do the gods and goddesses interact with one another? What do these interactions reveal about their characters?
- How do the gods and goddesses interact with humans? What do these interactions reveal about their characters?

ELL Frontload the Lesson—Set a Purpose for Reading. ELLs will find it easier to get through this challenging text if they know exactly what they are looking for.

Practice Students work independently and/or in small groups to apply today's teaching objective

Students read assigned sections from *D'Aulaires' Book of Greek Myths*. They will gather and analyze information about Greek gods using the Greek Gods and Goddesses graphic organizer (Appendix 8.1). The first row is filled in for them. **ELL** Enable Language Production—Reading and Writing. Consider having ELLs with prior schooling in their home language, particularly newer arrivals, read in the language they are most comfortable in and then write in English, or vice versa. Also, if you have students who have been in the United States for a while and are orally proficient in English but are struggling to read at grade level, consider creating a group that reads together with greater support from you. These students are often able to comprehend and discuss at a much higher level than the one at which they can currently read independently.

Greek Gods and Goddesses graphic organizer

God/ Goddess	Role	Relationship with Other Gods	Relationship with Humans	Character Traits
Zeus	God of thunder—most powerful god	Shared his powers with his brothers and sisters who became gods and goddesses	Has romantic relations with many humans and has half-god children	Powerful, controlling, loves women

Wrap Up Check understanding as you guide students to briefly share what they have learned and produced today

Ask volunteers to share and compare their Practice results. **ELL** Enable Language Production—Increasing Interaction. Sharing their work with English-proficient peers will expose ELLs to more examples of standard academic writing. Newer arrivals can be encouraged to use multilingual practices in their work: if they read a myth in English, perhaps they can discuss it in their home language with a bilingual peer; if they read a myth in their home language, perhaps now they can practice sharing their ideas in English. When searching for myths in a student's native language, it helps to use search terms translated to the native language rather than English. Example: To search for myths written in Greek, use "mitros griegos" (not "Greek myths") as your search terms.

To close, ask students to consider what they read in the stories of the gods and goddesses of Greek mythology compared with how the introduction of the book characterizes them. The distinction between the hero and the gods and goddesses will be important as the students develop a deeper understanding of heroism.

> In the introduction of this text, the narrator speaks of the gods as being beautiful, radiant, and incapable of doing wrong. Do you agree with this assessment of the Greek gods after having read these chapters? Why?

This discussion provides students with the opportunity to demonstrate their ability to present their findings in a focused, coherent manner with relevant evidence, sound valid reasoning, and well-chosen details. (SL.8.4)

Milestone Performance Assessment

Analyzing Character Roles, Relationships, and Traits

 PD TOOLKIT™

Collect and analyze the Greek Gods and Goddesses Graphic Organizer as a performance-based assessment to determine if students need additional instruction or support as a whole class, in small groups, or one on one. **ELL** Assess for Content and Language Understandings—Formative Assessment. This is an opportunity for you to assess your ELLs' language and content needs with regard to understanding the key figures in Greek mythology. Notice where their gaps are: Have they misunderstood something about the guiding questions you provided? Are they unclear about how to identify the relationships, roles, or traits of the gods and goddesses? Or do they struggle to find the language they need to express the ideas they have? Remember that strong content understanding is sometimes hidden behind "imperfect" uses of language! Use this information to plan upcoming lessons.

Use this checklist to assess student work on the Greek Gods and Goddesses Graphic Organizer.

Standards Alignment: RL.8.1, RL.8.3, W.8.4, W.8.9, W.8.10

Task	Achieved	Notes
Gather explicitly stated information from the text.		
Identify the role of the god or goddess in mythology.		
Describe the relationships of gods and goddesses with each other.		
Describe the relationships of gods and goddesses with humans.		
Draw accurate conclusions about the character traits of the Greek gods and goddesses.		

Reading Lesson 3

▼ Teaching Objective

Readers search for the archetypal hero's characteristics in mythological texts.

Close Reading Opportunity

▼ Standards Alignment

RL.8.1, RL.8.2, RL.8.3, RL.8.10, W.8.4, W.8.9, W.8.10, SL.8.1, SL.8.4, SL.8.6, L.8.1, L.8.3, L.8.6

▼ Materials

- *Sample Myth #1: The Tale of Perseus* (Appendix 8.2)
- *Sample Myth #2: The Quest of the Golden Fleece* (Appendix 8.2)

- Charting supplies or interactive whiteboard for the Characteristics of the Archetypal Hero chart
- Hero's Characteristics graphic organizer (Appendix 8.3)

▼ To the Teacher

This lesson guides students through a close reading of a myth with a focus on character. The lesson will probably take more than one session, as the Warm Up involves reading a new text and the Teach requires rereading that text.

▼ Procedure

Warm Up Gather the class to set the stage for today's learning

Pearson Education

Hero's Characteristic graphic organizer

Hero: _____ Text: _____ Brief Summary of the Text: _____

Characteristic	Evidence from the Text • Text quote or description • Page #
Mighty warrior	
Unusual birth circumstances	
Initiating event	
Epic quest	
Admirable qualities: bravery, selflessness	
Lives elsewhere	
Special weapons	
Help from gods/goddesses	

Ask students to share the previous day's discoveries about the gods and goddesses of Greek mythology. Help them to fill in any omissions as needed. **ELL** Frontload the Lesson—Make Connections. When you explicitly call up the work students have been doing around Greek myths, you help your ELLs orient themselves to the focus of this lesson.

In this lesson, students will begin to closely examine the characteristics of Greek heroes using the graphic organizer to the left (and in Appendix 8.3). Read *Sample Myth #1: The Tale of Perseus* (Appendix 8.2) with students. Again, bring the class definition of hero into view so students can reference it as they discuss *The Tale of Perseus*. **ELL** Frontload the Lesson—Make Connections. When you return repeatedly to the class definition of hero, your ELLs can connect their new learning to something familiar while refining and deepening their understanding of this core term. List what students notice about the character of Perseus.

> The gods are the ones with the serious power in mythology, but it is the hero who takes front stage and steals the show. Let's read the story of Perseus, the Greek hero. As we read, use the following questions to guide your thinking:

- What do you notice about this character's thoughts, words, or actions?
- What traits describe this character? What text evidence backs up this thinking?
- Do you think the character was a hero? Why or why not? What text evidence backs up this thinking?

Below are the questions with some sample responses:
What do you notice about this character's thoughts, words, or actions?

- He wants to save his mother from dangerous circumstances.
- He is willing to place himself in danger to save those he loves.
- He thinks about his actions and understands consequences, which is unusual for characters of Greek mythology.

What traits describe this character? What text evidence backs up this thinking?

- Clever because he tricked the Graeae into helping him; he warns his friends not to look at the Medusa but causes his enemies to look.
- Brave because he agreed to get the head of the Medusa; he confronts her and defeats her.
- Protective because he kept his mother from marrying Polydectes; he rescues his mom; protects his friends from the Medusa.

ELL Enable Language Production—Listening and Speaking. Realize that your ELLs might leverage familiar words to describe the traits they see in Perseus (e.g., *smart, not scared*). This shows that they are capable of making the intellectual inferences you require and provides a great opportunity for you to extend their vocabulary. Offer synonyms for their terms from the academic register of English. Finally, consider letting ELLs offer adjectives in their home language and then use a bilingual peer or a dictionary to help the class determine an English equivalent.

Do you think the character was a hero? Why or why not? What text evidence backs up this thinking?

- Responses will vary according to the thoughts of the class. Direct students to use text evidence to support their thinking about either stance.

Teach Model what students need to learn and do

Provide students with a definition of the classic mythological hero. Display a list of characteristics of the Greek hero. Next to each characteristic, model how to place specific evidence from the story to support the concept that Perseus fits the role of hero perfectly. Leave a few blank to allow students to discuss and fill in during the Try segment of the lesson.

There are certain characteristics possessed by nearly every Greek hero. This pattern is repeated in literature time and time again. We call this pattern an archetype. Define the term *archetype*: a pattern of character traits, behaviors, or events that recurs in stories again and again, most often in folklore and mythology.

> I am going to make a list of these archetypal characteristics and then together we are going to reread the story in search of evidence of these characteristics in Perseus.

Characteristics of the Archetypal Hero

- Usually a mighty warrior
- Has unusual birth circumstances; often the son or daughter of a god or goddess
- Experiences an initiating event that propels him or her to action
- Goes on epic quests as the result of some initiating event
- Displays certain admirable qualities: bravery, selflessness
- Leaves family or land to live with others
- Has special weapons
- Has supernatural help from the gods

> Let's go back into the text and look for evidence that matches up with this list of heroic characteristics.

ELL Provide Comprehensible Input—Organizers. This chart makes your teaching objective transparent to your students and gives them something concrete and permanent to refer back to during their independent work. Your ELLs in particular will benefit from this explicitness. Demonstrate how to use the information from Sample Myth #1: The Tale of Perseus (Appendix 8.2)

to complete the Hero's Characteristics graphic organizer (Appendix 8.3).
ELL Provide Comprehensible Input—Models. Here you are physically demonstrating for your students how to use specific evidence when analyzing a text and how to use the graphic organizer to keep track of what they have read. All students will benefit from watching you walk through the process, but it is especially helpful for ELLs. At this point in the lesson, your class chart might look like this:

Hero's Characteristics graphic organizer

Hero: <u>Perseus</u>   Text: <u>*The Tale of Perseus*</u>

Characteristic	Evidence from the Text • Text quote or description • Page #
Mighty warrior	Kills Medusa, doesn't look in eyes, page 69
Unusual birth circumstances	Birth information not in story, but when infant grandfather put him and mother in a chest sent out to sea, page 68
Initiating event	Polydectes demands that Danae marry him, page 68
Epic quest	Sets out to kill Medusa and bring her head home to Polydectes in order to kill him and retrieve his mother, page 68–69
Admirable qualities: bravery, selflessness	
Lives elsewhere	
Special weapons	
Help from gods/ goddesses	

ELL Provide Comprehensible Input—Organizers. Graphic organizers can make lesson content transparent for your ELLs and help them organize their thinking when they start working.

Try Guide students to quickly rehearse what they need to learn and do in preparation for practice

Have students work with a partner to find the evidence to support their thinking as they finish completing the Hero's Characteristics Graphic Organizer (Appendix 8.3). **ELL** Enable Language Production—Increasing Interaction. Partners can help ELLs understand the lesson requirements. If you have students who are just beginning to learn English, consider pairing them with bilingual peers (if possible in your class) who can use the home language to help them access the lesson.

> With your partner, reflect on the myth of Perseus and fill in the remainder of the chart from the category of "Admirable Qualities" to "Help from gods/goddesses."

Some possible responses are in the chart:

Admirable qualities: bravery, selflessness	Willing to risk his life to save his mother from marrying Polydectes
Lives elsewhere	Washed up on shores of beautiful island named Seriphos
Special weapons	Shield from Athena. A sword and winged sandals from Hermes. An invisibility cap from the Graeae, page 68
Help from gods/goddesses	The gods gave Perseus the special weapons, page 68

Clarify Briefly restate today's teaching objective and explain the independent task(s)

Explain to students that they will be reading the story of the hero Jason and using the same chart to catalog his heroic deeds. Restate the characteristics of a Greek hero and remind students to use specific evidence from Sample Myth #2: The Quest of the Golden Fleece (Appendix 8.2) to support the categories.

> Your task is to read about another hero, Jason. The text is called *The Quest of the Golden Fleece,* and because this is written as a myth, I recommend you slow down your reading pace until you feel comfortable with the language and style of writing. Please use a blank version of our Hero's Characteristics graphic organizer in order to determine whether Jason fits our definition of hero. Include text details to show your proof.

Practice Students work independently and/or in small groups to apply today's teaching objective

Students read *Sample Myth #2: The Quest of the Golden Fleece* (Appendix 8.2) and find evidence of hero characteristics. Students should record the evidence on their Hero's Characteristics Graphic Organizer (Appendix 8.3). **ELL** Enable Language Production—Reading and Writing. Check in with your ELLs to determine what kind of support they might need. Some middle school students who have been in this country for many years may still be classified as ELLs despite their fluency with oral English because they struggle with reading and writing or because they use nonstandard varieties of English. Such students should be supported to read a challenging text and take thoughtful notes; bear in mind that they might use "imperfect" English as they grow toward academic language proficiency.

Wrap Up Check understanding as you guide students to briefly share what they have learned and produced today

Ask volunteers to share the evidence they found about the character traits of a mythological hero.

Direct students to present their findings in a focused, coherent manner with relevant evidence and supporting details. Remind students to use appropriate eye contact, adequate volume, and clear pronunciation. (SL.8.4)

Milestone Performance Assessment

Character Traits of Mythological Heroes

Collect and analyze the Hero's Characteristics graphic organizer as a performance-based assessment to determine if students need additional instruction or support as a whole class, in small groups, or one on one. **ELL** Assess for Content and Language Understanding—Formative Assessment. Be sure to look for areas of success and challenge in both content and language as you examine your ELLs' work. For example, if students have a mismatch between the evidence they cite and the traits they claim the evidence shows, this might be because they did not completely understand the language of the graphic organizer or the language of the text. On the other hand, students may have understood everything quite well but have written their notes in nonstandard English. Carefully analyze the work to look for the root of any misunderstandings, and use this information to plan upcoming lessons.

Standards Alignment: RL.8.1, RL.8.3, W.8.4, W.8.9, W.8.10

Task	Achieved	Notes
Gather explicitly stated information from the text.		
Accurately articulate examples of hero characteristics from the text.		
Provide evidence to support thinking.		

153

Reading Lesson 4

▼ **Teaching Objective**

Readers search for the archetypal hero's journey in mythological texts.

Close Reading
Opportunity

▼ **Standards Alignment**

RL.8.1, RL.8.2, RL.8.3, RL.8.10, W.8.4, W.8.9, W.8.10, SL.8.1, SL.8.4, SL.8.6, L.8.1, L.8.3, L.8.6

▼ **Materials**

- The Stages of the Hero's Journey Defined (Appendix 8.4)
- *Sample Myth #1: The Tale of Perseus* (Appendix 8.2)
- "Theseus" in *D'Aulaires' Book of Greek Myths* by Ingri d'Aulaire and Edgar Parin d'Aulaire
- Hero's Journey graphic organizer (Appendix 8.5)

▼ **To the Teacher**

In this lesson, the students will be exploring the hero's journey. Remind students that an archetype is a pattern of character traits, behaviors, or events that recurs in stories again and again, most often in folklore and mythology. In the case of this lesson set, what patterns do we notice about the actions and characteristics of the literary hero?

Joseph Campbell identified a classic sequence of actions and events of literary heroes that recurs in stories across many cultures and time periods. He called this hero's journey a "monomyth" and first fully elaborated on it in *The Hero with a Thousand Faces* (1949). We have provided a modified version of Campbell's monomyth list for eighth graders, preserving the key elements of the hero's journey. See the Stages of the Hero's Journey Defined (Appendix 8.4). Campbell's original monomyth of the archetypal hero is somewhat more complex than the list provided.

Eighth graders are required to analyze how a modern work of fiction draws on themes, patterns of events, or character types from myths, traditional stories, or religious works and describe how the material is rendered new. By examining both traditional literature (in our case mythology) and modern literature through the lens of Joseph Campbell's monomyth, we are able to determine and compare themes and the aspects of the characters.

The terms *central idea* and *theme* are frequently used interchangeably. The theme (or central idea) of a piece of reading can often be expressed in one or two words, such as "friendship," "coming of age" or "family." However, the theme (or central idea) of a text may also be described in a longer, more specific sentence that describes the message or universal truth suggested by the events in the story. For example, "People should choose friends wisely," or "Growing up means making difficult choices."

▼ **Procedure**

Warm Up Gather the class to set the stage for today's learning

At this point in the lesson set, students should have established the concept that the mythological heroes share some common characteristics. Tap into students' interest in contemporary culture to conduct a brief discussion that connects the characteristics of Greek heroes to the superheroes of today. **ELL** Frontload the Lesson—Activate Prior Knowledge. When you let ELLs talk about topics that are of high interest to them, they are more likely to already be familiar with the language needed for the discussion. This will increase their motivation to participate in this lesson and will allow them to connect what they know already to the lesson's objective.

> Many of us have seen comics and movies that portray such heroes as Superman, Spiderman, and Batman. How do the Greek heroes compare with contemporary superheroes? Would the characteristics we list be the same? How might they be different?

Teach Model what students need to learn and do

The Stages of the Hero's Journey Defined

based on Joseph Campbell's monomyth theory
The Ordinary World: We are introduced to the hero, usually in his or her homeland. The hero must leave this world to enter the "special" world of the journey.
Call to Adventure: An initial event encourages the hero to accept a challenge or quest, such as choosing the fight for good over evil.
Refusal of the Call: The hero initially refuses, preferring the relative comfort of the ordinary world. He or she may be fearful, insecure, or worried that "the call" will be a hardship.

Meeting the Mentor:
The hero is introduced to one who will support and guide him or her on the journey with advice, training, or magical gifts. The mentor may be a living being or an object. The mentor provides the hero confidence to accept the call.

Crossing the Threshold:
The hero must cross the threshold and move into a new world from the ordinary world. The threshold may be an actual structure or another type of divider between the ordinary world and the special world. This crossing indicates commitment to the journey.

Tests/Allies/Enemies:
The hero must figure out how the rules in the special world work as he or she encounters minor challenges and meets others who may turn out to be supportive team members, sidekicks, or dangerous enemies.

Approach to the Innermost Cave:
The hero prepares for the "ordeal" or final challenge as he or she approaches the location where he or she will meet the greatest enemy. (Note that this may not literally be a cave.) For example, he or she might plan to advance toward the lair of the main enemy, plan an attack strategy, take a break for romance, or eliminate lesser enemies.

Ordeal:
The hero encounters a major life-or-death test and/or final battle with the greatest enemy. This is the climax of the journey. The hero usually experiences "death" from which he or she must be resurrected in a way that provides him or her the strength or wisdom to complete the journey.

Reward:
Also called "seizing the sword," in this stage, the hero receives a reward for facing and overcoming the ordeal. May be a magical tool, great wisdom, an elixir, the affection of another, or a combination of items.

The Road Back:
In this stage, the hero heads home to the ordinary world. The hero may resist returning, but circumstances often force him or her to commit to return.

Resurrection:
In this stage, the hero resolves his or her problem. He or she is "reborn" with his or her original characteristics from the ordinary world in combination with the new powers, strength, and wisdom gained from the journey. He or she must accept and sometimes must prove his or her new status as "hero" to others.

Return with the Elixir:
In this stage, the hero returns to the ordinary world with the "elixir," a great treasure or understanding to share from the journey. The hero becomes master of both worlds.

The Hero's Journey graphic organizer

Hero: _____ Text: _____

Brief Summary of the Text: _____

Stage of the Journey	Evidence from the Text • Text quote or description
The Ordinary World	
Call to Adventure	
Refusal of the Call	
Meeting the Mentor	
Crossing the Threshold	
Tests/Allies/Enemies	
Approach to the Innermost Cave	
Ordeal	
Reward	
The Road Back	
Resurrection	
Return with the Elixir	

In addition to sharing common characteristics, the heroes of mythology also shared common experiences and life journeys. Gather the class to discuss the steps of a Greek hero's journey.

> Practically every Greek hero goes on some kind of a quest or journey. What you may not know is that there are often predictable steps to these journeys. Who thinks they know some of those steps?

Briefly discuss ideas with the class and chart responses.

Introduce Campbell's monomyth, or "hero's journey," using The Stages of the Hero's Journey Defined (Appendix 8.4). Explain to students that there are typical steps in a hero's journey and that you are going to model a close read to determine these stages and steps.

ELL Provide Comprehensible Input—Organizers. This chart really demystifies the components of a myth, making it possible for your students to enter the world of literary criticism. ELLs in particular will likely benefit from being able to repeatedly come back to these core points. Consider enhancing the chart with visual icons to help students remember what the core points mean.

Use the Hero's Journey graphic organizer (Appendix 8.5) to identify the stages of the hero's journey in *Sample Myth #1: The Tale of Perseus* (Appendix 8.2).

> Let's walk step by step through Perseus's journey and discover the steps. Then you will read another myth and see if that hero goes through the same steps. For heroes to begin their journeys, they have to be called away from the ordinary world. This first stage, prior to their trials and battles, is called the Call to Adventure. But usually there is a discovery, an event that starts the hero on the heroic path. What was that in *The Tale of Perseus*?

The Hero's Journey in *The Tale of Perseus*

Stage of the Journey	Evidence from the Text • Text quote or description
The Ordinary World	Polydectes wants to marry mother, page 68
Call to Adventure	Told to bring back the head of Medusa, page 68
Refusal of the Call	No refusal in this myth
Meeting the Mentor	Athena and Hermes Given shield, sword, and flying sandals by Athena and Hermes, page 68
Crossing the Threshold	Approaching the rocky island on the boat, page 68
Tests/Allies/ Enemies	Perseus steals the eye from the Graeae and will not give it back until they help him, page 68
Approach to the Innermost Cave	Perseus approaches the lair where the Gorgons live. He is about to find Medusa, page 69
Ordeal	Perseus almost forgets to keep his eyes off Medusa, but he then uses her reflection. He severs her head and put its in his satchel, page 69
Reward	Perseus frees his mother and marries Andromeda, page 69

ELL Provide Comprehensible Input—Models. It is important for all your students, but particularly for your ELLs, to see *how* an expert reader uses close reading to analyze a myth.

Try Guide students to quickly rehearse what they need to learn and do in preparation for practice

Students review *The Tale of Perseus* and share plot developments from the story in order to substantiate the steps in the hero's journey. Have students work in partnerships to find evidence for the last three steps of the hero's journey.

Example of possible student responses:

The Road Back	We don't have any information about Perseus's return trip
Resurrection	Polydectes thought he had sent Perseus on a suicide mission, but Perseus reappears at the palace, page 69
Return with the Elixir	Perseus masters both the world of the Gorgons and the world where he lives, page 69

Circulate as groups are talking, highlighting the importance of key speaking and listening skills necessary for productive conversation and collaborative decision making. These skills include, but are not limited to, preparing for the discussion by reading the text closely, referring to evidence in the text, and reflecting on the ideas being discussed. (SL.8.1a, SL.8.1b)

Clarify Briefly restate today's teaching objective and explain the independent task(s)

Explain how students are going to examine "Theseus" in *D'Aulaires' Book of Greek Myths* by Ingri d'Aulaire and Edgar Parin d'Aulaire. As they read, they will be following the stages of the hero's journey with supporting evidence from the text.

> I would like to suggest that this map of the hero's quest is ageless and universal. Every myth you read from Ancient Greece or any other part of the world should fit this pattern of events. You are going to test this out. Your task is to read "Theseus," a hero myth from *D'Aulaires' Book of Greek Myths*. As you read, mark and detail with text evidence each stage and step in the journey. See if the conditions match this hero and his quest. I will provide the Hero's Journey graphic organizer for you to record your findings.

ELL Frontload the Lesson—Set a Purpose for Reading. ELLs will find it easier to work through the challenging language of this text if they know exactly what they are looking for. The Hero's Journey Graphic Organizer will help them do this.

Practice Students work independently and/or in small groups to apply today's teaching objective

Students read the Theseus myth and record the text details of the journey on the Hero's Journey Graphic Organizer (Appendix 8.5).

ELL Enable Language Production—Increasing Interaction. Language is developed through social interaction, and ELLs of all English proficiency levels might benefit from conducting their analyses in small groups. For students who are highly orally proficient, peer work can help them work through the unfamiliar academic register of the text; for students just learning English, peers can paraphrase the text content so that these newcomers can participate in the group's analysis.

Wrap Up Check understanding as you guide students to briefly share what they have learned and produced today

Working with a partner, students should share their organizers. Did you find the same evidence for the steps and stages in your hero's journey?

Use this opportunity to remind students to listen actively to their partner explain his or her evidence, then explain their own evidence and make any necessary changes based on the partner conversations. (SL.8.1d)

Reading Lesson 5

Close Reading Opportunity

▼ Teaching Objective

Readers develop understandings about the characteristics of Greek heroes through collaborative discussion.

▼ Standards Alignment

RL.8.1, RL.8.2, RL.8.3, RL.8.10, SL.8.1, SL.8.4, SL.8.6, L.8.1, L.8.3, L.8.6

▼ Materials

- Previously read Greek myth (such as Heracles from *D'Aulaires' Book of Greek Myths* by Ingri d'Aulaire and Edgar Parin d'Aulaire)
- Core Phrases
- Prepared hero guiding questions (see this lesson)
- A selection of myths for independent reading found in *D'Aulaires' Book of Greek Myths* (not previously read)
  - "Bellerophon"
  - "Theseus"
  - "The Apples of Love and the Apples of Discord" (Odysseus)

▼ To the Teacher

Prior to this lesson, read the myth of Heracles or another familiar myth with students. Also, choose a few new myths for students to read during Practice. If necessary, match students to a particular myth according to instructional needs. This is a good opportunity to use text level to differentiate instruction. ELL Enable Language Production—Reading and Writing. ELLs, like English-proficient students, are a diverse group. Each state (and even district) defines "English language learner" differently and sets different requirements for ELLs to be "reclassified" as English proficient. However, part of the definition of "ELL" nearly everywhere is that these students are not yet performing at grade level in an English-medium classroom. Some may be working at or above grade level in their home language; others may be highly orally proficient in English but struggle with reading and writing; still others may be on the verge of reclassification and therefore able to fully meet grade-level expectations. Regardless of where our students come in, our job is to take them further. This means finding a balance between giving students exposure to challenging grade-level text with support and giving them the opportunity to read texts at their independent levels while still demanding analytical thinking about this text.

This lesson focuses not only on the content discussed in previous lessons but also on the role collaborative discussion plays in deepening students' comprehension of a text. For true collaboration to occur, students must first engage with the text independently to develop their initial thoughts. Then students will meet in groups to develop new ideas around a common text.

▼ Procedure

Warm Up Gather the class to set the stage for today's learning

Ask students to review what they have learned with the class about the purpose and elements of myths thus far. Direct them to move forward and read mythology independently.

By now you should have enough mythology under your belt to go on your own journey and read your own myths. I have a selection of myths for independent reading.

Provide students with their myths for independent reading.

Teach Model what students need to learn and do

Model how to develop ideas while reading, and then explain how students can grow ideas in their discussions.

> Your job while reading your hero myth is to find out all you can about your hero. That means reading carefully in search of explicit and implicit information. Use these hero guiding questions:

Hero Guiding Questions

- Who is the hero?
- What do we know about the hero's birth and family?
- What is important about the hero's past? Why?
- What character traits are evident in this hero? Explain with text evidence.
- Does the hero have shortcomings? Explain with text evidence.

ELL Identify and Communicate Content and Language Objectives—Paraphrase. Your ELLs need exposure to academic English, but they also need to understand what you are saying. As you come to challenging vocabulary words in your model consider "stepping aside" to quickly explain the word with a common synonym. This will help ELLs develop their vocabulary.

> Keep track of your findings in your notes as you read. Watch me as I do this with my own myth, "Heracles."

- The hero of this myth is Heracles.
- He is the son of Zeus, a god, and Alceme, a human woman. He is half god, and half human, also known as a demigod.
- Hera, Zeus's wife, hates Heracles because she is jealous of her husband's tryst with another woman. She tries to destroy him as a baby by sending him poisonous snakes. Heracles kills both snakes with his hands. This is important because it shows he is more than human. He has unparalleled strength, which is tested by Hera throughout his life.
- He is extraordinarily strong and courageous. He completed the 12 labors, some of which include destroying beasts, stealing golden apples, and bringing a dog back from the underworld.
- His Achilles' heel, or his weakness, is his anger. Because he killed his teacher with a blow, his father sent him away.

> Now that I have read and thought about the hero of Heracles, I want to share my notes with my group.

Try Guide students to quickly rehearse what they need to learn and do in preparation for practice

Model a discussion with a group of students and ask the students watching to notice what they see and hear as well as to develop questions they have about the conversation.

Ask students to share what they noticed and wondered about the text discussion held with their peers. Direct students to focus on several key speaking and listening skills:

- Lead speaker reviews notes and presents findings, providing evidence and details from the text about the character.
- All speakers make eye contact and speak clearly.
- Listeners may pose questions to lead speaker asking for more evidence or clarification.
- Speaker responds to questions and ideas from group with relevant evidence. (SL.8.1a, SL.8.1b, SL.8.1c, SL.8.1d, SL.8.4)

ELL Enable Language Production—Listening and Speaking. Keep in mind that even these apparently basic listening conventions are culturally specific and may vary even among subcultures within the United States. For example, some children learn not to look at the speaker as a sign of respect; some cultures practice overlapping speech during conversation instead of strict turn-taking; and some groups use nonlinear patterns when conveying an idea, starting with indirect connections and circling back toward the main point. Look for behaviors that may indicate your students have been socialized differently than you, and think about how to encourage them to be culturally flexible depending on the demands of the context.

Clarify Briefly restate today's teaching objective and explain the independent task(s)

Explain how students will move from independent practice and thought to collaborative discussion.

> Our reading about a Greek hero will begin as an independent task. As you read, you will continue to note the characteristics of the hero as well as the stages of the hero's journey. Once that reading is completed, you will be meeting in groups to discuss your ideas about the hero and develop these ideas together.

Practice Students work independently and/or in small groups to apply today's teaching objective

Students read independent myth texts, looking for evidence of hero characters and recognizable patterns using the Hero Guiding Questions.

After reading, guide students to engage in a collaborative discussion in small groups or partnerships as modeled in Try. (SL.8.1a, SL.8.1b, SL.8.1c, SL.8.1d, SL.8.4)

ELL Enable Language Production—Listening and Speaking. As you check in with your ELL groups, you may hear some brilliant ideas packaged in nonstandard language. Remember that correcting students' language in front of their peers can shut down future contributions. Instead, pop into the conversation (drawing attention to good ideas or pushing the group's thinking) and rephrase students' ideas with more standard syntax or vocabulary. At the same time, remember that no one actually talks like a book—not even teachers—and that peer discussions are a context where some informal uses of language might be appropriate.

After the discussions, ask groups to reflect on their conversations:

Did the conversation with your peers help you deepen your understanding of the hero? Why or why not?

ELL Enable Language Production—Increasing Interaction. It is important to create an atmosphere of supportive sharing in your classroom so your ELLs feel comfortable sharing their ideas with the group and so they can be honest about their struggles and get help from their peers.

Wrap Up Check understanding as you guide students to briefly share what they have learned and produced today

Ask students to think about the heroes in their independent practice myths and compare the heroes to Heracles. Using their notes from class, they should be noticing very specific characteristics and patterns of events.

Provide a brief summary of your myth from independent practice. How is your hero the same as and different from Heracles? Be specific in your answers, using details from your texts.

Reading Lesson 6

▼ Teaching Objective

Readers preview contemporary novels to search for evidence of the archetypal hero and the monomyth structure.

Close Reading Opportunity

▼ Standards Alignment

RL.8.1, RL.8.2, RL.8.3, RL.8.9, RL.8.10, SL.8.1, SL.8.4, SL.8.6, L.8.1, L.8.3, L.8.6

▼ Materials

- "A Video Interview with Rick Riordan" at www.adlit.org or a print interview found at www.rickriordan.com
- *The Lightning Thief* by Rick Riordan
- A collection of fantasy novels for independent reading
- Book Group Calendar (downloadable PDF in the Core Ready PDToolkit)
- Charting supplies or interactive whiteboard for group predictions
- Book description for *Harry Potter and the Sorcerer's Stone* from www.amazon.com

▼ To the Teacher

In this lesson, we introduce the independent reading fantasy novel. Choose four to five fantasy novels from the Core Texts suggested at the beginning of the lesson set. These novels portray a strong hero whom students can analyze and discuss. Think about the accessibility of these texts as you develop small groups. Once groups are formed, students will read the texts individually and independently but discuss the texts as a group. Because a novel will take longer to read than the five sessions left in the lesson set, allow a few sessions for reading and discussion. In the PDToolkit you will find a blank version of the Book Group Calendar that you can customize to your schedule. **ELL** Enable Language Production—Reading and Writing. This is a great opportunity to differentiate instruction for your ELLs. Remember that our goal is to have all students master grade-level standards and work with complex text. If you have a group of recently arrived students with lots of prior schooling in their home language, consider having them read a fantasy novel in that language so they can fully practice your teaching objectives. If you have a group of orally proficient ELLs who are below grade level in reading, consider how you can give them a cognitive challenge in spite of their struggles with reading: Could they read in a group and support each other? Listen to a recording as they read? Have you read aloud to them? Do whatever you can to bring them to challenging text.

▼ Procedure

Warm Up Gather the class to set the stage for today's learning

Assess students' prior experiences with fantasy novels. Using books in the classroom or from the school or local library or texts read earlier in the school year, show students examples of fantasy texts. Begin a discussion about the fantasy genre and how it requires the author to create unbeliev-able situations that seem believable—which then require the reader to inter-act differently with the text. Readers must agree to the terms the new world sets forth; they cannot deny what is occurring in the text. Students must read closely and metaphorically, as many fantasy writers include fantastical places, people, and objects representing counterparts in reality. **ELL** Provide Comprehensible Input—Visuals. ELLs will grasp more clearly the idea of *fantasy* if you bring in physical examples of fantasy books and ask them to connect this term to novels they might already be familiar with.

Who has read a fantasy novel before? A book like *Harry Potter* or *The Hunger Games* or *A Wrinkle in Time*? What did you like about this genre? How was reading this genre different from reading realistic fiction?

Use this as an opportunity to assess students' understanding of the dif-ferences between fantasy and realistic fiction.

Sample responses:

- Realistic fiction allows for events that would happen only in real life. Fantasy includes magical events.

- Realistic fiction characters are human. Fantasy characters may be more than human and have certain powers.

- Realistic fiction takes place in a setting that may actually exist. Fantasy settings may involve places and times that exist only in the author's imagination.

Notice if students bring in any mention of heroes in fantasy text on their own, but don't prompt them to do so yet.

I want to start this journey by introducing you (if you do not already know his work) to a great writer by the name of Rick Riordan. He is the author of *Percy Jackson and the Olympians*. I will be reading from the first book in the series, *The Lightning Thief*.

Let's listen in on an interview of the author from Adolescent Literacy.org.

At www.adlit.org, search for "A Video Interview with Rick Riordan." At the main interview page, click the mythology tab next to the video screen.

Your job is to listen for the connections between mythology and fantasy.

ELL Provide Comprehensible Input—Audiovisual Aids. By eighth grade, all children (barring disability or severe deprivation) are highly proficient in the language of their home communities and often use language in very sophis-ticated ways. Young people of this generation are additionally often highly proficient at communicating through multimedia. A video interview can help form a bridge between ways of communication valued in schools (like book language) and the multilingual, nonmainstream, often visual ways that many ELL middle schoolers communicate with their peers and families.

Guide students to the following observations (among other excellent ones that they will come up with):

- characters have powers
- a clear hero
- characters who are allies to the hero
- imagined settings
- a villain
- imagined creatures

If you do not have access to the video link, you can find a print inter-view with Rick Riordan at www.rickriordan.com (click on "About Rick). Focus on the question about Greek gods and censorship.

After students share their observations on the content of the interview, discuss the following follow-up questions:

- Do you agree with the points Rick Riordan makes? Tell me why, referring to specific things you heard Mr. Riordan say.

- Do you see your lives as middle school kids relating a bit to the hero's journey? In what ways? Tell me some specifics about the relationship between your own lives and the important parts of the hero's journey.

ELL Frontload the Lesson—Make Connections. This discussion gives stu-dents a chance to make the hero's journey applicable to their own lives. This line of thinking can be especially powerful for ELLs, who are more likely to feel a mismatch between their experiences and school than many other students, and can increase their engagement with the lesson.

Goal	Low-Tech	High-Tech
Students make the connection between the mythical hero and the fantasy hero.	Students read a written version of an interview with Rick Riordan: www.rickriordan.com (click on "About Rick")	Students watch interview with Rick Riordan at www.adlit.org/authors/Riordan/. Search "A Video Interview with Rick Riordan." At the main interview page, click the mythology tab next to the video screen.

Teach Model what students need to learn and do

Explain that you will be shifting from previous lessons. Although stu-dents will still be using the knowledge gleaned from studying mythologi-cal heroes, their focus will shift to studying the heroic characters in fantasy novels. The goal is for students to identify and analyze how their modern fantasy texts draw on and renew the themes (heroism), pattern of events (the hero's journey), and character types (the hero) from myths. **ELL** Frontload the Lesson—Make Connections. When you explicitly draw students' attention to their earlier work and the work they will be doing in this lesson, you help your ELLs in particular build on what they've learned and extend their thinking further.

> We will now begin reading contemporary fantasy novels. Our goal is to make the connection between ancient myth and contemporary fantasy. I want you to see just how many modern storytellers use the structure of the monomyth to create and tell their stories.

Model how to read the blurb (from *The Lightning Thief*) and analyze it to make predictions about the character of Percy and the events that might take place in the story. The blurb is a short, engaging synopsis that appears on the back of a book or on a book's webpage, usually designed to entice a reader.

> So if fantasy novels follow the hero's journey, what do you think will happen to Percy Jackson? Let's read the blurb and make some thoughtful predictions based on what we know about the monomyth.

Read the blurb aloud.

> If we hadn't just read mythology, I would say this book is a mystery. Zeus's lightning bolt has been stolen and the main character Percy is the prime suspect. I know mysteries well. I read in search of clues to find the person who committed the crime. My guess is part of this novel will read like the genre of mystery, with Percy trying to find the lightning bolt and prove his innocence.

Model how you reference the mythology knowledge you have gathered in the previous lessons. Notice the recognizable:

- character names from Greek mythology
- places from Greek mythology
- characteristics of the hero
- events of the hero's journey/monomyth

> On the other hand, in this fantasy book in particular, it is hard to ignore the connections to mythology. Mount Olympus is the home of the Immortals. Zeus is the most powerful of these gods. So the mythology that Percy is studying in school seems to be coming to life all around him. This makes me want to search for clues of a hero's journey. And I think I can find a few just in the blurb . . .

- Who will most likely be the hero?
- What characteristics of an archetypal hero will this character most likely display?
- Which stages of the hero's journey seem to be referenced in the blurb?

> Based on the phrase that he angered monsters and gods, I think these could be some of Percy's trials, during the "Tests" and "Ordeal" parts of his journey. When we read about Percy's friends, it sounds like they'll be going on the journey with him. They could end up being his allies on the journey. There is an Oracle and a prophecy, which sound like part of the hero's quest.

ELL Provide Comprehensible Input—Models. Here you are showing your students how they can use knowledge of genre to make predictions about the arc of a story. When you are explicit with your students about how authors use such "templates" to structure their texts, you are inducting your ELLs into the world of literary readers and writers. This can increase both the accuracy of their predictions and their overall comprehension of a text.

Try Guide students to quickly rehearse what they need to learn and do in preparation for practice

Show students another book blurb from a fantasy novel. Using the same questions you used during the model, students will develop a prediction and share this prediction with a partner. One possibility is the description of *Harry Potter and the Sorcerer's Stone* on www.amazon.com. If this description is not available to you, feel free to use another blurb from a fantasy novel.

Remind students to refer to specific text in the blurb to support the opinions and conclusions they are reaching.

As students engage in their discussions, listen in to ensure that they are arriving at the conversations prepared and are adequately referencing the fantasy book blurb under discussion. (SL.8.1a)

There are several possible parallels to the hero's journey in the brief description of the book, including:

- Ordinary World: Harry's miserable aunt and uncle
- Call to Adventure: the summoning to wizard school
- Meeting of the Mentor: greeting by a lovable giant
- Tests/Allies/Enemies: unique curriculum, colorful faculty

There is also a suggestion of the extraordinary birth circumstances of the archetypal hero: Harry's wizard parents, birthright, and noble destiny.

Clarify Briefly restate today's teaching objective and explain the independent task(s)

Explain that students will be reading the blurb of the book, looking for signs of the hero's journey, and writing group predictions on the materials provided.

> Your reading goal is to begin by reading the blurb of your book. Using what you know about mythology and Greek heroes, see if you recognize any signs of the archetypal hero's characteristics or typical hero's journey in the text. Make some logical predictions based on what you know about the monomyth and/or the hero's characteristics, referring to specific words or lines from the blurb.

> When you have completed this initial discussion, sit side by side and begin to read your first chapter.

Practice Students work independently and/or in small groups to apply today's teaching objective

Students meet in book groups to collaborate and make predictions based on their blurbs and knowledge of the monomyth. They should write their findings on chart paper to share with the rest of the class. When they have completed their predictions, students should begin reading their books. **ELL** Enable Language Production—Increasing Interaction. Group work can be a good way for ELLs to gain entry to the lesson. If they are still unsure of what is expected of them, their peers can help. Consider putting ELLs in groups with bilingual students who share their home language as well as with monolingual English-speaking peers so the discussion can occur in both languages.

Please note that if a group's blurb does not reveal much that seems to parallel the elements of the classic hero and hero's journey, the group might have more success reading book reviews online on sites such as Amazon.com. Reviews often provide additional plot and character clues that may connect to students' knowledge about heroes. If a group truly comes up empty-handed, those students still should write about their findings and be able to provide evidence to support the claim that they were not able to make any connections.

Reading Lesson 7

▼ Teaching Objective

Readers search for the archetypal hero's characteristics in independent novels.

Close Reading Opportunity

▼ Standards Alignment

RL.8.1, RL.8.2, RL.8.3, RL.8.9, RL.8.10, W.8.4, W.8.9, W.8.10, SL.8.1, SL.8.4, SL.8.6, L.8.1, L.8.3, L.8.6

▼ Materials

- Hero's Characteristics graphic organizer (Appendix 8.3)
- Charting supplies or interactive whiteboard to create Heroic Quality of Character/Evidence and Impressions chart
- *The Lightning Thief* by Rick Riordan
- A collection of fantasy novels for independent reading

▼ To the Teacher

In this lesson, students will be exploring the qualities of the hero in their fantasy novels. You will be modeling how to gather evidence of the hero's

Wrap Up Check understanding as you guide students to briefly share what they have learned and produced today

Student groups share their findings from their blurbs.

Also, take an opportunity to develop some parameters for the fantasy book discussions that will occur at later times. Setting guidelines will teach students to come prepared for discussion as well as how to develop and meet goals. (SL.8.1a, SL.8.1b, SL.8.1c, SL.8.1d)

You may wish to use a calendar as a tool to support students and yourself in laying out a schedule that allows students to complete reading their fantasy novels in a timely manner, as they will be using the evidence from these texts to develop the literary essay in the writing portion of the lesson set.

> We will be using the Wrap Up time for you to meet in groups and make reading plans for your books. I have given you a blank calendar, and I want you to plot your reading plans on the calendar and then keep it with you so you have a reference for the pages you must read each night. Because you will talk from time to time about your novels, you need to keep up with the schedule to be prepared for your group. If you read ahead of schedule, please be sensitive to your group members' desire to enjoy the story—no spoilers!

characteristics, so you will need to have read through Chapter 6 ("I Become Supreme Lord of the Bathroom"). In order to do the work of character analysis, be sure students have read about six chapters or a sizeable chunk of the novel they are reading independently. You can use some of the following ideas to manage the reading:

- Provide set days for reading of the text
- Use the Book Club Calendars completed in the previous lesson
- Stretch lessons over a few days to reiterate more difficult objectives while allowing students more time to practice and read the text

▼ Procedure

Warm Up Gather the class to set the stage for today's learning

Revisit the Hero's Characteristics graphic organizer (Appendix 8.3) that outlined the characteristics of the archetypal hero. Students will begin to examine the concept of the protagonist from the fantasy novel as the hero and how these heroes compare with previously studied heroes.

ELL Frontload the Lesson—Activate Prior Knowledge. Make the relationship between this lesson and earlier work explicit to help your ELLs orient themselves to work they are about to do.

Let's review our Hero's Characteristics graphic organizer. If you look up the elements of the genre of fantasy and focus on character, one thing you'll find is that most fantasy characters have some special powers. The main characters in modern fantasy novels tend to be called heroes or heroines, and they are usually characterized as brave, a bit innocent, and selfless. How does your knowledge of modern fantasy characters match up with our mythology character description?

Responses will vary, but some things students might share about familiar modern fantasy characters in comparison with the archetypal hero characteristics include:

- Modern fantasy characters tend to be courageous. They knowingly place themselves in danger to prove themselves, save others, or save a higher ideal.
- Most modern characters take on conflicts that require them to use physical and/or mental strength.
- Some modern characters are self-sacrificing. At a point in the story, the hero realizes that his or her own life is worth sacrificing if it is for the greater good.
- The modern character is often a good friend, brother/sister, or son/daughter. The relationships between the hero and those he or she holds dear make him or her a stronger and better leader.

Teach Model what students need to learn and do

Explain to students that they will be comparing the archetypal characters from the previous lessons with the characters present in their fantasy novels. Demonstrate this with the character Percy from *The Lightning Thief*.

We are going to start our investigation of our fantasy novels and our comparison of the stories in these novels to mythology by thinking first about the main character. I am going to reflect on what we have read aloud from *The Lightning Thief* and how the main character fits our working definition of a hero.

The first thing I notice is that Percy refers to himself as half blood. This seems to be an example of an unusual birth circumstance. I know that Greek heroes are demigods—half human, half god. So that is a big hint that Percy is likely to be the hero of my story. And as I read, Percy talks about how bad stuff happens when he is on field trips, and while he's not specific about what those things are, it does sound like he has some untapped powers that he hasn't realized yet. That sounds a bit like Heracles and the power he had as a child to kill those snakes. By the way, when Percy talks about himself, he doesn't seem to feel particularly powerful or successful. He doesn't do well in school, he is always getting in trouble, and clearly, as the story begins, after the initial flashback, Percy has no idea that he is the son of a Greek god. He thinks he is just a regular kid.

Complete the first items on the following chart to mark the heroic quality of the character and the evidence from the text. Model the inclusion of evidence through paraphrased information and details as well as direct quotes from the text. (*Important:* We do not include direct quotes due to publishing restrictions, but we certainly recommend that teachers model providing quotes as evidence for students.)

Hero's Characteristics graphic organizer

Characteristic	Evidence from the Text • Text quote or description • Page # (*)
Mighty warrior	Percy Jackson fights the minotaur, rips off its horn, and uses it as a weapon to kill him, page XX
Unusual birth circumstances	Son of Poseidon—a half blood. Lives with his human mother and stepfather. Remembers seeing his father looking at him in his cradle when he was a baby, page XX
Initiating event	Doesn't know what to do when Mrs. Dodds turns into a beast and shows her talons, page XX
Epic quest	Must return the lightning bolt to Zeus in order to free his mother from the Underworld and return into the living world, page XX
Admirable qualities: bravery, selflessness	Percy feels that he is no longer afraid, but strong enough to face what comes his way, page XX Distracted and fought the Minotaur to save Grover, page XX

Page numbers will vary depending on edition.

Try Guide students to quickly rehearse what they need to learn and do in preparation for practice

Tell students to work in partnerships in order to determine the last three parts of the hero's characteristics graphic organizer for Percy Jackson.

As students work in their partnerships, have them consider whether they should be speaking in formal English or more casual conversational language. (SL.8.6) **ELL** Enable Language Production—Listening and Speaking. Remember that some students might not use what you consider formal English because they don't know that particular register of the language. Newcomer ELLs may still be acquiring the mechanics of English; orally proficient ELLs may be accustomed to a nonstandard variety of English. It is important to notice how students use language and to give them the tools to make conscious choices about what style of language they will use in different settings. At the same time, be careful not to "correct" students in front of their peers if they use nonstandard language, as this is likely to make them reluctant to contribute their ideas in the future.

> Now that I have modeled the first few heroic characteristics of Percy Jackson, work with a partner to determine the last three: the hero lives elsewhere, he has special weapons, and he receives help from gods and goddesses.

Lives elsewhere	Percy lived at boarding school, page XX
Special weapons	Mr. Brunner gives him a bronze sword nicknamed Riptide, page XX
Help from gods/ goddesses	Chiron (Mr. Brunner) and Grover (a satyr) are his protectors, page XX

Students share their comparisons of Percy to the archetypal hero.

Clarify Briefly restate today's teaching objective and explain the independent task(s)

Direct students to read their fantasy novels and analyze their characters. Students should connect their analyses to specific events, descriptions, and background information provided in the plots of the novels they are reading.

> Your reading challenge is to read your fantasy novel in order to identify the hero and some of his or her character traits, just as we did for *The Lightning Thief*. You will place the evidence of these characteristics in the Hero's Characteristics graphic organizer.

Practice Students work independently and/or in small groups to apply today's teaching objective

Students revisit the texts they have read to date in their groups and together identify the hero and his or her traits. Students will then continue reading their fantasy novels. Students record the characteristics and evidence on the Hero's Characteristics graphic organizer (Appendix 8.3). **ELL** Identify and Communicate Content and Language Objectives—Check for Understanding. Check in with your ELLs to make sure they understand the lesson objective, know what constitutes evidence of a hero's traits, and can read and comprehend the text they are analyzing.

Wrap Up Check understanding as you guide students to briefly share what they have learned and produced today

To assess and support a deeper class understanding of heroic characters, ask students to share the hero of their novel as well as their impressions and

analyses and reasons supporting them. This type of sharing also provides students with other titles they may find compelling enough to read at a later date. Provide students with the opportunity to revisit their organizers across the book to see if they have discovered new evidence of the hero archetype.

Milestone Performance Assessment

Finding Hero's Characteristics in Fantasy Novels

Collect and analyze the Hero's Characteristics graphic organizer as a performance-based assessment to determine if students need additional instruction or support as a whole class, in small groups, or one on one. **ELL** Assess for Content and Language Understanding—Formative Assessment. Make sure your ELLs know how to do the performance tasks described. If they do not, study their work thoughtfully to determine why: Are they confused about what the traits in the graphic organizer mean? Did they misunderstand your instructions about how to complete the organizer? Are they having trouble expressing their ideas in a way that is clear to you as a reader? Each will require a different sort of instructional response from you. Consider having a conversation with these students to get a deeper understanding of their thought process.

 Use this checklist to assess student work on the Hero's Characteristics graphic organizer.

Standards Alignment: RL.8.1, RL.8.2, RL.8.3, RL.8.9, W.8.4, W.8.9, W.8.10

Task	Achieved	Notes
Analyze the modern character and describe how the character demonstrates archetypal heroic traits.		
Support analysis with explicit evidence from the text.		

Reading Lesson 8 . . . .

▼ Teaching Objective

Readers search for the archetypal hero's journey in independent novels.

Close Reading Opportunity

▼ Standards Alignment

RL.8.1, RL.8.2, RL.8.3, RL.8.9, RL.8.10, W.8.4, W.8.9, W.8.10, SL.8.1, SL.8.4, SL.8.6, L.8.1, L.8.3, L.8.6

▼ Materials

- *The Lightning Thief* by Rick Riordan
- The Stages of the Hero's Journey Defined (Appendix 8.4)
- Hero's Journey graphic organizer (Appendix 8.5)
- A collection of fantasy novels for independent reading

▼ To the Teacher

To model the stages of the hero's journey for *The Lightning Thief*, you will need to have read to at least Chapter 11 of the text.

▼ Procedure

Warm Up Gather the class to set the stage for today's learning

Refer to the previous lesson that modeled gathering of evidence that connects the characteristics of a hero and the character of Percy Jackson.

Teach Model what students need to learn and do

Explain to students that they will be looking to connect the monomyth from mythology to modern fantasy novels. Using the Hero's Journey graphic organizer (Appendix 8.5) which was used to catalog the hero's journey in mythology, model how to gather evidence from *The Lightning Thief* to correlate with the stages of the journey. **ELL** Frontload the Lesson—Make Connections. It will be great for your ELLs to clearly see that they have already learned this skill and now are just applying it to a new text.

> In a typical fiction novel, the first several chapters are dedicated to exposition—we learn the basics—the characters, the setting, and some hint of the problem or challenge. The same is true in the first part of a myth or the exposition in a fantasy novel. But we know we are moving into new territory in fiction when the action begins to rise. In the case of a myth, the real action begins when the hero agrees to the adventure and crosses the threshold into the new unfamiliar world. Let's notice how Percy, just like the heroes of mythology, follows the stages of the monomyth. We'll use our Hero's Journey graphic organizer to keep track of the evidence.

Hero's Journey graphic organizer

Stage of the Journey	Evidence from the Text • Text quote or description • Page # (*)
The Ordinary World	Percy is just an unhappy kid at boarding school. He was 100 percent in the real world, page XX
Call to Adventure	Mrs. Dodds confronts Percy in the museum and reveals herself as a monster, page XX
Refusal of the Call	Percy dismisses what happened at the museum, page XX
Meeting the Mentor	Mr. Brunner is in fact Chiron, a centaur who I know from mythology was a teacher and mentor to Jason and Achilles and other Greek heroes. He gives Percy the pen/sword, page XX
Crossing the Threshold	Percy might have crossed into that new world when he escaped from the Minotaur and arrived at Camp Half-Blood, a summer camp where nothing seems normal, page XX
Tests/Allies/Enemies	In this story, Percy uses a similar trick, a reflecting glass ball, to find Medusa without looking her in the eyes and then chop off her head, page XX
Approach to the Innermost Cave	Percy and the rest of the demigods are developing a plan to defeat the Titans. Percy also has romantic feelings for Annabeth, page XX
Ordeal	Percy has gone west, to California, and is now in the Underworld looking for Hades, who he thinks has "turned" and stolen the lightning bolt to cause trouble between Poseidon and Zeus. The prophecy promises he will find the bolt and will return it to Zeus, page XX

Page numbers will vary depending on edition.

Try Guide students to quickly rehearse what they need to learn and do in preparation for practice

Provide students with The Stages of the Hero's Journey Defined (Appendix 8.4) and Hero's Journey graphic organizer (Appendix 8.5) and instruct them to work with a partner to determine the evidence that supports the stages in the hero's journey in *The Lightning Thief*.

> With a partner, determine the evidence for the last four stages of the hero's journey. Record the evidence in the Hero's Journey graphic organizer.

Sample of completed student graphic organizer:

Reward	Percy gets to meet his father, page XX
The Road Back	Percy harnesses the power of water to defeat Luke, the real lightning thief, page XX
Resurrection	Percy belongs with his mother in the real world but also in the new world of demigods, page XX
Return with the Elixir	Percy returns the lighting bolt to Zeus at Mount Olympus, page XX

Clarify Briefly restate today's teaching objective and explain the practice task(s)

Explain that students will be gathering evidence to support the stages of the hero's journey in their own fantasy novels.

> Your task is to use the Hero's Journey graphic organizer to gather evidence from your independent fantasy novels, just as I did with *The Lightning Thief.* Use the blank graphic organizer provided.

Practice Students work independently and/or in small groups to apply today's teaching objective

Students will complete the Hero's Journey graphic organizer using the evidence from their fantasy novels. Confer with students to make sure they are citing specific quotes and supplying accurate information from their novels.

Wrap Up Check understanding as you guide students to briefly share what they have learned and produced today

Ask students to share examples of their completed hero's journey graphic organizers with evidence from their fantasy novels.

> What have we learned about the monomyth?

Milestone Performance Assessment

Finding the Hero's Journey in Fantasy Novels

Analyze the Hero's Journey Graphic Organizer as a performance-based assessment to determine if students need additional instruction or support as a whole class, in small groups, or one on one. **ELL** Assess for Content and Language Understanding—Formative Assessment. Check that your ELLs are making progress in both content mastery and language development. Be especially considerate of how content and language overlap—for example, if a student seems unable to find evidence of the hero's journey in the fantasy novel, is this because he or she doesn't understand the parts of the hero's journey, or because he or she is unable to understand the language the author uses to present the stages of the journey, or because he or she is unable to clearly communicate understanding? Use this information to plan upcoming lessons.

 Use this checklist to assess student work on the Hero's Journey Graphic Organizer.

Standards Alignment: RL.8.1, RL.8.2, RL.8.3, RL.8.9, W.8.4, W.8.9, W.8.10

Task	Achieved	Notes
Analyze the modern character and describe how the character's experiences parallel the archetypal monomyth (hero's journey).		
Support analysis with explicit evidence from the text.		

Reading Lesson 9 ·

▼ Teaching Objective

Readers recognize the importance of secondary characters in fantasy novels.

Close Reading Opportunity

▼ Standards Alignment

RL.8.1, RL.8.2, RL.8.3, RL.8.10, W.8.4, W.8.6, W.8.9, W.8.10, SL.8.1, SL.8.4, SL.8.5, SL.8.6, L.8.1, L.8.2, L.8.3, L.8.6

▼ Materials

- *The Lightning Thief* by Rick Riordan
- A collection of fantasy novels for independent reading
- Charting supplies or interactive whiteboard to create the Secondary Character Analysis chart
- Secondary Character Analysis graphic organizer (downloadable PDF in the Core Ready PDToolkit)

▼ To the Teacher

During this lesson, the students will be exploring the ever-important allies, or secondary characters, in heroic tales. The students will consider the purpose of these characters and notice how they interact with the hero, help propel the action, and compare across texts. This lesson will also require students to go back and gather text evidence of the secondary characters' actions and qualities. As you will have completed at least 11 chapters in *The Lightning Thief*, the allies will be clearly present.

▼ Procedure

Warm Up Gather the class to set the stage for today's learning

During this Warm Up, engage students in a brief discussion about their progress with their fantasy novels. Use the language of the hero's journey to ascertain where students are in the novels.

> One of the factors that seemed to bring our Greek heroes closer to their Call to Adventure was leaving the safety of their homes. When I read *The Lightning Thief*, I discovered that Percy found out he would not be invited back to his private school the following year. And then he talked to Mr. Brunner who hinted to him that he was not normal.
>
> Has anyone reached a similar point in his or her books yet? Is anyone helping your hero?

ELL Frontload the Lesson—Activate Prior Knowledge. By helping ELLs ground this lesson in the work they have already been doing, you enable them to root what they will learn from this lesson in the novel they are already very familiar with.

Teach Model what students need to learn and do

Secondary Character Analysis graphic organizer

Secondary Character(s)	Ally or Enemy	Actions of Secondary Character	Values/Hopes of Secondary Character	Relationship between Hero and Secondary Character

In this lesson, students will be shifting their focus from the protagonist as the hero to the secondary characters in their novels. Using references from some well-known movies and books such as *Star Wars* and *Harry Potter*, discuss the concept of the ally and how these characters often display heroic characteristics themselves. It is also imperative that students understand how the allies help create the full identity of the hero.

Frontload this lesson by presenting students with the terms *enemies* and *allies:*

Enemies: Characters whose role is to prevent the hero from beginning the journey, succeeding with a quest, or completing the journey.
Allies: Characters who serve to help and support the hero on his or her journey.

ELL Identify and Communicate Content and Language Objectives—Key Content Vocabulary. Make this essential vocabulary transparent to your ELLs by adding visuals and familiar examples as well as home-language translations if possible.

> Fantasy novels have another characteristic or element worth noting. Typically the hero or heroine travels on the journey with allies—people who are there to help and support the hero on his path. Think about Harry Potter—he had Hermione and Ron. Luke Skywalker had R2D2 and C3PO. Usually these sidekicks do not have the same powers as the hero, but they do have value and resources.
>
> In this lesson, I am going to broaden my lens and look at the other characters around Percy. My goal is to try to find evidence that Percy will have allies help him on his quest and/or enemies that try to stand in his way. I will use the following questions to guide my thinking about the secondary characters, or allies and enemies.

- What secondary character(s) does the hero encounter who seem(s) to have the same values or hopes as the hero?
- What secondary character(s) does the hero encounter who seem(s) to want to prevent the hero from continuing on his journey?
- Is the secondary character(s) an ally or an enemy? Does the character mean to help or harm your hero?
- What are the actions of the secondary characters(s) that allow the hero to continue or temporarily prevent the hero from continuing on the journey?
- How do the hero and the secondary character(s) interact? How would you describe their relationship, and why?

Read aloud from the first few pages of the chapter "Grover Unexpectedly Loses His Pants." Model the analysis of Percy's relationship with Grover using the Secondary Character Analysis chart.

> It turns out that Percy's friend Grover is traveling on the same bus home for the summer and that Grover isn't quite what he seems. Since one person has already turned into a harpy and tried to kill Percy, I think that Grover is some-thing more than he appears as well. The bus has broken down, and Grover seems panicked to get Percy away from the three old women at the roadside stand. Is he an ally or an enemy? Why? Let's chart our thinking.

Secondary Character Analysis graphic organizer

Secondary Character	Ally or Enemy	Actions of Secondary Character	Values/ Hopes of Secondary Character	Relationship between Hero and Secondary Character
Grover	Ally	Seems panicked to get Percy away from the three old women at the roadside stand.	He feels connected to nature. He hopes to find Pan. His task is to protect Percy, and he takes this task seriously.	They are best friends. Grover is helpful and understands Percy's emotions. He is a satyr, and it is his role to protect Percy and deliver him safely to Camp Half-Blood.

Try Guide students to quickly rehearse what they need to learn and do in preparation for practice

> Now it's your turn to help me. The bus has broken down, and Grover seems panicked to get Percy away from the three old women at the roadside stand. Let's use our chart to analyze their role in the story.

Three old women	Enemy	The three old women seem to be staring directly at Percy. One takes out a pair of giant gold scissors and cuts a piece of yarn. It looks almost like a ritual.	They represent the three fates from Greek mythology. They wish to prevent Percy from beginning his journey and returning the lightning bolt to Zeus.	Percy and Grover see them on the side of the road on their way back to Manhattan. The three old ladies are knitting. They are strangers, but they are fixated on Percy. While staring, one cuts the yarn. Grover is frightened that the yarn represents Percy's lifeline.

Clarify Briefly restate today's teaching objective and explain the independent task(s)

> Your reading task is to continue your novels and pay particular attention to the secondary characters surrounding your hero.

- What secondary character(s) does the hero encounter who seem(s) to have the same values or hopes as the hero?
- What secondary character(s) does the hero encounter who seem(s) to want to prevent the hero from continuing on his or her journey?
- Is the secondary character(s) an ally or a enemy? Does the character mean to help or harm your hero?
- What are the actions of the secondary characters(s) that allow the hero to continue or temporarily prevent the hero from continuing on the journey?
- How do the hero and the secondary character(s) interact? How would you describe their relationship, and why?

ELL Enable Language Production—Reading and Writing. These guiding questions will help your ELLs zero in on the most important information about secondary characters so they will be more successful as they read and analyze.

> Use the Secondary Character Analysis graphic organizer (PDToolkit) to guide your thinking and note taking.

Practice Students work independently and/or in small groups to apply today's teaching objective

Students read and draw conclusions about secondary characters using the guiding questions posed during the lesson and take notes in the Secondary Character Analysis graphic organizer (PDToolkit).

Secondary Character Analysis graphic organizer

Secondary Character	Ally or Enemy	Actions of Secondary Character	Values/ Hopes of Secondary Character	Relationship between Hero and Secondary Character

Wrap Up Check understanding as you guide students to briefly share what they have learned and produced today

Tell students to meet with their book groups and discuss their findings of allies and/or enemies.

Direct students to carefully listen to the ideas of their group and to ask thoughtful, relevant, and detailed questions that connect the ideas of different members of their group. (SL.8.1c)

> Meet with your book groups to discuss the allies and enemies found in your own fantasy novels. Use the graphic organizers to guide your discussion.

- Did you determine the same allies and enemies?
- Which evidence did you choose from the text to support your thinking?

Extension as Students Complete Independent Books

As a culmination to the students' novel reading work, provide students an opportunity to show what they have learned from this lesson set with a visual display they create either by hand or digitally (see high-tech and low-tech options provided). Have them develop a poster comparing the fantasy heroes with ones they read about in Greek mythology. After students complete their visual display, provide them with an opportunity to present their work to the class. One option might be to create a "Hallway of Heroes" and to invite students' families or other classes to listen to student presentations.

When students share their posters, remind them to clarify information, strengthen claims and evidence, and add interest by highlighting the visual displays they integrated into their presentations. (SL.8.5)

Criteria for Hero Poster
Presents at least two important connections between the modern hero and the classic hero
Presents at least one important difference between the modern hero and the classic hero
Draws one critical conclusion about the heroes' traits

Graphics are relevant and sourced and make the information easier to understand
Labels are succinct and to the point and express an important concept
Design is logical and easy to follow
If digital, presentation brings message to life through different modalities (links, sound effects, voice-over)
Uses digital and/or multimedia components to strengthen, clarify, and add interest to oral presentation
Presents findings in a clear, focused manner with relevant evidence, reasoning, and details
Uses appropriate eye contact, adequate volume, and clear pronunciation

Goal	Low-Tech	High-Tech
After completing their fantasy novels, students develop a visual display comparing the fantasy hero with those read about in Greek mythology. Use the criteria to support students as they create a handwritten or digital poster.	Using visual aids from magazines, drawings, or printed pictures, students develop a poster that shows the way their heroes are the same as or different from one another and what connections, if any, exist between them.	Develop a Glogster page (www.glogster .com) that shows the way students' heroes are the same as or different from one another and what connections, if any, exist between them.

Milestone Performance Assessment

Fantasy vs. Greek Mythological Heroes Poster

PD **pd** TOOLKIT™

Analyze students' posters as a performance-based assessment to determine if students need additional instruction or support as a whole class, in small groups, or one on one. **ELL** Assess for Content and Language Understanding—Formative Assessment. Use the visual displays to check your ELLs' ability to compare and contrast heroes. This is a relatively nonlinguistic assessment that should help you get a clear picture of your students' content understanding, one that doesn't leave ELLs bogged down by language challenges.

 Use this checklist to assess student posters.

Standards Alignment: RL.8.1, RL.8.2, RL.8.3, RL.8.9, W.8.4, W.8.6, W.8.10, SL.8.4, SL.8.5

Task	Achieved	Notes
Present at least two important connections between the modern hero and the classic hero.		
Present at least one important difference between the modern hero and the classic hero.		
Draw one critical conclusion about the hero's traits.		
Include graphics that are relevant, sourced, and make the information easier to understand.		
Include labels that are succinct and to the point and express an important concept.		

Task	Achieved	Notes
Design is logical and easy to follow.		
If digital, presentation brings message to life through different modalities (links, sound effects, voice-over)		
Use digital and/or multimedia components to strengthen, clarify, and add interest to oral presentation.		
Present findings in a clear, focused manner with relevant evidence, reasoning, and details.		
Use appropriate eye contact, adequate volume, and clear pronunciation.		

Reading Lesson 10

▼ Teaching Objective

Readers reflect on connections between mythology and modern literature by comparing and contrasting a novel to the filmed version.

Close Reading Opportunity

▼ Standards Alignment

RL.8.1, RL.8.2, RL.8.3, RL.8.7, RL.8.9, RL.8.10, W.8.4, W.8.9, W.8.10, SL.8.1, SL.8.4, SL.8.6, L.8.1, L.8.3, L.8.6

▼ Materials

- *The Lightning Thief* by Rick Riordan
- Film adaptation of *The Lightning Thief*
- Film vs. Text Analysis graphic organizer (Appendix 8.6)

▼ To the Teacher

Prior to the lesson, be sure to have completed the read-aloud of *The Lightning Thief* or provide students with the opportunity to read the remainder of the book.

For this lesson, acquire a copy of the film version *The Lightning Thief* to enable students to make comparisons between the text and the film. This lesson will ask the students to examine how film compares with the written novel.

ELL Provide Comprehensible Input—Audiovisual Aids. ELLs who are highly orally proficient but who are behind in reading and writing can usually tackle difficult concepts and abstract ideas. However, when nearly all their classwork and assessments are based on reading and writing, it can be hard for a teacher to determine what they really understand about the content of the lesson set. This lesson allows you to see what kind of critical thinking your ELLs can do because it is based on a read-aloud and a film, both of which are accessible to struggling readers. Even newcomer ELLs who are not yet strong in oral English will be able to get a lot out of the movie because it provides substantial visual support.

▼ Procedure

Warm Up Gather the class to set the stage for today's learning

Explain the history of storytelling: how one's storytelling ability and how one viewed the story led to various adaptations of the same tale. You may even reference how there are many versions of *Cinderella* or *Little Red Riding Hood*.

> When myths were told long ago, a storyteller or family member would share the story around the fire. At every retelling, something might have been a bit different—a detail, an addition, an omission. The tales were refined and revised over time as people added their own perspective and style to the telling of these ancient stories.

Teach Model what students need to learn and do

Film vs. Text Analysis graphic organizer

Observations from the Book	Observations from the Film	Why Do You Think the Filmmaker Made Changes, If Any?	My Evaluation of These Changes	Describe Evidence of the Hero's Characteristics from Film	Describe Evidence of the Hero's Journey from Film
In the book . . .	In the film . . .	The filmmaker probably chose to make changes because . . .	I agree/ disagree with the decisions the filmmaker made . . . (explain) I prefer the book/ the movie because . . .	The hero's characteristics are evident when . . .	The hero's journey is evident when . . .

Engage students in a discussion on the process of turning a book into a film.

Filmmakers have a complicated job when they adapt a book into a film. They read the book like the rest of us do, and then they imagine bringing it to life for the audience. A filmmaker needs to think differently when preparing to make a movie than an author does when preparing to write a novel.

Discuss things like the time restraints for film, budget for actors, scenery and special effects, casting, and appropriateness for audience as just some of the elements that filmmakers must consider when telling a story in film. Also, briefly discuss the role of director and actor in the filmmaking process.

Explain the main task of comparing the film version to the book version of the story.

> As you view the film:

- How does the film compare with the book? What is the same? What is different?

- Why do you think the filmmaker may have portrayed things differently in the film than in the book?

- Do you agree with these decisions? Why or why not? Which version do you prefer—the book or the movie? Why do you feel this way?

- Is the hero portrayed with the same characteristics in the book and film? Are these qualities revealed in the same way?

- Does the film follow the hero's journey (monomyth)? How?

> I am going to model this by playing the opening scene in the film and then stopping the film and sharing my written observations with you. This should help you see what your independent work should look like. Keep in mind it is very challenging to watch a story and jot notes at the same time, but this is your job.

Play the opening scene and share your written observations with the class in the Film vs. Text Analysis chart. Model the suggested sentence starters to help students frame their ideas. **ELL** Identify and Communicate Content and Language Objectives—Language Form and Function. Through this model, you show ELLs how to express their observations and opinions in a structured way. The columns in the Film vs. Text Analysis graphic organizer help them think through each required part of a film–text comparison. The sentence frames found in the graphic organizer can be powerful tools for ELLs struggling to put their thinking into words.

The Film vs. Text Analysis graphic organizer is available in Appendix 8.6. Students may use the organizer to record their observations at various stopping points as they view the film. Note that we purposely use the general term *filmmaker* to allow for commentary and evaluation of any decisions made in the filmmaking process including actor, director, screenwriter, and so on.

Film vs. Text Analysis

Observations from the Book	Observations from the Film	Why Do You Think the Filmmaker Made Changes, If Any?	My Evaluation of These Changes	Describe Evidence of the Hero's Characteristics from Film	Describe Evidence of the Hero's Journey from Film
In the book . . .	In the film . . .	The filmmaker probably chose to make changes because . . .	I agree/ disagree with the decisions the filmmaker made . . . (explain) I prefer the book/ the movie because . . .	The hero's characteristics are evident when . . .	The hero's journey is evident when . . .
In the book, Percy defeats the Minotaur at Half-Blood Hill.	In the film, Percy defeats the Minotaur at the entrance to Half-Blood Camp.	The filmmaker probably chose to make changes because he wanted to compress events for the sake of time.	I prefer the book because the author writes with more detail than can be expressed by the film.	The hero's characteristics are evident when he shows fearlessness in the face of danger—the Minotaur.	The hero's journey is evident when he defeats the Minotaur and essentially accepts his demigod status.

Try Guide students to quickly rehearse what they need to learn and do in preparation for practice

Play another significant chunk of the film, and then stop and ask students to share what they have noticed. Share similarities and differences between the film and text versions.

Clarify Briefly restate today's teaching objective and explain the independent task(s)

Direct students to their task while viewing the film.

> Your job is to notice the ways in which the versions of the story differ, which version you prefer, and why you think the filmmaker made this choices. Jot all your thoughts and observations in your reading notebooks.

ELL Frontload the Lesson—Set a Purpose for Reading. In this case, you are setting a purpose for *listening*, which will help your ELLs to follow the movie and identify the most relevant information.

Practice Students work independently and/or in small groups to apply today's teaching objective

Students watch the film, jot notes on the Film vs. Text Analysis graphic organizer (Appendix 8.6), and think critically about the choices the filmmaker has made. Split up the viewing according to your class needs.

Wrap Up Check understanding as you guide students to briefly share what they have learned and produced today

Conduct a discussion that allows students to share their insights as they watched the film.

> What were some of the big differences between the book and movie? Why do you think the filmmaker made these decisions? Do you agree with the decisions? Why? What evidence of the hero archetype did you find?

After students have recorded their observations and thinking on the entire film, collect their writing as a performance-based assessment of their ability to compare the film and book.

Milestone Performance Assessment

Film vs. Text Analysis   PD **pd** TOOLKIT™

Collect and analyze students' Film vs. Text Analysis graphic organizers as a performance-based assessment to determine if students need additional instruction or support as a whole class, in small groups, or one on one. **ELL** Assess for Content and Language Understanding—Formative Assessment. Examine your ELLs' work thoughtfully, looking for students' mastery of content objectives as well as their ability to present their understanding in standard English. Remember that brilliant ideas may be packaged in nonstandard English. Remember also that an apparent misunderstanding about the content might actually be rooted in a miscommunication about the directions for the lesson.

 Use this checklist to assess student work on the Film vs. Text Analysis graphic organizer.

Standards Alignment: RL.8.1, RL.8.2, RL.8.3, RL.8.7, RL.8.9, W.8.4, W.8.9, W.8.10

Task	Achieved	Notes
Provide accurate analysis of the similarities and differences between the film and text version of the story.		
Evaluate the effectiveness of the decisions made by the filmmakers.		

Task	Achieved	Notes
Articulate evidence of the hero's characteristics from the film.		
Articulate evidence of the hero's journey from the film.		

Grade 8

Writing Lessons

The Core I.D.E.A. / Daily Writing Instruction at a Glance table highlights the teaching objectives and standards alignment for all 10 lessons across the four stages of the lesson set (Introduce, Define, Extend, and Assess). It also indicates which lessons contain special features to support English language learners, technology, speaking and listening, close reading opportunities, and formative ("Milestone") assessments.

Grade 8 Revealing Character: The Hero's Journey

Instructional Stage	Lesson	Teaching Objective	Core Standards	Special Features
Introduce: *notice, explore, collect, note, immerse, surround, record, share*	1	Writers determine the characteristics of a literary essay.	RL.8.1 • RL.8.2 • RL.8.3 • RL.8.9 • RL.8.10 • W.8.2 • W.8.4 • W.8.9 • W.8.10 • SL.8.1 • SL.8.4 • SL.8.6 • L.8.1 • L.8.2 • L.8.3 • L.8.6	S&L ELL Close Reading Opportunity
	2	Writers reflect on their research of an archetypal hero's characteristics in independent texts.	RL.8.1 • RL.8.2 • RL.8.3 • RL.8.9 • RL.8.10 • W.8.2 • W.8.4 • W.8.9 • W.8.10 • SL.8.1 • SL.8.4 • SL.8.6 • L.8.1 • L.8.2 • L.8.3 • L.8.6	S&L ELL Close Reading Opportunity
	3	Writers reflect on their research of the archetypal hero's journey in independent texts.	RL.8.1 • RL.8.2 • RL.8.3 • RL.8.9 • RL.8.10 • W.8.2 • W.8.4 • W.8.9 • W.8.10 • SL.8.1 • SL.8.4 • SL.8.6 • L.8.1 • L.8.2 • L.8.3 • L.8.6	S&L ELL Close Reading Opportunity Milestone Assessment
Define: *name, identify, outline, clarify, select, plan*	4	Writers create thesis statements and outline their literary essay.	RL.8.1 • RL.8.2 • RL.8.3 • RL.8.9 • RL.8.10 • W.8.2 • W.8.4 • W.8.9 • W.8.10 • SL.8.1 • SL.8.4 • SL.8.6 • L.8.1 • L.8.2 • L.8.3 • L.8.6	ELL Close Reading Opportunity Milestone Assessment
Extend: *try, experiment, attempt, approximate, practice, explain, revise, refine*	5	Writers craft introductory paragraphs for their literary essays.	W.8.2 • W.8.4 • W.8.5 • W.8.9 • W.8.10 • SL.8.1 • SL.8.4 • SL.8.6 • L.8.1 • L.8.2 • L.8.3 • L.8.6	S&L ELL
	6	Writers develop body paragraphs with evidence to support the thesis of their essays.	W.8.2 • W.8.4 • W.8.5 • W.8.9 • W.8.10 • SL.8.1 • SL.8.4 • SL.8.6 • L.8.1 • L.8.2 • L.8.3 • L.8.6	ELL
	7	Writers draft conclusions for their literary essays that follow and support their thesis.	W.8.2 • W.8.4 • W.8.5 • W.8.9 • W.8.10 • SL.8.1 • SL.8.6 • L.8.1 • L.8.2 • L.8.3 • L.8.6	ELL
	8	Writers add and cite a direct quote from their fantasy novels as evidence in their literary essays.	RL.8.1 • RL.8.10 • W.8.2 • W.8.4 • W.8.9 • W.8.10 • SL.8.1 • SL.8.6 • L.8.1 • L.8.2 • L.8.3 • L.8.6	ELL Close Reading Opportunity Milestone Assessment
	9	Writers revise and edit and title their literary essays.	W.8.2 • W.8.4 • W. 8.5 • W.8.9 • W.8.10 • SL.8.1 • SL.8.6 • L.8.1 • L.8.2 • L.8.3 • L.8.6	ELL
Assess: *reflect, conclude, connect, share, recognize, respond*	10	Writers reflect on final drafts and provide feedback to others.	W.8.2 • W.8.4 • W.8.5 • W.8.6 • W.8.10 • SL.8.1 • SL.8.4 • SL.8.6 • L.8.1 • L.8.2 • L.8.3 • L.8.6	S&L ELL Tech Milestone Assessment

Writing Lesson 1

▼ Teaching Objective

Writers determine the characteristics of a literary essay.

Close Reading Opportunity

▼ Standards Alignment

RL.8.1, RL.8.2, RL.8.3, RL.8.9, RL.8.10, W.8.2, W.8.4, W.8.9, W.8.10, SL.8.1, SL.8.4, SL.8.6, L.8.1, L.8.2, L.8.3, L.8.6

▼ Materials

- Common Archetypes in "The Lion King" Sample Essay (Appendix 8.7), copies for students
- Deconstructing the Literary Essay Questionnaire (Appendix 8.8)

▼ To the Teacher

Before beginning the writing lessons, allow students the opportunity to be well into their fantasy novels. **We suggest you begin these lessons after Reading Lesson 6.**

In a literary essay, a reader shares their analysis or interpretation of selected elements of a text, such as theme, character or structure. This kind of writing about reading goes beyond the classic book report. It requires students to display their understanding of the elements of a text in a well-thought-out way. Students are required not just to simply recall the events of the text, but to analyze the text, consider the larger message the author wished to convey, and then use specific evidence from the text to demonstrate a deeper understanding.

The writing lessons in this set will lead students through the steps of writing a literary essay that focuses on the characters in their fantasy novels.

▼ Procedure

Warm Up Gather the class to set the stage for today's learning

It is important to let students know that the task before them may pose a challenge as they think deeply about a text and develop their own ideas.

Writing well about our reading is challenging. It requires that we understand what we read, can draw important conclusions from this material, and then present this analysis in writing. In our age of information, it will be our responsibility to gather evidence, facts, and quotes from various sources and effectively communicate our ideas about what we have gathered. Both reading and writing are essential communication skills for 21st-century citizens. When we write about our reading, we comprehend at a much deeper level. We reread important sections, we choose specific lines of dialogue or specific actions, and we analyze them closely. We think deeply about the themes conveyed and how the author presents them with evidence from the text.

Teach Model what students need to learn and do

During this lesson, model how to examine the structure and content of a literary essay. Once students have a visual representation of the task before them, it will allow them to understand the expectations you have for their literary essays.

We will be writing literary essays about the archetype of the hero in literature. What is an archetype? An archetype is a pattern of character traits, behaviors, or events that recurs again and again in literature, most often in folklore and mythology. It comes from the Greek *arkhetupon*, which means "something molded first as a model."

If mythology gave birth to the hero, writers of fantasy texts have been using this character type in their stories for thousands of years. Each writer puts his or her own spin on that hero, but often much of the hero character is patterned on that original mold, that original set of characteristics that defined the quintessential hero.

Let's look at an example of a literary essay that explores the hero archetype. It is an example of a student-developed essay.

Conduct a shared reading of Common Archetypes in "The Lion King" Sample Essay (Appendix 8.7)

Ask students to discuss:

What seems to be the purpose of this essay? What is the main point the author is trying to make?

Guide students to recognize that the essay attempts to prove an idea about "The Lion King" by providing support and examples from the story.

Then focus on the structure of the essay:

What do you notice about how this essay is set up?

Examine the paragraph structure that includes an introduction, three body paragraphs, and a concluding paragraph. Explain that each main section, introduction, body, and conclusion has a unique and important purpose. **ELL** Identify and Communicate Content and Language Objectives—Language Form and Function. Here you are being transparent with your ELLs that the structure of essays is not arbitrary: Writers use certain forms for certain purposes, and experienced readers come to expect these parts. Conventions—like paragraphing—make communication easier among members of the world of literary analysis.

Try Guide students to quickly rehearse what they need to learn and do in preparation for practice

Briefly review the Deconstructing the Literary Essay Questionnaire (Appendix 8.8) that requires students to read like writers and examine each section of the text with a lens on content and purpose. Ask students to paraphrase the task each question requires of them to ensure they comprehend the questions. **ELL** Enable Language Production—Reading and Writing. You are inducting your students into the genre of literary analysis by demystifying its characteristics. Your ELLs are less likely to pick this information up from osmosis; your guiding questions set them up to be successful as they deconstruct the sample essay.

1) REVIEW:

Read the essay again closely. As you read, mark up the text by underlining important points and noting any confusions or questions you have about ideas or vocabulary. Clear up confusions and define any unfamiliar vocabulary with classmates or the teacher before moving on with the questionnaire.

2) INTRODUCTION:

Label the introduction. What does the writer say (brief summary) and do in the introductory paragraph? What seems to be the purpose of the introductory paragraph?

3) THESIS:

Double underline and label the thesis. What is the thesis of the essay? What seems to be the job of the thesis?

4) BODY PARAGRAPHS:

Label and number each body paragraph. What does the writer say (brief summary) and do in each body paragraph? What seems to be the job of the body paragraphs?

5) CONCLUSION:

Label the conclusion. What does the writer say (brief summary) and do in the conclusion? What seems to be the job of the concluding paragraph?

6) OTHER OBSERVATIONS:

What else do you notice about what the writer says and does in the essay?

Clarify Briefly restate today's teaching objective and explain the independent task(s)

Explain how students will revisit the Common Archetypes in "The Lion King" Sample Essay to develop a deeper understanding of the parts and characteristics of the literary essay. They will use the Deconstructing the Literary Essay Questionnaire (Appendix 8.8) to guide them.

Practice Students work independently and/or in small groups to apply today's teaching objective

Pearson Education

Students read the Common Archetypes in "The Lion King" Sample Essay to develop a deeper understanding of the parts and characteristics of the literary essay using the Deconstructing the Literary Essay Questionnaire as a guide. Students work in partnerships on the questionnaire. Remind students that when they engage in a collaborative discussion they should respond to one another's questions and comments with relevant evidence, observations, and ideas. (SL.8.1c) The essay is a challenging read, but it provides a strong model of the methods and language of a literary essay. Circulate among students and guide them to read closely, monitoring and clarifying their comprehension as they work through the questionnaire. After everyone completes Step 1, you may opt to reduce the size of the task by assigning the written analysis of a single paragraph to each group and pooling the answers later.

Responses will vary but some possibilities are listed here:

1) REVIEW:

Read the essay again closely. As you read, mark up the text by underlining important points and noting any confusions or questions you have about ideas or vocabulary. Clear up confusions with classmates or the teacher before moving on with the questionnaire.

Annotations will vary with each partnership, but check to see that students have noted important points and monitored their reading for unfamiliar vocabulary words or ideas that confuse them. Guide partnerships to problem-solve comprehension challenges together.

2) INTRODUCTION:

Label the introduction. What does the writer say (brief summary) and do in the introductory paragraph? What seems to be the purpose of the introductory paragraph?

What the introduction says and does:

- Defines what a hero is.
- Connects real-life heroism and heroism in literature/film.
- Defines *archetype*.
- Says that there are archetypal patterns found in the characteristics of the hero and his journey in "The Lion King."
- Says Simba is like the archetypal hero.

Purpose of introduction: to connect to the reader, provide background on the topic, and say what the essay is mainly about.

3) THESIS:

Double underline and label the thesis. What is the thesis of the essay? What seems to be the job of the thesis?

Thesis: "Simba is like the archetypal hero because he goes on a classic journey of self-discovery and develops the characteristics of the hero he is meant to be."

Purpose of thesis: to say what the essay is mainly about in a single sentence.

4) BODY PARAGRAPHS:

Label and number each body paragraph. What does the writer say (brief summary) and do in each body paragraph? What seems to be the job of the body paragraphs?

What body paragraph 1 says and does:

- Simba has the qualities of the archetypal hero.
- Lists the qualities he has with examples and details from the film.
- Clear connection to the thesis.

What body paragraph 2 says and does:

- Simba's journey is like the archetypal hero's journey.
- Lists parts of the journey with examples and details from the film.
- Clear connection to the thesis.

What body paragraph 3 says and does:

- Says there is more evidence of the journey.
- Provides more details and examples about the journey in the film.
- Clear connection to the thesis.

Purpose of body paragraphs: to provide details from the text (film) to prove the thesis.

5) CONCLUSION:

Label the conclusion. What does the writer say (brief summary) and do in the conclusion? What seems to be the job of the concluding paragraph?

What the conclusion says and does:

- Says why archetypes are important to understanding a story and characters.
- Says what we (viewers of a film) do to understand a character and story.
- Says Simba and his journey were similar to archetypal heroes; re-states thesis but in slightly different words.
- Connects the Lion King to heroes of old.
- No new details from the film.

Purpose of conclusion: to wrap up the essay and restate the main point of the essay.

6) OTHER OBSERVATIONS:

What else do you notice about what the writer says and does in the essay?

Responses will vary but may include:

- Use of sophisticated vocabulary (academic language)
- Formal English
- Complex sentences. One exception is the opening "grabber."
- Refers to characters by name
- Refers to the film by name
- Lots of details from the film
- Title is related to the thesis

Ask students to share what they noticed about the structure and content of the literary essay. Chart their responses with the purpose of creating a visual model of the parts and purpose of the literary essay. Ask students to read lines from the text that exemplify the elements they identify. **ELL** Provide Comprehensible Input—Build Background. By explicitly introducing the core elements of a literary essay, you demystify the characteristics of this genre for your students. Your ELLs in particular benefit from this explicitness.

Explain to students that they will be able to use these characteristics of the essay as a checklist while developing their literary essays. Tell them they will need to gather evidence that will eventually support their thinking and help them compose their essay.

Have students save the sample essay. It may be useful as a structural model and academic language bank later. **ELL** Identify and Communicate Content and Language Objectives—Language Form and Function. Students will be able to refer back to this sample essay throughout the lesson set to study how its author accomplishes his or her purposes by crafting language. ELLs in particular will benefit from having this expert model to refer to.

Writing Lesson 2

▼ Teaching Objective

Writers reflect on their research of an archetypal hero's characteristics in independent texts.

Close Reading
Opportunity

▼ Standards Alignment

RL.8.1, RL.8.2, RL.8.3, RL.8.9, RL.8.10, W.8.2, W.8.4, W.8.9, W.8.10, SL.8.1, SL.8.4, SL.8.6, L.8.1, L.8.2, L.8.3, L.8.6

▼ Materials

- *The Lightning Thief* by Rick Riordan
- Hero's Characteristics graphic organizer from Reading Lesson 7 (Appendix 8.3)
- The Stages of the Hero's Journey Defined (Appendix 8.4)
- Students' fantasy novels for independent reading

▼ To the Teacher

This lesson refers to the hero character trait chart from Reading Lesson 7 that gathered specific evidence from a text. During this lesson, students will be preparing for writing by developing a quick-write that reflects on evidence of archetypal hero characteristics in the main character of their independent text.

The lesson also proposes two approaches to the topic of a literary essay on heroes. We suggest that you allow students to choose one approach or the other based on the strength of the evidence they gather for each. If you feel students need more scaffolding with writing a literary essay, however, you might assign them the first approach, as several of the upcoming

lessons highlight a model essay that compares a contemporary story hero with the archetypal hero.

▼ Procedure

When writing a literary essay, the writer must choose a focus and engage in a research process on that focus. In this case, the topic of students' essays will be the hero character in their independent novels. Provide students with one or more ways to approach a literary essay on the hero of a fantasy text. We provide two sample approaches, but feel free to suggest and accept other ways of focusing the essay. **ELL** Enable Language Production—Reading and Writing. Offering two options for essays is a good way to scaffold the composition process for your ELLs. They may choose the one that they feel most capable of tackling.

Note that the sample essay on *The Lion King* in Writing Lesson 1 models both of the following approaches in one piece. In some of the following lessons, a model essay on Percy from *The Lightning Thief* will take the first approach listed. Because this essay is the modeled one, students will have the most support if this is the essay path they follow and if such support is needed.

First Approach: Essay comparing your story's hero to the archetypal hero:

One possible topic of a literary essay about your text's hero is to examine and evaluate whether he or she is similar to or different from the archetypal hero. Do this by studying the characteristics of the archetypal hero we explored in the reading lessons and seeing whether you can find evidence of them in your hero. Maybe you will find a close match or no match at all. Maybe you will find that the hero matches in some ways or not in others. You can write about any of these results as long as you have evidence to prove it.

In forming your thesis, you would answer the question: Does your character possess the characteristics of an archetypal hero? Your job would be to prove whether the character possesses the characteristics of an archetypal hero.

See the Hero's Characteristics chart on page 151 in Reading Lesson 3. **ELL** Enable Language Production—Reading and Writing. By providing a specific prompting question, you help your ELLs narrow the focus of their essays and give them a jumping-off point from which to form their thesis.

Second Approach: Essay comparing your story's hero's quest to the archetypal hero's journey:

> Another way to approach an essay on your hero is to see how the archetypal hero's journey is the same as or different from your hero's experiences. Do this by studying the experiences of your hero and searching for similarities between these and the archetypal hero's journey. Like with the hero's characteristics, maybe you will find a close match or no match at all. Maybe you will find that your hero's journey matches in some ways and not in others. You can write about any of these results as long as you have evidence to prove it.

> In forming your thesis, you would answer the question: Does the character follow an archetypal hero's journey (monomyth)? Your job would be to prove whether the character follows the archetypal hero's journey.

See The Stages of the Hero's Journey Defined (Appendix 8.4) on page 154 in Reading Lesson 4.

Explain that students will be gathering evidence around both of these approaches and then selecting the thesis they think they can do the best job explaining.

Teach   Model what students need to learn and do

Model how students will use the Hero's Characteristics graphic organizer (Appendix 8.3) to focus on specific evidence about the hero in their fantasy texts. Students can either use exact quotes from the text or describe the actions, thoughts, and feelings of the character. Let students know that today is a research day. They will be continuing to gather evidence from their independent texts to use as possible evidence in their literary essays. They will then use the information gathered to develop a quick-write. They will confirm a thesis based on the evidence or lack thereof that they discover during this research process.

> In this lesson, we are going to begin with the first approach to the literacy essay: comparing your story's hero to the archetypal hero's characteristics. I want you to spend your writing time today revisiting our list of hero's characteristics and mapping the traits of your hero as evidence of whether your hero is similar to the archetypal hero. Revisit your books and find evidence of these characteristics. Write a quote or paraphrase the evidence from the text and include the page number where this evidence was found. Here is my modeled organizer from Reading Lesson 7 on the hero's characteristics.

Hero's Characteristics graphic organizer

Characteristic	Evidence from the Text • Text quote or description • Page # (*)
Mighty warrior	Percy Jackson fights the minotaur, rips off its horn, and uses it as a weapon to kill him, page XX
Unusual birth circumstances	Son of Poseidon—a half-blood. Lives with his human mother and stepfather. Remembers seeing his father looking at him in his cradle when he was a baby, page XX
Initiating event	Doesn't know what to do when Mrs. Dodds turns into a beast and shows her talons, page XX
Epic quest	Must return the lightning bolt to Zeus in order to free his mother from the Underworld and return into the living world, page XX
Admirable qualities: bravery, selflessness	When Percy feels that he is no longer afraid, but strong enough to face what comes his way, page XX Distracted and fought the Minotaur to save Grover, page XX
Lives elsewhere	Percy lived at boarding school, page XX
Special weapons	Mr. Brunner gives him a bronze sword nicknamed Riptide, page XX
Help from gods/ goddesses	Chiron (Mr. Brunner) and Grover (a satyr) are his protectors, page XX

*Page numbers will vary depending on edition.

Model how to develop a working thesis. You will be explicitly teaching students to develop a thesis in Writing Lesson 4, but the evidence gathered will be more relevant if students know what they will be proving. Model how to then use the evidence and working thesis to develop a quick-write. **ELL** Provide Comprehensible Input—Models. The typical structure of a thesis statement is a linguistic convention. When you begin your modeling during this lesson, you show your ELLs how to develop and express an assertion that connects to the evidence they have discovered.

> Now that I have researched and gathered evidence about Percy Jackson from *The Lightning Thief*, I want to develop a working thesis to guide my thinking as I continue to search for evidence. I think I want to prove that Percy is an archetypal hero, which means he has the characteristics of the Greek heroes we read about in mythology.

Model the quick-write in front of students. Base your writing on the following questions:

- Does your character possess the characteristics of the archetypal hero?
- What might your thesis be at this point?
- Do you have enough evidence to prove this thesis?

Here is how your modeled writing might begin:

Percy Jackson, like the Perseus of Greek mythology, is an archetypal hero. He exhibits the same heroic qualities throughout the novel. In the beginning of the story, he is portrayed as an innocent young boy living at a boarding school with no particular powerful characteristics. He is in constant trouble at his boarding school and has ADD. However, unusual circumstances keep occurring. When Mrs. Dodd, the substitute teacher, turns into a beast with talons at the museum, it alerts Percy that something is truly different about his circumstances. Upon realizing his unusual birth circumstances—that he is the son of the god Poseidon—Percy accepts his fate and knows he must accomplish the task of returning the lightning bolt to Zeus. His heroic qualities of bravery and selflessness shine through as he defeats the Minotaur in order to save his friend, ally, and "protector," Grover.

Evaluate the evidence you have to prove your thesis. For example:

I think that I have enough evidence to prove the working thesis: Percy, like the Perseus of Greek mythology, possesses many characteristics of the archetypal hero. I might need to search for more details to include in an essay, though.

ELL Provide Comprehensible Input—Visuals. Consider physically highlighting for students which sentence is your thesis and which sentences provide evidence for the thesis. You may also want to physically point to each piece of evidence and point back at the thesis, asking students, "Does *this* support my claim that Percy is an archetypal hero?" ELLs will better understand the purpose of the thesis and its connection to the evidence if they can see these visual links.

Try Guide students to quickly rehearse what they need to learn and do in preparation for practice

Direct students to revisit the notes they made in Reading Lesson 3 when they were asked to identify the hero and his or her traits and share their findings in discussion with a partner. This will help them gather their thoughts for the quick-write in Practice.

As you listen in to students' discussions, direct them to present their findings, emphasizing salient points in a focused, coherent manner with relevant evidence, sound valid reasoning, and well-chosen details. (SL.8.4) Then instruct students to develop a working thesis.

Based on the evidence you have, what thesis could you develop about your main character in comparison with the archetypal hero? Do you need more evidence? Discuss.

ELL Enable Language Production—Increasing Interaction. When ELLs interact with their peers, they can deepen their content understanding, clarify any confusion they may have, and further their skill with English. In this case, English-proficient peers may be able to help ELLs formulate their theses according to the conventions of standard English so they are clearer to a monolingual-English-speaking audience.

Clarify Briefly restate today's teaching objective and explain the independent task(s)

Give students the task of adding evidence to the Hero's Characteristics graphic organizer they developed during Reading Lesson 7. Remind them that the more evidence they place in the chart, the stronger their literary essays will be.

Your writing job is to add to your list of traits, based on your newest reading progress, as well as collect evidence for those traits from the chapters you have already read. You will also develop a quick-write based on the evidence gathered, like the model of Percy Jackson. Use the following questions to guide you:

- Does your character possess the characteristics of the archetypal hero?
- What might your thesis be at this point?
- Do you have enough evidence to prove this thesis?

Practice Students work independently and/or in small groups to apply today's teaching objective

Students revisit their independent novels, searching for any additional helpful evidence of character traits that denote the archetypal hero's characteristics, and jot findings and quotations on the Hero's Characteristics graphic organizer (Appendix 8.3).

Students then develop quick-writes about how their hero compares with the archetypal hero. As you meet with individual students, be sure they are including and referencing specific evidence from the text. **ELL** Identify and Communicate Content and Language Objectives—Check for Understanding. At this stage in the writing process, you may want to focus on making sure that your ELLs are on track with the concepts of archetypal hero, thesis statement, and supporting evidence. Do not be too worried at this stage if their notes or quick-writes have nonstandard English features in them—there will be time later to focus on how they can adjust their language to a more academic register. Coach instead around how to make a clear, concise thesis.

Wrap Up Check understanding as you guide students to briefly share what they have learned and produced today

Review the idea that this part of writing a literary essay is akin to researching for an informational piece of writing.

You might recognize that part of what you did during Practice was a kind of research. You weren't learning new facts on a topic, but you were searching for evidence that would support the thesis you will be developing. The evidence in a literary essay comes from the book you are reading. Who added more evidence that will help you prove your thesis? What did you add?

Writing Lesson 3 ●

▼ Teaching Objective

Writers reflect on their research of the archetypal hero's journey in independent texts.

Close Reading Opportunity

▼ Standards Alignment

RL.8.1, RL.8.2, RL.8.3, RL.8.9, RL.8.10, W.8.2, W.8.4, W.8.9, W.8.10, SL.8.1, SL.8.4, SL.8.6, L.8.1, L.8.2, L.8.3, L.8.6

▼ Materials

- Hero's Journey graphic organizer (Appendix 8.5) as developed in Reading Lesson 8, teacher model and students' pieces
- Students' fantasy novels for independent reading

▼ To the Teacher

In this lesson, you will be using the filled-in version of the Hero's Journey graphic organizer (Appendix 8.5) from Reading Lesson 8.

▼ Procedure

Warm Up Gather the class to set the stage for today's learning

Reference the previous lesson's task, and reinforce the goal for the literary essay.

> In Writing Lesson 2, you searched for evidence of the classic hero in your fantasy hero. You gathered text evidence in the form of quotes from the text or descriptions that will help you prove or disprove that your fantasy character is patterned after the hero archetype.

Teach Model what students need to learn and do

Model how to do a quick-write that reflects the evidence of the hero's journey using the characteristics chart that references quotes and descriptions from *The Lightning Thief*.

Our job is to continue to gather text evidence of the archetype of the journey using the Hero's Journey Graphic Organizer developed in Reading Lesson 8. We will then use this chart to develop a quick-write about Percy Jackson's hero's journey.

Here is the chart I filled out for *The Lightning Thief*. Let's take a close-up look at the way I am quoting or describing text.

Hero's Journey Graphic organizer

Stage of the Journey	Evidence from the Text • Text quote or description • Page # (*)
The Ordinary World	Percy is just an unhappy kid at boarding school. He was 100% in the real world, page XX
Call to Adventure	Mrs. Dodds confronts Percy in the museum and reveals herself as a monster, page XX
Refusal of the Call	Percy dismisses what happened at the museum, page XX
Meeting the Mentor	Mr. Brunner is in fact Chiron, a centaur who I know from mythology was a teacher and mentor to Jason and Achilles and other Greek heroes. He gives Percy the pen/sword, page XX
Crossing the Threshold	Percy might have crossed into that new world when he escaped from the Minotaur and arrived at Camp Half-Blood, a summer camp where nothing seems normal, page XX
Tests/Allies/Enemies	In this story, Percy uses a similar trick, a reflecting glass ball, to find Medusa without looking her in the eyes and then chop off her head, page XX
Approach to the Innermost Cave	Percy and the rest of the demigods are developing a plan to defeat the Titans. Percy also has romantic feelings for Annabeth, page XX

Stage of the Journey	Evidence from the Text • Text quote or description • Page # (*)
Ordeal	Percy has gone west, to California, and is now in the Underworld looking for Hades, who he thinks has "turned" and stolen the lightning bolt to cause trouble between Poseidon and Zeus. The prophecy promises he will find the bolt and will return it to Zeus, page XX
Reward	Percy gets to meet his father, page XX
The Road Back	Percy harnesses the power of water to defeat Luke, the real lightning thief, page XX
Resurrection	Percy belongs with his mother in the real world but also in the new world of demigods, page XX
Return with the Elixir	Percy returns the lighting bolt to Zeus at Mount Olympus, page XX

*Page numbers will vary depending on edition.

Now, watch as I model a quick-write about Percy's journey as a hero.

Model the quick-write for students. Base your thinking on the following questions:

- Does the hero's journey in your fantasy text follow the archetypal characteristics?
- What might your thesis be at this point?
- Do you have enough evidence to prove this thesis?

Percy Jackson travels the path of a hero. Like the heroes of mythology before him and like his namesake Perseus, Percy takes on a quest that will change him and, ultimately, the world around him. He begins the story in the ordinary world as an innocent, awkward young boy who finds it difficult to concentrate at his boarding school. All this changes, however, as a substitute teacher, Mrs. Dodds, reveals herself to be more than human. This is the initiating event of his journey. At first, Percy dismisses this, refuses his call to adventure, and tries to continue his ordinary life. Once he defeats the Minotaur, Percy has crossed the threshold into his new life as he discovers he is the son of a god—Poseidon. He then takes on the task of returning Zeus's lightning bolt, which had been stolen. Along the way, he must undertake a number of ordeals, such as battling Medusa, chopping off her head, and sending it to Mount Olympus. Like Perseus before him, Percy does not travel this path alone. With Annabeth and Grover at his side, he travels west, to California, and visits the Underworld looking for Hades, who he thinks has "turned" and stolen the lightning bolt to cause trouble between Poseidon and Zeus. The prophecy promises he will find the bolt and will return it to Zeus. Percy does just this as he harnesses the power of water to defeat Luke, the real lightning thief. With the bolt in hand, Percy is

allowed to resurrect his mother and bring her from the Underworld back to the world of the living. Once the lightning bolt is returned to its rightful owner at Mount Olympus, Percy realizes that he now belongs to two worlds: the ordinary world with his mother and the world of the demigods.

Evaluate the evidence you have to prove your thesis.

I seem to have a lot of evidence that Percy's journey is an archetypal hero's journey. A possible thesis could be: In *The Lightning Thief*, Percy's experiences mirror those of the archetypal hero in many ways. But I am going to try to gather more evidence to prove this even more clearly.

ELL Provide Comprehensible Input—Models. Watching you think through your hero's journey and compose your quick-write will help ELLs understand how to do this better than just listening to an explanation would. This second example reinforces your teaching objectives from the prior lesson, showing your ELLs yet again how to express a thesis statement and how to connect text evidence back to that assertion.

Try Guide students to quickly rehearse what they need to learn and do in preparation for practice

Direct students to revisit the notes on the Hero's Journey graphic organizer they made in Reading Lesson 8 and share their findings in discussion with a partner. This will help them gather their thoughts for the quick-write in Practice. **ELL** Enable Language Production—Increasing Interaction. Oral language proficiency often runs ahead of writing proficiency. When you give your ELLs a chance to get their ideas out through peer discussion, you set them up for success when they begin to write independently later in the lesson.

Then instruct students to develop a working thesis.

Based on the evidence you have, what thesis could you develop about your main character's journey in comparison with the archetypal hero's journey? Do you need more evidence? Discuss.

Clarify Briefly restate today's teaching objective and explain the independent task(s)

Give students the task of adding evidence to the Hero's Journey Graphic Organizer they developed during Reading Lesson 8. Remind them that the more evidence they place in the chart, the stronger their literary essays will be. **ELL** Identify and Communicate Content and Language Objectives—Language Form and Function. Language consists not just of grammar and vocabulary but of larger units, like essays and discussions, used to accomplish particular purposes. In literary essays, authors wish to persuade their readers of their thesis statement (*function*). To do this, they assert their statement and back it up with textual evidence (*form*). When you encourage your students to find as much evidence as possible, you are giving your ELLs a tool for making their assertions more believable to other English-speaking academics.

Your writing job is to add to your evidence of the hero's journey, based on your newest reading progress, as well as collect evidence from the chapters you have already read. You will also develop a quick-write based on the evidence gathered, like my model of Percy Jackson. Use the following questions to guide you:

- Does the hero's journey in your fantasy text follow the archetypal characteristics?
- What might your thesis be at this point?
- Do you have enough evidence to prove this thesis?

Practice Students work independently and/or in small groups to apply today's teaching objective

Students revisit their independent novels, searching for any additional helpful evidence of parallels to the archetypal hero's journey in their novels and jot findings and quotations on their Hero's Journey graphic organizer. Students develop quick-writes about their hero's journey. As you meet with individual students, be sure they are including and referencing specific evidence from the text.

Wrap Up Check understanding as you guide students to briefly share what they have learned and produced today

Ask students to work in their groups to share their individual quick-writes. Remind them to utilize each other as resources. As they listen to one another, do they think their peer could add more evidence from the text? If so, where?

 Remind students to provide relevant evidence, observations, and ideas when responding to their classmates' questions. (SL.8.1c)

Milestone Performance Assessment

Hero's Characteristics and Hero's Journey Graphic Organizers and Working Thesis Statements

 PD TOOLKIT™

Collect and analyze the Hero's Characteristics graphic organizer and the Hero's Journey graphic organizer with the accompanying working thesis statements as a performance-based assessment to determine if students need additional instruction or support as a whole class, in small groups, or one on one. **ELL** Assess for Content and Language Understanding—Formative Assessment. Be sure, at this stage, to focus specifically on your ELLs' ability to accomplish the objectives found in the table. ELLs who are just acquiring English may have trouble

forming sentences and finding the words they need; ELLs with high oral proficiency may use features of nonstandard varieties of English. Look past these different uses of language to see what students are doing right in their work—there will be time to focus on linguistic form as they draft and revise.

Use this checklist to assess student work on the Hero's Characteristics and Hero's Journey graphic organizers and working thesis statements.

Standards Alignment: RL.8.1, RL.8.2, RL.8.3, RL.8.9, W.8.2, W.8.4, W.8.9, W.8.10

Task	Achieved	Notes
Include descriptions from the text in the evidence column of the hero's characteristics organizer.		
Insert direct quotes from the text in the evidence column in the hero's characteristics organizer.		
Develop a working thesis about the hero's characteristics based on the quotes and descriptions from the text.		
Insert descriptions from the text in the evidence column of the hero's journey organizer.		
Insert direct quotes from the text in the evidence column in the hero's journey organizer.		
Develop a working thesis about the hero's journey based on the quotes and descriptions from the text.		

Writing Lesson 4

Close Reading Opportunity

▼ Teaching Objective

Writers create thesis statements and outline their literary essay.

▼ Standards Alignment

RL.8.1, RL.8.2, RL.8.3, RL.8.9, RL.8.10, W.8.2, W.8.4, W.8.9, W.8.10, SL.8.1, SL.8.4, SL.8.6, L.8.1, L.8.2, L.8.3, L.8.6

▼ Materials

- *The Lightning Thief* by Rick Riordan
- Student graphic organizers and quick-writes from Writing Lessons 2 and 3
- Hero Literary Essay Outline (Appendix 8.9)
- Students' fantasy novels for independent reading

▼ To the Teacher

Students have been gathering evidence about their characters' similarity to archetypal heroes and keeping a working thesis statement in mind when researching. With this lesson, they will understand why so much time was spent researching for their essay as they confirm a thesis based on the evidence they have at hand. Too often, we ask them to develop a thesis first, causing the thesis, and sometimes even the essay, to end up needing major revision later. Now that they have the power of information from the text, their thesis statements will be stronger from the get-go as they will be based on actual evidence. Developing a thesis statement may be difficult for some students who may be unfamiliar with this type of writing. Be sure to model many examples. In the days following this lesson, be sure to highlight and share examples of strong thesis statements developed by other students. **ELL** Enable Language Production—Reading and Writing. ELLs in particular will likely need to see many models of effective thesis statements as they learn how to package their ideas in conventional academic forms.

▼ Procedure

Warm Up Gather the class to set the stage for today's learning

By eighth grade, many students have written informational texts that require a thesis statement. You want them to use this understanding as they begin to develop thesis statements for their literary essays. Return to the purpose of the thesis established in Writing Lesson 1.

In the previous writing lesson, what did we say the purpose of the thesis in a literary essay is?

Teach Model what students need to learn and do

Develop the concept that the literary essay is an argument, and like all quality arguments, the writer needs to make a clear point with supporting evidence.

When you write a literary essay, especially one requiring research, you are essentially making an argument. You are arguing for your interpretation, your evaluation, your point of view. And like any argument or opinion-based writing, you must have a specific thesis that presents your interpretation. Once you generate your thesis, you then prove it, with the evidence from your text.

Model examples of literary essay thesis statements.

So what does a thesis look like for a literary essay? A critical thesis about a text presents a conclusion you have drawn about that text. Your thesis is not something you can find in the text directly. You have to draw a conclusion from what you read and then prove it with evidence in your essay.

ELL Provide Comprehensible Input—Models. Crafting a thesis statement is conceptually challenging, but expressing it effectively can be equally difficult. Stress to students that a thesis statement is a general assertion that launches the essay and that the thesis itself typically does not contain specific examples from the text. Show them that they can use terms like *many ways* or *some characteristics* or *typical journey* to make general claims, saving specifics for later. When you are clear about this, you will especially help your ELLs focus on composing original, concise thesis statements.

Review the following thesis options for students as they will relate to their fantasy novels. (If you would like to have additional options, list those as well.)

- Explain how the main character possesses the qualities of a classic hero.
- Explain how the main character's experiences are parallel to Joseph Campbell's hero's journey/monomyth.

Your thesis statement for this essay needs to draw a conclusion about your main character as a hero.

Model how to review the notes gathered in the charts from Writing Lessons 2 and 3 for support as you develop a couple of options for thesis statements.

Depending upon your book and what you want to say about that hero, you could have a thesis statement like this:

Percy Jackson is a classic archetypal hero—other than the contemporary setting, he is the picture of Perseus.

or

Percy Jackson is in many ways a classic Greek hero, but in other ways he is quite different.

or

The quest that Percy Jackson takes in *The Lightning Thief* is dangerous and complicated, but it is the same journey that every hero has taken for thousands of years.

or

The Lightning Thief might be a relatively new fantasy story, but it is really based on a very old myth.

Try   Guide students to quickly rehearse what they need to learn and do in preparation for practice

During Try, students will verbally rehearse the development of their thesis statements. Direct students to use their graphic organizers and quick-writes as thinking tools to develop possible thesis statements for their literary essays.

> I want you to rehearse your thinking about your hero and his or her journey. With your graphic organizers and quick-writes in hand, I want you to brainstorm possible interpretations of your hero relative to all that you have learned about the archetypal hero and Greek mythology. Think about possible thesis statements and then talk them through with a partner. You have to feel confident that you can prove your statement with the text evidence you have collected.

> **ELL** Frontload the Lesson—Set a Purpose for Reading. Here you are arming your ELLs with a focus as they review their work. This will help them to choose the strongest possible thesis statement as they check their ideas against this important guiding question.

Clarify   Briefly restate today's teaching objective and explain the independent task(s)

Reiterate the importance of textual evidence in a literary essay. It is wise to choose a thesis that you feel you have evidence to prove. In Practice, students will use their notes, quick-writes, and conversations with partners to develop a written thesis statement they feel they can successfully prove based on the evidence they have gathered.

Practice   Students work independently and/or in small groups to apply today's teaching objective

Students develop the thesis statement about which they will write in their individual essays. Direct students to write down their thesis in a single, clear sentence that identifies the main character by name. The statement should articulate what the essay will prove but should not provide any

specific evidence yet. **ELL** Identify and Communicate Content and Language Objectives—Check for Understanding. Your ELLs probably have some great ideas at this point but may struggle to craft a powerful, concise thesis. Check in with them and coach them about how to formulate their theses in academic English. Always frame such feedback in terms of purpose and audience: As they are writing literary essays, they will want to follow the conventions of literary analysis in order to have a powerful effect on their readers.

Wrap Up   Check understanding as you guide students to briefly share what they have learned and produced today

Students each share their chosen thesis statement with the class.

> Let's go around the room and listen to each student read his or her thesis out loud for us to hear. Be sure to use the main character's name in your thesis statement.

Finally, present the outline and requirements students will be using to develop their literary essays. These requirements will be referenced in subsequent lessons. See the Hero Literary Essay Outline (Appendix 8.9).

Milestone Performance Assessment

Writing Thesis Statement   PD **pd** TOOLKIT™

Collect and analyze students' written thesis statements as a performance-based assessment to determine if students need additional instruction or support as a whole class, in small groups, or one on one. **ELL** Assess for Content and Language Understanding—Formative Assessment. When you evaluate your ELLs' work, thoughtfully examine both the ideas contained in their thesis statements and the language they used to express these ideas. One area might be strong even though the other is weak—tease out the areas where they truly need support.

 Use this checklist to assess student written thesis statements.

Standards Alignment: W.8.2, W.8.4, W.8.9, W.8.10

Task	Achieved	Notes
Choose a thesis for the literary essay by evaluating the strength of the evidence to prove the thesis.		

Task	Achieved	Notes
Express thesis in a single, clear sentence that identifies the main character by name and articulates what the essay will prove but does not provide specific evidence yet.		

Writing Lesson 5

▼ Teaching Objective

Writers craft introductory paragraphs for their literary essays.

▼ Standards Alignment

W.8.2, W.8.4, W.8.5, W.8.9, W.8.10, SL.8.1, SL.8.4, SL.8.6, L.8.1, L.8.2, L.8.3, L.8.6

▼ Materials

- *The Lightning Thief* by Rick Riordan
- Hero Literary Essay Outline (Appendix 8.9)

▼ To the Teacher

In this lesson, you will be modeling multiple ways for the writer to develop an engaging introductory paragraph that will both hook the reader and state a thesis. **ELL** Provide Comprehensible Input—Models. Introductions are a convention of literary analysis in the English-speaking world. Printed examples will help ELLs understanding what a good introduction looks like better than an explanation of the concept could. Remember to reference the Hero Literary Essay Outline (Appendix 8.9) students will be using as they navigate their way through the development of the literary essay.

▼ Procedure

Warm Up Gather the class to set the stage for today's learning

Show students the Hero Literary Essay Outline (Appendix 8.9) that was first introduced during the Wrap Up of Writing Lesson 4. Ask students to recall some ways they know how to introduce their writing.

In Writing Lesson 4, I showed you the outline for our literary essays. Our first task is to think of the introduction. There are lots of interesting ways to begin a literary essay. What tools do you think you have in your writer's toolbox that could be used to introduce a thesis, a book, and a character?

Teach Model what students need to learn and do

Explain the various ways to begin literary essay writing and model examples of these techniques:

- a narrative snippet
- a rhetorical question
- background information or description of topic
- a relevant definition
- a quote
- the thesis

You can start with a narrative snippet from the book that clearly illustrates the topic of your thesis. This snippet would retell part of the plot without copying the text. Because it reads like a story, the introduction is more interesting and appealing to the reader. For example:

In the opening pages of The Lightning Thief, *Percy Jackson was completely unaware that he would meet the Furies, make friends with a satyr, battle a Minotaur, and find himself surrounded by demigods.* The Lightning Thief *might be a contemporary fantasy story, but it is really based on a very old myth, the myth of Perseus . . .*

You can start with a rhetorical question—a question that pulls the reader in but that you already know the answer to. For example:

What has kept the concept of the hero's journey alive for thousands of years? When the reader recognizes himself in this archetype and enjoys traveling alongside the storyteller on this quest. Readers will recognize themselves in the pages of The Lightning Thief, *a new fantasy novel that presents an old but trustworthy storyline . . .*

Another way of beginning your essay is by providing background information or a description about the topic.

The Lightning Thief *is a modern fantasy story by Rick Riordan based on a very old myth. In fact, nearly everything about the main character, Percy Jackson, matches the archetype of the Greek hero . . .*

or

Perseus is a classic Greek hero whose tale has been told for centuries. In fact, he possesses specific characteristics that appear again and again in stories from across time and around the world. We call a repeating pattern in literature an archetype. The archetype of the hero may even be found in literature today . . .

Defining a relevant term, such as *heroism, journey,* or *archetype,* gives the reader a glimpse into the topic you are about to address in your essay. For example:

Heroism, by definition, is an action exhibited in fulfilling a high purpose or attaining a noble end. Percy Jackson, the hero of The Lightning Thief *by Rick Riordan, demonstrates the qualities of a hero as defined here . . .*

A writer may also begin an essay with a relevant quote from the text. Present the quote, and then explain it in a way that connects with the thesis you plan to discuss. For example:

"Being a half blood is dangerous. It's scary. Most of the time, in painful, nasty ways" (1). So begins the tale of the heroic Percy Jackson: son, student, demigod . . .

Lastly we can start with your thesis. This is probably the most straightforward approach, as the readers will know right away what you are planning to tell them. However, this essay starter is not necessarily an attention grabber. An example might look like this:

Percy Jackson is a classic archetypal hero. Other than the contemporary setting, he is the picture of Perseus, a classic hero of old . . .

Try Guide students to quickly rehearse what they need to learn and do in preparation for practice

Students share their interests in the different choices for leads. Choose a student and walk him or her through developing a lead in front of the class. With a different type of lead, work with a student to develop another beginning to the literary essay.

Which type of lead might you want to try as you write your introductory paragraph for your literary essay?

Pearson Education

ELL Enable Language Production—Reading and Writing. By letting your students decide which introduction format works best for them and showing them how to compose it, you are demystifying what is essentially a linguistic skill for your ELLs. Writing strong introductions is part of mastering academic language.

Clarify Briefly restate today's teaching objective and explain the independent task(s)

Require students to craft *two* different introductory paragraphs.

Your writing task is to try at least two different approaches for your introductory paragraph. You might want to start with the straightforward approach, leading with your thesis. But then try one of the more creative approaches. When you are done, share your introductions with a classmate who has read your book. Can they find your thesis? Which paragraph do they like better, and why?

Practice Students work independently and/or in small groups to apply today's teaching objective

Students draft two introductory paragraphs that each include the thesis and then choose their favorite through discussion with a classmate.

Wrap Up Check understanding as you guide students to briefly share what they have learned and produced today

Choose students to share their process in crafting introductions. Once other students hear or see clear examples of quality introductions, they may wish to revise their paragraphs.

Where did you put your thesis in your introduction? Was it at the beginning of your paragraph? The end? Was your partner able to find your thesis? Revise your introductory paragraph for clarity, thesis, and interest. Use a different-colored pen (or colored font) for your revisions.

💬 Take this opportunity to reinforce good speaking and listening etiquette, including carefully listening to new information expressed by others and qualifying or justifying their own views in light of the evidence presented. (SL.8.1d) **ELL** Enable Language Production—Increasing Interaction. Group sharing is a valuable way for ELLs to get feedback on their work from English-proficient peers. They can find out whether their efforts at developing an introductory paragraph are having the intended effect, and they can hear how others have applied the writing techniques you have taught.

Writing Lesson 6 •••••••••••••••••••••••••

▼ Teaching Objective

Writers develop body paragraphs with evidence to support their theses.

▼ Standards Alignment

W.8.2, W.8.4, W.8.5, W.8.9, W.8.10, SL.8.1, SL.8.4, SL.8.6, L.8.1, L.8.2, L.8.3, L.8.6

▼ Materials

- *The Lightning Thief* by Rick Riordan
- Hero Literary Essay Outline (Appendix 8.9)
- Perseus and Percy: Classic and Contemporary Heroes Model Literary Essay (Appendix 8.10)

▼ To the Teacher

You will be modeling an example of body paragraphs that include multiple pieces of textual evidence.

▼ Procedure

Warm Up Gather the class to set the stage for today's learning

Explain to students that they should be ready to write their body paragraphs in this lesson. Advise them to be aware that the literary essay is not about just listing events from the text but is a true analysis of a text.

> In crafting the body paragraphs of our literary essays, be sure to remember not to just list events. If we aren't careful, our body paragraphs in literary essays end up like a big pile of text details and quotes with little or no organization or logic. It is not enough for the text evidence to be in the essay: it has to be in the essay in a meaningful, logical way.

Teach Model what students need to learn and do

Explain the job of the body paragraphs, then model how to develop one that supports the thesis statement and uses specific details from the text. **ELL** Provide Comprehensible Input—Models. Your students have already studied one model essay, but watching you go through the process of composing body paragraphs will clarify *how* to create a polished piece for your ELLs in particular.

Review the requirements in the Hero Literary Essay Outline (Appendix 8.9) students will be using to develop their literary essays.

Body paragraphs

- Usually two or more body paragraphs
- Paragraphs organized into broad categories
- Topic sentence establishes focus of paragraph
- Commentary from the student writer
- Details/evidence/quotes from text to support thesis

Other requirements

- Use names and vocabulary from the text with accuracy
- Transitions connect ideas
- Formal style and language

> The job of body paragraphs is not just to list your evidence. Their job is to develop your argument.

> If you present your thesis in a single sentence in the introduction, the body paragraphs allow you to share the specifics of your analysis—your thoughts, or commentary, alongside the evidence from the text. The evidence should be interspersed between your thoughts and explanations. If you are going to state that Percy is an archetypal hero, then you need to explain that with your thoughts and the text evidence that guided your thinking.

> Topic sentence: Rick Riordan chose to bring the classic Perseus myth to life in the pages of *The Lightning Thief,* but in doing so put his own spin on things.

Guide students to think about how to organize their body paragraphs.

> I have a lot of proof that Percy possesses the characteristics of the archetypal hero, but I need to think about how to group my thinking and evidence. There is

no requirement as to how many body paragraphs are in your essay. Just make sure that each paragraph has a purpose and a focus. There are many ways to cluster ideas in an essay, and you may have your own logic about how to do this.

Present the following:

1. Compare/contrast

Paragraph 1: Ways the character/journey is the like the archetype
Paragraph 2: Ways the character/journey is unlike the archetype

2. Parts of the story

Paragraph 1: In the beginning of the story . . .
Paragraph 2: Later in the story . . .
Paragraph 3: As the story concludes . . .

3. Similar elements

Paragraph 1: Character background (birth circumstances, living elsewhere)
Paragraph 2: Admirable qualities (bravery and selflessness)
Paragraph 3: Help completing the quest (special weapons, help from gods)

Direct students to refer to the body paragraphs that are modeled in the Perseus and Percy: Classic and Contemporary Heroes Model Literary Essay (Appendix 8.10). Which structural choice did the writer make? **ELL** Enable Language Production—Reading and Writing. By explicitly discussing these components of the text, you are making it easier for your ELLs to produce work of similar quality. Consider breaking things down further by explaining what makes a good topic or concluding sentence (makes a mini-claim that supports the thesis statement) or pointing out transitional phrases that connect claims to evidence.

Try Guide students to quickly rehearse what they need to learn and do in preparation for practice

Read the body paragraphs of the Perseus and Percy: Classic and Contemporary Heroes Model Literary Essay (Appendix 8.10) with students and ask them to locate the following:

- Topic sentence establishes focus of paragraph
- Commentary from the student writer
- Details/evidence/quotes from text to support thesis

ELL Enable Language Production—Reading and Writing. When you lead students in an analysis of an exemplary body paragraph, you offer ELLs a chance to see the language of a strong literary analysis. This writing model will become the structure your students will refer to when writing their own analyses.

Clarify Briefly restate today's teaching objective and explain the independent task(s)

Explain to students that their Practice task is to use their outline, text evidence, and their own thoughts to compose their body paragraphs.

Practice Students work independently and/or in small groups to apply today's teaching objective

Students draft their body paragraphs. While students are drafting, they should refer to the outline content for "body paragraphs" and "other requirements." As you coach students, direct them to review their paragraphs for coherence. Guide them as needed. **ELL** Identify and Communicate Content and Language Objectives—Check for Understanding. Be sure your ELLs understand the purpose of each piece of the required paragraphs, and how to structure their sentences so as to clearly convey their analysis to readers.

After you have started writing, if you find you have competing ideas in a single paragraph, turn that into two body paragraphs. If you find you have added extra information that is not really helping your paragraph make its point, remove those sentences altogether.

Wrap Up Check understanding as you guide students to briefly share what they have learned and produced today

As students are developing their body paragraphs, have students work with a partner and share how they align the evidence from the text with the essay's thesis statement.

The body paragraphs of your literary essay are probably the most important part of the writing piece. They hold the evidence that you have read, understood, and analyzed the text at a higher level. With a partner, share your thesis statement, as well as at least five pieces of evidence. Ask your partner: Does the evidence I provided support my thesis statement?

Writing Lesson 7

▼ **Teaching Objective**

Writers draft conclusions for their literary essays that follow and support their theses.

▼ **Standards Alignment**

W.8.2, W.8.4, W.8.5, W.8.9, W.8.10, SL.8.1, SL.8.6, L.8.1, L.8.2, L.8.3, L.8.6

▼ Materials

- *The Lightning Thief* by Rick Riordan
- Hero Literary Essay Outline (Appendix 8.9)
- Perseus and Percy: Classic and Contemporary Heroes Model Literary Essay (Appendix 8.10)

▼ To the Teacher

As students craft their concluding paragraph, it is important to remind them that they should be reiterating their thesis statement but not repeating it. You may wish to support students in individual conferences or in small groups to help them paraphrase the thesis to show that the writer has, in fact, made his or her case.

▼ Procedure

Warm Up Gather the class to set the stage for today's learning

Review the job of a conclusion at the end of an essay.

> Just as with all essay conclusions, the conclusion of a literary essay brings your journey of thought to an end. The reader should feel you tie up your argument and bring your "speech" to a close.

Teach Model what students need to learn and do

Model how to develop a conclusion for the literary essay using the Hero Literary Essay Outline (Appendix 8.9).

> You should not introduce new topics into your conclusion. But you can write a brilliant conclusion by making a relevant comment about the literature that relates to your thesis but leaves the reader considering your thoughtful idea. You should consider the following requirements:

Conclusion

- Reiterate but not restate the thesis
- Follow from and support the information provided in the essay
- Should not present new evidence

ELL Identify and Communicate Content and Language Objectives— Language Form and Function. This is an excellent opportunity to remind your ELLs about the connection between the *form* of a conventional conclusion and its *function,* which is to leave the reader feeling convinced and also contemplative. When you discuss the purpose of particular structures, you empower your ELLs to use English writing to affect their audience.

Explain how writers may strengthen a basic conclusion with a memorable final thought. Some possibilities:

- Why the topic or thesis is important to the reader
- A connection between the topic and something important: real life experience, history, literature, and so on
- A succinct answer to any questions posed in the introduction
- A question that will leave the reader thinking about the topic

Review the conclusion in the Perseus and Percy: Classic and Contemporary Heroes Model Literary Essay (Appendix 8.10):

> *The Lightning Thief* is a 375-page myth full of immortal, bickering gods, the battle for good and evil, and a reluctant hero trying to keep alive on his quest. The tales of heroes told by the ancient Greeks are tightly woven into the fabric of our culture. Riordan's development of Percy is a clear indicator of that. He loves and is inspired by Greek myths. But it is also clear that he will spin the tale in his own direction to tell a good story. The characters of Perseus and Percy both tell us, through their bravery, selflessness, and overall heroic deeds, that it is our responsibility to help others when we can. After all, isn't that the true definition of a hero?

Once students have read the conclusion once, guide them through your thought process and how you addressed the characteristics of the concluding paragraph.

> Now that you have read the conclusion, which parts meet the criteria? What else do you notice?

Guide students to point out the following:

Reiterate but not restate the thesis:

> The tales of heroes told by the ancient Greeks are tightly woven into the fabric of our culture. Rick Riordan's development of Percy is a clear indicator of that.

Follow from and support the information provided in the essay

> The characters of Perseus and Percy both tell us, through their bravery, selflessness, and overall heroic deeds, that it is our responsibility to help others when we can.

Leave the reader with a thought-provoking question:

> After all, isn't that the true definition of a hero?

Try Guide students to quickly rehearse what they need to learn and do in preparation for practice

Tell students to jot down notes on how they will address the following characteristics of a concluding paragraph:

- Reiterate but not restate the thesis
- Follow from and support the information provided in the essay
- Should not present new evidence

> Using the characteristics of the concluding paragraph, jot down notes on how you think you will accomplish each with your own books. Share with a partner

in your book group. Then consider how you might strengthen your conclusion with a memorable final thought, such as:

- Why the topic or thesis is important to the reader
- A connection between the topic and something important: real-life experience, history, literature, and so on
- A succinct answer to any questions posed in the introduction
- A question that will leave the reader thinking about the topic

Clarify Briefly restate today's teaching objective and explain the independent task(s)

As you task students with drafting their conclusion, make sure you reiterate the importance of revisiting the thesis statement while not restating it.

> Your writing challenge is to craft your own conclusion. Make sure to make the conclusion bigger than a simple restating of your thesis. Comment on that thesis, but don't repeat it exactly. Make sure that your conclusion follows and supports the information presented in the essay.

Practice Students work independently and/or in small groups to apply today's teaching objective

Students craft their own conclusions for their literary essays. As you circulate to confer with students, be sure that they are including the four

components of the concluding paragraph. If you find students restating their thesis statements word for word, guide them to paraphrase the statement instead. **ELL** Enable Language Production—Reading and Writing. Your ELLs in particular might struggle to rephrase their thesis statements, as they simply may not know the words and structures they would need in order to paraphrase them. You might offer them some basic paraphrasing strategies, such as turning the original statement around (e.g., from "Percy is the archetypal hero" to "Percy represents the archetypal hero") or using synonyms. Regardless, push them to include all the components of a strong conclusion, knowing that their ability to compose these parts will increase in sophistication as they see more models and get more practice.

Wrap Up Check understanding as you guide students to briefly share what they have learned and produced today

Task students with sharing their conclusions with a partner.

> Share your conclusion with a partner. How did you reiterate but not repeat your thesis? Did you expand the basic conclusion with any of the techniques suggested in the lesson?

Writing Lesson 8

▼ Teaching Objective

Writers add and cite a direct quote from their fantasy novels as evidence in their literary essays.

Close Reading Opportunity

▼ Standards Alignment

RL.8.1, RL.8.10, W.8.2, W.8.4, W.8.9, W.8.10, SL.8.1, SL.8.6, L.8.1, L.8.2, L.8.3, L.8.6

▼ Materials

- *The Lightning Thief* by Rick Riordan
- Perseus and Percy: Classic and Contemporary Heroes Model Literary Essay (Appendix 8.10)
- Students' fantasy novels for independent reading

▼ To the Teacher

During the reading lessons, it is important that students have gathered specific notes, as they will be using these quotes and specific pieces of evidence to prove their thesis statements.

▼ Procedure

Warm Up Gather the class to set the stage for today's learning

Begin this lesson with what you have noticed about students' writing. Affirm their attempts at including specific details from their texts.

> I noticed that as some of you began writing your essays, you wanted to use the quote from the book in your essay rather than your own paraphrased description of that moment in the text. In this lesson, we are going to revise our essays with this goal in mind. Everyone will get some practice learning to embed a quote in the essay and properly cite that quote.

Teach Model what students need to learn and do

Using the Perseus and Percy: Classic and Contemporary Heroes Model Literary Essay (Appendix 8.10), model how to go back into the actual text to add in a specific quote. First, think aloud about where a quote would support a specific statement in the literary essay. Students should be aware of not only the process but of the punctuation used to cite the quote. Explain the rules for punctuating the quote.

> Now I am going to show you how to consider where a specific quote would enhance your statement. Then I will model how to cite this quote using the correct punctuation. Here is my essay at the end of my first draft of writing.

Present the following piece of the essay draft:

> Both Perseus and Percy are mighty warriors. They are brave, spirited, and natural-born leaders. Time and time again, they battle against forces to protect friends, family, and even enemies. In the classic myth, Perseus battles Medusa. In the book, Medusa now runs a statue store and enjoys turning visiting satyrs into stone. Percy still gets to kill her, but he sends her head back to Zeus in a FedEx package this time. An entirely different beast, the Minotaur, half-man, half-bull, is killed by Theseus in the ancient tales but stabbed by Percy in the novel. In killing the Minotaur, Percy saved his friend Grover. Characters throughout the novel remark on Percy's bravery. As the Minotaur is defeated, they realize whom they have on their hands. Selflessness is yet another quality these two heroes display as they risk life and limb to protect and save their mothers. Perseus battles Medusa, while Percy returns Zeus's lightning bolt in order to retrieve his mother from the Underworld. Percy's newfound abilities matter little to him. His priority is bringing his mother back to the world of the living.

Stop and model the think-aloud to show where a quote would make sense and strengthen the idea that Percy is a hero.

> When I read the first body paragraph, I think I would like to focus on the part that indicated that others are beginning to understand that Percy is a hero. Most often, the hero himself will not have this self-awareness, so we will choose another character that understands the heroic qualities on display. Annabeth, on page 56, recognizes Percy for the hero he is. I will add that quote. To embed this quote, I will use the following rules to punctuate correctly:

- Use quotation marks around the quote from the text.
- Put the page number, in parentheses, before the period for that sentence.

Examples of Quote Citations: Literary Essay

A direct quote from a character:
"'Your courage is truly admirable,' whispered Keith" (32).

Quoting a description from the text:
He was a "small, skinny, and inconspicuous boy," and he seemingly had few friends (7).

Try Guide students to quickly rehearse what they need to learn and do in preparation for practice

Tell students to review their notes and their drafted essays. Then ask them to choose a spot where they feel a quote would add description and enhance a statement from the essay.

> Review your notes and examine the draft of your essay. Where would a direct quote enhance a statement made in your essay? Which quote might you choose?

Clarify Briefly restate today's teaching objective and explain the independent task(s)

Explain to students that they will be embedding quotes and citations directly from the fantasy novel into the literary essay using the correct format.

> Your job is to find at least one place to embed a quote directly from your novel. If you have already done so, check your conventions and see that you have done it properly. If not, look at your organizer. What direct quote would enhance your essay?

> Use quotation marks to surround your text quote, just as you would dialogue. Then remember to put the page number, in parentheses, before the period for that sentence.

Practice Students work independently and/or in small groups to apply today's teaching objective

Students embed direct quotes from their fantasy novels into their literary essays. Remind them to use the charts that organize the important events and page numbers. They should also have visual access to the modeled text as a guide for their citations. **ELL** Enable Language Production—Reading and Writing. Help your ELLs to use the advanced skill of embedding a quotation in another sentence midstream. Alternatively, make sure that even if their quotations are standing alone as complete sentences, they use language on either side of the quotation to introduce and explain it.

Wrap Up Check understanding as you guide students to briefly share what they have learned and produced today

Share clear examples of citing embedded quotes with the entire class.

> Let's look at a few embedded quotes in essays so we can see how our fellow classmates revised their writing.

Milestone Performance Assessment

Literary Essay Quotations

Collect and analyze student literary essays as a performance-based assessment to determine if students need additional instruction or support as a whole class, in small groups, or one on one. **ELL** Assess for Content and Language Understanding—Formative Assessment. Verify that your ELLs are making good judgments about where quotations would enhance their work. If they have done this, consider if they are using the language on either side of the quotation to set it up and explain it effectively.

 Use this checklist to assess student literary essays.

Standards Alignment: RL.8.1, W.8.2, W.8.4, W.8.9, W.8.10, L.8.1, L.8.2, L.8.3

Task	Achieved	Notes
Embed a character quote as evidence.		
Reference a particular part of the text using page number.		
Use punctuation correctly when citing evidence from the text.		

Writing Lesson 9

▼ Teaching Objective

Writers revise, edit, and title their literary essays.

▼ Standards Alignment

W.8.2, W.8.4, W.8.5, W.8.9, W.8.10, SL.8.1, SL.8.6, L.8.1, L.8.2, L.8.3, L.8.6

▼ Materials

- Perseus and Percy: Classic and Contemporary Heroes Model Literary Essay (Appendix 8.10)
- Literary Essay Editing Checklist (Appendix 8.11)

▼ To the Teacher

This lesson is an opportunity for students to refine their writing through the editing process. Students should be putting the finishing touches on their essays by also adding a title.

▼ Procedure

Warm Up Gather the class to set the stage for today's learning

Introduce the Literary Essay Editing Checklist (Appendix 8.11) and briefly explain each item as needed.

Teach Model what students need to learn and do

Literary Essay Editing Checklist

Task	Yes/No
Revisions	
Did I write a unique introduction with a clear and focused thesis?	
Did I write body paragraphs with relevant text details and insightful commentary/conclusions?	

Task	Yes/No
Did I write a conclusion that reiterates the thesis?	
Did I write a title that captures the thesis and the attention of the readers?	
Does my writing show a command of embedding and citing direct quotes?	
Does my writing show a sophisticated understanding of proper comma usage?	
If produced digitally: Did I use technology to produce and publish writing and present the relationships between information and ideas effectively?	
COPS Editing	
Did I check and correct my **c**apitalization?	
Did I check and correct my **o**rder and usage of words?	
Did I check and correct my **p**unctuation?	
Did I check and correct my **s**pelling?	

Explain the job and importance of a title. Model how to develop a title for a literary essay, using the Perseus and Percy: Classic and Contemporary Heroes Model Literary Essay (Appendix 8.10).

The title of an essay should capture your thesis in an interesting way. It is essential that your title be descriptive of your stance, your point of view. And just as you did with your introductory paragraph, you want to get the reader's attention. Just using the title of your novel is unacceptable. So is rewriting your thesis as a title.

Watch me as I consider a number of options for titling an essay. When choosing a title, I want to remember my thesis, the central idea of the essay. For example, my thesis might be: Rick Riordan modeled his modern-day hero, Percy, after the classic hero, Perseus, but with a twist. So how can I hint at this in a clever way? How about:

A Name Is Just a Name. Or Is It?

Will the Real Perseus Please Stand Up?

Everything Old Is New Again

The Myth That Never Died

Ask students to help you choose the title for the literary essay.

Which do you like best? Why? You want the title to be interesting but also smart. Clever but silly will not reflect well on your piece. Help me choose.

Once the title is chosen, model how to use the checklist to revise and edit your writing.

Now that I have revised my literary essay by including a title, I want to use my Literary Essay Editing Checklist (Appendix 8.11) to make sure that I have all other components as well.

Go through each point of the checklist and show students the evidence in the essay. Use the following to guide you.

Checklist Examples to Highlight for Students

Checklist Criteria	Evidence from the Text
Introduction with a clear and focused thesis	There is plenty of evidence in *The Lightning Thief* to prove that Percy is based on Perseus and embodies the archetypal heroic characteristics.
Body paragraphs with relevant text details and my own insightful commentary/conclusions	Selflessness is yet another quality these two heroes display as they risk life and limb to protect and save their mothers. Perseus battles Medusa to prevent his mother from marrying a horrific man, while Percy returns Zeus's lightning bolt in order to retrieve his mother from the Underworld. Percy's newfound abilities matter little to him. His priority is bringing his mother back to the world of the living.
Conclusion that reiterates the thesis	The tales told by the ancient Greeks are tightly woven into the fabric of our culture. Rick Riordan's development of Percy is a clear indicator of that.
A title that captures the thesis and the attention of the readers.	Perseus and Percy: Classic and Contemporary Heroes
Shows a command of embedding and citing direct quotes.	Quote from Annabeth (56). She was looking at a real-life hero.

Try Guide students to quickly rehearse what they need to learn and do in preparation for practice

Direct students to review their essays with a partner and draft two or three options for titles. Have a few volunteers share their titles and the thinking behind them. **ELL** Enable Language Production—Increasing Interaction. Peer discussion gives your ELLs a low-pressure environment to hear another example of how to revise and to practice the language they need to express their own ideas about revision. Working with English-proficient peers can also help ELLs learn new techniques for accomplishing their goals with their essays.

Clarify Briefly restate today's teaching objective and explain the independent task(s)

Remind students that they are to use their writing time for the development of titles, revision, and editing.

> Your writing task is to edit your writing for the proper conventions, spelling, and grammar. You have brainstormed titles for your essay. Choose the one you want to keep and place it at the top of your final draft.

Practice Students work independently and/or in small groups to apply today's teaching objective

Students edit and title their essays using the Literary Essay Editing Checklist (Appendix 8.11). **ELL** Enable Language Production—Reading and Writing.

Make sure your ELLs understand that revision is a normal part of writing and that it's good to find areas to improve. Then help them to figure out *how* to add what is missing: Was it an oversight, or are they not sure how to make their meaning clear in English?

Wrap Up Check understanding as you guide students to briefly share what they have learned and produced today

Choose students to share their final titles. Also, ask students to articulate some of the things they found that needed attention during the revision and editing process.

Writing Lesson 10 ·

▼ Teaching Objective

Writers reflect on final drafts and provide feedback to others.

▼ Standards Alignment

W.8.2, W.8.4, W.8.5, W.8.6, W.8.10, SL.8.1, SL.8.4, SL.8.6, L.8.1, L.8.2, L.8.3, L.8.6

▼ Materials

- Student literary essays
- Perseus and Percy: Classic and Contemporary Heroes Model Literary Essay (Appendix 8.10)
- Literary Essay Editing Checklist (Appendix 8.11)
- Essay Feedback Sheet (Appendix 8.12)

▼ To the Teacher

To celebrate the final product of the literary essay, this lesson asks students to read their classmates' writing and reflect upon the skills and craft techniques that make a quality piece of writing in a collaborative feedback exercise called a gallery walk.

▼ Procedure

Warm Up Gather the class to set the stage for today's learning

As with all writing pieces, we will be asking students to reflect on not just their writing piece but on themselves as writers. Engage students in discussion.

> Now we come to the end of a productive writing lesson set. Let's talk about what you have learned as a writer in these lessons.

As students reflect on their writing, remind them to speak clearly and use appropriate eye contact, adequate volume, and clear pronunciation. (SL.8.4)

Teach Model what students need to learn and do

Essay Feedback Sheet

Student Writer: _____

Title of Essay: _____

Student Writer's Statement (something that makes you proud about your essay):

Reader's name	Feedback *Please be specific.*

Reader's name	Feedback *Please be specific.*

Describe the process of a student writing gallery walk. Students should place their writing on a desk next to an Essay Feedback Sheet (Appendix 8.12). Model how to craft a statement that explains the favorite part of an essay:

> I am most proud of the second paragraph where I made sure to include an exact quote from a character in the novel.

ELL Provide Comprehensible Input—Models. ELLs will understand how to talk about their favorite parts of their essays by studying your example. Remember that talking about what one has done well is a socially high-stakes practice that can sometimes get a person accused of bragging. It is governed by conventions in every language and culture, and your students may be accustomed to practices that are different from yours. Be clear with students that there are appropriate ways to talk in English about what we are proud of, and highlight this point as students discuss your example.

Try Guide students to quickly rehearse what they need to learn and do in preparation for practice

Ask students to notice what you wrote in your statement. Then ask them to provide examples of positive and specific feedback on the Perseus and Percy: Classic and Contemporary Heroes Model Literary Essay (Appendix 8.10).

Some examples of what students might say:

- Your first sentence grabbed my attention and made me want to read more.
- Your thesis was clear and concise.
- To prove your thesis about the hero or hero's journey, you added specific and accurate evidence from the text.
- You used accurate and vivid descriptions to describe the hero and his qualities.
- Your conclusion helped me connect heroes across multiple texts.
- Your essay left me thinking about . . .

> I want you to use our independent time to provide one another with positive feedback about your pieces. First, write a brief statement in the space on the Essay Feedback Sheet to explain which part of the essay is your favorite, and put this note next to the draft on your desk.

Distribute feedback sheets and coach students in this task. Remind students that their Literary Essay Editing Checklist (Appendix 8.11) checklist may be a useful tool for finding specifics for self-evaluation and providing feedback to others during the gallery walk.

ELL Enable Language Production—Reading and Writing. This is a moment when ELLs can learn the structure of a compliment from their peers and from your recasts of students' ideas. Keep in mind that complimenting is another socially high-stakes practice and is typically governed by particular conventions that determine when and how it is appropriate to give a compliment. The conventions of English compliments may differ from the conventions of compliments in your ELLs' home cultures. This discussion empowers your ELLs to be culturally flexible.

Clarify Briefly restate today's teaching objective and explain the independent task(s)

> Now, you will walk about the room and read one another's pieces. Your responsibility as a reader is to comment on a positive element of three different pieces during our time. We will leave the Essay Feedback Sheet next to each writing piece so that readers can leave their thoughtful comments along with their names. You are all accountable for reading and commenting as described.

Practice Students work independently and/or in small groups to apply today's teaching objective

Students participate in the gallery walk, reading published pieces from this lesson set and articulating a favorite element of each literary essay in writing and why. You may also wish to invite guests to the gallery walk such as parents, other students, administrators, faculty, and school support staff. **ELL** Enable Language Production—Listening and Speaking, Reading and Writing. If you are inviting students' families to join the gallery walk, consider how ELLs will share their work if their guests do not read English. Can they record a home-language translation for their families to listen to? Can they draft a second version in their home language? These accommodations show respect for all the linguistic and cultural resources your students bring to the classroom.

Wrap Up Check understanding as you guide students to briefly share what they have learned and produced today

Focus on the positive aspects of one another as writers, and ask students to share what they noticed about their classmates as writers.

> What did you notice about your classmates' writing that impressed you? Be specific in the skill, but not by naming the writer.

Goal	Low-Tech	High-Tech
Student publishes and shares his or her literary essay in a meaningful way.	Students publish the literary essay with pen and paper. Gallery walk is conducted using notepaper or sticky notes.	Students digitally publish the literary essay and respond to one another's writing with digital posts.

Milestone Performance Assessment

Literary Essay Checklist

 PD TOOLKIT™

Collect and analyze students' literary essays as a performance-based assessment to determine if students need additional instruction or support as a whole class, in small groups, or one on one. **ELL** Assess for Content and Language Understandings—Summative Assessment. Remember to examine ELLs' work for both content mastery and language mastery. This process is complicated by the fact that the field of literary analysis (content) calls for particular forms of language—not just grammar and vocabulary, but textual organization, tone, and what counts as evidence, among other things. Study how your ELLs have progressed in their ability to use discipline-specific language practices to communicate in an academic context. Are they using topic sentences to orient their readers? Are they making claims and linking them clearly to supporting evidence? Do they attempt to make stylistic choices appropriate to purpose and audience, like standard grammar and specific vocabulary?

 Use this checklist to assess student work on their literary essays.

Standards Alignment: W.8.2, W.8.4, W.8.5, W.8.6, W.8.9, W.8.10, L.8.1, L.8.2, L.8.3, L.8.6

Task	Achieved	Notes
Revising		
Write a unique introduction with a clear and focused thesis.		

Task	Achieved	Notes
Write body paragraphs with relevant text details and insightful commentary/conclusions.		
Write a conclusion that makes a judgment or decision.		
Write a title that captures the thesis and the attention of the readers.		
Show a command of embedding and citing direct quotes.		
If produced digitally: Use technology to produce and publish writing and present the relationships between information and ideas effectively.		
COPS Editing		
Capitalization.		
Order and usage of words.		
Punctuation.		
Spelling.		

GLOSSARY

allies: characters who serve to help and support the hero on his or her journey.

archetype: a pattern of character traits, behaviors, or events that recurs in stories again and again, most often in folklore and mythology.

central idea (theme): the terms *central idea* and *theme* both can be used to describe the unifying idea or subject of the story. A well-developed central idea/theme often suggests a universal truth about life or human behavior.

enemies: characters whose role is to prevent the hero from beginning the journey, succeeding with a quest, or completing the journey.

fantasy text: in the genre of fantasy, there are magical events, characters who often have special powers, and imagined settings.

hero: a contemporary hero is a person admired for courage and admirable qualities; a classic mythological hero is a figure, often of divine descent, who has great strength or special abilities. This archetypal pattern occurs across many stories; a literary hero is the main character in a story, often with admirable characteristics.

journey: a voyage or trip from one place to another.

monomyth: the journey of the archetypal hero. Joseph Campbell originally used the term *monomyth* to describe the journey of a hero, but it refers to a pattern found in many myths and narratives.

myth: a traditional story that often describes the adventures of heroes and/or explains a custom or belief.

mythology: a collection of ancient stories, passed down first by oral storytelling, which a culture uses to help explain the world.

quest: a long and difficult search for something

theme: [See "central idea."]

traditional literature: ancient stories, passed down first by oral storytelling; includes myths, legends, folktales, and so on.

threshold: the place or point where something begins.

trials: the act of testing or trying something or someone.

PD TOOLKIT™

Accompanying *Core Ready for Grades 6–8*, there is an online resource site with media tools that, together with the text, provides you with the tools you need to implement the lesson sets.

The PDToolkit for Pam Allyn's *Core Ready* Series is available free for 12 months after you use the password that comes with the box set for each grade band. After that, you can purchase access for an additional 12 months. If you did not purchase the box set, you can purchase a 12-month subscription at **http://pdtoolkit.pearson.com.** Be sure to explore and download the resources available at the website. Currently the following resources are available:

- Pearson Children's and Young Adult Literature Database
- Videos
- PowerPoint Presentations
- Student Artifacts
- Photos and Visual Media

- Handouts, Forms, and Posters to supplement your Core-aligned lesson plans
- Lessons and Homework Assignments
- Close Reading Guides and Samples
- Children's Core Literature Recommendations

In the future, we will continue to add additional resources. To learn more, please visit **http://pdtoolkit.pearson.com.**

Directions: Use the organizer to think about and record the key elements of a short story.

Character(s) (identify and describe protagonist, antagonist, and minor characters)	Narrator (identify narrative mode and narrator, if possible)	Setting (describe the time and place of the story)
Key Plot Episodes (include conflict and resolution)	Brief Summary of Story (include all elements)	Central Idea

Here is a list of central ideas, or themes, that are common to literature written for middle school students.

Adventure	Friendship	Patriotism
Beauty	Growing up	Power
Bravery	Greed	Religion
Bullying	Guilt	Society
Childhood	Health	Social class
Citizenship	Heroism	Social cliques
Compassion	Honesty	Survival
Confidence	Hope	Trust
Courage	Justice	Violence
Ethnicity	Love	War
Evil	Morality	Wisdom
Family relationships	Nature	
Freedom	Overcoming challenges	

Directions: Use the following questions as a guide to analyzing central idea in multiple stories.

Story 1:

Story 2:

Common Central Idea:

Discussion Questions

1. Summarize the gist of each text. What was similar about these texts? What was different?

2. What methods did each author use to convey a central idea? (Consider literature elements, narration, point of view, narrative techniques, and so on.)

3. What is the author's message related to a central idea of the text in each piece? How do you know? Are the messages the same in both texts? Explain.

4. Which text's approach to a central idea was more effective in your opinion? Why?

1. Why do you think O. Henry called the story "The Last Leaf?"

2. The author uses lots of figurative language, descriptive detail, and imagery in the story. What do you think are the strongest examples?

3. Why do you think O. Henry chooses to personify pneumonia? Was this an effective use of figurative language? Explain.

4. How would you describe the mood of the story after Johnsy becomes sick? What actions, dialogue, and language help convey the mood?

5. How would you describe the relationship between Johnsy and Sue? How is their relationship important to the story?

6. Do you think Johnsy really believes that she will pass away with the last leaf? Why or why not? Cite evidence from the text to support your thinking.

7. This story was published in 1907 and takes place around that time. Does the time period have an impact on the story? If the story took place today, would anything be different or not? Explain.

8. How does Johnsy's point of view change across the story? How is this important to the central idea(s)?

9. O. Henry is famous for writing stories with a "twist," or surprise at the end. What was the twist in this story? Were you surprised? Explain?

10. The author describes Behrman as a failed artist. Why is this significant to the story? Do you agree?

11. One of the central ideas of the story is hope. How is hope an important theme? What do you think O. Henry message is about hope? What other central ideas may be found in this story?

12. What is your overall opinion of the story? What other comments do you have to share?

APPENDIX 6.5 Microblog Paper

Directions: Use the following paper to plan a tweet with up to 140 spaces. One character per box, including spaces.

	Yes/No
Revising	
Did I answer all components of the question/prompt?	
Are my ideas in a logical sequence?	
Did I include sufficient text evidence by using direct quotations and/or paraphrasing?	
COPS Editing	
Did I check and correct my **c**apitalization?	
Did I check and correct my **o**rder and usage of words?	
Did I check and correct my **p**unctuation?	
Did I check and correct my **s**pelling?	

Name: _____ **Date:** _____ **Story Title and Author:** _____

Directions: Choose one of the following prompts to write about the short story.

- Determine a central idea of the short story, explain what the author's message is about the central idea, and discuss how the author conveys that message. Include specific evidence from the text.

- Choose an important character in the short story whose point of view changes as the story unfolds. Explain how the point of view changes and why. Explain how this change connects to a central idea of the story.

- Name the narrative techniques used by the author to enhance the experience of reading the short story. How does the use of these narrative techniques work to contribute to the meaning, tone, and/or mood of the text?

- Choose one key episode or event from the short story. Why is this significant? How does it contribute to your understanding of a central idea, or how is it important to the development of the plot?

Sample Short Story Version #1 (Few Narrative Techniques)

The London Eye

01. The day that Nick Connell learned he could become invisible began like any other. When he woke up, it was raining. Nick lived in Stepney, in the East End of London. A hundred years ago, the street where Nick lived had been a tire factory, and on humid days the air still smelled of rubber.

02. One morning, Nick woke up and put on his school uniform. He was eleven and looked like a lot of other boys his age, with a round face and black hair. The only thing different about Nick was that he had one green eye and one brown eye. Everyone told Nick he was special—that having two different-colored eyes was a mark of greatness—but he hated it.

03. Nick had recently lost all three of his family's umbrellas, and so he walked to school through the cold wet rain. At lunch he got in a fight with his best friend, Jules. They stopped speaking to each other.

04. At home, Nick made toast and tea and started on his homework. But then, out of the blue, while he was staring, bored, at a page of fractions, Nick thought, "Maybe I should go look in Rosie's room." Nick's older sister Rosie was sixteen, and she was always out with her friends.

05. Nick pushed open the door to his sister's room, then stood for a moment in the hallway, debating whether to go inside. He listened for any sounds downstairs, but the house was quiet, and so Nick went into the room. He read her diary, snooped around a little, and was sitting on the floor eating her stash of chocolate caramels when he heard footsteps on the stairs.

06. The footsteps on the stairs turned louder. Rosie was nearly at the hall. He was scared. He held the chocolate wrapper in his hand, closed his eyes, and waited to hear his sister begin to scream.

07. But she didn't. She came into the room, put her schoolbag on the bed, and took off her shoes. Nick opened one eye. His sister's shoe had landed a few inches from his knee. He opened the other eye, expecting to see Rosie looking at him. But she wasn't. She was lounging on the bed now, flipping through a magazine.

08. After a few more minutes, Rosie went downstairs. Once he heard noises from the kitchen, Nick went downstairs.

He asked if she had seen him earlier, and she said no.

Nick went upstairs and looked in the bathroom mirror. He looked the same, if a little more bedraggled than usual. He frowned. He raised one eyebrow, then the other, at his reflection. He didn't know what he was expecting to see, and he sighed. Then he decided to do an experiment. He closed his eyes and opened them again. He was invisible.

Nick practiced in his bathroom every day for a week before he tried to turn invisible outside. He became used to the popping sensation in his chest, and after seven days of practicing he could summon it in seconds.

And then, just like that, all of London was his.

Nick's favorite soccer team was Arsenal. The first thing he did was sneak into the Arsenal stadium. He had never been so happy in his life.

It was the best summer ever. Nick explored Buckingham palace without getting caught. He snuck into restaurants, but he never stole food.

He'd set two rules for himself:

1. No stealing.
2. No snooping on people you know.

The first rule was hard because Nick's family was poor, but the second rule was easy. Nick had thought about following friends, but the idea scared him.

Instead Nick explored his city. He went into all the rooms that he'd never be allowed in otherwise—without money, without a noble title. He snuck into a mansion in Mayfair and went in a members' club. He watched a gambling circle and went in Harrods, the department store. He watched every Arsenal match and sometimes went to the team's practices.

One night in August, Nick rode the London Eye, the Ferris wheel by the river. He'd already snuck onto it a dozen times that summer. The city was below him. Nick looked out and felt good. And then he felt the pop in his chest, and suddenly he was there. He wasn't invisible any longer. Nick could never turn invisible again. After a few months, he stopped trying. But for the rest of his life, he remembered the season when all of London was his.

Sample Short Story Version #2 (Many Narrative Techniques)

The London Eye

01. The day that Nick Connell learned he could become invisible began like any other. When he woke up, rain was bucketing down from a low gray sky. Nick lived in Stepney, in the East End of London, in a small brick house surrounded by identical small brick houses. A hundred years ago, the street where Nick lived had been a tire factory, and on humid days the air still smelled of rubber.

02. On this cold spring morning, Nick woke up and put on his school uniform. He was eleven and looked like a lot of other boys his age, with a round face and black hair. The only thing different about Nick was that he had one green eye and one brown eye. Everyone told Nick he was special—that having two different colored eyes was a mark of greatness—but he hated it. "It just makes me look funny," he said.

03. Nick had recently lost all three of his family's umbrellas, and so he walked to school through the cold wet rain. When he arrived, his school uniform was soaked, and he sat, dripping, through Math, Geography, and History. At lunch he got in a fight with his best friend, Jules, when she said there were seven oceans on the planet and he said there were five. Neither of them cared much about it either way, but by the time lunch was over they weren't speaking to each other.

04. At home, Nick made toast and tea and started on his homework. But then, out of the blue, while he was staring, bored, at a page of fractions, Nick thought, "Maybe I should go look in Rosie's room."

05. Nick's older sister Rosie was sixteen, and she was always out with her friends. "I just want to find out where they go," Nick whispered aloud as he climbed the stairs to her room. "I just want to know what they do."

06. Nick pushed open the door to his sister's room, then stood for a moment in the hallway, debating whether to go inside. He listened for any sounds downstairs, but the house was quiet, and so Nick went into the room. He read her diary, snooped around on her computer, and was sitting on the floor eating her stash of chocolate caramels when he heard footsteps on the stairs.

07. "No, no, no," Nick whispered. How had he not heard the front door? He must have been rustling the candy wrappers too loudly.

08. The footsteps on the stairs turned louder. Rosie was nearly at the hall. All the blood had left Nick's face, turning him pale. He scrunched up the chocolate wrapper in his hand, closed his eyes, and waited to hear his sister begin to scream.

09. But she didn't. She came into the room, dumped her schoolbag on the bed, and kicked off her shoes. Nick opened one eye. His sister's shoe had landed a few inches from his knee. He opened the other eye, expecting to see Rosie with her arms folded over her chest, glaring at him. But she wasn't. She was sitting on the bed now, flipping through a magazine.

10. After a few more minutes, Rosie yawned and padded downstairs. Once he heard noises from the kitchen, Nick bolted up and ran down the stairs and into the kitchen.

11. "Nick!" Rosie yelped. "You scared me. I didn't think anyone was home."

12. "You didn't see me earlier?"

13. "No," said Rosie, as though he were very stupid.

14. Nick went upstairs and looked in the bathroom mirror. He looked the same, if a little more bedraggled than usual. He frowned. He raised one eyebrow, then the other, at his reflection. He didn't know what he was expecting to see, and he sighed. Then he decided to do an experiment. He closed his eyes and remembered hearing his sister's footsteps coming up the stairs. His heart began to pound in his chest. His eyes were

squinted shut. *I'm not here,* he thought to himself, *I'm not here.* And then he felt something pop, like a bubble bursting in his chest, and he opened his eyes.

15. He wasn't there. His reflection, in the mirror, was gone. Nick laughed, and the sound seemed to come from nowhere at all, from thin air. Nick reached his hand toward the mirror, and his fingers grazed the cold glass, and still nothing appeared in the reflection. He was invisible.

16. Nick practiced in his bathroom every day for a week before he tried to turn invisible outside. He became used to the popping sensation in his chest, and after seven days of practicing he could summon it in seconds.

17. And then, just like that, all of London was his.

18. Nick's favorite soccer team was Arsenal, and the first thing he did was sneak into the Arsenal stadium. He jumped, invisible, from the stands down onto the pitch and watched the game from the sidelines. After the striker missed a goal, the Arsenal coach, Arsène Wenger, stood right next to Nick and shouted at the team, throwing his hands in the air, his face turning purple. The players ran inches away from Nick's face. When Arsenal scored the winning goal, Nick ran out onto the field, his arms in airplanes, circling the huddle of cheering players. He had never been so happy in his life.

19. It was the best summer ever. Nick hopped the fence in front of Buckingham Palace and lay under a cherry tree a few inches from the queen's window. He wandered through noisy bustling restaurant kitchens in Shoreditch and Hackney, careful not to bump into the chefs with their steaming pots and pans. He spent a lot of time in the kitchen of his favorite Indian restaurant on Brick Lane, but he never stole any food.

20. He'd set two rules for himself:

1. No stealing.
2. No snooping on people you know.

21. The first rule was hard because Nick's family was poor, but the second rule was easy. Nick had thought about following Jules and his other friends from school, but the idea unsettled him. He didn't want to be untrustworthy. And after thinking about it for a long time, he decided he didn't really want to hear what people said about him when he wasn't there.

22. Instead Nick explored his city. He went into all the rooms that he'd never be allowed in otherwise— without money, without a noble title. He snuck into a mansion in Mayfair that looked like a great white cake and went into a members' club down the block full of round men with red cheeks. He watched a gambling circle in the basement of a kebab shop in Islington. In June, he told his mom he was staying with Jules's family and then spent the night in Harrods, the best department store in London. He watched every Arsenal match and sometimes went to the team's practices, dribbling alongside the players, pretending to take shots on goal.

23. One night in August, Nick rode the London Eye, a huge Ferris wheel on the banks of the river. He'd already snuck onto it a dozen times that summer. The city glittered below him. Nick pressed his hands to the glass compartment. He felt completely content and completely himself. And then, as though he knew it was coming, he felt the pop in his chest, and suddenly he was there. He wasn't invisible any longer. His reflection looked back at him, surprised, in the glass.

24. Nick could never turn invisible again. After a few months, he stopped trying. But for the rest of his life, he remembered the season when all of London was his. One day, when Nick was eighteen, Jules's dad won tickets to an Arsenal match in a raffle. The seats were the best in the stadium, right above the pitch.

25. "Can't get any closer than this, can you?" asked Jules's dad.

26. "No," said Nick, laughing, "you can't."

	Yes/No
Revising	
Is my short story inspired by at least one clear central idea (theme)?	
Did I establish a narrator?	
Did I include only a few important characters?	
Did I include a clearly defined setting?	
Did I include a problem or complication?	
Did I use several narrative techniques to enhance the short story? • Character dialogue • Detailed description • Word choice • Pacing	
Did I include a conclusion that reveals a message or truth about the central idea?	
COPS Editing	
Did I check and correct my **c**apitalization?	
Did I check and correct my **o**rder and usage of words?	
Did I check and correct my **p**unctuation?	
Did I check and correct my **s**pelling?	

Standards Alignment: RL.6.1, RL.6.2, RL.6.3, RL.6.5, W.6.4, W.6.9, W.6.10

Reading Lesson 3
Milestone Performance Assessment:

Use this checklist to assess student work on the Elements of a Short Story Graphic Organizer.

Task	Achieved	Notes
Identify and briefly describe character(s).		
Identify and briefly describe the narrator.		
Identify and briefly describe setting(s).		
Identify and briefly describe key plot episodes (including conflict and resolution).		
Provide a brief, accurate summary.		
Identify and briefly describe a central idea and the author's message about it.		
Cite several points of evidence that support thinking about the central idea.		

Standards Alignment: RL.6.1, RL.6.4, W.6.4, W.6.10, L.6.4, L.6.5, L.6.6

Reading Lesson 5
Milestone Performance Assessment:

Use this checklist to assess student work analyzing the use of language and narrative techniques.

Task	Achieved	Notes
Choose two words from independent reading and examine and evaluate the words for denotation and connotation.		
Write a brief summary of the short story.		
Highlight the exact words or lines from the text as an example of a narrative technique.		
Name the narrative technique identified.		
Explain how the use of this narrative technique contributes to overall meaning, tone, and/or mood of the story.		

Standards Alignment: RL.6.1, RL.6.2, RL.6.3, RL.6.6, W.6.4, W.6.9, W.6.10

Reading Lesson 6
Milestone Performance Assessment:

Use this checklist to assess student paragraphs based on the four-step process.

Task	Achieved	Notes
Identify the narrative mode of a story.		
Identify an important situation (possibly the conflict) in the text.		
Explain how a main character's point of view toward the situation develops across the text.		
Articulate how the development of the point of view connects to a central idea.		
Provide sufficient textual evidence to support thinking.		

Standards Alignment: RL.6.1, RL.6.2, RL.6.3, RL.6.4, RL.6.6, W.6.4, W.6.9, W.6.10

Reading Lesson 9
Milestone Performance Assessment:

Use this checklist to assess the content and effectiveness of student short story discussion guides.

Task	Achieved	Notes
Compose at least eight discussion questions.		
Demonstrate knowledge of the short story genre and the teaching objectives of the lesson set through content of questions.		
Demonstrate comprehension of the target short story by including references to specific story elements and details in several questions.		
Include questions that have potential to engage others in prolonged open-ended discussion of the target short story.		

Standards Alignment: RL.6.1, W.6.4, W.6.6, W.6.9, W.6.10

Writing Lesson 2
Milestone Performance Assessment:

Use this checklist to assess student work on their six-word memoirs and tweets.

Task	Achieved	Notes
Craft a six-word memoir that effectively captures a central idea of the writer's life.		
Write a reflection paragraph and include an image that clearly elaborates on the words chosen for the memoir.		
Concisely articulate thinking about the short story using the microblogging format.		

Standards Alignment: W.6.4, W.6.5, W.6.9, W.6.10, L.6.1, L.6.2, L.6.3, L.6.6

 **Writing Lesson 5**

Milestone Performance Assessment:

Use this checklist to assess student revisions.

Task	Achieved	Notes
Revising		
Craft a strong written literary commentary that answers all components of the question/prompt.		
Compose ideas in a logical sequence.		
Include text evidence with effective use of direct quotations and/or paraphrasing.		
COPS Editing		
Capitalization.		
Order and usage of words.		
Punctuation.		
Spelling.		

Standards Alignment: W.6.3, W.6.4, W.6.5, W.6.10, L.6.1, L.6.2, L.6.3, L.6.6

Writing Lesson 9
Milestone Performance Assessment:

Use this checklist to assess student revisions.

Task	Achieved	Notes
Revising		
Short story inspired by at least one clear central idea (theme).		
Establish a narrator.		
Include only a few important characters.		
Include a clearly defined setting.		
Include conflict or resolution.		
Use several narrative techniques to enhance the short story. • Character dialogue • Detailed description • Word choice • Pacing		
Include a conclusion that reveals a message or truth about the central idea.		
COPS Editing		
Capitalization.		
Order and usage of words.		
Punctuation.		
Spelling.		

Core Ready Reading Rubric

The following Core Ready Reading Rubric is designed to help you record each student's overall understanding across four levels of achievement as it relates to the lesson set goals. We recommend that you use this rubric at the end of the lesson set as a performance-based assessment tool. Use the Milestone Performance Assessments as tools to help you gauge student progress toward these goals. Reteach and differentiate instruction as needed. See the foundational book, *Be Core Ready: Powerful, Effective Steps to Implementing and Achieving the Common Core State Standards,* for more information about the Core Ready Reading and Writing Rubrics.

Lesson Set Goal	Emerging	Approaching	Achieving	Exceeding	Standards Alignment
Examine how the details (story elements and plot episodes) of a short story contribute to the overall development of the central idea.	Student is unable to explain how the details (story elements and plot episodes) of a short story contribute to the overall development of the central idea. Lacks specific textual evidence.	Student accurately identifies the details of a short story (story elements and plot episodes). May have difficulty describing how they contribute to the overall development of the central idea or lack sufficient textual evidence.	Student accurately identifies the details of a short story (story elements and plot episodes) and how they contribute to the overall development of the central idea. Provides sufficient, relevant evidence to support points.	Student accurately identifies the details of a short story (story elements and plot episodes) and how they contribute to the overall development of the central idea. Provides detailed and insightful evidence of to support points. May describe and effectively support multiple central ideas.	RL.6.1 RL.6.2 RL.6.3 RL.6.5 RL.6.10 W.6.4 W.6.9 W.6.10 SL.6.1 SL.6.2 SL.6.4 SL.6.6 L.6.1 L.6.3 L.6.6
Examine the development of a short story and identify key elements.	Student demonstrates little or no evidence of success examining the development of a short story and identifying key elements. Lacks accuracy and/or evidence.	Student demonstrates some success examining the development of a short story and identifying key elements. May have some gaps or sequencing issues or lack sufficient textual evidence.	Student examines the development of a short story and identifies key elements with accurate content and sequence. Provides sufficient textual evidence to support thinking.	Student examines the development of a short story and identifies key elements with accurate content and sequence. Provides thorough and detailed textual evidence. May demonstrate deep inferential thinking and comprehension. May demonstrate success with highly challenging text.	RL.6.1 RL.6.3 RL.6.5 RL.6.10 W.6.4 W.6.9 W.6.10 SL.6.1 L.6.1 L.6.3 L.6.6

Core Ready Reading Rubric, Grade 6, *continued*

Lesson Set Goal	Emerging	Approaching	Achieving	Exceeding	Standards Alignment
Determine the figurative and connotative meaning of words and phrases as they are used in a text and analyze the impact of a specific word choice on meaning and tone.	Student is unable to determine the figurative and connotative meaning of words and phrases as they are used in a text and analyze the impact of a specific word choice on meaning and tone.	Student demonstrates some success determining the figurative and connotative meaning of words and phrases as they are used in a text and analyzing the impact of a specific word choice on meaning and tone. May contain some inaccuracies or lack sufficient textual evidence.	Student demonstrates success determining the figurative and connotative meaning of words and phrases as they are used in a text and analyzing the impact of a specific word choice on meaning and tone. Explanations are accurate and contain sufficient detail.	Student demonstrates solid success determining the figurative and connotative meaning of words and phrases as they are used in a text and analyzing the impact of a specific word choice on meaning and tone. Demonstrates significant evidence of deep understanding.	RL.6.1 RL.6.4 RL.6.10 W.6.4 W.6.9 W.6.10 SL.6.1 SL.6.4 SL.6.6 L.6.1 L.6.3 L.6.4 L.6.5 L.6.6
Determine the narrative mode of a short story and explain the impact of the mode on the story.	Student is unable to determine the narrative mode or explain the impact on the short story. Lacks accuracy and/or evidence.	Student demonstrates some success determining the narrative mode of short story and explaining the impact. May contain some inaccuracies or lack sufficient textual evidence.	Student demonstrates solid success determining the narrative mode and explaining the impact of a short story. Explanations are accurate and logical and contain sufficient detail.	Student demonstrates outstanding success determining the narrative mode and explaining the impact on a short story. Explanations demonstrate accurate and insightful observations about aspects of the narration.	RL.6.1 RL.6.6 RL.6.10 W.6.4 W.6.9 W.6.10 SL.6.1 SL.6.2 SL.6.4 SL.6.6 L.6.1 L.6.3 L.6.6

Lesson Set Goal	Emerging	Approaching	Achieving	Exceeding	Standards Alignment
Articulate how the narrator or a main character's point of view develops across a story.	Student shows little or no success articulating how the narrator or a main character's point of view develops across a story.	Student shows some evidence of articulating how the narrator or a main character's point of view develops across a story. Descriptions may be unevenly developed. May have some gaps or lack sufficient textual evidence	Student shows solid evidence of articulating how the narrator or a main character's point of view develops across a story. Provides accurate and sufficient textual evidence.	Student shows outstanding evidence of articulating how the narrator or a main character's point of view develops across a story. Provides thoughtful and detailed textual evidence. Demonstrates deep inferential thinking and comprehension.	RL.6.1 RL.6.2 RL.6.3 RL.6.6 RL.6.10 W.6.4 W.6.9 W.6.10 SL.6.1 SL.6.2 SL.6.4 SL.6.6 L.6.1 L.6.3 L.6.6
Readers compare and contrast how short stories across different genres approach a similar central idea.	Student shows little or no success of comparing and contrasting how short stories across different genres approach a similar central idea.	Student compares and contrasts with some success how short stories across different genres approach a similar central idea. Descriptions may be unevenly developed. May have some gaps or lack sufficient textual evidence.	Student shows solid evidence of successfully comparing and contrasting how short stories across different genres approach a similar central idea. Provides accurate and sufficient textual evidence.	Student shows outstanding evidence of comparing and contrasting how short stories across different genres approach a similar central idea. Provides thorough and detailed textual evidence. Demonstrates deep inferential thinking and comprehension.	RL.6.1 RL.6.2 RL.6.3 RL.6.6 RL.6.9 RL.6.10 SL.6.1 SL.6.4 SL.6.6 L.6.1 L.6.3 L.6.6
By the end of the year, read and comprehend literature, including stories, dramas, and poems, in the grades 6–8 text complexity band proficiently, with scaffolding as needed at the high end of the range.	Student shows little or no evidence of reading and comprehending texts appropriate for the grades 6-8 text complexity band even with scaffolding.	Student shows some evidence of reading and comprehending texts appropriate for the grades 6-8 text complexity band with scaffolding.	Student shows solid evidence of reading and comprehending texts appropriate for the grades 6-8 text complexity band proficiently but may need scaffolding at the high end of the range.	Student shows solid evidence of reading and comprehending texts above the grades 6-8 text complexity band proficiently.	RL.6.10

Core Ready Reading Rubric, Grade 6, *continued*

Lesson Set Goal	Emerging	Approaching	Achieving	Exceeding	Standards Alignment
In collaborative discussions, demonstrate evidence of preparation and exhibit responsibility for the rules and roles and purpose of conversation.	Student demonstrates little or no success at coming to discussions prepared and often disregards the rules, deadlines, and roles of conversation even with prompting and redirection.	Student participates in collaborative discussions with some success. Lacks thorough preparation at times. Sometimes observes the rules, deadlines, and roles of conversation but needs frequent prompting or redirection.	Student consistently participates in collaborative discussions and comes to discussions prepared. Student observes the rules, deadlines, and roles of conversation with little prompting or redirection.	Student participates in collaborative discussions with purpose and enthusiasm. Arrives to all discussions thoroughly prepared. Student carefully observes the rules, deadlines, and roles of conversation with no prompting or redirection.	SL.6.1a SL.6.1b
In collaborative discussions, identify, share, and develop ideas in a manner that enhances understanding of the topic, text, or issue being discussed and demonstrate an understanding of multiple perspectives.	Student demonstrates little or no success asking and answering specific questions with relevant comments that enhance discussion or demonstrating comprehension of multiple perspectives through reflection and paraphrasing, even with prompting.	Student demonstrates some success asking and answering specific questions with relevant comments that enhance discussion or demonstrating comprehension of multiple perspectives through reflection and paraphrasing. May need frequent prompting or redirection.	Student demonstrates solid success asking and answering specific questions with relevant comments that enhance discussion or demonstrating comprehension of multiple perspectives through reflection and paraphrasing with little prompting or redirection.	Student demonstrates outstanding success asking and answering specific questions with relevant, insightful comments that consistently enhance discussion. Demonstrates thorough comprehension of multiple perspectives through reflection and paraphrasing. No prompting or redirection needed.	SL.6.1c SL.6.1d
Adapt speech to a variety of contexts and tasks, demonstrating command of formal English when indicated or appropriate.	Student shows little or no evidence of success adapting speech to a variety of contexts and tasks. Demonstrates very little command of formal English when indicated or appropriate.	Student shows some evidence of success adapting speech to a variety of contexts and tasks. Demonstrates basic command of formal English when indicated or appropriate.	Student effectively adapts speech to a variety of contexts and tasks. Demonstrates solid command of formal English when indicated or appropriate.	Student shows exceptional evidence of adapting speech to a variety of contexts and tasks. Demonstrates sophisticated command of formal English when indicated or appropriate.	SL.6.6

Lesson Set Goal	Emerging	Approaching	Achieving	Exceeding	Standards Alignment
Demonstrate command of standard English and its conventions and use the knowledge when writing, speaking, reading, and listening.	Student demonstrates very little command of standard English and its conventions. Little or no evidence of application of knowledge when writing, speaking, reading, and listening.	Student shows some command of standard English and its conventions and attempts to use the knowledge when writing, speaking, reading, and listening.	Student shows solid command of standard English and its conventions and uses the knowledge when writing, speaking, reading, and listening.	Student shows exceptional command of standard English and its conventions and demonstrates sophisticated use of the knowledge when writing, speaking, reading, and listening.	L.6.1 L.6.2 L.6.3
Acquire and use accurately grade-appropriate general academic and domain-specific words and phrases, strategically building vocabulary knowledge when needed.	Student shows little or no evidence of the acquisition and accurate use of grade-appropriate general academic and domain-specific words and phrases. Little or no success using vocabulary building strategies.	Student shows some evidence of the acquisition and accurate use of grade-appropriate general academic and domain-specific words and phrases. Effectively uses vocabulary building strategies at times.	Student shows solid evidence of the acquisition and accurate use of grade-appropriate general academic and domain-specific words and phrases. Effectively uses vocabulary building strategies with frequency.	Student shows outstanding evidence of the acquisition and accurate use of grade-appropriate general academic and domain-specific words and phrases sophisticated for the grade level. Proactively uses a wide variety of vocabulary building strategies with success.	L.6.6

Core Ready Writing Rubric

Grade 6   Packing a Punch: The Art and Craft of Short Stories

The following Core Ready Reading Rubric is designed to help you record each student's overall understanding across four levels of achievement as it relates to the lesson set goals. We recommend that you use this rubric at the end of the lesson set as a performance-based assessment tool. Use the Milestone Performance Assessments as tools to help you gauge student progress toward these goals. Reteach and differentiate instruction as needed. See the foundational book, *Be Core Ready: Powerful, Effective Steps to Implementing and Achieving the Common Core State Standards,* for more information about the Core Ready Reading and Writing Rubrics.

Lesson Set Goal	Emerging	Approaching	Achieving	Exceeding	Standards Alignment
Compose formal written literary commentary of a short story.	Student writing does not address the prompt (off topic) and/or lacks any relevant textual evidence.	Student writing answers the prompt with partial focus or accuracy and contains some textual evidence. Use of quotations and/or paraphrasing may be ineffective or inaccurate.	Student writing accurately answers the prompt and contains sufficient textual evidence. Use of quotations and/or paraphrasing is effective and accurate.	Student writing accurately answers the prompt and contains detailed and highly effective textual evidence. Use of quotations and/or paraphrasing is very thorough, effective, and accurate.	RL.6.1 RL.6.3 RL.6.10 W.6.4 W.6.5 W.6.6 W.6.9 W.6.10 SL.6.1 SL.6.4 SL.6.6 L.6.1 L.6.2 L.6.3 L.6.6
Write and share short stories that convey a central idea (theme) and demonstrate the use of a variety of narrative techniques (dialogue, descriptive details, word choice, pacing) to enhance key elements of the story.	Student writing lacks a clear central idea and/or contains no narrative techniques.	Student writing loosely connects to a central idea and contains some attempts to use narrative techniques to enhance key elements of the story. Use of some techniques may be ineffective.	Student writing conveys a central idea and uses narrative techniques to enhance key elements of the story.	Student writing clearly conveys one or more central idea and very effectively uses a wide variety of narrative techniques to enhance key elements of the story.	W.6.3 W.6.4 W.6.5 W.6.10 SL.6.1 SL.6.2 SL.6.4 SL.6.6 L.6.1 L.6.2 L.6.3 L.6.6

Lesson Set Goal	Emerging	Approaching	Achieving	Exceeding	Standards Alignment
By the end of the year, read and comprehend literature, including stories, dramas, and poems, in the grades 6–8 text complexity band proficiently, with scaffolding as needed at the high end of the range.	Student shows little or no evidence of reading and comprehending texts appropriate for the grades 6-8 text complexity band even with scaffolding.	Student shows some evidence of reading and comprehending texts appropriate for the grades 6-8 text complexity band with scaffolding.	Student shows solid evidence of reading and comprehending texts appropriate for the grades 6-8 text complexity band proficiently but may need scaffolding at the high end of the range.	Student shows solid evidence of reading and comprehending texts above the grades 6-8 text complexity band proficiently.	RL.6.10
With some guidance and support from peers and adults, develop and strengthen writing as needed by planning, revising, editing, rewriting, or trying a new approach.	Student makes little or no attempt to develop and strengthen writing as needed by planning, revising, editing, rewriting, or trying a new approach. Shows little or no attention to the conventions of standard English.	Student attempts to develop and strengthen writing as needed by planning, revising, editing, rewriting, or trying a new approach. Shows some command for the conventions of standard English. May contain significant errors or lacks clarity.	Student develops and strengthens writing as needed by planning, revising, editing, rewriting, or trying a new approach. Shows solid command for the conventions of standard English. May contain some errors or lack of clarity.	Student extensively develops and strengthens writing as needed by planning, revising, editing, rewriting, or trying a new approach. Shows exceptional command for the conventions of standard English. Few or no errors or lapses of clarity evident.	W.6.5
Use a variety of techniques, including the Internet, to publish and share writing with a larger audience.	Student demonstrates little or no success at publishing and sharing writing with a larger audience.	Student attempts to publish and share writing with a larger audience. Use of publishing techniques may be uneven or ineffective at times.	Student successfully publishes and shares writing with a larger audience using a variety of techniques.	Student successfully publishes and shares writing with a larger audience using a variety of techniques. May demonstrate outstanding variety, creativity, or effect on audience.	W.6.6
In collaborative discussions, demonstrate evidence of preparation and exhibit responsibility for the rules and roles and purpose of conversation	Student demonstrates little or no success at coming to discussions prepared and often disregards the rules, deadlines, and roles of conversation even with prompting and redirection.	Student participates in collaborative discussions with some success. Lacks thorough preparation at times. Sometimes observes the rules, deadlines, and roles of conversation but needs frequent prompting or redirection.	Student consistently participates in collaborative discussions and comes to discussions prepared. Student observes the rules, deadlines, and roles of conversation with little prompting or redirection.	Student participates in collaborative discussions with purpose and enthusiasm. Arrives to all discussions thoroughly prepared. Student carefully observes the rules, deadlines, and roles of conversation with no prompting or redirection.	SL.6.1a SL.6.1b

Core Ready Writing Rubric, Grade 6, *continued*

Lesson Set Goal	Emerging	Approaching	Achieving	Exceeding	Standards Alignment
In collaborative discussions, identify, share, and develop ideas in a manner that enhances understanding of the topic, text, or issue being discussed and demonstrate an understanding of multiple perspectives.	Student demonstrates little or no success asking and answering specific questions with relevant comments that enhance discussion or demonstrating comprehension of multiple perspectives through reflection and paraphrasing, even with prompting.	Student demonstrates some success asking and answering specific questions with relevant comments that enhance discussion or demonstrating comprehension of multiple perspectives through reflection and paraphrasing. May need frequent prompting or redirection.	Student demonstrates solid success asking and answering specific questions with relevant comments that enhance discussion or demonstrating comprehension of multiple perspectives through reflection and paraphrasing with little prompting or redirection.	Student demonstrates outstanding success asking and answering specific questions with relevant, insightful comments that consistently enhance discussion. Demonstrates thorough comprehension of multiple perspectives through reflection and paraphrasing. No prompting or redirection needed.	SL.6.1c SL.6.1d
Adapt speech to a variety of contexts and tasks, demonstrating command of formal English when indicated or appropriate.	Student shows little or no evidence of success adapting speech to a variety of contexts and tasks. Demonstrates very little command of formal English when indicated or appropriate.	Student shows some evidence of success adapting speech to a variety of contexts and tasks. Demonstrates basic command of formal English when indicated or appropriate.	Student effectively adapts speech to a variety of contexts and tasks. Demonstrates solid command of formal English when indicated or appropriate.	Student shows exceptional evidence of adapting speech to a variety of contexts and tasks. Demonstrates sophisticated command of formal English when indicated or appropriate.	SL.6.6
Demonstrate command of standard English and its conventions and use the knowledge when writing, speaking, reading, and listening.	Student demonstrates very little command of standard English and its conventions. Little or no evidence of application of knowledge when writing, speaking, reading, and listening.	Student shows some command of standard English and its conventions and attempts to use the knowledge when writing, speaking, reading, and listening.	Student shows solid command of standard English and its conventions and uses the knowledge when writing, speaking, reading, and listening.	Student shows exceptional command of standard English and its conventions and demonstrates sophisticated use of the knowledge when writing, speaking, reading, and listening.	L.6.1 L.6.2 L.6.3

Lesson Set Goal	Emerging	Approaching	Achieving	Exceeding	Standards Alignment
Acquire and use accurately grade-appropriate general academic and domain-specific words and phrases, strategically building vocabulary knowledge when needed.	Student shows little or no evidence of the acquisition and accurate use of grade-appropriate general academic and domain-specific words and phrases. Little or no success using vocabulary building strategies.	Student shows some evidence of the acquisition and accurate use of grade-appropriate general academic and domain-specific words and phrases. Effectively uses vocabulary building strategies at times.	Student shows solid evidence of the acquisition and accurate use of grade-appropriate general academic and domain-specific words and phrases. Effectively uses vocabulary building strategies with frequency.	Student shows outstanding evidence of the acquisition and accurate use of grade-appropriate general academic and domain-specific words and phrases sophisticated for the grade level. Proactively uses a wide variety of vocabulary building strategies with success.	EL.6.6

Name _____ **Date** _____ **Photograph** _____

Directions: Use this graphic organizer to analyze historical photos.

Describe the photo. What do you notice?	
What might these details tell you about this historical time period?	
How are the individuals in your photo affected by the events taking place?	
What conclusions might you draw?	
What questions might you ask?	

Name _____ **Date** _____ **Title and Author** _____

Directions: Use these graphic organizers to record observations and thoughts about the elements of historical fiction.

Historical Fiction Element: Characters	Evidence from the Text (include page number)	Describe what you are thinking at this point.
-Characters are realistic. They may include fictional people created by the author, real people who lived at the time, or both. -Fictional or real, all characters' actions, words, thoughts and experiences are consistent with people of the time period. What are we learning about the characters in general? What about the characters is realistic to the historical time period and place?		

Historical Fiction Element: Setting Setting is an authentic historical time period and location. The setting is very important in historical fiction because it influences all other elements. -What historical time period and location are represented in the book?	Evidence from the Text (include page number or percentage)	Describe what you are thinking at this point. (e.g. your background knowledge, questions, conclusions, predictions)

Historical Fiction Element: Key Plot Events -Events may be fictional, real, or both. The problems and experiences faced by the characters are realistic to the historical setting. -What plot details are representative of the time period and place? -What, if any, real events are part of the plot?	Evidence from the Text (include page number)	Describe what you are thinking at this point.

Historical Fiction Element: Description What descriptive language does the writer use to bring the time period alive?	Evidence from the Text (include page number)	Describe what you are thinking at this point.

Historical Fiction Element: Dialogue Is there dialogue? If so, how does it help show thoughts/perspectives of the time period? Is the language/slang typical of the time period?	Evidence from the Text (include page number)	Describe what you are thinking at this point.

Narrative Mode	Explanation
First-Person	The narrator reveals the plot through a character, usually the protagonist, who is a participant in the story and relates the events through his or her eyes. Uses the pronouns *I, me,* or *we* to refer to himself or herself.
Second-Person	The narrator reveals the plot by telling the story to another character, usually the protagonist, or directly addressing the reader. Refers to the addressee as "you." Also known as the imperative point of view. This perspective is found very seldom in fiction. A writer would be more likely to use second person in a nonfiction piece.
Third-Person	The narrator does not participate in the action and is not a character in the story. Tells the story as an outside observer. Uses the pronouns *he, she,* and *they*. There are three types of third-person point of view. They are: • Third-person omniscient: This narrator is all-knowing and shares thoughts, feelings, and opinions of any and all characters in the story or event. • Third-person limited: This narrator shares only the thoughts, feelings, and opinions of a single character in the story or event. • Third-person objective: When writing from this perspective, the writer does not share any thoughts, feelings, or opinions. It is left to the reader to interpret these things from information given (dialogue, action, setting, and so forth).

Name: _____

Directions: Use this graphic organizer to record thinking.

Historical facts that the author uses in the historical fiction story	Elements and details in the historical fiction story that were imagined by the author
The Great Depression caused a lack of money. Schools were segregated. Schools for black students and schools for white students were not equal. Less money went to schools for black students. Schools for white students discarded materials and gave them to schools for black students. Many families were sharecroppers. Children had to help work the farm. Many children walked very long distances on dirt roads to schools. Some children had buses. The school year was shorter than it is now.	

In 1961, the American South was deeply segregated. Buses, trains, schools, libraries, restaurants, and movie theaters—even water fountains—had separate areas for African-Americans and for White Americans. In 1960, the Supreme Court had ruled in Boynton v. Virginia that segregation was illegal in public transportation.

Nevertheless, public transportation in the South was still segregated. A group named, the Congress of Racial Equality (CORE), decided to do something about it. On May 4, 1961, thirteen riders—ten men and three women, seven of whom were black and six of whom were white—boarded two buses in Washington, D.C., and headed south. Instead of dividing the seating on the bus along color lines, the riders sat together. That was all.

But by riding an integrated bus across the Deep South, the Freedom Riders were making one of the most dramatic and courageous stands against segregation in the entire Civil Rights movement. Their route would take them through towns and cities that supported segregation, places where they faced tremendous danger.

Maybe the most amazing thing about the Freedom Rides is that the riders were, in a way, completely ordinary. A lot of them were college students. No one pushed them to sign up—many of their families actually tried to stop them from going. They could have carried on with their lives as regular students, studying, seeing their friends. But they decided to take a stand, and the nation and the world watched.

In Alabama, one of the buses was firebombed. In Montgomery, more than a thousand people attacked the bus after it pulled into the station. The riders were beaten very badly. But they practiced nonviolence. No matter what they faced from the angry crowd, they wouldn't fight back.

Across the country, people were shocked by the violence against the Freedom Riders. How could the government allow peaceful citizens to be treated that way? The police had not protected the buses and even sometimes encouraged the violence against them. Newspaper photographs of the riders after the attack in Montgomery swept around the world.

The United States could no longer turn a blind eye to segregation, and the systematic prejudice and violence against African-Americans in the South. In 1964, the Civil Rights Act outlawed racial discrimination. Despite the odds against them, every one of the Freedom Riders survived.

Reference:

Nelson, S. (Director). (2011). *Freedom Riders* [Motion picture]. United States: PBS.

Selecting a Topic

Focus event:

Why is it important to tell the story of _____?

What can we learn from the actions of people involved in this event?

What were the consequences of this event?

Charles Person

I was the youngest person on the bus. I came to Washington, D.C., from Atlanta, where I was a freshman at Morehouse College, studying math and physics. I always wanted to be a nuclear physicist, and I was accepted at MIT, but the tuition was too expensive for my parents. The Georgia Institute of Technology would have been more affordable, but it's an all-white university and wouldn't even consider my application.

There were 22 people on our bus. We left Washington, D.C., on May 4, 1961. On May 5, the United States sent its first man into space on the Freedom 7. This seemed like a good sign. The Freedom 7, it had to mean something, didn't it? The country couldn't go into space, we couldn't move forward, while still keeping things the way they were.

This all started for me with the lunch counter sit-ins, when I was still in high school. I went after my classes finished and settled in at the counter. None of the waiters would serve me so I would just sit. Meanwhile, they just moved around behind the counter, in their little white hats like folded boats, and pretended I wasn't there. It's how I got all my homework done. You'd be amazed how much work you can get done while waiting to be served at a lunch counter. The waiters poured sodas from the red Coca-Cola machine. They fixed root beer floats and chocolate milkshakes, and cut thick slices of pie with a scoop of vanilla ice cream, and served them to the white customers.

Sometimes, outside the lunch counter, on the sidewalk, there would be other student activists, holding signs that said "The Golden Rule Does Not Apply Here" and "How Do We Get an Invitation to Lunch?" Sometimes one of the other protesters would catch my eye and nod at me. I was arrested just for sitting at the counter and spent 16 days in jail. I wanted to do more, so when CORE came to Atlanta to find a representative for the Freedom Ride, I signed up.

When at last we pulled into Charlotte, North Carolina, the bus station was quiet. Nothing bad happened. We milled around a waiting room marked "Whites Only." I took a sip of water from a fountain, and then I noticed that my shoes were scuffed.

In one corner of the station was a shoeshine counter with a wooden sign that read "Whites Only." A man sat on a stool with a rag over his shoulder and jars of open polish beside him. I handed him the correct change and settled into a chair. Nothing happened; he didn't move.

"May I have a shoeshine?" I asked.

"No," he said. He wouldn't look me in the eye. "Please leave."

Frank

I'm not a bad man. I don't want it to be like this. But I work here, and I really need to keep this job. When he sat down, everyone in the station was watching me, waiting to see what I would do.

If I said yes, I knew what would happen. There were men in the station who believe in segregation. They'd come to my house in the night. They'd ring the bell while my daughters and I were cleaning up after dinner, and then they'd stand back and wait on the lawn until I came outside.

Before long, they'd beat me up. You might not believe me, but I swear, they would. Just last week it happened to a doctor in Charlotte who treated an African-American patient instead of sending him to the other hospital.

"May I have a shoeshine?" he asked.

"No," I said. I couldn't look him in the eye. "Please leave."

The young man stayed very still, waiting for me to say more. I tried to swallow, but my mouth had gone dry. I wanted to tell him I was sorry. I admired how brave he was.

But I didn't say anything. Instead, I simply repeated, "Please leave."

After what felt like a very long time, he nodded, stood up, and walked away.

Joseph Perkins

As soon as Charles climbed down from the seat, I climbed up. The man looked at me like he was about to get upset. He looked grim and nervous.

"Hello, sir," I said. "I'd like a shoe shine, please."

He put down his rag and walked outside. Everyone in the station was quiet, watching us. It was only a matter of time before the police came. All of us rode the bus knowing we might be arrested, without reason, without a fair trial. I'd heard of judges who listened to entire trials with their backs to the defendants. But if I were arrested, the country would know about it. We had reporters with us, and photographers, and they would make sure the word got out.

While this was happening, I waited for the police, and I thought about our drive south. Our first stop was in Richmond, Virginia, then we continued on to Greensboro, North Carolina, and High Point, and Salisbury. We traveled east of the Smoky Mountains into Charlotte. We drove through the city, "Will You Still Love Me Tomorrow" by the Shirelles playing on the radio.

During the lunch counter sit-ins, we'd sit quietly on the red vinyl stools, and white men and women would come to jeer at us. One of the other protesters had a container of sugar poured over her hair. An angry red-faced man threw ketchup onto my charcoal sweater. We waited it out. We talked quietly to each other and read the signs above the counter: Cherry Pie 15¢, Sundae 12¢. The thing is, if you don't give them anything to fight against, they get bored.

The police car was outside the station, its lights flashing blue across the walls. I could see the shoeshine man talking to one of the officers, his shoulders hunched. In a minute, they'll come inside and take me away. But that's fine.

Fifty years later, after more than 400 students and activists have driven on buses all through the South, after the Civil Rights Act and the Voting Rights Act,

I know I'll be thinking about this moment, the moment after the officers arrive and before they push through the swinging doors. The station is so quiet. Everyone's holding their breath. And I feel completely calm.

(Story based on real people and real events in the Charlotte, N.C. bus station.)

References:

Bennett, K. (2011). *Charles Person Was on Freedom Riders Bus 50 Years Ago*. Retrieved from http://www.aarp.org/politics-society/history/info-05-2011/freedom-riders-charles-person.html

PBS. (2010). *Biography: Charles Person*. Retrieved from http://www.pbs.org/wgbh/americanexperience/freedomriders/people/charles-person

Transitions that signal time has passed

> After a few days/hours/minutes
> After that
> Along the way
> An hour later
> Before long
> Eventually
> Later on
> Later that same day
> Much later
> Next
> Shortly after that
> Some time later
> Soon
> Then

Transitions that signal something is happening at about the same time

> As soon as
> At that very moment
> During all of this
> Immediately
> Meanwhile
> Suddenly
> While this was happening
> Without delay

Transitions that signal an ending to the story

> At last
> Finally
> In the end

Transitions that signal an event that occurs just in time

> In the nick of time
> Just in time
> Not a moment too soon

Transitions that signal location [brackets indicate examples, fill in your own noun]

> Across [town]
> At the [park]
> Elsewhere
> In another part of [the museum]
> Inside the [apartment]
> Outside the [house]
> Opposite [the store], there was a
> Somewhere else in [the city]

Task	Yes/No
Revising	
Historical Fiction Narrative	
Is my story based on a true event?	
Did I use a consistent first-person narrative mode?	
Does my narrative contain three sections, each with its own narrator?	
Are my main characters (narrators) realistic with clear points of view toward the focus event that reflect their background experiences?	
Did I include a realistic historical setting with details based on researched facts?	
Does my dialogue enhance development of character point of view?	
Did I use transitions to move the story from one idea to the next?	
Did I include a logical conclusion to each of the three parts?	
Author's Note	
Did I include my own personal reasons for writing about this particular historical event/time period?	
Did I provide brief historical information about the event(s)/time period?	
Did I share my opinion about the event(s) that took place during the time period?	
Did I provide information on sources used for research?	
Did I reflect on the process of research and/or writing?	
Did I include an explanation of why this is a topic worth writing about?	
COPS Editing	
Did I check and correct my **c**apitalization?	
Did I check and correct my **o**rder and usage of words?	
Did I check and correct my **p**unctuation?	
Did I check and correct my **s**pelling?	

Standards Alignment: RL.7.1, RL.7.3, W.7.4, W.7.10

 Reading Lesson 2

Milestone Performance Assessment: Identifying the Elements of Historical Fiction

Use this checklist to assess student work on their Elements of Historical Fiction Graphic Organizers.

Task	Achieved	Notes
Identify as many elements of historical fiction as possible at this point in their reading.		
Use information from the text to draw conclusions about the historical time period.		

Standards Alignment: RL.7.1, RI.7.1, RL.7.2, RI.7.2, RI.7.3, RL.7.3, RL.7.9, W.7.4, W.7.9, W.7.10

 Reading Lesson 5

Milestone Performance Assessment: Comparing and Contrasting Historical Fiction and Nonfiction

Use this checklist to assess student short essays or infographics.

Task	Achieved	Notes
Compare and contrast the depiction of a historical period in a fictional source and in an informational source.		
Provide sufficient textual evidence to support thinking.		

Standards Alignment: RL.7.7, W.7.4, W.7.9, W.7.10

Reading Lesson 7
Milestone Performance Assessment: Identifying and Analyzing Filmmakers' Techniques

Use this checklist to assess student Exit Slips and Filmmaking Techniques Evaluation Charts.

Task	Achieved	Notes
Identify techniques such as lighting, camera angle and focus, sound, and color.		
Analyze the way the use of these techniques contributes to the overall effect of the film and the development of literary elements.		
Articulate and evaluate similarities and differences between the book and the film.		
Provide sufficient textual evidence to support thinking.		

Standards Alignment: RI.7.1, RI.7.3, RI.7.6, RI.7.8, RI.7.9, RI.7.10, W.7.4, W.7.9, W.7.10

Reading Lesson 9

Milestone Performance Assessment: Written Response to a Speech

Use this checklist to assess student written responses.

Task	Achieved	Notes
Analyze the focus speaker's point of view/perspective.		
Include evidence from the text to trace the development of the POV/perspective of the focus speaker across the text.		
Compare how the two speakers shape their argument through differing interpretations and evidence.		
Reflect on the experience of hearing the opposition's point of view.		
Use evidence from the text to support analysis and reflection.		

✂ -

Writing Lesson 1

Standards Alignment: RI.7.1, RI.7.2, RI.7.3, RI.7.10, W.7.3, W.7.4, W.7.5, W.7.9, W.7.10

Milestone Performance Assessment: Selecting a Topic

Use this checklist to assess student Selecting a Topic graphic organizers.

Task	Achieved	Notes
Select a focus event and explain its importance.		
Articulate what might be learned through the example put forth by the people involved in this focus event.		
Explain the consequences of this focus event.		

✂ -

Standards Alignment: W.7.3, W.7.4, W.7.5, W.7.10

Writing Lesson 4

Milestone Performance Assessment: Selecting and Establishing Character, Narrator, and Setting

Use this checklist to assess student drafts.

Task	Achieved	Notes
Select and describe a realistic setting.		
Select three narrators.		
Articulate point of view/perspective of each narrator.		
Create realistic characters.		
Provide a brief character description.		

- -

Standards Alignment: W.7.3, W.7.4, W.7.5, W.7.10, L.7.1, L.7.2, L.7.3

Writing Lesson 8
Milestone Performance Assessment: Author's Notes

Use this checklist to assess student work on author's notes.

Task	Achieved	Notes
Include explanation of why the author chose to write about the events/time period.		
Provide brief historical information about the events/time period.		
Include opinion about the events that took place during the time period.		
Provide information on sources used for research.		
Include a reflection on the process of research and/or writing.		
Include an explanation of why this is a topic worth remembering and honoring.		

✂ -

 Writing Lesson 9

Standards Alignment: W.7.4, W.7.5, W.7.10, L.7.1, L.7.2, L.7.3

Milestone Performance Assessment: Revising and Editing Writing

Use this checklist to assess student revisions and editing.

Task	Achieved	Notes
Revising		
Historical Fiction Narrative		
Story based on a true event.		
Use consistent first-person narrative mode.		
Contains three sections, each with its own narrator.		
Main characters (narrators) are realistic with clear points of view toward the focus events that reflect their background experiences.		
Include realistic historical setting with details based on researched facts.		
Dialogue enhances development of character point of view.		
Use transitions to move story from one idea to the next.		
Logical conclusion to each of the three parts.		
Author's Note		
Include own personal reasons for writing about this particular historical event/time period.		
Provide brief historical information about the event(s)/time period.		
Share opinion about the event(s) that took place during the time period.		
Provide information on sources used for research.		
Reflect on the process of research and/or writing.		
Include an explanation of why this topic is worth writing about.		

Task	Achieved	Notes
COPS Editing		
Capitalization.		
Order and usage of words.		
Punctuation.		
Spelling.		

Core Ready Reading Rubric

Grade 7 Examining Cultural Perspectives: Historical Fiction and Drama

Lesson Set Goal	Emerging	Approaching	Achieving	Exceeding	Standards Alignment
Examine how the historical setting shapes the plot of the story.	Student is unable to identify the setting or how the setting shapes the plot of the story. Lacks textual evidence.	Student accurately identifies the historical setting. May have difficulty describing how the historical setting shapes the plot of the story. May lack sufficient textual evidence to support ideas.	Student accurately identifies the historical setting and describes how the setting shapes the plot of the story. Provides sufficient, relevant evidence to support points.	Student accurately identifies and describes how the historical setting shapes the plot of a story. Provides detailed and insightful evidence to support points. May describe and effectively support several examples.	RI.7.1 RL.7.1 RL.7.3 RI.7.3 RI.7.10 RL.7.10 W.7.4 W.7.10 SL.7.1 SL.7.4 SL.7.6 L.7.1 L.7.3 L.7.6
Identify the narrator of a story and analyze the point of view the narrator conveys.	Student is unable to identify the narrator of a story and analyze the point of view the narrator conveys.	Student identifies the narrator of a story and provides some analysis of the point of view the narrator conveys. Analysis may lack sufficient detail and clarity.	Student identifies the narrator of a story and analyzes the point of view the narrator conveys. Analysis is clear and contains sufficient detail.	Student identifies the narrator of a story and analyzes the point of view the narrator conveys. Analysis is thorough and accurate with detailed textual evidence.	RL.7.1 RL.7.3 RL7.6 RL.7.10 W.7.4 W.7.9 W.7.10 SL.7.1 SL.7.6 L.7.1 L.7.2 L.7.3 L.7.6

Lesson Set Goal	Emerging	Approaching	Achieving	Exceeding	Standards Alignment
Compare and contrast a written story to its filmed version and analyze the effects of techniques unique to each medium.	Student shows little or no evidence of success comparing and contrasting a written story to its filmed version and analyzing the effects of techniques unique to each medium.	Student compares and contrasts with some success a written story to its filmed version and analyzes the effects of techniques unique to each medium. Descriptions may be unevenly developed. May have some gaps or lack sufficient textual evidence.	Student shows solid evidence of successfully comparing and contrasting a written story to its filmed version and analyzing the effects of techniques unique to each medium. Provides accurate and sufficient textual evidence.	Student shows outstanding evidence of comparing and contrasting a written story to its filmed version and analyzing the effects of techniques unique to each medium. Provides thorough and detailed textual evidence. May demonstrate deep inferential thinking and comprehension.	RL.7.1 RL.7.2 RL.7.7 R.7.10 W.7.4 W.7.9 W.7.10 SL.7.1 SL.7.2 SL.7.4 SL.7.6 L.7.1 L.7.3 L.7.6
Compare and contrast how stories in both film and print examine the way the cultural background influences point of view.	Student shows little or no evidence of success comparing and contrasting how stories in both film and print examine the way the cultural background influences point of view.	Student compares and contrasts with some success how stories in both film and print examine the way the cultural background influences point of view. Descriptions may be unevenly developed. May have some gaps or lack sufficient textual evidence.	Student shows solid evidence of successfully comparing and contrasting how stories in both film and print examine the way the cultural background influences point of view. Provides accurate and sufficient textual evidence.	Student shows outstanding evidence of comparing and contrasting how stories in both film and print examine the way the cultural background influences point of view. Provides thorough and detailed textual evidence. May demonstrate deep inferential thinking and comprehension.	RL.7.1 RL.7.3 RL.7.6 RL.7.7 RL.7.10 W.7.4 W.7.9 W.7.10 SL.7.1 SL.7.2 SL.7.4 SL.7.6 L.7.1 L.7.3 L.7.6

Core Ready Reading Rubric, Grade 7, *continued*

Lesson Set Goal	Emerging	Approaching	Achieving	Exceeding	Standards Alignment
Compare and contrast a fictional portrayal and a historical account of the same event.	Student shows little or no evidence of success comparing and contrasting a fictional portrayal and a historical account of the same period.	Student compares and contrasts with some success a fictional portrayal and a historical account of the same period. Descriptions may be unevenly developed. May have some gaps or lack sufficient textual evidence.	Student shows solid evidence of successfully comparing and contrasting a fictional portrayal and a historical account of the same period. Provides accurate and sufficient textual evidence.	Student shows outstanding evidence of comparing and contrasting a fictional portrayal and a historical account of the same period. Provides thorough and detailed textual evidence. Demonstrates deep inferential thinking and comprehension.	RL.7.1 RI.7.1 RI.7.2 RI.7.3 RL.7.9 RL.7.10 RI.7.10 W.7.4 W.7.9 W.7.10 SL.7.1 SL.7.2 SL.7.4 SL.7.6 L.7.1 L.7.3 L.7.6
Examine the balance of historical fact and imagined elements in a historical fiction text.	Student demonstrates little or no evidence of success describing both historical fact and imagined elements in a historical fiction text. Lacks accuracy and/or evidence.	Student describes with some success both historical fact and imagined elements in a historical fiction text. May have some gaps or lack sufficient textual evidence.	Student accurately describes both historical fact and imagined elements in a historical fiction text. Provides sufficient textual evidence.	Student describes both historical fact and imagined elements in a historical fiction text. Provides thorough and detailed textual evidence. May demonstrate deep inferential thinking and comprehension.	RL.7.1 RI.7.1 RI.7.2 RI.7.3 RL.7.9 RL.7.10 RI.7.10 W.7.4 W.7.9 W.7.10 SL.7.1 SL.7.2 SL.7.4 SL.7.6 L.7.1 L.7.3 L.7.6

Lesson Set Goal	Emerging	Approaching	Achieving	Exceeding	Standards Alignment
Examine the development of point of view across historical accounts.	Student demonstrates little or no evidence of success examining the development of point of view across historical accounts. Lacks accuracy and/or evidence.	Student examines with some success the development of point of view across historical accounts. May have some gaps or lack sufficient textual evidence.	Student accurately examines the development of point of view across historical accounts. Provides sufficient textual evidence.	Student examines the development of point of view across historical accounts. Provides thorough and detailed textual evidence. May demonstrate deep inferential thinking and comprehension.	RI.7.1 RI.7.2 RI.7.5 RI.7.6 RI.7.8 RI.7.9 RI.7.10 SL.7.1 SL.7.2 SL.7.4 SL.7.6 L.7.1 L.7.3 L.7.6
By the end of the year, read and comprehend literature, including stories, dramas, and poems, in the grades 6–8 text complexity band proficiently, with scaffolding as needed at the high end of the range.	Student shows little or no evidence of reading and comprehending texts appropriate for the grades 6-8 text complexity band even with scaffolding.	Student shows some evidence of reading and comprehending texts appropriate for the grades 6-8 text complexity band with scaffolding.	Student shows solid evidence of reading and comprehending texts appropriate for the grades 6-8 text complexity band proficiently, but may need scaffolding at the high end of the range.	Student shows solid evidence of reading and comprehending texts above the grades 6-8 text complexity band proficiently.	RL.7.10
By the end of the year, read and comprehend literary nonfiction in the grades 6–8 text complexity band proficiently, with scaffolding as needed at the high end of the range.	Student shows little or no evidence of reading and comprehending texts appropriate for the grades 6-8 text complexity band even with scaffolding.	Student shows some evidence of reading and comprehending texts appropriate for the grades 6-8 text complexity band with scaffolding.	Student shows solid evidence of reading and comprehending texts appropriate for the grades 6-8 text complexity band proficiently but may need scaffolding at the high end of the range.	Student shows solid evidence of reading and comprehending texts above the grades 6-8 text complexity band proficiently.	RI.7.10

Core Ready Reading Rubric, Grade 7, *continued*

Lesson Set Goal	Emerging	Approaching	Achieving	Exceeding	Standards Alignment
In collaborative discussions, demonstrate evidence of preparation and exhibit responsibility for the rules and roles and purpose of conversation.	Student demonstrates little or no success at coming to discussions prepared and often disregards the rules, deadlines, and roles of conversation even with prompting and redirection.	Student participates in collaborative discussions with some success. Lacks thorough preparation at times. Sometimes observes the rules, deadlines, and roles of conversation but needs frequent prompting or redirection.	Student consistently participates in collaborative discussions and comes to discussions prepared. Student observes the rules, deadlines, and roles of conversation with little prompting or redirection.	Student participates in collaborative discussions with purpose and enthusiasm. Arrives to all discussions thoroughly prepared. Student carefully observes the rules, deadlines, and roles of conversation with no prompting or redirection.	SL.7.1a SL.7.1b
In collaborative discussions, share and develop ideas in a manner that enhances understanding of a topic and contribute and respond to the content of the conversation in a productive and focused manner.	Student demonstrates little or no success asking and answering specific questions with appropriate details, making comments that contribute to the discussion, or acknowledging new information and adjusting own thinking to reflect new ideas if necessary even with prompting.	Student demonstrates some success asking and answering specific questions with appropriate details, making comments that contribute to the discussion, and acknowledging new information and adjusting own thinking to reflect new ideas if necessary but needs frequent prompting or redirection.	Student demonstrates solid success asking and answering specific questions with appropriate details, making comments that contribute to the discussion, and acknowledging new information and adjusting own thinking to reflect new ideas if necessary. May need occasional support or prompting or redirection.	Student demonstrates outstanding success asking and answering specific questions with appropriate details, making comments that contribute to the discussion, and acknowledging new information and adjusting own thinking to reflect new ideas if necessary. Proactively uses this strategy to support own learning. No prompting or redirection needed.	SL.7.1c SL.7.1d
Adapt speech to a variety of contexts and tasks, demonstrating command of formal English when indicated or appropriate.	Student shows little or no evidence of success adapting speech to a variety of contexts and tasks. Demonstrates very little command of formal English when indicated or appropriate.	Student shows some evidence of success adapting speech to a variety of contexts and tasks. Demonstrates basic command of formal English when indicated or appropriate.	Student effectively adapts speech to a variety of contexts and tasks. Demonstrates solid command of formal English when indicated or appropriate.	Student shows exceptional evidence of adapting speech to a variety of contexts and tasks. Demonstrates sophisticated command of formal English when indicated or appropriate.	SL.7.6

Lesson Set Goal	Emerging	Approaching	Achieving	Exceeding	Standards Alignment
Demonstrate command of standard English and its conventions and use the knowledge when writing, speaking, reading, and listening.	Student demonstrates very little command of standard English and its conventions. Little or no evidence of application of knowledge when writing, speaking, reading, and listening.	Student shows some command of standard English and its conventions and attempts to use the knowledge when writing, speaking, reading, and listening.	Student shows solid command of standard English and its conventions and uses the knowledge when writing, speaking, reading, and listening.	Student shows exceptional command of standard English and its conventions and demonstrates sophisticated use of the knowledge when writing, speaking, reading, and listening.	L.7.1 L.7.2 L.7.3
Acquire and use accurately grade-appropriate general academic and domain-specific words and phrases, strategically building vocabulary knowledge when needed.	Student shows little or no evidence of the acquisition and accurate use of grade-appropriate general academic and domain-specific words and phrases. Little or no success using vocabulary building strategies.	Student shows some evidence of the acquisition and accurate use of grade-appropriate general academic and domain-specific words and phrases. Effectively uses vocabulary building strategies at times.	Student shows solid evidence of the acquisition and accurate use of grade-appropriate general academic and domain-specific words and phrases. Effectively uses vocabulary building strategies with frequency.	Student shows outstanding evidence of the acquisition and accurate use of grade-appropriate general academic and domain-specific words and phrases sophisticated for the grade level. Proactively uses a wide variety of vocabulary building strategies with success.	L.7.6

Core Ready Writing Rubric

Grade 7 Examining Cultural Perspectives: Historical Fiction and Drama

Lesson Set Goal	Emerging	Approaching	Achieving	Exceeding	Standards Alignment
Write historical fiction narrative that includes key elements of historical fiction.	Student demonstrates little or no success writing historical fiction narrative. Few or no key elements evident.	Student demonstrates some success writing historical fiction narrative. Some elements may be weak or uneven.	Student demonstrates solid success writing historical fiction narrative. All elements are present and effective.	Student demonstrates outstanding success writing historical fiction narrative. All elements are well-developed and highly effective.	W.7.3 W.7.4 W.7.5 W.7.10
Conduct research to craft a realistic setting with authentic details in the narrative.	Student writing shows little or no evidence of research to craft a realistic setting with authentic details.	Student writing shows some evidence of research to craft a realistic setting with authentic details. May be somewhat underdeveloped or lack clarity.	Student shows solid evidence of research to craft a realistic setting with authentic details.	Student shows outstanding evidence of research to craft a well-developed, realistic setting with several authentic details that fit seamlessly in the narrative.	RI.7.1 RI.7.2 RI.7.3 RI.7.10 W.7.3 W.7.4 W.7.5 W.7.6 W.7.7 W.7.10 SL.7.1 SL.7.2 SL.7.6 L.7.1 L.7.2 L.7.3 L.7.6
Articulate a character/narrator's background and illustrate its influence on his or her perspective.	Student shows little or no evidence of articulating a character/narrator's background and illustrating its influence on his or her perspective. Character/narrator and his or her background and perspective are underdeveloped and/or irrelevant.	Student shows some evidence of articulating a character/narrator's background and illustrating its influence on his or her perspective. Character/narrator and his or her background and perspective may be somewhat underdeveloped or lack relevance.	Student shows solid evidence of articulating a character/narrator's background and illustrating its influence on his or her perspective. Character/narrator and his or her background and perspective are sufficiently developed.	Student shows outstanding evidence of articulating a character/narrator's background and illustrating its influence on his or her perspective. Character/narrator and his or her background and perspective are well-developed and insightfully connected.	W.7.3 W.7.4 W.7.5 W.7.10

Lesson Set Goal	Emerging	Approaching	Achieving	Exceeding	Standards Alignment
Employ dialogue to reinforce characters' point of view.	Student uses little or no dialogue to reinforce characters' point of view.	Student uses some dialogue. Dialogue may be irrelevant or ineffective in conveying point of view.	Student successfully uses dialogue that is relevant and effective in conveying point of view.	Student successfully uses highly effective dialogue to convey point of view. May also reveal other key aspects of characters.	RL.7.1 RL.7.6 RL.7.10 W.7.3 W.7.4 W.7.5 W.7.10
Write a reflective author's note to explain their thinking and writing process.	Student shows little or no evidence of success writing a reflective author's note to explain thinking and writing process, even with support.	Student shows some evidence of success writing a reflective author's note to explain thinking and writing process. Some elements may be missing or underdeveloped.	Student shows solid evidence of success writing a reflective author's note to explain thinking and writing process. All required elements evident.	Student shows outstanding evidence of success writing a reflective author's note to explain thinking and writing process. All required elements evident. Insightful and detailed.	W.7.4 W.7.5 W.7.10
By the end of the year, read and comprehend literary nonfiction in the grades 6–8 text complexity band proficiently, with scaffolding as needed at the high end of the range.	Student shows little or no evidence of reading and comprehending texts appropriate for the grades 6-8 text complexity band even with scaffolding.	Student shows some evidence of reading and comprehending texts appropriate for the grades 6-8 text complexity band with scaffolding.	Student shows solid evidence of reading and comprehending texts appropriate for the grades 6-8 text complexity band proficiently, but may need scaffolding at the high end of the range.	Student shows solid evidence of reading and comprehending texts above the grades 6-8 text complexity band proficiently.	RI.7.10
With some guidance and support from peers and adults, develop and strengthen writing as needed by planning, revising, editing, rewriting, or trying a new approach, focusing on how well purpose and audience have been addressed.	Student makes little or no attempt to develop and strengthen writing as needed by planning, revising, editing, rewriting, or trying a new approach. Shows little or no attention to the conventions of standard English.	Student attempts to develop and strengthen writing as needed by planning, revising, editing, rewriting, or trying a new approach. Shows some command for the conventions of standard English. May contain significant errors or lacks clarity.	Student develops and strengthens writing as needed by planning, revising, editing, rewriting, or trying a new approach. Shows solid command for the conventions of standard English. May contain some errors or lack of clarity.	Student extensively develops and strengthens writing as needed by planning, revising, editing, rewriting, or trying a new approach. Shows exceptional command for the conventions of standard English. Few or no errors or lapses of clarity evident.	W.7.5

Core Ready Writing Rubric, Grade 7, *continued*

Lesson Set Goal	Emerging	Approaching	Achieving	Exceeding	Standards Alignment
Use technology, including the Internet, to complete required tasks: to produce and publish writing, link to and cite sources, and interact and collaborate with others.	Student demonstrates little or no success at using technology to accomplish required tasks. May refuse to participate, use technological tools inappropriately, or lack the skills to use technological tools effectively.	Student attempts to use technology for required tasks, but may have some ineffective or underdeveloped elements, occasionally neglect to follow proper procedures, or lack some key skills to be solidly successful.	Student demonstrates solid success in using technology to accomplish required tasks. All elements are effective and complete, and student follows proper procedures and possesses necessary skills for success.	Student demonstrates outstanding success in using technology to accomplish required tasks. May demonstrate outstanding skills, innovative thinking, or creativity.	W.7.6
In collaborative discussions, demonstrate evidence of preparation and exhibit responsibility for the rules and roles and purpose of conversation.	Student demonstrates little or no success at coming to discussions prepared and often disregards the rules, deadlines, and roles of conversation even with prompting and redirection.	Student participates in collaborative discussions with some success. Lacks thorough preparation at times. Sometimes observes the rules, deadlines, and roles of conversation but needs frequent prompting or redirection.	Student consistently participates in collaborative discussions and comes to discussions prepared. Student observes the rules, deadlines, and roles of conversation with little prompting or redirection.	Student participates in collaborative discussions with purpose and enthusiasm. Arrives to all discussions thoroughly prepared. Student carefully observes the rules, deadlines and roles of conversation with no prompting or redirection.	SL.7.1a SL.7.1b
In collaborative discussions, share and develop ideas in a manner that enhances understanding of a topic and contribute and respond to the content of the conversation in a productive and focused manner.	Student demonstrates little or no success asking and answering specific questions with appropriate details, making comments that contribute to the discussion, or acknowledging new information and adjusting own thinking to reflect new ideas if necessary even with prompting.	Student demonstrates some success asking and answering specific questions with appropriate details, making comments that contribute to the discussion, and acknowledging new information and adjusting own thinking to reflect new ideas if necessary but needs frequent prompting or redirection.	Student demonstrates solid success asking and answering specific questions with appropriate details, making comments that contribute to the discussion, and acknowledging new information and adjusting own thinking to reflect new ideas if necessary. May need occasional support or prompting or redirection.	Student demonstrates outstanding success asking and answering specific questions with appropriate details, making comments that contribute to the discussion, and acknowledging new information and adjusting own thinking to reflect new ideas if necessary. Proactively uses this strategy to support own learning. No prompting or redirection needed.	SL.7.1c SL.7.1d

Lesson Set Goal	Emerging	Approaching	Achieving	Exceeding	Standards Alignment
Adapt speech to a variety of contexts and tasks, demonstrating command of formal English when indicated or appropriate.	Student shows little or no evidence of success adapting speech to a variety of contexts and tasks. Demonstrates very little command of formal English when indicated or appropriate.	Student shows some evidence of success adapting speech to a variety of contexts and tasks. Demonstrates basic command of formal English when indicated or appropriate.	Student effectively adapts speech to a variety of contexts and tasks. Demonstrates solid command of formal English when indicated or appropriate.	Student shows exceptional evidence of adapting speech to a variety of contexts and tasks. Demonstrates sophisticated command of formal English when indicated or appropriate.	SL.7.6
Demonstrate command of standard English and its conventions and use the knowledge when writing, speaking, reading, and listening.	Student demonstrates very little command of standard English and its conventions. Little or no evidence of application of knowledge when writing, speaking, reading, and listening.	Student shows some command of standard English and its conventions and attempts to use the knowledge when writing, speaking, reading, and listening.	Student shows solid command of standard English and its conventions and uses the knowledge when writing, speaking, reading, and listening.	Student shows exceptional command of standard English and its conventions and demonstrates sophisticated use of the knowledge when writing, speaking, reading, and listening.	L.7.1 L.7.2 L.7.3
Acquire and use accurately grade-appropriate general academic and domain-specific words and phrases, strategically building vocabulary knowledge when needed.	Student shows little or no evidence of the acquisition and accurate use of grade-appropriate general academic and domain-specific words and phrases. Little or no success using vocabulary building strategies.	Student shows some evidence of the acquisition and accurate use of grade-appropriate general academic and domain-specific words and phrases. Effectively uses vocabulary building strategies at times.	Student shows solid evidence of the acquisition and accurate use of grade-appropriate general academic and domain-specific words and phrases. Effectively uses vocabulary building strategies with frequency.	Student shows outstanding evidence of the acquisition and accurate use of grade-appropriate general academic and domain-specific words and phrases sophisticated for the grade level. Proactively uses a wide variety of vocabulary building strategies with success.	L.7.6

God/Goddess	Role	Relationship with Other Gods	Relationship with Humans	Character Traits
Zeus	God of thunder—most powerful god	Shared his powers with his brothers and sisters who became gods and goddesses	Has romantic relations with many humans and has half-god children	Powerful, controlling, loves women

Sample Myth # 1: The Tale of Perseus

When Perseus was an infant, his grandfather, King Acrisius, received a prophecy that Perseus would one day kill him. And so he sent his daughter Danae and her son to sea in a wooden chest. After three days, the chest washed up on the shores of a beautiful green island called Seriphos.

The island's king was named Polydectes. Polydectes wanted to marry Danae, who refused him. While Perseus was able to protect his mother, Polydectes would never get his way, and so he developed a scheme to send Perseus far from the island.

One summer night, Polydectes threw a great banquet. He served wine and olives and bread with honey. There was beautiful music, and candles glowed in the dark corners of the palace gardens. Everyone on the island was invited, and each guest was required to bring a gift.

"What did you bring me?" Polydectes asked Perseus.

"Nothing," said Perseus. "I am very poor, and I had nothing to bring you."

Polydectes and his courtiers laughed, and Perseus grew angry.

"What do you want?" he asked. "I will bring you anything you ask."

"Bring me the head of Medusa."

Medusa was one of the three Gorgons, dangerous women with twisting snakes on their heads. Perseus agreed to the king's demand and left on his quest at once. To help him slay the Gorgon, Hermes gave Perseus winged sandals and a sword and Athena gave him a shield.

"When you meet Medusa, look into the shield instead of at her," said Athena. "If you look at her, you will be turned to stone. But her reflection cannot harm you."

Next Perseus visited the Graeae, three quarrelsome old women who shared one eye. While they were bickering, Perseus stole the eye and refused to give it back unless they helped him. They gave him a cap that made its wearer invisible, and finally Perseus was ready.

The Gorgons lived on a rocky island buffeted by strong waves. As Perseus's boat drew closer, he realized that the rocks on the island were actually men whom the Gorgons had turned to stone. As Perseus approached the Gorgons' lair, he grew more and more afraid. Poisonous snakes twisted from their heads, and their eyes were black and cruel. Perseus was so scared that he almost forgot Athena's advice and looked at Medusa. Instead he fixed his eyes on the shield. He cut off Medusa's head, put it in a satchel, and flew home on the winged sandals.

When he returned to Seriphos, Perseus discovered that Polydectes was holding Danae captive. He ran to the palace to free her.

"If you are my friend, close your eyes!" he shouted. Then he drew Medusa's head from his bag, and Polydectes and his followers were turned to stone.

Soon after, Perseus married Andromeda. They lived a long and happy life together, and when they died they were cast into the sky as constellations.

Sample Myth #2: The Quest of the Golden Fleece

Jason was raised in the wooded mountains of Thessaly by a centaur named Chiron. When he turned twenty, he returned to the city of Iolcus to claim the throne his uncle, Pelias, had stolen from his father.

King Pelias refused to surrender the crown unless Jason completed a heroic quest. He was tasked with bringing home the golden fleece, which hung from the branch of an oak tree in a grove in Colchis. The grove was protected by a dragon, and Colchis lay hundreds of miles away across the treacherous Bosphorus Strait. Still, Jason accepted. He had a beautiful ship built and

invited heroes like Hercules, Orpheus, Castor and Pollux, and Atalanta to join him. Soon the *Argo* set sail.

When the Argonauts arrived in Colchis, King Aietes would only relinquish the golden fleece if Jason performed three tasks: He had to yoke the Khalkotauri, two fire-breathing bulls; plow a field; and sow it with dragon's teeth. Jason agreed, though everyone knew he was doomed to fail.

He would have certainly failed, if not for one thing: King Aietes had a daughter, Medea, who fell in love with Jason the moment she saw him. Using her knowledge of sorcery, Medea helped Jason with each task. She gave him a salve to keep the bulls' fire from burning his skin, and when the dragon's teeth sprouted into warriors defending the grove, she told Jason to throw a rock into the melee. The warriors began to bludgeon each other until all of them were dead.

The golden fleece was guarded by a dragon that never closed its eyes. But Medea gave it a sleep potion, and while it dozed Jason crept inside the grove and stole the fleece.

When King Aietes realized his daughter had helped Jason, he was furious. He chased them through Colchis and down to the harbor. To slow him down, Medea slayed her brother and threw his body into the sea. King Aietes was horrified and frantically tried to retrieve his son from the water. While he was distracted, Jason and Medea escaped and sailed home across the Aegean. When they returned to Iolcus, Jason was crowned king.

But misfortune followed them, and Jason soon lost the throne. Worse, he betrayed Medea and abandoned her for another woman. Medea killed his new bride by giving her a wedding dress that burst into flames when she put it on. She then killed her and Jason's two sons and fled in a winged chariot to Mount Olympus, where the gods protected her. For the rest of his days, Jason was beset by grief and regret.

Hero: _____ **Text:** _____

Brief Summary of the Text: _____

Characteristic	Evidence from the Text • Text quote or description • Page #
Mighty warrior	
Unusual birth circumstances	
Initiating event	
Epic quest	
Admirable qualities: bravery, selflessness	
Lives elsewhere	
Special weapons	
Help from gods/goddesses	

based on Joseph Campbell's monomyth theory

The Ordinary World:

We are introduced to the hero, usually in his or her homeland. The hero must leave this world to enter the "special" world of the journey.

Call to Adventure:

An initial event encourages the hero to accept a challenge or quest, such as choosing the fight for good over evil.

Refusal of the Call:

The hero initially refuses, preferring the relative comfort of the ordinary world. He or she may be fearful, insecure, or worried that "the call" will be a hardship.

Meeting the Mentor:

The hero is introduced to one who will support and guide him or her on the journey with advice, training, or magical gifts. The mentor may be a living being or an object. The mentor provides the hero confidence to accept the call.

Crossing the Threshold:

The hero must cross the threshold and move into a new world from the ordinary world. The threshold may be an actual structure or another type of divider between the ordinary world and the special world. This crossing indicates commitment to the journey.

Tests/Allies/Enemies:

The hero must figure out how the rules in the special world work as he or she encounters minor challenges and meets others who may turn out to be supportive team members, a sidekick, or dangerous enemies.

Approach to the Innermost Cave:

The hero prepares for the "ordeal" or final challenge as he or she approaches the location where he or she will meet the greatest enemy. (Note that this may not literally be a cave.) For example, he or she might plan to advance toward the lair of the main enemy, plan an attack strategy, take a break for romance, or eliminate lesser enemies.

Ordeal:

The hero encounters a major life-or-death test and/or final battle with the greatest enemy. This is the climax of the journey. The hero usually experiences "death" from which he or she must be resurrected in a way that provides him or her the strength or wisdom to complete the journey.

Reward:

Also called "seizing the sword," in this stage, the hero receives a reward for facing and overcoming the ordeal. May be a magical tool, great wisdom, an elixir, the affection of another, or a combination of items.

The Road Back:

In this stage, the hero heads home to the ordinary world. The hero may resist returning, but circumstances often force him or her to commit to return.

Resurrection:

In this stage, the hero resolves his or her problem. He or she is "reborn" with his or her original characteristics from the ordinary world in combination with the new powers, strength, and wisdom gained from the journey. He or she must accept and sometimes must prove his or her new status as "hero" to others.

Return with the Elixir:

In this stage, the hero returns to the ordinary world with the "elixir," a great treasure or understanding to share from the journey. The hero becomes master of both worlds.

Hero: _____   **Text:** _____

Brief Summary of the Text: _____

Stage of the Journey	Evidence from the Text • Text quote or description • Page #
The Ordinary World	
Call to Adventure	
Refusal of the Call	
Meeting the Mentor	
Crossing the Threshold	
Tests/Allies/Enemies	
Approach to the Innermost Cave	
Ordeal	
Reward	
The Road Back	
Resurrection	
Return with the Elixir	

Observations from the Book	Observations from the Film	Why Do You Think the Filmmaker Made Changes, If Any?	My Evaluation of These Changes	Describe Evidence of the Hero's Characteristics from Film	Describe Evidence of the Hero's Journey from Film
In the book . . .	In the film . . .	The filmmaker probably chose to make changes because . . .	I agree/disagree with the decisions the filmmaker made . . . (explain) I prefer the book/ the movie because . . .	The hero's characteristics are evident when...	The hero's journey is evident when . . .

Heroes are everywhere. The world is full of self-sacrificing individuals who look to make the world a better place. They are on the news, on talk shows, and even in our imaginations. Heroism is not a characteristic that blossoms overnight. Real-life heroes have values that have developed throughout their lives and affect their actions. Heroes in literature and film often go on similar journeys that allow them to develop and display classic heroic qualities. These predictable patterns in literature are called archetypes. Archetypes are character traits, behaviors, or events that recur again and again in literature, most often in folklore and mythology. Archetypal patterns may also be found in modern books and films. This is the case with the characteristics of the hero and his journey in the film "The Lion King." It tells a story about a main character called Simba, the soon to be "lion king." Simba is like the archetypal hero because he goes on a classic journey of self-discovery and develops the characteristics of the hero he is meant to be.

In this film, the most obvious archetype is the hero. The hero pattern is one that appears in both mythology and contemporary literature. Simba possesses many of the characteristics of an archetypal hero. His birth is unusual as the son of the lion king Mufasa. The movie opens with all of the animals of Pride Rock attending a celebration of his important birth. Traditional heroes often live away from their families for some time. When Simba's father is killed by Scar, Simba does not stand up to fight, but instead runs away to live in the jungle with Timon and Pumbaa. In the jungle, Simba is on a quest to find out who he really is. Like the heroes of myths who often receive help from gods, Simba is helped by his father from heaven and Rafiki, the wise baboon. They both inspire him to return to Pride Rock to fight his evil Uncle Scar. When Simba returns, he exhibits the brave and selfless qualities of a mighty warrior, fighting and winning over Scar to become the new lion king.

Another archetype present in "The Lion King" is the hero's journey. Some of Simba's experiences follow this pattern. He begins in the ordinary world with his family, but he runs away when Scar blames him for his father's death. Simba's call to adventure is to become the next lion king after his father dies, but he refuses the call to save the rest of the lion pride from enemy Uncle Scar. He chooses to run away to a different world and live with allies Timon and Pumbaa instead. Nala, his ally from Pride Rock, finds Simba and asks him to return to help defeat Scar. Simba refuses again, but then he has a vision of his father who mentors him along with Rafiki to return to Pride Rock, his true home. There his ordeal is a fight with Scar and his minions, the hyenas. His reward is killing Scar and becoming king with Nala as his queen.

There is more evidence of the archetypal journey in "The Lion King." Death and resurrection are often a part of a classic hero's experience. Although he does not actually die, Simba's life as he knows it comes to an end when he runs from Pride Rock into the dangerous desert after the death of his father. When he meets Timon and Pumbaa, they save him by giving him a reason to live. When Simba goes back to the pridelands, his family and friends are surprised to discover he is alive. It is like a resurrection as they welcome him and he becomes the new lion king.

Recognizing the archetypes of the hero in a story is very important to the understanding of a story and its characters. In order to do this, we must analyze the actions, words, and feelings of the characters to find patterns that occur time and time again in stories. We discover how these characters demonstrate the special characteristics of a hero and travel on a journey to overcome their past and become greater individuals. This helps us deeply understand a character and make connections to other texts, stories, and genres. Simba, the main character of "The Lion King," is a classic hero with a classic journey. "The Lion King" may be a movie, but it reminds us of the heroes of old.

1) REVIEW:
   Read the essay again closely. As you read, mark up the text by underlining important points and noting any confusions or questions you have about ideas or vocabulary. Clear up confusions and define any unfamiliar vocabulary with classmates or the teacher before moving on with the questionnaire.

2) INTRODUCTION:
   Label the introduction. What does the writer say (brief summary) and do in the introductory paragraph? What seems to be the purpose of the introductory paragraph?

3) THESIS:
   Double underline and label the thesis. What is the thesis of the essay? What seems to be the job of the thesis?

4) BODY PARAGRAPHS:
Label and number each body paragraph. What does the writer say (brief summary) and do in each body paragraph? What seems to be the job of the body paragraphs?

5) CONCLUSION:
Label the conclusion. What does the writer say (brief summary) and do in the conclusion? What seems to be the job of the concluding paragraph?

6) OTHER OBSERVATIONS:
What else do you notice about what the writer says and does in the essay?

You will write a literary essay about your modern fantasy texts on one of the following topics:
- Explain how the main character possesses the qualities of a classic hero.
- Explain how the main character's experiences are parallel to Joseph Campbell's hero's journey/monomyth.

Your essay should include:

Introduction
- Grab the readers' attention
- Introduce the topic clearly
- Present thesis in a single, clear sentence
- Preview of what is to follow in essay

Body Paragraphs
- Usually two or more body paragraphs
- Paragraphs organized into broad categories
- Topic sentence establishes focus of each paragraph
- Commentary from the student writer
- Details/evidence/quotes from text to support thesis

Conclusion
- Reiterate but not restate the thesis
- Follow from and support the information provided in the essay
- Should not present new evidence

Other requirements:
- Use names and vocabulary from the text with accuracy
- Transitions connect ideas
- Formal style and language

The Lightning Thief is a modern fantasy story by Rick Riordan based on a very old myth. In fact, nearly everything about the main character, Percy Jackson, matches the archetype of the Greek hero. But the question is, did the author explicitly design Percy Jackson to be a modern-day Perseus, the famous hero of Greek mythology? I think so. There is plenty of evidence in *The Lightning Thief* to prove that Percy is based on Perseus and embodies the archetypal heroic characteristics.

Riordan chose to bring Perseus and the hero archetype to life in the pages of *The Lightning Thief*, but in doing so put his own spin on things. Both Perseus and Percy have unusual birth circumstances. In the classic myth, Perseus is the son of Zeus. In *The Lightning Thief*, he is now the son of Poseidon. Same demi-god, different dad. Both heroes were raised by their mothers with no knowledge of their fathers. Neither had a carefree childhood or believed himself to be anything extraordinary. Before uncovering the fact that he is a demi-god, Percy is an unlikely hero. He is considered a troublemaker in school, with a track record of expulsions. His dyslexia makes learning and reading difficult, and his ADHD makes it hard for him to be attentive or to sit still in class. He has never been one of the "cool" kids in school. Although the beginnings of these young men's lives were less than ideal, they become who they were meant to be: heroes.

Both Perseus and Percy are mighty warriors. They are brave, spirited, and natural-born leaders. Time and time again, they battle against forces to protect friends, family, and even enemies. In the classic myth, Perseus battles Medusa. In the book, Medusa now runs a statue store and enjoys turning visiting satyrs into stone. Percy still gets to kill her, but he sends her head back to Zeus in a FedEx package this time. An entirely different beast, the Minotaur, half-man, half-bull, is killed by Theseus in the ancient tales but stabbed by Percy in the novel. In killing the minotaur, Percy saves his friend Grover. Characters throughout the novel remark on Percy's bravery. As the minotaur is defeated, they realize whom they have on their hands. "'He's the one. He must be,' said Annabeth" (56). She is looking at a real-life hero. Selflessness is yet another quality these two heroes display as they risk life and limb to protect and save their mothers. Perseus battles Medusa, while Percy returns Zeus's lightning bolt in order to retrieve his mother from the Underworld. Percy's newfound abilities matter little to him. His priority is bringing his mother back to the world of the living.

Usually, when a hero gets called to adventure, he or she is given special weapons and assistance. Perseus receives assistance from the gods Hermes and Athena. He is given a curved sword from Hermes and a highly polished bronze shield from Athena. Percy has multiple mentors, but the main one is Chiron. He begins the novel as Percy's Latin teacher, Mr. Brunner. He is seemingly the only non-family member who has any faith in Percy. Later, he is revealed to be Chiron, known as a very wise centaur and somewhat favored by the gods. He provides Percy with a three-foot-tall, double-edged celestial bronze sword to fight the monsters he knows Percy will encounter. Riptide is usually kept as a ballpoint pen when not in use and will always return to Percy's pocket.

The Lightning Thief is a 375-page myth full of immortal, bickering gods, the battle for good and evil, and a reluctant hero trying to keep alive on his quest. The tales of heroes told by the ancient Greeks are tightly woven into the fabric of our culture. Riordan's development of Percy is a clear indicator of that. He loves and is inspired by Greek myths. But it is also clear that he will spin the tale in his own direction to tell a good story. The characters of Perseus and Percy both tell us, through their bravery, selflessness, and overall heroic deeds, that it is our responsibility to help others when we can. After all, isn't that the true definition of a hero?

Task	Yes/No
Revisions	
Did I write a unique introduction with a clear and focused thesis?	
Did I write body paragraphs with relevant text details and insightful commentary/conclusions?	
Did I write a conclusion that reiterates the thesis?	
Did I write a title that captures the thesis and the attention of the readers?	
Does my writing show a command of embedding and citing direct quotes?	
Does my writing show a sophisticated understanding of proper comma usage?	
If produced digitally: Did I use technology to produce and publish writing and present the relationships between information and ideas effectively?	
COPS Editing	
Did I check and correct my **c**apitalization?	
Did I check and correct my **o**rder and usage of words?	
Did I check and correct my **p**unctuation?	
Did I check and correct my **s**pelling?	

Student Writer: _____

Title of Essay: _____

Student Writer's Statement (something that makes you proud about your essay): _____

Reader's name	Feedback *Please be specific.*

Lesson Set Goal	Emerging	Approaching	Achieving	Exceeding	Standards
In collaborative discussions, share and develop ideas in a manner that enhances understanding of a topic and contribute and respond to the content of the conversation in a productive and focused manner.	Student demonstrates little or no success asking and answering specific questions with appropriate details, making comments that contribute to the discussion, or acknowledging new information and adjusting own thinking to reflect new ideas if necessary, even with prompting.	Student demonstrates some success asking and answering specific questions with appropriate details, making comments that contribute to the discussion, and acknowledging new information and adjusting own thinking to reflect new ideas if necessary, but needs frequent prompting or redirection.	Student demonstrates solid success asking and answering specific questions with appropriate details, making comments that contribute to the discussion, and acknowledging new information and adjusting own thinking to reflect new ideas if necessary. May need occasional support, prompting, or redirection.	Student demonstrates outstanding success asking and answering specific questions with appropriate details, making comments that contribute to the discussion, acknowledging new information and adjusting own thinking to reflect new ideas if necessary. Proactively uses this strategy to support own learning. No prompting or redirection needed.	SL.8.1c SL.8.1d
Adapt speech to a variety of contexts and tasks, demonstrating command of formal English when indicated or appropriate.	Student shows little or no evidence of success adapting speech to a variety of contexts and tasks. Demonstrates very little command of formal English when indicated or appropriate.	Student shows some evidence of success adapting speech to a variety of contexts and tasks. Demonstrates basic command of formal English when indicated or appropriate.	Student effectively adapts speech to a variety of contexts and tasks. Demonstrates solid command of formal English when indicated or appropriate.	Student shows exceptional evidence of adapting speech to a variety of contexts and tasks. Demonstrates sophisticated command of formal English when indicated or appropriate.	SL.8.6
Demonstrate command of standard English and its conventions and use the knowledge when writing, speaking, reading, and listening.	Student demonstrates very little command of standard English and its conventions. Little or no evidence of application of knowledge when writing, speaking, reading, and listening.	Student shows some command of standard English and its conventions and attempts to use the knowledge when writing, speaking, reading, and listening.	Student shows solid command of standard English and its conventions and uses the knowledge when writing, speaking, reading, and listening.	Student shows exceptional command of standard English and its conventions and demonstrates sophisticated use of the knowledge when writing, speaking, reading, and listening.	L.8.1 L.8.2 L.8.3
Acquire and use accurately grade-appropriate general academic and domain-specific words and phrases, strategically building vocabulary knowledge when needed.	Student shows little or no evidence of the acquisition and accurate use of grade-appropriate general academic and domain-specific words and phrases. Little or no success using vocabulary building strategies.	Student shows some evidence of the acquisition and accurate use of grade-appropriate general academic and domain-specific words and phrases. Effectively uses vocabulary building strategies at times.	Student shows solid evidence of the acquisition and accurate use of grade-appropriate general academic and domain-specific words and phrases. Effectively uses vocabulary building strategies with frequency.	Student shows outstanding evidence of the acquisition and accurate use of grade-appropriate general academic and domain-specific words and phrases sophisticated for the grade level. Proactively uses a wide variety of vocabulary building strategies with success.	L.8.6

References

Allington, D. (2012). Private experience, textual analysis, and institutional authority: The discursive practice of critical interpretation and its enactment in literary training. *Language and Literature, 21*(2).

Carrier, K. A., & Tatum, A. W. (2006). Creating sentence walls to help English-language learners develop content literacy. *The Reading Teacher, 60*(3), 285–288.

Ehri, L. C., Dreyer, L. G., Flugman, B., & Gross, A. (2007). Reading rescue: An effective tutoring intervention model for language-minority students who are struggling readers in first grade. *American Educational Research Journal, 44*, 414–448.

Goldenberg, C. (2008). Teaching English Language Learners: What the research does—and does not—say. *American Educator, 32*(2), 8–23, 42–44.

Lewis, M. (1993). *The lexical approach: The state of ELT and the way forward.* Hove, England: Language Teaching Publications.

Nattinger, J. R. (1980). A lexical phrase grammar for ESL, *TESOL Quarterly, XIV*(3), 337–334.

PARCC Model. (2012). *PARCC model content frameworks: English language arts/literacy grades 3–11.*